AMISTAD LITERARY SERIES

GLORIA NAYLOR

Critical Perspectives
Past and Present

ALSO IN THE
Amistad Literary Series

LANGSTON HUGHES
ZORA NEALE HURSTON
TONI MORRISON
ALICE WALKER
RICHARD WRIGHT

Also by Henry Louis Gates, Jr.

Figures in Black: Words, Signs, and the "Racial" Self
Signifying Monkey: Toward a Theory of Afro-American Literary Criticism
Loose Canons: Notes on the Culture Wars
Black Literature and Literary Theory (editor)
The Classic Slave Narratives (editor)
Reading Black, Reading Feminist (editor)

Also by K. A. Appiah

Assertion and Conditions
For Truth in Semantics
Necessary Questions: An Introduction to Philosophy
Avenging Angel (fiction)
In My Father's House: Africa in the Philosophy of Culture
Early African-American Classics (editor)

AMISTAD LITERARY SERIES

GLORIA NAYLOR

Critical Perspectives
Past and Present

EDITED BY
Henry Louis Gates, Jr., and K. A. Appiah

NEW YORK, NEW YORK

Critical Perspectives Past and Present

MICHAEL C. VAZQUEZ, *Project Coordinator*

WAYNE L. APONTE
LISA GATES
SONJA OKUN

Amistad Press, Inc.
1271 Avenue of the Americas
New York, NY 10020

Distributed by:
Penguin USA
375 Hudson Street
New York, NY 10014

Designed by Stanley S. Drate, Folio Graphics Company, Inc.
Produced by March Tenth, Inc.

10 9 8 7 6 5 4 3 2 1

Library of Congress Cataloging-in-Publication Data

Gloria Naylor : critical perspectives past and present / edited by
    Henry Louis Gates, Jr., and K. A. Appiah.
        p.   cm. — (Amistad literary series)
    Includes bibliographical references and index.
    ISBN 1-56743-017-1 : $24.95. — ISBN 1-56743-030-9 (pbk.) : $14.95
    1. Naylor, Gloria—Criticism and interpretation. 2. Afro-American
women in literature. I. Gates, Henry Louis. II. Appiah, Anthony.
III. Series.
PS3564.A895Z68   1993
813'.54—dc20
                                                           92-45758
                                                           CIP

Contents

Preface

◆◆◆◆◆◆◆◆◆◆◆◆◆◆

Gloria Naylor
(1950–   )

In the history of the African-American literary tradition, perhaps no author has been more immersed in the formal history of that tradition than Gloria Naylor. As an undergraduate student of African-American literature at Brooklyn College and a graduate student of Afro-American Studies at Yale (where she served as a teaching assistant in a course entitled "Black Women and Their Fictions"), Naylor has analyzed the works of her male and female antecedents in a manner that was impossible before the late seventies. And, while she is a citizen of the republic of literature in the broadest and most cosmopolitan sense, her work suggests formal linkages to that of Ann Petry, James Baldwin, and more recently, Toni Morrison.

Gloria Naylor was born in 1950 into the family of Roosevelt and Alberta McAlpin Naylor. Her father was a transit worker and her mother a telephone operator. Between her graduation from high school in 1968 and 1975, Naylor served as a missionary for the Jehovah's Witnesses in Florida, North Carolina, and New York. Between 1975 and 1981, she worked as a telephone operator in several New York hotels. Since 1981, when she graduated from Brooklyn College, she has been a professional writer. She has also taught literature and writing at Yale, Cornell, Brandeis, George Washington University, Princeton, and at Penn.

In addition to *The Women of Brewster Place*, which received the American Book Award and has been adapted for television, Naylor is the author of *Linden Hills* (1985), *Mama Day* (1988), and *Bailey's Cafe* (1992). *The Women of Brewster Place* launched her career quite dramatically with its bold return to, and rejuvenation of, naturalism as a mode of narration and plot development. While her contemporaries were turning to the lyrical modernism of Zora Neale Hurston for literary inspiration, Naylor used Ann Petry's *The Street*, the classic work of black feminist naturalism, as her silent second text. Like Petry and Richard Wright before her, Naylor found in the resources of naturalism the means through which to indict a social structure that could tolerate the economic underdevelopment of so much of Black America. Considering the fact that the eighties witnessed the creation of the largest underclass in the history of Black Americans, *Brewster Place*, standing at the beginning of that decade, can be read as an augury of events to come.

But even within her practice of naturalism, Naylor refuses to paint completely diminished lives. The seven-part structure of the novel allows for a rendering of a range of sensibilities with a subtlety not commonly found in such fiction. Hers is a *lyrical* naturalism, with its roots in James Baldwin's gospel-inspired riffs on Richard Wright's *Native Son* and *Black Boy*. What's more, Naylor demonstrated a powerful manner of depicting sexuality—in its varied permutations—linking her again to Baldwin, but also registering a more open and complex way to depict the vagaries of desire in Black fiction. These pioneering efforts have helped to make the decade of the eighties a new era, indeed, a renaissance, in Black women's writings.

Naylor's subsequent novels have been enormously ambitious. *Linden Hills*, her master's thesis at Yale, is structured as an elaborate play upon Dante's *Inferno*. Naylor is concerned here, in part, to indict the moral bankruptcy of the Black nouveau riche. If *Linden Hills* is widely seen as less successful than *Brewster Place*, it is perhaps because her grasp on the mores of the Black bourgeoisie seems less sure than is her understanding of the lives of the Black under- and working classes. *Mama Day* is a beautifully lyrical rewriting both of Shakespeare's *The Tempest* and Toni Morrison's *Song of Solomon*. And her most recent novel, *Bailey's Cafe*, is almost Faulknerian in its experimental narrative voice, bearing an important resemblance to Toni Morrison's *Jazz*, published in the same year. Naylor, it seems clear, is not afraid to experiment formally, and her works, like the best of her predecessors, engage European as well as American traditions.

The pieces collected in the opening review section attest to Naylor's important, if sometimes controversial, place in the expanding canon of American letters. The reviews, selected from an array of magazines, journals, and newspapers, showcase the evolving literary culture of the eighties and nineties and her vibrant contribution to the emerging renaissance of African-American women's writing.

The fourteen critical essays that follow map out the diversity of Naylor's accomplishments and concerns. Observing the convergence of form and content in *The Women of Brewster Place*, Michael Awkward argues that the disparate stories of individual women come to form a community characterized by both cohesion and diversity. For Awkward, the novel can be read as a revision of both Toomer's *Cane* and Morrison's *The Bluest Eye*. Redacting Harold Bloom's model of anxious male influence-peddling, Awkward argues for a noncompetitive model of creative misreading he finds in recent African-American writing.

Reading *The Women of Brewster Place* alongside Duchamps's photographic installation "Etant Donnes" and William Faulkner's *Sanctuary*, Laura Tanner argues that Naylor's naturalism breaks with literary convention by portraying the rape from the victim's perspective.

Celeste Fraser reads *The Women of Brewster Place* as a counterargument to the New Right discourse of "Black welfare motherhood" and single-parent families, exemplified by the Moynihan report. By presenting the living diversity of Black female experience, struggling to survive in the ghetto, Naylor undermines conservative stereotypes of Black poverty.

Elaborating further upon the social and economic topos of Naylor's fiction, Barbara Christian notes that Naylor's explicit treatment of class and geography in her first two novels is a remarkable achievement in African-American writing. Christian describes the way in which Black "progress" and the creation of a Black middle class is played out spatially, and explores the complexity of Naylor's treatment of gender in relation to class.

The role of dreams—and deferral—in *The Women of Brewster Place* is the subject of Jill L. Matus's essay. Observing that the sense of closure in the final story of the book is undermined by the fact that the "block party" that would unite the female community only occurs in a dream, Matus maintains that Naylor's refusal to definitively end her story—the novel's sense of irresolution—marks a revision of the meaning of Langston Hughes's deferral: that a dream deferred is a dream alive, a life still in progress.

Returning to some of the issues charted out by Barbara Christian, Luke Bouvier notes the interplay and instability of language, race, gender, and geographical space in *Linden Hills*. In his reading, Linden Hills itself is the site of a struggle to control names and meaning. Animating the novel is a conflict between essentialism (the assertion of fundamental identity, i.e., definitive meanings, races, boundaries, as practiced by the patriarch Nedeed) and the rough-and-tumble multiplicity of social reality.

From an intertextual perspective, Catherine C. Ward observes that Naylor patterns *Linden Hills* after Dante's *Inferno*. She finds that the choice of Dante as a model lends a moral seriousness and a universal mythic dimension to her story of Black middle-class "success" and its price.

The allegorical structure of *Linden Hills* is explored even further in Margaret Homans's intricate reading of the novel as a work of visionary feminism. Homans finds that Naylor transforms Virgil and Dante in the same way that the feminist theorist Luce Irigaray transforms Plato: by locating a specifically female creativity (and procreativity) within a masculine tradition of paternal self-duplication.

The theme of patriarchy is also central to Keith Sandiford's reading of *Linden Hills*, which sees it as an instance of Black American gothic, with Black patriarchy functioning as a narrative locus of abiding evil. In an approach informed by the Russian theorist Mikhail Bakhtin, Sandiford attends to the multiple voices or texts competing throughout.

Another sort of tension—one between personal identity and cultural history—is the subject of Theresa Goddu's essay on *Linden Hills*. In her view, Naylor counterposes an autobiographical or poetic "subjective" approach to history to the willed amnesia of the Black middle class, the "mythic," ahistoricist pretensions of patriarchy, and the "objective" history of the white male historians.

Peter Erickson argues that Naylor employs Shakespeare to thematize the split between white male and Black female literary traditions, as well as between "white" high culture and "Black" everyday experience. He astutely notes that Naylor's revision of *The Tempest* breaks with twentieth-century revisions by creating a Black female Prospero rather than a victorious (Black) Caliban. The use of precursor texts is also the concern of James Robert Saunders, who finds that the strategy lends Naylor's own work tragic resonance, even though Naylor's revisions tend to be more hopeful than the originals.

Helen Fiddyment Levy's discussion of Naylor's first three novels revolves around a Black communal life dissolved by the agencies of the modern social bureaucracies. Naylor's increasing use of magic, myth, and the elements is shown to be an attempt to recover the vital connection and strong community of the home place.

In the volume's concluding essay, Larry R. Andrews takes up Naylor's first three novels and the evolving themes of folk tradition, history, magic, and nature. Naylor, he argues, presents a new picture of relations among women, of female friendship, sisterhood, and community.

—Henry Louis Gates, Jr.

REVIEWS

THE WOMEN OF BREWSTER PLACE (1982)

ANNIE GOTTLIEB

The New York Times Book Review, August 22, 1982

Ten or twelve years ago, the vanguard of the women's movement began exhorting the rest of us to pay attention to our relationships with other women: mothers, daughters, sisters, friends. How important those neglected bonds were, said representatives, how much of the actual substance of life they were. But it was hard, at first, for most women to see clearly the significance of those bonds; all our lives those relationships had been the backdrop, while the sexy, angry fireworks with men were the show.

Now, it seems, that particular lesson of feminism has been not only taken to heart but deeply absorbed. Here are two first novels in which it feels perfectly natural that women are the foreground figures, primary both to the reader and to each other, regardless of whether they're involved with men. In Gloria Naylor's fierce, loving group portrait of seven black women in one housing development and in Valerie Miner's somewhat less successful portrayal of a three-generation Irish clan, the bonds between women are the abiding ones. Most men are incalculable hunters who come and go. They are attractive—but weak and/or dangerous—representatives of nature and of violence who both fertilize and threaten the female core.

Gloria Naylor's *The Women of Brewster Place* is set in one of those vintage urban-housing developments that black people (who are, in truth, "nutmeg," "ebony," "saffron," "cinnamon-red," or "gold") have inherited from a succession of other ethnic groups. The difference is that while the Irish and Italians used it as a jumping-off place for the suburbs, for most of its "colored daughters" Brewster Place is "the end of the line": "They came because they had no choice and would remain for the same reason." But the end of the line is not the end of life. With their backs literally to the wall—a brick barrier that has turned Brewster

3

Place into a dead end—the women make their stand together, fighting a hostile world with love and humor.

There's Mattie Michael, dark as "rich, double cocoa," who defied her overprotective father to take man who was pure temptation, almost a force of nature—a Pan. Pregnant and disowned, she made the instinctive matriarchal decision (I mean that word in the mythic, not the sociological sense) to live without a man and invest all her love back into her child. Left in the lurch by the grown, spoiled son who results, she becomes the anchor for the other women of Brewster Place.

There's Etta Mae Johnson, survivor and good-time woman, who comes home to Mattie when her dream of redemption by marrying a "respectable" preacher is sordidly ended. There's Ciel Turner, whose husband, Eugene, ominously resents her fertility: "With two kids and you on my back, I ain't never gonna have nothin' . . . nothin'!" There's Kiswana (formerly Melanie) Browne, idealistic daughter of middle-class parents, who has moved to Brewster Place to be near "my people." Cora Lee, a welfare mother, likes men only because they provide babies, but she can't cope with children once they are older. She is almost lifted out of the inertia of her life by the power of art when Kiswana takes her to see a black production of Shakespeare in the park. And, finally, there are Theresa and Lorraine, lovers who embody the ultimate commitment of woman to woman and yet arouse unease or loathing in most of the other women of Brewster Place.

Despite Gloria Naylor's shrewd and lyrical portrayal of many of the realities of black life (her scene of services in the Canaan Baptist Church is brilliant), *The Women of Brewster Place* isn't realistic fiction—it is mythic. Nothing supernatural happens in it, yet its vivid, earthy characters (especially Mattie) seem constantly on the verge of breaking out into magical powers. The book has two climaxes, one of healing and rebirth, one of destruction. In the first, Mattie magnificently wrestles Ciel, dying of grief, back to life. In the second, Lorraine, rejected by the others, is gang raped, a blood sacrifice brutally proving the sisterhood of all women. Miss Naylor bravely risks sentimentality and melodrama to write her compassion and outrage large, and she pulls it off triumphantly.

DOROTHY WICKENDEN

The New Republic, September 6, 1982

Like any ghetto, Brewster Place has its horrors and its desperate charms. A dead-end street, cut off from the city's main arteries by a

brick wall, this neighborhood is inhabited by decaying apartment buildings, children who "bloom in colorful shorts and tops plastered against
gold, ebony, and nut-brown arms and legs," and women who "pin their
dreams to wet laundry hung out to dry." There are men who live here
too, of course. They visit their women like nightmares, leaving behind
them babies and bile. But Gloria Naylor's women, much like those of
Toni Morrison and Alice Walker, are daunting even in desolation. Most
of them find that through laughter and companionship they can make
themselves virtually impregnable.

The Women of Brewster Place is subtitled "a novel in seven stories,"
and Naylor has blended the lives of these distinctive characters just as
fluidly as the women do in their long kitchen talks, "so that what lay
behind one and ahead of the other became indistinguishable." Their personal histories share a common theme: violence and abuse at the hands
of men. Adoring fathers beat their young daughters senseless and turn
them out of the house when they get pregnant; lovers fracture their jaws
when they burn a pot of rice; sons mysteriously change from affectionate
boys to juvenile delinquents who pick them clean of money and love. But
these women are astoundingly resilient. The novel's standard-bearer,
Mattie Michael, holds together the lives of the others through strength
of will, and it is Naylor's knowing characterization of Mattie that makes
The Women of Brewster Place more than a patchwork of stories about
seven women. Mattie is described in her old age as someone who "chose
her words with the grinding precision of a diamond cutter's drill." The
same can be said of Gloria Naylor, who has written a polished story
about how individuals adapt when their aspirations for better lives are
met repeatedly with ridicule and random brutality.

It won't come as a surprise to readers of contemporary fiction by
black women that Gloria Naylor has few kind words to waste on members
of the other sex. Yet The Women of Brewster Place, like Alice Walker's
extraordinary The Color Purple, a new epistolary novel about marital
love and hate, love among women, and love of God—and unlike much
current fiction by privileged white feminists—is not simply a self-indulgent celebration of female solidarity. Naylor and Walker write with equal
lucidity about the cruelty that poverty breeds and the ways in which
people achieve redemption. Nor is there a wariness about traditional
women's roles. The Women of Brewster Place is a novel about motherhood, a concept embraced by Naylor's women, each of whom is a surrogate child or mother to the next.

Despite the simple elegance of Naylor's prose, there is a risk that the
accumulation of horrific experiences may deaden some readers' senses
before the novel builds to its devastating climax. Yet the spirit with
which these women cope is, finally, more powerful than the circumstances of their lives. When the granddaughter of one of Mattie's closest

friends wills her own death after her baby dies and her lover abandons her, Mattie surges into Luciela Louise's sick room:

'No! No! No!' Like a black Brahman cow, desperate to protect her young, she . . . approached the bed with her lips clamped shut in such force that the muscles in her jaw and the back of her neck began to ache.

She sat on the edge of the bed and enfolded the tissue-thin body in her huge ebony arms. And she rocked. Ciel's body was so hot it burned Mattie when she first touched her, but she held on and rocked. Back and forth, back and forth—she had Ciel so tightly she could feel her young breasts flatten against the buttons of her dress. The black mammoth gripped so firmly that the slightest increase of pressure would have cracked the girl's spine. But she rocked.

LINDEN HILLS (1985)

◆◆◆◆◆◆◆◆◆◆◆◆◆

MEL WATKINS

The New York Times Book Review, March 3, 1985

Gloria Naylor's first novel, *The Women of Brewster Place*, which won an American Book Award in 1983, chronicled the plight of eight black women living in an urban lower-class cul-de-sac. With few exceptions—most notably the portrayal of a ghastly gang rape, which took on mythic proportions—that book realistically portrayed the characters' efforts to overcome the poverty and anguish of their lives. "Linden Hills," Miss Naylor's second novel, also uses a confined geographic setting to construct a tale about the interconnected lives of a group of black characters. It is, however, a much more ambitious work in which realism is subordinated to allegory. Although flawed, it tackles a controversial subject with boldness and originality.

Like Amiri Baraka in *The Systems of Dante's Hell* (1965), Miss Naylor has adapted Dante's *Inferno* to her own fictional purposes—in this instance a tale of lost black souls trapped in the American dream. The setting is Linden Hills, an upper-middle-class black community built on a huge plot of land owned by the mysterious Nedeed family (the locale is not specified). Purchased by Luther Nedeed in 1820—after he had sold his octoroon wife and six children into slavery and moved from Tupelo, Mississippi, we are told—the land has remained under the proprietorship of the Nedeeds for more than 150 years. Luther (read Lucifer), as all the males in the Nedeed family are named, opened a funeral parlor, then developed the land and leased sections to black families. His sons and grandsons, all of whom are physical copies of the original landowner, furthered his plan—to establish a showcase black community. That community, as the original Luther says, would not only be an "ebony jewel" representing black achievement, but also "a beautiful, black wad of spit right in the white eye of America."

When Miss Naylor picks up the story in the present, Luther's vision has been realized. Linden Hills is a thriving community of successful black professionals. But Luther's domain is not all it seems. We discover why when introduced to the residents of Linden Hills by Willie and Lester (read Dante and Virgil), two young poets who take odd jobs with the Hills inhabitants to earn money for Christmas. As they work their way down the circular drives—a structural hierarchy wherein the wealthier and more successful families live closer to the Nedeed home, which is surrounded by a frozen lake at the bottom of the hill—Miss Naylor strips away the facade of material success to reveal a netherworld of chaos and despair.

Among the characters we meet are Norman, who is periodically felled by an attack of "the pinks," a strange malady that causes him to tear at his own skin to remove the imagined slimy substance that he feels is consuming him, and the Rev. Michael T. Hollis, who has forsaken his Baptist background to adopt the staid practices of the Episcopal Church and in the process becomes an alcoholic. Then there is Maxwell Smyth (formerly Smith), who, in pursuit of perfection and an untainted image, exercises so much control that even his bodily excretions are without odor. And, of course, there is the tormented Luther Nedeed himself—plagued by a baffling disruption of his sovereignty that threatens his kingdom, but maintaining his strange dominance over the inhabitants of Linden Hills.

Simply stated, Miss Naylor's version of the *Inferno* suggests that blacks who aspire to the white world and material success are pawns of the Devil and will experience the torments of hell. It is an intriguing allegory, and for the most part Miss Naylor presents it with wit and insight into the tensions and anxieties that plague assimilated blacks. (There is even a sense of tongue-in-cheek humor here—why else would the author's Dante and Virgil bear the names of a well-known ventriloquist-and-dummy team?) The problem is that, perhaps because of the rigid allegorical structure, the narrative lists toward the didactic. Moreover, intimations of some bizarre rituals are never made quite clear. Why does one of the Nedeed wives order snakeroot, powdered dove's heart and castor oil for her kitchen? And what exactly are the strange ministrations Luther performs on the corpses in his mortuary?

Although Miss Naylor has not been completely successful in adapting the *Inferno* to the world of the black middle class, in *Linden Hills* she has shown a willingness to expand her fictional realm and to take risks. Its flaws notwithstanding, the novel's ominous atmosphere and inspired set pieces—such as the minister's drunken fundamentalist sermon before an incredulous Hills congregation—make it a fascinating departure for Miss Naylor, as well as a provocative, iconoclastic novel about a seldom-addressed subject.

♦♦♦♦♦♦♦♦♦♦♦♦♦

SHERLEY ANNE WILLIAMS

Ms., June 1985

At the turn of the century, stories about what was then called "the better class of colored people" dominated fiction written by Afro-Americans. But with the Harlem Renaissance (1917–1939), the black bourgeoisie passed out of fashion as a literary topic. Writers such as Zora Neale Hurston, Sterling A. Brown, and Langston Hughes began to celebrate the rich verbal and musical culture of the black masses—music and lore that the black middle class deplored as examples of the backwardness of the lower classes and as reminders of the slave past. Nonetheless, there were Harlem Renaissance writers who still followed a tradition epitomized in an earlier generation by Frances E.W. Harper and W. E. B. Du Bois, in whose fictional work black middle-class character and setting were coupled with the theme of racial uplift. (Harper and Du Bois directed their literary efforts toward refuting the commonplace racist argument that blacks were "too primitive" to participate or achieve in American society on an equal basis with whites.) In the 1920s, Walter White, who became the NAACP's executive secretary, and Jessie Fauset, the woman who served as literary editor of the NAACP's *Crisis* magazine under Du Bois, both wrote first novels in order to present authentic portrayals of "Negroes of breeding."

In other Harlem Renaissance novels where black middle-class characters held center stage (including the work of Nella Larsen; see *Ms.*, December, 1980), the protagonists were at odds with their middle-class background, and as often as not sought some kind of common cause and identity with the masses of black folk. But by the mid-1930s, with the increasing emphasis on the lives of average, workaday blacks in literature, Afro-American writers more often treated the black bourgeoisie as the object of scorn, deriding them for intellectual superficiality and conspicuous consumption, as well as for their shame of the slave past, of the culture that spawned blues and jazz, and of physical features that linked them to Africa.

Now, 50 years later, three recent novels—all by young black women writers—once again turn our attention to the black bourgeoisie. Gloria Naylor's *Linden Hills* updates the critical view of the black elite in a clever allegory with gothic elements. Andrea Lee's *Sarah Phillips* and Ntozake Shange's *Betsey Brown* add to the slim store of novels that focus on the childhood and adolescence of black female protagonists. Black life has always been more various than the literature has been at liberty to show. These novels indicate a broadening of subject matter that is welcome.

In *Linden Hills*, Naylor broadly transmogrifies Dante's *Inferno:* two young black men take on odd jobs in the affluent black suburb of the book's title. Willie (audaciously nicknamed Willie White because his skin is so black) is an oral poet, who grew up in the Putney Wayne Projects, a very different kind of community from its near neighbor, plush Linden Hills. Willie White has committed over 600 poems to memory and can cast the ingredients of a cereal box into heroic couplets at a single glance. Lesterfield Tilson (known as "Shit" because his skin is the color of a baby's stool), though born and raised in Linden Hills (in its more modest section) and a writer in the more formal sense, is maverick enough to prefer the education of the streets that he gets while hanging out with his partner. Together they embody the best of the oral and literate traditions in Afro-American experience.

At the bottom of Linden Hills where the most opulent homes are (Naylor plays on the black idiomatic sense of "down") is the seat of the successive generations of the dark-skinned "satanic" Luther Nedeed. The original Luther was a freedman who, having bought the land in the 1820s, rented shacks to blacks who were too poor to farm. The later Luther Nedeeds, prosperous morticians all, follow in the patriarch's footsteps—each acquires an "octoroon bride" to bear the next generation and presides over the increasingly wealthy Linden Hills of his particular day.

Naylor also revoices motifs and devices from the recent fiction of Toni Morrison and Alice Walker, often with remarkable effectiveness, as in the relationship between Willie and Lester which echoes, without imitating a similar one between the major characters in Morrison's *Song of Solomon.* Naylor is at her best, powerful and chilling, where the last Mrs. Nedeed unravels the stories of previous generations of Nedeed women. Letters (like Walker's Celie in *The Color Purple,* Mrs. Nedeed writes to herself), recipes, shopping lists, photographs are all a means of piecing together these women's histories, of excavating their buried lives.

Although *Linden Hills* has many compelling moments, the "sins" of this community—hypocrisy, loveless marriages and marital infidelities, idleness—seem too trivial to carry the weight of Naylor's expert literary attentions. Still, in this second novel, Naylor serves notice that she is a mature literary talent of formidable skill.

The way the heroine of Andrea Lee's *Sarah Phillips* describes herself—"light-skinned, quite pretty with an unfocused snobbery, vague literary aspirations, and a lively appetite for white boys"—sounds like a satiric limning of a contemporary "bourgie babe" (the black equivalent of a Jewish princess). But what Lee's first novel holds up to mockery is not the pretensions of her upper-middle-class heroine, but the "outworn rituals" of black community. *Sarah Phillips*, the memoir of a privileged girlhood, oddly enough, resembles nothing in Afro-American letters so much as Richard Wright's autobiographical *Black Boy*, one of the most searing accounts of a deprived boyhood in the literature. In *Black Boy*, Wright literally and figuratively renounces oral culture and black traditions for personal autonomy. Andrea Lee seems bent on something of the same sort in *Sarah Phillips*.

Sarah, the daughter of an affluent Baptist minister, lives in an exclusive black suburb of Philadelphia, attends a private, integrated school and summer camp, graduates from Harvard, and escapes the constraints of her stodgy, middle-class background by going to France. The loosely connected episodes that make up this novel are consistently well observed and precisely crafted, and record Sarah's initiation into a knowledge of her status as it is perceived by the white world. Like Wright in *Black Boy*, Sarah's rite of passage involves a rejection of black community rather than a renewed sense of identification with blacks. Hearing the outrage expressed by a group of gypsies who happen to wander into the well-tended suburb where she lives ("it's a real crime for colored people to live like this"); confronting the "servant problem" at her exclusive girls' school (Sarah is the only black person there who is not a servant and she is at pains to keep her distance from them); observing what happens when an inner-city black gang comes to her expensive summer camp for a week; being embarrassed during a visit with an elderly parishioner confined to a nursing home (who matter-of-factly interrupts their small talk with the startling story of the rape which resulted in her giving birth at age 12)—each becomes an occasion that emphasizes Sarah's own sense of distance from black people.

Through all this, Lee maintains a stance as a careful, though sometimes ironic reporter of detail and incident, rather than as an interpreter. But when the novel ends, leading us back to its beginning, the ambivalence Sarah projects in the first chapter is gone: Sarah is free in France, laughing at racist jokes, sexual pet to a trio of white boys. I suspect that Jessie Fauset, the arch-defender of bourgeois breeding, is turning in her grave.

One of the implicit messages of *Linden Hills* and *Sarah Phillips* is that the only *real* black is a poor black. That proposition, of course, is by no means unique. Ntozake Shange, however, in *Betsey Brown*, depicts an affluence that is not incompatible with black culture and community. Her protagonist has upper-class origins that include a surgeon/artist/activist father (a black music aficionado who takes his four kids to see Chuck Berry, and a proud "race man" who encourages their participation in civil rights demonstrations), as well as a fragile-nerved mother (who works outside the home as a social worker in the black community), and a color-struck grandmother (whose taste for lyric reverie Betsey has inherited). Consequently, the book speaks to some of the deeper complexities and paradoxes that have helped sustain and perpetuate the positive aspects of the Afro-American experience; I only wish I could be more enthusiastic about it as a literary achievement.

Despite the fact that the novel is told in the third person and the narrative freely dips into the thoughts of other characters, the narrative voice and perspective remains that of Betsey, a dreamy and childish 13-year-old. Shange never expands or corrects the limitations or inaccuracies of this naïve and therefore unreliable center of consciousness. For example, the Browns (a dual-career couple back in the 1950s and 1960s in St. Louis) cope with a "servant problem" of their own. And while Betsey emphasizes that the succession of black lower-class women hired as housekeepers sleep in the attic because Betsey's mother would never "put a Negro in the basement" (the traditional servants' quarters), there's never any acknowledgment that Betsey responds to these women in much the same way as white children have traditionally related to black servants—as surrogate parents who guide the children through the shoals of childhood and adolescence. Such unremarked sentimentality is permissible in 13-year-old Betsey; it is inexcusable in Shange.

Another difficulty—one that complicates the problems of the narrative—is language. The characters and the narrator all talk and think alike. The point is not, of course, nonstandard usage as such—but the doubt that this usage sometimes casts on the credibility of the upper-class adult characters. To have Betsey's grandmother voice her pretensions in the same dialect as the dark-skinned characters she despises is to make her into an object of fun, if not outright contempt; and while she is snobbish, she's meant, I think, to be a likable character. Shange proves over and over again in the novel that she is able to approximate the rhythms and reproduce the idioms of vernacular black speech without resorting to what is, in this case, the literary equivalent of black-face minstrelsy.

It is noteworthy that three important young black women novelists have chosen to write about the black middle class, but, with the possible exception of the disappointing *Betsey Brown*, these books do not revise the literary image of the black bourgeoisie. On the contrary, they go a long way toward confirming that the colored gentry are just as trifling now as they were said to have been 60 years ago.

◆◆◆◆◆◆◆◆◆◆◆◆◆◆◆◆◆◆◆◆◆◆◆◆◆◆◆◆◆◆◆◆◆◆◆◆

MAMA DAY (1988)

◆◆◆◆◆◆◆◆◆◆◆◆◆

RITA MAE BROWN

The *Los Angeles Times*, March 6, 1988

God created the universe in six days. It took her longer, but Gloria Naylor has created her own universe in *Mama Day*.

The novel's title is the pet name of the most powerful figure in Willow Springs, a fictional Southern island. Miranda Day, born in 1895, is the great-aunt of Cocoa Day, a young, too-smart woman who moves to New York City.

Just why Cocoa would want to live among both the cold and the Yankees mystifies the residents of Willow Springs. Mama Day figures, observing the male inhabitants of the island, that there have to be better men in New York, even if they do talk funny.

Cocoa does find a husband, although her real intention was to find a job. Throughout the novel, Cocoa's observations run an uncharitable but accurate course. At a New York party after a weary day of job hunting, Cocoa remarks that finding employment might have been easier when want ads were listed under "colored" and "white." Attacked for wanting to bring back segregation, she thinks, "Where had it gone? I just wanted to bring the clarity about it back—it would save me a whole lot of subway tokens."

Since Willow Springs is an imaginary island off the coasts of South Carolina and Georgia, Naylor can turn the world upside down. The descendants of the slaves of white Bascombe Wade (murdered by Mama Day's great-grandmother) own their own land. If set on the mainland, this twist could not be possible since South Carolina and Georgia had laws preventing slaves from owning land. The land gives people power and place, and no resident of Willow Springs will sell to an outsider.

The world is also turned upside down in that the women possess the real power, and are acknowledged as having it.

This doesn't mean that Mama Day and her sister Abigail don't resort to feminine wiles to get their way. Cocoa, watching her husband, George, manipulated by her grandmother and great-aunt, thinks, "You've been

13

allowed to overhear the quiet whisper about how marvelous you are, to witness glimpses of melting awe at the strength of your back, your arms. Yeah, they would lie back now, your ego would take over."

Cocoa straddles two worlds, that of island women and that of mainland women—which is to say quasi-men, for mainland women have forgotten their mysteries. She struggles to make herself whole, to find a synthesizing power.

Other characters struggle with their search for power. Dr. Buzzard, a moonshine maker and quack doctor, parodies the women's power. Ruby is an example of women's power serving the self which is a form of evil. And everyone's power in Willow Springs was born with Sapphira Wade in 1799, the "witch" who killed the Master.

In this upside-down world comes George Andrews, Cocoa's new husband. George's power comes from his logical Western mind. He is an engineer and values precision. He is also an orphan cut off from his roots, and therefore beguiled by Willow Springs where bloodlines can be traced through the centuries.

George's scientific outlook does not prevent him from possessing a sharp sense of his own emotional life. One of the ironies of *Mama Day* is that Cocoa gets angry with him for not being more overtly emotional. She can't understand that he is never going to display his emotions the way she displays hers. George says that living with a female is "a day-to-day balancing act, and I really enjoyed the challenge. Because the times I got it right, your being different made all the difference in the world."

George also thinks, "Only a fool would spend his life looking for some dream woman. The right woman is the one you can live with, not the one in your head."

George is the linchpin of *Mama Day*. His rational mind allows the reader to experience the island as George experiences it. Mama Day and Cocoa are of the island and therefore less immediately accessible to the reader.

The turning point of the book comes when George is asked not only to believe in Mama Day's power but to act on it. Cocoa is desperately ill. A hurricane has washed out the bridge so that no mainland doctor can be summoned. Only Mama Day can show George the way to save his wife. He is told to go into the chicken coop and search in the northwest corner for the nest of an old red hen. He is to bring back to Mama Day what he finds there. He tries to do as he is told, but George needs a quantifiable result. He misses the symbolism of the eggs, of the old hen, and of the objects he must carry into the hen house. And so he "fails," but his action allows his wife to live even though the result of this task is horrible for him.

The formula for heterosexual salvation in conventional novels is for the man and woman either to understand one another and live happily ever after or to understand each other and realize they can't life together. The key is thinking, not necessarily feeling. Not so here. George must let go of his rigidity, his "male" mind. When he can't do that, he sacrifices himself on the altar of love. Success is a form of surrender: the opposite of the desire to control.

When you read *Mama Day*, and surely you will read it, "surrender" to it. Don't worry about finding the plot. Let the plot find you. The different voices are beautifully realized, but Naylor's technique can be a confusing one to read. Occasionally the narrator's voice is not so cleanly, stylistically marked, and the reader must press on doggedly before knowing who is speaking, realizing that a plot is developing through these fragmented viewpoints.

A writer's first work of fiction is usually a surprise to the reader and the writer, too. A writer's second book is almost always a disappointment. A writer's third novel determines whether the writer has a real career. It's also the show-off novel because the writer is beginning to feel her/his power, but the lessons of self-restraint are up the road.

Mama Day is Naylor's show-off novel. She has a dazzling sense of humor, rich comic observation and that indefinable quality we call "heart." She has a lot to show off.

LINDA SIMON

The *Women's Review of Books*, September 1988

In *The Women of Brewster Place* Gloria Naylor created a community of Black women living in an urban cul-de-sac, a city within a city. In *Linden Hills*, her suburban Black community was as isolated as any urban ghetto, its inhabitants fixed on the acquisition of material goods and exemplary table manners, trading their heritage and sense of their own identity as Blacks for the superficialities that the outside world calls signs of success.

Now, in *Mama Day*, Naylor gives us Willow Springs, a fictional island off the coast of South Carolina and Georgia. Its inhabitants are the descendants of slaves, their ties to mainstream American culture as fragile as the bridge that connects the island to the mainland. Naylor's protagonist is Cocoa, born Ophelia Day, a young woman in her twenties with roots in Willow Springs, who is trying to establish herself in New York City when we first meet her.

What interests Naylor is her heroine's identity as a rural Black woman and her confrontation with urban America. Can Cocoa live in

New York and still retain a sense of her heritage? For the first half of the book it seems she can. Through work, marriage and eventually motherhood, she could no doubt learn what is transferable from Willow Springs besides the lavender cologne that her great-aunt sends her—what, from her personal and racial history, could help her in the urban experience. From a sassy, street-smart, insecure and cynical young woman she might develop into someone more trusting, tolerant and self-assured, if Naylor allowed that.

She doesn't. At mid-point in the book she returns Cocoa to Willow Springs, weakens her physically and emotionally (she is near death throughout the book's climax) and forces changes in her life through supernatural intervention. The message is that in traveling north Cocoa has been a trespasser. Tempted to forget her rural southern past, to reject her ancestors' sustaining superstition and belief in magic, she incurs a wrathful punishment—one that has nothing to do with the changes that could have taken place in her if Naylor had decided to opt for character development in a more realistic setting. After Cocoa's struggle for health she is reborn as a southerner resolved to accept her unbreakable ties to island culture.

If we are to take this protagonist's portrait as representative of urban Black women transported from the South, then they are fearful, defensive, vulnerable. Trying to protect herself from the assaults of the city, Cocoa exhibits a defensive surface to the world, judging it through superficial impressions. In doing so she often deceives herself, but while she admits "I was always thrown off balance," she persists in trying to convince herself that the finely honed intuition that served her in Willow Springs will work for her in New York. She thinks she can determine by the look of a briefcase or appointment book whether or not a woman is unemployed, "which briefcases that swung with the right weight held only pounds of resumés, or which Gucci appointment books had the classifieds neatly clipped out and taped onto the pages so you'd think she was expected where she was heading instead of just expected to wait."

Though she recognizes underlying racism and sexism in the city, Cocoa herself resorts to ethnic slurs in the form of food-names for people: "fudge sticks, kumquats, bagels, zucchinis." Later she admits that her bigotry resulted from fear: "Nothing's just black and white here like in Willow Springs," she tells her lover George. "Nothing stays put. So I guess the way I talk is my way of coming to terms with never knowing what to expect from anything or anybody."

For background Naylor drew on her visits to the Sea Islands off the coast of Georgia, but in her imagination Willow Springs becomes even more isolated and inbred, and more resolutely Black. It exists as it must have been hundreds of years ago, a homogeneous Black culture nurtured by folklore and tradition, defiantly refusing to move into modern times.

Its woods contain herbs, roots, stems and leaves that can be used for good or for evil—as medicine or as poison. There is a secret part of the woods, "the other place," where the supernatural can and does occur. Conjurors and spirits lurk in these woods; the rational gives way to the irrational.

Dominating the island is Miranda Day, Mama Day, Cocoa's great-aunt. She is the descendant of the legendary Sapphira, a slave with knowledge of witchcraft, and of Sapphira's white owner Bascombe Wade, whom she married, persuading him to deed his land to his slaves. Sapphira bore seven sons, then killed Wade.

Cocoa struggles to retain this cultural heritage in New York, but she cannot enact the conjuror role of Sapphira Wade's heir, attuned to dark, unnamable forces. Yet abandoning this role means abandoning her history with nothing to replace it. Accepting white culture as another part of her heritage, so she fears, will betray her and her face. When George asks her out on their second date, for example, she finds herself thinking, "Surely, he jests," and worries that she may be quoting Shakespeare. "Just proves," she responds quickly, "that Shakespeare didn't have a bit of a soul—I don't care if he did write about Othello, Cleopatra, and some slave on a Caribbean island. If he had been in touch with our culture, he would have written somewhere, 'Nigger, are you out of your mind?'"

From her great-aunt Cocoa has learned ways of dealing with the world that allow her to retain her belief in Black rural superiority. Her perceptions of New York are paralleled by Mama Day's perceptions of urban America, gleaned by examining the faces in the audience on television shows (only the faces; she turns the sound off). Mama Day judges these people on the basis of the way they laugh, "the slump of the shoulders. And always, always the eyes. She can pick out which ladies in the audience have secretly given up their babies for adoption, which fathers have daughters making pornographic movies, exactly which homes have been shattered by Vietnam, drugs, or 'the alarming rise of divorce'." Contemporary America, according to Mama Day, is not a place in which she—or Cocoa—can thrive.

Contrasted with Cocoa, so burdened by her past, is George Andrews, her lover, then her husband. Cocoa first meets him (and writes him off at first as a "bonbon") when he interviews her for a job. George was brought up in an orphanage where he was taught a creed the opposite of Cocoa's. "Only the present has potential," the orphaned boys would recite, and George had come to live by that creed. He does not believe in fate or predestination. He has no childhood models for behavior, except the pragmatic head of the orphanage. George can invent the present with equanimity and feels comfortable in New York, where the past is easily obliterated and the future only tentatively envisioned. He wants to create his own history, and it is this difference between them—Cocoa's need to conserve and his to invent—that tells us that Naylor will now allow their relationship to endure even after she has gotten them married.

George goes to Willow Springs with Cocoa. The place "smelled like forever," feels like paradise. He urges Cocoa to try to conceive their child in the big mahogany bed that belonged to Bascombe and Sapphira. It doesn't matter to him that the bed, weighted with legend, portends evil and tragedy. "I was sure about us," he says; "we could defy history." He learns otherwise. Soon he comes to see that this paradise has its underside, and that he and Cocoa risk being trapped there forever unless he can assist in the magic necessary to free them. Instead, he insists on living in the present. Cocoa strives to join him there, but in the end she must suffer and sacrifice George to survive.

After eliminating George from the story, Naylor supplies Cocoa with a new husband and two sons and moves everyone to Charleston, which is urban but still southern enough. "It was easier . . . and I drew strength from moving in the midst of familiar ground," observes Cocoa. Forty-seven at the end of the book, she is quieter and mellower; but the changes in her have not unfolded in the course of daily events. Rather, they are magical transformations worked by the extravagant tragedy Naylor has fashioned here. The questions set out at the beginning are never resolved. For instance, how will Cocoa manage her life with a husband who exults in watching football games, is determined to emulate the material lifestyle of the professional middle class, and who, despite his sensitivity to women, seems to expect his wife to devote herself primarily to bearing and raising his family? ("I'd gladly stay home and have four babies," George had offered, "if you promise to go out and break your back for me.")

How will Cocoa manage to hand down to her children her own sense of history and heritage, far from her family in Willow Springs? How will she find a way to use her heritage to strengthen herself? How will she transform herself from an insecure young woman into a mature one? How will she integrate her knowledge of white culture and history with Black culture and history? All these issues remain unexplored. And it is too bad, because they are important, more important than the tale of terror and suspense that *Mama Day* becomes.

◆◆◆◆◆◆◆◆◆◆◆◆◆◆

BHARATI MUKHERJEE

The New York Times Book Review, February 21, 1988

On a note card above my writing desk hang the words of the late American original, Liberace: "Too much of a good thing is simply wonderful."

Excess—of plots and subplots, of major characters and walk-ons, of political issues and literary allusions—is what Gloria Naylor's *Mama Day,* her third and most ambitious book, is blessed with. "There are just too many sides to the whole story," Cocoa, Mama Day's grandniece, explains at the end of this longish novel, and the story obviously feels urgent enough to both Cocoa and to Ms. Naylor that they present it to us whole.

If novels are viewed as having the power to save, then novelists are obliged, first, to relive the history of the errors of earlier chroniclers and filling in the missing parts. Recent novels like *Mama Day,* Toni Morrison's *Beloved* and Louise Erdrich's *Love Medicine* resonate with the genuine excitement of authors discovering ways, for the first time it seems, to write down what had only been intuited or heard. These are novelists with an old-fashioned "calling" (to bear witness, to affirm public virtues) in a post-modernist world; their books are scaled down for today's microwavable taste, but still linked to the great public voice of 19th-century storytelling.

Mama Day has its roots in *The Tempest.* The theme is reconciliation, the title character is Miranda (also the name of Prospero's daughter), and Willow Springs is an isolated island where, as on Prospero's isle, magical and mysterious events come to pass. As in *The Tempest,* one story line concerns the magician Miranda Day, nicknamed Mama Day, and her acquisition, exercise, and relinquishment of magical powers. The other story line concerns a pair of "star-crossed" (Ms. Naylor's phrase, too) lovers: Ophelia Day, nicknamed Cocoa, and George Andrews.

Willow Springs is a wondrous island, wonderfully rendered. We learn its secrets only if we let ourselves listen to inaudible voices in boarded-up houses and hard-to-reach graveyards. We find out the way the locals do, "sitting on our porches and shelling June peas, quieting the midnight cough of a baby, taking apart the engine of a car—you done heard it without a single living soul really saying a word."

On this wondrous island, slavery and race relations, lovers' quarrels, family scandals, professional jealousies all become the "stuff as dreams are made on." The island itself sits just out of the legal reaches of Georgia and South Carolina. "And the way we saw it," ghosts whisper, "America ain't entered the question at all when it come to our land. . . . We wasn't even Americans when we got it—[we] was slaves. And the laws about slaves not owning nothing in Georgia and South Carolina don't apply, 'cause the land wasn't then—and isn't now—in either of them places."

America, with all its greed and chicanery, exists beyond a bridge. The island was "settled" (if that word is ever appropriate in American history) in the first quarter of the 19th century by an African-born slave, a spirited woman named Sapphira who, according to legend, bore her master, a Norwegian immigrant named Bascombe Wade, and maybe person or persons unknown, a total of seven sons. She then persuaded Bascombe to deed the children every square inch of Willow Springs, after which she either poisoned or stabbed the poor man in bed and vanished ahead of a posse. We find out the conditions of Sapphira's bondage only at the end of the novel: love, and not a bill of sale, had kept Bascombe and Sapphira together. Bascombe had given up his land to her sons willingly. This disclosure may make for "incorrect" politics, but it is in keeping with the "Tempest"-like atmosphere of benevolence, light and harmony that Ms. Naylor wishes to have prevail on Willow Springs.

Mama Day, who made a brief appearance in Ms. Naylor's earlier novel, "Linden Hills," as the toothless, illiterate aunt, the wearer of ugly, comfortable shoes, the hauler of cheap cardboard suitcases and leaky jars of homemade preserves, the caster of hoodoo spells, comes into her own in this novel. The portrait of Mama Day is magnificent:

> Miranda, Sister, Little Mama, Mama Day. Melting, melting away under the sweet flood waters pouring down to lay bare a place she ain't known existed: Daughter. And she opens the mouth that ain't there to suckle at the full breasts, deep greedy swallows of a thickness like cream, seeping from the corners of her lips, spilling onto her chin. Full. Full and warm to rest between the mounds of softness, to feel the beating of a calm and steady heart. She sleeps within her sleep.

Mama Day—over 100 years old if we are to believe what folks in Willow Springs say, unmarried, stern, wise, crotchety, comforting—is the true heir of Sapphira Wade. Sapphira and Bascombe's love nest, a yellow house set deep in the woods, yields secrets about the future as well as the past to the witch-prophet-matriarch Mama Day. She is the ur-Daughter to Sapphira's ur-Mother and, in turn, through a Leda-and-the-Swan kind of mysterious dead-of-night visitations, she peoples the land herself.

Mama Day has special powers. She and her people believe in a pre-Christian, pre-rational reality in which the good magician can sprinkle love powders and speed up happy events, and the bad magician can very nearly ruin things by brewing up pots of poisoned tea and rubbing fatal oils into brides' braids. Mama Day's observations have the simple force of parables. She can use a torn-up chicken coop to get across her moral message: "Just like that chicken coop, everything got four sides: his side, her side, an outside, and an inside. All of it is the truth." The truth, however, requires belief in the existence of alternate realities, in ghosts and spells.

While Ms. Naylor emphasizes the ur-Mother aspect of the Day women, this novel is also partially in a dialogue with 19th-century slave narratives, one aim of which, as young scholars like Barbara McCaskill of Emory University have pointed out, was for black women writers to convince pro-abolitionist Northern white women that blacks had as much capacity for maternal feelings as whites; propaganda to the contrary was cooked up by slave traders interested in facilitating guiltless sales.

As long as the narrative confines itself to Mama Day and daily life on the bizarre island full of rogues, frauds, crazies, martyrs and clairvoyants, the novel moves quickly. Curiously, the slow sections are about the love story of 27-year-old Cocoa, who has relocated from Willow Springs to New York, and George Andrews, who is meant to be emblematic of the good-hearted, hard-driving but culturally orphaned Northern black man. The courtship occurs all over Manhattan—in greasy diners, in three-star restaurants, in midtown offices, on subways—giving Ms. Naylor a chance to accommodate several set pieces. But she is less proficient in making the familiar wondrous than she is in making the wondrous familiar. Discussions of black bigotry (Cocoa uses kumquats, tacos, and bagels as race-related shorthand and has to be scolded into greater tolerance) or of the alienating effects of Bernard College on black women ("those too bright, too jaded colored girls" is George's put-down) seem like arbitrary asides.

The love story suffers from a more serious flaw. Ms. Naylor, through strident parallels, wants us to compare Cocoa and George to Romeo and Juliet, and their courtship process to the taming of Katharina, the "shrew." The literary plan calls for George to sacrifice his life so that Cocoa might be saved, but the lovers never quite fill out their assigned mythic proportions. Cocoa just seems shallow and self-centered; and George is a priggish young man who wears dry-cleaned blue jeans for roughing it on weekends. For their love story to overwhelm us, with "all passion spent," the lovers' intensity should make whole paragraphs resonate. This, unfortunately, Ms. Naylor does not do. It seems the unchallenged domain of the 19th-century novel to link personal passion with the broader politics of an age. Cocoa is not Madame Bovary, Anna Karenina, Jane Eyre, Dorothea Brooke.

But I'd rather dwell on "Mama Day"'s strengths. Gloria Naylor has written a big, strong, dense, admirable novel; spacious, sometimes a little drafty like all public monuments, designed to last and intended for many levels of use.

◆◆◆◆◆◆◆◆◆◆◆◆◆

RACHEL HASS

The Boston Review, June 1988

Gloria Naylor's new novel takes us to places rarely seen inside the contemporary black experience. *Mama Day* wrestles with a central question for blacks, Jews, and immigrants in America: how does one excel in society without losing or compromising cultural history?

Naylor takes us to Willow Springs, an island off the southeast coast of the United States, where in 1823 a black slave woman who had married her master took her husband's life after forcing him to deed his land to all the slaves and their descendants. Isolated for 150 years, Willow Springs in the eighties is an unaffiliated state with its own codes and rituals that make history a part of everyday life.

The leader and representative spirit of Willow Springs is Miranda Day, known to all as Mama Day. Not an old lady sitting on her front porch in a rocking chair, swaying back in time, Mama Day lives in the present tense, feeding the chickens, healing the sick, organizing candlelight ceremonies. Grounded by history and directed by instinct, Mama Day wields the power and authority of a magician. She can tell if life has begun inside a chicken egg by holding it to the light of a candle; she can diagnose internal cysts of a pregnant woman by slipping her hand inside "a path she knew so well that the slightest change of moisture, the amount of give along the walls, or the scent left on her hands could fix a woman's cycle within less than a day of what was happening with the moon." In a dark forest, "she knows every crook and bend, every tree that falls and those that are about to sprout."

When native islanders leave Willow Springs, they "go Mainside: and stay there. Those who remain believe that if you 'cross over' you leave something behind which may be your soul. Mama Day's niece Cocoa is one of the few to leave the island and return. In doing so she becomes the agent of change and continuity. Cocoa goes to New York where she meets and starts a relationship with George, a football fanatic. . . . Because the times I got it right, your being different made all the difference in my world."

Naylor takes us beyond the conflict of gender to show how everyone has a history. Cocoa carries the strength of Willow Springs; George is the son of a prostitute who abandons him as an infant. Cocoa is fueled by her family history; George must discover his own. Together they unpack their emotional luggage and we're never sure when the suitcase will come out again.

Mama Day's loosely distributed narrative allows many voices to sing at once. Characters shout off the page; whisper in your ear. The scenes between Cocoa and George read as a series of monologues, providing insight into both sides.

The author rarely bothers to tell who is talking; language identifies people with their own particular history. Naylor uses the island dialect and modern English to place her novel on Willow Springs or in New York. In doing so she brings separate worlds onto the same page, without explanation or translation, and demands coexistence of the past with the present. The rhythm of the prose pulls you inside the story like a magnet.

Gloria Naylor makes magic, as well as fiction. Like her characters, she has the ability to believe and writes with the power of knowing that anything is possible.

◆◆◆◆◆◆◆◆◆◆◆◆◆◆

ROSELLEN BROWN

Ms., February 1988

Gloria Naylor is building a world. *Mama Day* is the third in a set of novels whose locales and characters are loosely interrelated. *The Women of Brewster Place* come to their ghetto street when hope and possibility run out; on the other side of a dividing wall their rich but equally desperate neighbors in *Linden Hills* live trapped in artifice and greed.

In search of yet another kind of destiny, *Mama Day* plays out a preoccupation of black writers in general, and black women in particular, with the gains and losses that have come with the move from rural to urban, from intuitive to rational, life. Alice Walker's mother's garden, Toni Morrison's faith in the *other* reality of hauntings and magical powers—all are related to the contest in *Mama Day* between the two ways of knowledge. Naylor's book is a paean to the old mysteries of the irrational, and to the heroines who have, throughout history, wielded enormous powers of healing and wholeness.

Ophelia, nicknamed Cocoa, is a smart, appealing young New Yorker with a mouth on her, the kind of woman who gets tips on sharp dressing from *Essence*, who shops for a job with an impressive résumé in her big stylish purse. She addresses, in her chapters, a young man named George Andrews who looks like the same kind of yuppie, cool black version, and who's clearly a terrific husband for Cocoa once they get past some initial hostilities; in his chapters he talks back.

But as so often happens, especially among first generation high achievers, both have been shaped irrevocably by backgrounds invisible to the eye. Cocoa grew up in the island town of Willow Springs, neither in Georgia nor in South Carolina, a sort of bastard beauty of a place connected to the inferior civilization of both states by a bridge. She is the latest and last extension of an extraordinary family founded in 1823 by the union of a slave owner and spirited slave named Sapphira. Cocoa is the much-loved and petted daughter of the daughter of the seventh son. (Her cousin, Willa Nedeed, perished in the conflagration that brought *Linden Hills* to its apocalyptic conclusion.)

George, on the other hand, as sympathetic as any man to appear in the recent fiction of black women, has no family history. He has grown up a perfect representative of the benign but fiercely focused philosophy of the directors of his boys' shelter who help their charges overcome the bleakness of their beginnings by exhorting them to "Keep it in the now, fellas." This has made him a succesful engineer, a sincere pursuer of culture at the same time that he's a fanatic football fan, a connoisseur of the here-and-now pleasures of New York City, a thoughtful lover.

This opening quarter of *Mama Day* gives us a side of Gloria Naylor we haven't seen before in its amplitude and wit. More conversational than her previous books, *Mama Day* show us the young black couple's "social smarts," as opposed to the "street smarts" we've had in so much fiction about the urban poor. George and Cocoa go at each other with a charming nastiness born of their weariness with certain familiar patterns in office, friendship, bedroom politics. (Cocoa talks about blacks who are "the disciples of a free market with a Christ complex: they went to the Cross and rose without affirmative action." George tells Cocoa that people are like food to her: fudge sticks, kumquats, bagels, zucchinis, a litany of insulting metaphors by which she characterizes the types around her.) Has anyone else written about characters like this?

But the author's purpose is not to dwell "beyond the bridge" with Cocoa. With a nearly audible sigh of relief, Naylor takes her back south and puts her in the hands of her great-aunt, Mama Day, a canny, confident mix of midwife and conjure-woman, of soul and psychology, who knows dangerous secrets and can cure almost anything if she can get her patient's commitment. Mama Day is the essence of all good things to Naylor: respect for life, for family and nature, a comprehension of the way to harness natural forces, an acceptance of death. Hers is the single face "that's been given the meaning of peace."

To simplify a complicated plot that is alternately affecting and silly, though never less than interesting, someone is out to get Cocoa, not merely by badmouthing her but by putting a hex on her and augmenting it with real poison.

Between Cocoa's problem and nearly everyone else's, Naylor keeps Mama Day busy arranging powerful currents: there are taints, curses, cooperative forces, there is luck and fate, there is hope, belief, and finally the primacy of the inexplicable to which George and his rational convictions, the essence of life "beyond the bridge," are sacrificed. There is not much irony in this—although Cocoa insists there are many ways to look at the tragic denouement of her marriage to George, the ineluctable power of island wisdom wins out.

The schematic parts of *Mama Day*, when the power of the old wisdom is at hand, are clearly what Naylor wants us to pay close attention to, and they are lively and specific enough to go down more easily than many literary lessons. But, heretical or not, I can't help but wish she felt less of a need to elevate by making symbolic, or by fitting everything into a larger scheme—*Linden Hills* used nothing less than the *Inferno* as an armature. Most black novelists, granted, might call it a white folks' luxury to write, in novelist Paula Fox's memorable phrase, "uncompromised by purpose." But when she is not didactically fostering our spiritual instruction, Gloria Naylor serves another worthy purpose beautifully: she invites us to imagine the lives of complex characters at work and play, and gives us a faithfully rendered community in all its seasons. I hope she'll choose to continue to move, in a loose and unconstrained stride, in that direction.

BAILEY'S CAFE (1992)

◆◆◆◆◆◆◆◆◆◆◆◆◆

KAREN JOY FOWLER

The Chicago Tribune, October 4, 1992

Geographically, Bailey's Cafe is everywhere. It can be entered from the real world at any point; its address is despair.

In *Bailey's Cafe*, the audacious and mesmerizing new novel from Gloria Naylor *(The Women of Brewster Place, Linden Hills* and *Mama Day)*, the author tells us the stories of some of the people who find the cafe. Memorable and musical, harsh and funny, strange and familiar, these stories are narrated, for most of the book, by the cafe's cook and manager. Bailey is not his name, but he lets us call him that. He is a wonderful character, full of humor and insight, and his voice sings us through the painful parts of his own story. Yet Naylor's finest achievement remains the cafe itself.

Bailey's Cafe is a halfway house—halfway between the finite and the infinite, halfway between the belief that the universe cares for us as individuals and the evidence that it does not. Because these two positions would seem to be mutually exclusive, it is delightful to watch as Naylor manages not only to argue on both sides but also to embody the contradiction as an actual restaurant. The edge of the world is at the front door of Bailey's Cafe and the void at the back.

A person finds Bailey's when he or, more often, she reaches a certain level of hopelessness. The cafe offers its customers a menu of indifferent food—except for the weekends, when anything desired is available—and a period of time in which no time passes. "Unless there's some space, some place, to take a breather for a while, the edge of the world—frightening as it is—could be the end of the world, which would be quite a pity," says Bailey.

It's only a way station, Eve tells us, with no guarantees. Eve runs the equally phantasmagorical boarding house, unless it's a brothel, down the street. Eve's brownstone is surrounded by a garden of wildflowers; each of the women who stays there has her own totemic bloom. To see a particular woman a man must buy her particular flower from Eve and take it as an offering.

We hear several stories about the women in Eve's boarding house, and Eve's is one of them. Thrown out of her home by her godfather for a display of sexuality, she makes a perilous journey to New Orleans. This trial destroys and remakes her. No later challenge the world holds can do more than bore her. "If I could get through all I'd gotten through, then I was overqualified to be the mayor of New Orleans. And much too overqualified to be the governor of Louisiana. And when I kept thinking on up the line, the comparisons were beneath contempt."

Eve is a customer in the cafe, but as proprietor of the boarding house she holds more power within this quasi-nether world than anyone else seems to. Only she makes actual decisions about who may stay and who will go. She is not moved by charity. We see her refuse one of the saddest cases, and Bailey, in whose judgment we place a certain amount of trust on such matters, assures us that Eve is not a charitable woman. Her powers and motives remain elusive and mysterious.

The book contains a second forceful woman, less powerful but equally knowing. She is Nadine, Bailey's wife. Bailey tells us about his courtship of her. He saw her at a baseball game, followed her and then, afraid to attract her attention in any way that would make him seem a masher, dumped a sherbet cone down her dress. "Then she smacked me in the head with her straw purse," he tells us. "The courtship was on."

Bailey loves his wife, but has a hard time liking her. Yet they are "the right kind of fit." Bailey is loquacious, Nadine supernaturally taciturn. Her silence has such a powerful, magical feel that one of the book's few disappointments is the chapter in which she begins to talk. She gives us the story of Mariam, a story she warns us is so horrifically female, Bailey has sneaked off rather than tell it to us. (A lie, Bailey assures us later.) The story is a moving one, but Nadine's voice is insufficiently differentiated from the other women's and too ordinary to belong to Nadine.

In fact, two of the most successful stories are the two about men—Bailey's own and the one told by Miss Maple, the thoroughly male, cross-dressing bouncer at Eve's boarding house. It is not that these stories are any less or any more painful than the women's, but the men's voices have a lighter touch.

The book is clearly religious—filled with Biblical references and retorts to Biblical stories—and, just as clearly, magical. It posits the destructive power of real events and argues that fiction is equally powerful. It encompasses history, myth, imagination and quotidian detail. So much is packed into a relatively short book, so little left out, that it spills into the imagination of the reader and travels in a hundred different directions.

This abundance plays against the particular pains contained in the various character's stories. Pain is one thing the world contains in excessive amounts; Naylor doesn't hesitate to show us this. But the world contains everything else in excessive amounts as well. Through her beautiful prose and by way of a reckless inclusion, Gloria Naylor achieves an exuberance that prevents "Bailey's Cafe," pain-filled as it is, from being an unhappy book.

DONNA RIFKIND

The Washington Post, October 11, 1992

Gloria Naylor's is a commanding fictional voice: sonorous, graceful, sometimes piercing, often spellbinding. At its best, it's the kind of voice that moves you along as if you were dreaming. But it runs the risk, at its worst, of overpowering the voices of her own carefully imagined characters.

Naylor offers characteristic highs and lows in her fourth book, *Bailey's Cafe*. Like the author's 1983 prize-winning novel, *The Women of Brewster Place*, the new book is set up as a series of interweaving life portraits. We are in Brooklyn, 1948: Bailey, the cafe's proprietor, presides over the grill while his taciturn wife Nadine runs the cash register.

The coffee here is bad and the food worse, but the place has a mystical pull that attracts people with long histories and invites them to remember. "It's the last place before the end of the world for some," says Bailey; and, he warns, if you go out the back door you'll find nothing there. "Since the place sits right on the margin between the edge of the world and infinite possibility, the back door opens out to a void."

So the cafe is part dream allegory, part greasy-spoon reality. If it reminds you a little bit of *The Canterbury Tales*, it's supposed to: Chaucer's host at the Tabard Inn was Harry Bailly, and Naylor's chorus of tale-telling voices echoes its 14th-century ancestor. (This is an author accomplished at giving world literature an African-American spin. Her *Linden Hills* was based on Dante's *Inferno*, while *Mama Day*, her third novel, owed much to *The Tempest*.)

Who are the latter-day pilgrims swapping stories and eating peach cobbler at Bailey's? There is Sadie, a wino and two-bit prostitute who lives on the streets but is perfecting an immaculate dream house in her imagination. There's Peaches, whose self-hatred drives her to mutilate her beautiful face, and Jesse Bell, who is haunted by a scandal-ridden marriage, and a heroin habit she can't shake.

For the most part, Naylor steps aside and lets her characters tell their own tales of hopes abandoned and dreams deferred—and some of the stories, most notably Sadie's, are extraordinarily poignant. But here and there the author falters, as in the tale of Mariam, a 14-year-old black Ethiopian Jewess who was ostracized from her village because she is pregnant. Somehow her wandering through the continents has brought her to Brooklyn and Bailey's, where the cafe owner/narrator delivers some distinctly unfictional opinions about the state of Israel.

"Israel isn't gonna be run any differently from any other country," exhorts Bailey. (It is 1948, remember, the year Israel's status as a nation became official.) "Inside those borders it's the same old story: You got your haves and your have nots. You got those who are gonna be considered inferior to others because of the type of Jew they are, the color of Jew they are, or whatever. But above all, the groups who are in power are going to do whatever they can to stay in power."

Opinions like these have every right to be expressed. The trouble is that Naylor does not quite convince us that Bailey is doing the expressing. These views suffer from the harshness of hindsight: They sound much more like those of a novelist in the 1990s than a cafe owner in the 1940s. The fictional dream has been interrupted, abruptly, by an argument that is supposed to be a plea for tolerance but in fact comes dangerously close to sounding like a soapbox denunciation from the author's own mouth. (At one point she even writes that Mariam would not have been allowed into Israel under the Law of Return because she's unfamiliar with the Talmud, an accusation that is entirely untrue.)

And this from a writer who has just finished giving a touching portrait of a Stanford graduate, a Ph.D. in statistics who can't get hired anywhere in America because he is black and who—somehow not at all improbably—takes to wearing women's clothing: Computing the odds, he finds that he has as much chance of employment if he cross-dresses as if he does not. Through the statistician's own persuasive voice Naylor manages to make a genuine appeal for tolerance—there are many such appeals throughout her fiction—and one that makes the criticisms of Israel all the more incongruous.

Fortunately, jarring authorial interruptions in the novel are few, and are more than balanced by many beautifully realized set pieces. Listen to the lyricism in this passage as Bailey watches the statistician, known as Miss Maple, toast the New Year:

"The bells outside begin to toll for midnight, 1949. He takes his full champagne glass to the rear of the cafe . . . He steps off boldly into the midst of nothing and is suspended midair by a gentle wind that starts to swirl his cape around his knees. It's a hot, dry wind that could easily have been born in a desert, but it's bringing, of all things, snow . . . He holds his glass up and turns to me as a single flake catches on the rim before melting down the side into an amber world where bubbles burst and are born, burst and are born."

This is no ordinary writing. It leaves one with the impression that, while she has already distinguished herself as a formidable novelist, Gloria Naylor's best work has yet to be done.

◆◆◆◆◆◆◆◆◆◆◆◆◆◆

DAN WAKEFIELD

The New York Times Book Review, October 4, 1992

At first I was fooled by the folksy touches of *Bailey's Cafe*—the home-sewn red checkered curtains hanging from the brass rail, the peach cobbler that Nadine only dishes up when the mood hits her, nostalgic tales of Smokey Joe Williams and other stars of the old Negro baseball leagues winningly told by the owner and grill man, a native of Flatbush who says he is "majoring in Life"—even the name of his place, which is also the name of the book. All this seemed to suggest a warmhearted, mom-and-pop-store philosophy in a neighborhood of citizens known then as "colored people" in the Brooklyn of 1948.

The first two patrons we meet are familiar stock types—Sister Carrie, the pious, scripture-quoting lady who is a "Cornerstone of the Temple of Perpetual Redemption," and Sugar Man, the "all-around hustler and pimp" with the fancy clothes and the 1936 Duesenberg. The grill-man narrator known as Bailey admits after introducing the pair that "if you don't listen below the surface, they're both one-note players. Flat and predictable. But nobody comes in here with a simple story. Every one-liner's got a life underneath it. . . . Let's just take 'em one key down."

Gloria Naylor, the author of "The Women of Brewster Place" and other novels, takes us many keys down, and sometimes back up, in this virtuoso orchestration of survival, suffering, courage and humor, sounding through the stories of these lives. They are told in a variety of voices, sometimes of Bailey (not his name, but he didn't want to change the sign when he bought the cafe), sometimes the customers, sometimes as third-person narration, blending historical and personal data ("This summer the talk is of Dewey's upcoming election—and Eve") with surreal beauty ("Cascades of light flowing in, breaking up, and rolling like fluid diamonds over the worn tile. . . . It went on for hours").

The pain that is a natural component of these lives is seared into our consciousness, as it is in the flesh of a woman who comes to the boardinghouse-bordello down the street who "had Lucky Strike spelled out on the inside of her thigh with a lit cigarette butt. A reminder to get the right brand the next time she was sent to the store." A "cocoa-butter dream" named Mary, in order to escape the imprisonment of her lover with his pearl-handled razor and his clubfoot, tries to destroy her own beauty by cutting her face with a beer opener. She explains she couldn't hold the opener when her hands got too slippery from the gushing blood after the first incision: "I made a poor job of it. I had to resort to sawing my way down, leaving hunks of flesh wedged between the two prongs of the opener. That took so much time that when I'd only reached the bottom jawbone, the pain was so intense I passed out."

Sadie the wino, Jesse Bell the heroin addict and the others we meet all know, like the self-scarred Mary, "You can find Bailey's Cafe in any town," for this setting is not the geography of Brooklyn but the territory of the soul. Bailey's "sits right on the margin between the edge of the world and infinite possibility." You step out the back door "into the midst of nothing" and there are people who come in and head straight for that door and are never seen again. Yet others with the same intention stay, and find some quirky, unexpected, singular kind of salvation (is there any other?)—like Stanley, whose middle names are Beckwourth Booker T. Washington Carver, but who is now called Miss Maple.

Stanley earned his Ph.D. in mathematics at Stanford and traveled across America the summer of '48 in search of a job as a statistical analyst in marketing ("The offers accumulated: bellboy, mailroom clerk, sleeping-car porter, elevator operator"). Along the way, in the process of collecting 99 job rejections, he traded in his sweltering gray flannel suit for what he discerned as the practical comfort of a light percale housedress, realizing the garb made no difference at all in his chance as a Negro in '48 America of getting the job he sought.

Stanley is transformed from a sweating gray-flannel corporate aspirant to a cool housekeeper (and nighttime bouncer) at Eve's boarding-house-bordello, where he wears light percale housedresses to work. Bailey attests to the manhood of Miss Maple, explaining that "in the summer, when he takes a day off he might show up in here with a backless sundress or a little cotton romper. We're talking no wigs. We're talking no makeup. No padded falsies. No switching. And if it's near the evening, we're talking a five o'clock shadow that he runs his hands over like any tired man after a day of hard work."

Bailey says he doesn't believe in happy endings (I'm sure he means the unearned kind), yet the finale of all these stories is not madness or darkness but light and birth. All those on the street gather for the delivery of a son by a pregnant 14-year-old Ethiopian Jew named Mariam who claims "No man has ever touched me." She is brought to Bailey's Cafe by Gabe, the neighborhood pawnbroker from the Caucasus ("His spine is bent from straddling so much of the world for so long and his eyes water constantly from the strain of all he's seen").

When the baby's first thin cry is heard, the place goes wild—customers climb on tables and chairs, or join hands and stomp the floor, and someone starts singing a spiritual:

"Soon we were all singing, a bit ragged and off-key. But all singing."

Ms. Naylor has earned the song.

PETER ERICKSON

Kenyon Review 15, Summer 1993

Bailey's Cafe (Harcourt Brace Jovanovich) is the fourth in a sequence of novels that Gloria Naylor has conceived as a quartet. Hitherto, she has used two devices to create a sense of linkage from one novel to the next. The first is to develop a character or situation referred to in a previous novel; the second is to continue a pattern of allusions to Shakespeare. In this final novel of the quartet, however, Naylor teases us by deferring fulfillment of these expectations for so long that we have just about forgotten or given up. For example, Mama Day, the third novel, has planted George's reference to his birth at Bailey's Cafe. Yet Naylor makes us wait until the last three pages of the novel Bailey's Cafe before mentioning George and revealing who his mother is and where (unbeknownst to George) he fits in the overall scheme. The comment of one of the characters—"in this business you could use a sense of humor"— applies to Naylor's role as novelist.

Initially, the strongest connection Bailey's Cafe demonstrates with Naylor's previous work is to her first novel, The Women of Brewster Place. Like the earlier novel, Bailey's Cafe presents a series of stories about down-and-out women. The resemblance is sufficiently close that the basic approach now seems routine, predictable, at times even trite. Having delayed almost too late until the last third of the novel, Naylor springs a surprise. The last, longest, and most important story is devoted to a man. This is where Naylor breaks new ground. The legacy from the first three novels in the quartet is a line of failed, incomplete, or uncertain male characters: from the negative instances of the brutal young rapists and the helplessly alcoholic Ben in The Women of Brewster Place to the shaky efforts of Lester and Willie in Linden Hills and George in Mama Day to break out and to seek alternative modes of masculine identity. In Bailey's Cafe Naylor provides a positive model of masculinity. It is a sign of Naylor's humor that the man capable of this masculinity bears the name Miss Maple and wears women's dresses.

However, Naylor emphasizes that Miss Maple represents a case neither of sexual ambiguity nor gender indeterminacy. Sugar Man, the epitome of traditional manhood, demonstrates the false perception created by anxiety: "And it does no good to tell him for the thousandth time that Miss Maple isn't a homosexual. Sugar Man has had to cling onto that or he would just about lose his senses when Miss Maple is around." In order to reach a different definition of manhood, Miss Maple, then Stanley, has had to overcome the same anxiety: "Manhood is a pervasive preoccupation when you're an adolescent boy, and you tend to see a fairy under every bush." This fear is concentrated on his father, whom the son regards according to convention as "a coward" for his refusal to fight back against white racist harassment: "I didn't see him as a man at all." Eventually the boy's view is reversed: he breaks out of the impasse in which his resentment toward his father has trapped him and comes to realize that his father is instead the model for an alternative manhood: "how to be my own man." How Naylor brings about this transformation is testimony to the brilliance of her comic imagination.

In the funniest moment of the book, Naylor has father and son stripped naked and locked in a storeroom by four uncouth white brothers, whereupon the two black men put on female clothing, break out of their prison, and take revenge by summarily dispatching each of the four whites in turn. The scene could not be more cartoonish, slapstick, and farcical, yet the secret of Naylor's comic inventiveness is that its effects are both hilarious and deeply moving at the same time, as though the hilarity gave access to deeper levels of feeling. Under the duress of their imprisonment, Stanley's angry outburst against his father suddenly gives way to the physical contact he had earlier shunned: "Papa reached out to me in the darkness and I jerked my shoulder away from his hands. Don't you touch me. My teeth were clenched. Just don't touch me."

> You don't even amount to the ape they [the white men] called you—you're nothing. And you've always been nothing. Nothing . . . nothing . . . noth. . . .
> My whole body started vibrating, my teeth chattering, my hands and leg muscles moving with a will of their own. He caught me in his arms before I fell to the floor. And then he placed me down gently to hold me as I cried like the child I was.
> My flesh againt his flesh. . .

Forced by the occasion, the father for the first time expresses his hope that his son "identify yourself as a man" and the son begins to have a new understanding of what—from his father's perspective—it means "to become a man."

Of course, this reconciliation of father and son is confirmed by the father's abandonment of passive resistance and his recourse to violent retaliation. Ironically, what finally provokes his heroic attack is the white men's desecration of the complete set of Shakespeare volumes the father has purchased as a "legacy" for his son: "They had gotten to the books. The silk cover was gouged with holes, the spine busted and bent over double. They'd torn out handfuls of pages, crushed what was left between their fists, and then urinated on the whole thing. The stench of

The Tempest was quickly filling the whole room." The entire network of Shakespearean allusions through the previous three novels is compressed into one image—the Shakespeare corpus represented in the most literal way possible as a set of books, physical objects shipped in a crate. The image illustrates the complex, multiple effects of Naylor's comedy. On one level, the educated, self-confident black man is moved to defend the Shakespearean heritage against ignorant whites. Yet on another level the humor turns in a different direction to make the Caliban-like gesture of destroying the books a magnificent act of exorcism. As a fitting conclusion to her long engagement with Shakespeare over the course of the quartet, this farewell is a riddance ritual that announces the end of Naylor's artistic apprenticeship. The moment is not only unaccountably funny but also satisfying. The taboo surrounding Shakespeare as sacred icon is broken; we are allowed to experience Naylor's outrageous comic violation as a release.

The final section of the novel that follows Miss Maple's story continues the focus on male identity and enters what might be considered non-Shakespearean territory: the relationship between blacks and Jews. The problems of black anti-Semitism and Jewish racism have recently received new attention. Naylor's contribution to this discussion is deeply affecting because she is able to use the medium of fiction to convey the possibility of cooperation. The black male proprietor of Bailey's Cafe and Babe the Jewish owner of the pawnshop are brought together specifically to bless the baby boy to whom Miriam, an Ethiopian Jew, has given birth. The festive response by the novel's three key male figures to "the baby's first thin cry" is touching: "Then Gabe grabbed me, whirled me around, and we started to dance. He could kick pretty high for an old goat. Miss Maple took his other hand and the three of us were out in the middle of the floor, hands raised and feet stomping." The same three men preside over the formal ceremony of circumcision: "I had to stand in as the honorary *sandek*, the godfather. And Miss Maple took the role of the other male guests to help me respond to the blessing. Don't worry, Gabe said; God will forgive you for not being Jews." Through this cross-cultural nurturant concern, the novel provides a final suggestion of a new male identity. At the risk of sounding ungrateful in the face of the genuine gratitude I feel, I must also register the negative side of this positive outcome. Political and ceremonial discourse is made to seem a largely male affair. The one explicit protest against this state—that of Miriam's mother—is not fully or clearly stated.

ESSAYS

◆◆◆◆◆◆◆◆◆◆◆◆◆

Authorial Dreams of Wholeness: (Dis)Unity, (Literary) Parentage, and *The Women of Brewster Place*

MICHAEL AWKWARD

I wrote because I had no choice, but that was a long road from gathering the authority within myself to believe that I could actually be a writer. The writers I had been taught to love were either male or white. And who was I to argue that Ellison, Austen, Dickens, the Brontës, Baldwin and Faulkner weren't masters? They were and are. But inside there was still the faintest whisper: Was there no one telling my story? And since it appeared there was not, how could I presume to? . . . [Reading] The Bluest Eye [was] the beginning [of my ability to conceive of myself as a writer]. . . . The presence of the work . . . said to a young black woman, struggling to find a mirror of her worth in this society, not only is your story worth telling but it can be told in words so painfully eloquent that it becomes a song.

—Gloria Naylor,
"A Conversation" (with Toni Morrison)

In his essay "Art as a Cultural System," Clifford Geertz says of the coalescence of form and content in art:

> The unity of form and content is, where it occurs and to the degree it occurs, a cultural achievement, not a philosophical tautology. If there is to be a semiotic science of art it is that achievement it will have to explain.[1]

While my discussion of form-content coalescence (and concurrent explorations of double consciousness) is certainly not offered as a "science" of Afro-American textual reading, it does, I hope, serve to exemplify the semiotic notion that art forms, as Geertz puts it, "materialize a way of experiencing, bring a particular cast of mind out into the world of objects, where men can look at it." What my readings in this study allow men and women to look at, if these readings are successfully lucid, is Black culture's insistence on unity, even in the face of powerfully divisive opposition.

The unity of form and content in Gloria Naylor's *The Women of Brewster Place* is, like that of its female-authored precursors, essentially related to its exploration of the redemptive possibilities of female coalescence. But because it is a work that consists of the narratively *disconnected* stories of individual women, such coalescence does not involve simply an individual protagonist's inside and outside as it does in *Their Eyes Were Watching God* and *The Bluest Eye*. Rather, it involves demonstrating—both by exhibiting essential psychological and circum-

37

stantial affinities between the women and by offering significant evidence of these women's recognition of such affinities—that the protagonists of the individual texts actually form, at the novel's conclusion, a community of women. As is the case in both of the texts on which this study has concentrated to this point, textual explorations of female unity in Naylor's novel are unmistakably related to the work's narrative strategies, strategies whose ends are underscored by the novel's subtitle, "A Novel in Seven Stories": to demonstrate that the narratively disconnected texts of individual protagonists can be forged into a unified whole.

Naylor's narrative tasks are seemingly complicated by the means she chooses to demonstrate an achieved Afro-American woman's community. In a novel in which unrealistic dreams are the source of much of the female characters' pain, the author's depiction of the scene of female coalescence—the women's unified efforts to tear down the wall that separates Brewster Place from the rest of the city—as the grief-inspired dream of one of these characters prevents a reading of Naylor's portrait of female nexus as either an actual narrative event or a realistic possibility. *The Women of Brewster Place*'s totalizing gesture, then, evidences the work's textual disjunctions. If Naylor's novel displays a unity of form and content, it is a unity based on a common *disunity*, on a shared failure to achieve wholeness.

My subsequent discussion will demonstrate that despite its various disjunctive elements, *The Women of Brewster Place*'s relation to the novels previously discussed in this study is not essentially a parodic one. In other words, Naylor's novel does not employ *Their Eyes Were Watching God* or *The Bluest Eye* as misinformed works whose correction offers—as is the case with Baldwin's "corrections" of Wright and Morrison's revisions of both the primer and Ellison's Trueblood episode—dramatic entry into the Afro-American literary tradition. Rather, these texts, along with other key Afro-American works which provocatively explore women's lives and the impediments to the development of cooperative Afro-American communities (namely, Ntozake Shange's *for colored girls*[2] and Jean Toomer's *Cane*), provide the textual foundation and material for the author's provocative explorations of the potential richness of narrative disunity.

II

Elaine Showalter's essay "Feminist Criticism in the Wilderness" argues that one means of advancing the study of women's literature is to describe and systematically account for the presence of both female and male precursorial influence in women's texts. She says:

> Our current theories of literary influence . . . need to be tested in terms of women's writings. If a man's text, as Bloom and Edward Said have main-

tained, is fathered, then a woman's text is not only mothered but parented; it confronts both paternal and maternal precursors and must deal with the problems and advantages of both lines of inheritance. . . . [A] woman writing unavoidably thinks back through her fathers as well [as her mothers].[3]

The notion of a female author's confrontation with a dual ancestry, of her text's "parented" status, is certainly applicable to the Afro-American woman's literary tradition which has—as much as its white woman's counterpart—been forced to develop (until very recently) in the shadows of an overwhelmingly male canon. My preceding chapter offers a detailed account of Toni Morrison's confrontations with such a dual parentage.

Morrison's refiguration of Ellison provides a suggestive literary example of the feminist revisionary impulse whose radically subversive goals the critic Sandra Gilbert characterize in the following way: "We [feminists] must redo our [Western] history . . . , we must review, reimagine, rethink, rewrite, revise, and reinterpret the events and documents that constitute [a thousand years of Western culture]."[4] Showalter, however, appears to condemn feminist criticism's revisionary emphasis, arguing that it "retards our progress in solving our own theoretical problems" and speaking approvingly of the fact that feminist criticism has "gradually shifted its center from revisionary readings to sustained investigation of literature by women." Showalter's views to the contrary notwithstanding, it seems to me that such a revisionary emphasis was a necessary moment in the history of contemporary feminist criticism. It allowed feminist critics and writers to expose the phallocentric myths that have long contaminated Western culture and literary history, clearing space for the types of sustained investigations Showalter desires.

Taken together, Gilbert's and Showalter's comments suggest a profitable way to conceptualize the primary differences between Morrison's and Naylor's first novels. *The Bluest Eye* stands as a revisionary reading whose textual struggles with white and Afro-American male-authored texts clear imaginative space for Naylor's sustained investigation of Afro-American women's life in *The Women of Brewster Place*. Morrison's stunning critical revision of Ellison's phallocentric *Invisible Man*, the Afro-American literary canon's most highly esteemed text, offers subsequent writers like Naylor a freedom from such corrective revisionary chores and an opportunity to establish less adversarial relationships with male writers whose work seriously and conscientiously considers Afro-American women.

Showalter argues that a parented woman's text "must deal with the problems and advantages of both lines of inheritance." It is difficult to discern in Morrison's revisionary ratios anything but the "problems" offered by *The Bluest Eye's* paternal precursor. With Naylor's text, however, one can observe both the provocative "advantages" and perplexing "problems" represented by *Cane*. (Interestingly, as we shall see, what is for Naylor perhaps the most significant advantage of *Cane* also serves as its most perplexing problem.) Toomer's influence is felt first in *The Women of Brewster Place*'s opening sentence: "Brewster Place was the bastard child of several clandestine meetings between the alderman of the sixth district and the managing director of Unico Realty Company."[5] The sentence is a direct echo of the first sentence of *Cane*'s "Seventh Street"—the text that introduces the movement northward of the narrative's focus: "Seventh Street is a bastard of Prohibition and War."[6]

The narrative structure of *The Women of Brewster Place* is, in fact, akin to *Cane*'s first section. For the novel presents, like the first section of Toomer's text, the self-titled stories of female protagonists followed by a concluding story that explores a female community's reaction to an ominous natural event. There is, thus, evidence of Naylor's refiguration of *Cane*'s content. But any literary descendant of Toomer more interested in the *form* of his presentation of women than in the *content* of such presentations—as I believe Naylor is—must confront the perplexing problem of *Cane*'s form: that is, its apparent disjunctiveness and refusal to fit comfortably into any Western generic category. Clearly, no current generic designation is appropriate to describe the curious admixture of vernacular songs, imagistic verse, experimental fiction and drama that make up *Cane*. An artist attempting to use Toomer's text as a model must come to terms, I believe, with how it achieves its "chaotic" unity.

Naylor's technical refigurations of Toomer, which I shall discuss more fully toward the close of this chapter, manifest her creative responses to the problem of *Cane*'s form. Before such responses can be demonstrated, however, it is necessary to chart her more content-oriented refigurations of *The Women of Brewster Place*'s maternal precursorial text, *The Bluest Eye*. Only when one comprehends the later work's revisionary gestures with respect to elements of Morrison's novel can one successfully describe Naylor's recapitulation of a Toomerian effect to compose a specifically Afro-American text.

III

Perhaps the most fruitful starting point in an exploration of Naylor's relationship to Morrison is the author's own comments about *The Bluest Eye* and its potential assistance to a beginning writer. In a *New York Times Book Review* article entitled "Famous First Words" in which various authors answer the question "What is your favorite opening passage in a work of literature, and why?", Naylor cites Claudia's preface to *The Bluest Eye*.

> Each writing seminar I teach begins with having my students read Toni Morrison's *Bluest Eye*. I believe that by taking apart the first novel of any great

writer, we can see plainly what strategies failed since it is a first work and where the germ of artistic brilliance lies since it is that particular author. With this passage [Claudia's preface], one of the novel's opening sections, I can demonstrate all the major elements of a writer's art simply through an exegesis of three short paragraphs. While the novel handles a weighty subject—the demoralization of black female beauty in a racist society—it *whispers* in the mode of minimalist poetry, thus resulting in the least common denominator for all classics: the ability to haunt. It alerts my students to the fact that fiction should be about storytelling, the "why" of things is best left to sociologists, the "how" is more than enough for writers to tackle, especially beginning writers.[7]

Naylor's statement is significant for my present discussion for two reasons: (1) it discloses its author's view of how one begins the struggle to become a successful writer, and (2) it justifies in a quite curious way its own insistence that Claudia's preface constitutes the most analytically provocative "first words" of Morrison's novel. In the first instance, Naylor suggests that becoming a writer requires development of a very specific *interpretive* skill. According to Naylor, the beginning writer must become analytically sophisticated enough to expose the artistic "flaws" in the "weak" first products of great writers. While Baldwin's discussions of his problematic relation to Wright are perhaps best understood in terms of Freudian theories of Oedipal struggles between fathers and usurping sons, Naylor's comments are more fully elucidated when they are viewed as calls for deconstructive exegesis.[8]

Although she disagrees with deconstructionist theories about the perfectibility of expressive forms (her statement suggests a view that great writers *are* great by virtue of their ability to conceive and execute successfully inde(con)structible narratives), Naylor seems nevertheless to feel that the apparent unity of a lesser work of even the greatest writers falls apart under the weight of an exegesis that concentrates on exposing textual disjunctions. Her view, for example, that "by taking apart the first novel of any great writer, we can see plainly what strategies failed" compares analytically with Jonathan Culler's suggestion that "[d]econstructive readings characteristically undo narrative schemes by focusing instead on internal difference."[9] Such readings, in other words, expose the disunity of apparently unified narrative structures. By taking apart the precursor text in order to reveal its failed strategies of narration in the manner Naylor suggests, the aspiring author operates much like the deconstructive critic who, according to Culler, "attends to structures that resist a text's unifying narrative schemes."

Apparently, however, such self-oriented utilizations of texts as Naylor and Culler suggest also occasion what Harold Bloom characterizes as creative misreadings. For Bloom, the novice writer attempts to appropriate and then correct a precursor's meaning, an act which, because there is no such thing as "interpretations but only misinterpretations,"[10] leads necessarily to misreadings that serve to advance the novice writer's perspective at the expense of those of the precursor. While Naylor makes no mention of what she feels are the specific flaws in *The Bluest Eye*'s narrative strategies, her strategic misreadings of Morrison's text, and their self-interested purpose, are, I believe, plainly evident in her discussion of Claudia's preface.

In asserting her view that Claudia's preface is of greater importance than the primer to Morrison's subsequent text, Naylor even goes so far as to argue that Claudia's preface contains qualities that clearly belong to the primer. She says that the first sentence of Claudia's preface, "Quiet as it's kept, there were no marigolds in the fall of 1941,"[11] "is the DNA [of the novel], spawning the second sentence, the second the third,"[12] though Morrison herself, in her employment of the primer's sentences as epigraphs to sections of the text, plainly implies a more essential generative relationship (albeit an inversive one) between primer and text.

The motivation for Naylor's misreading is not far to seek, for it lies in the most pronounced differences between *The Bluest Eye* and *The Women of Brewster Place*. White presence and influence are represented in Morrison's novel as powerful institutional forces that render blacks unable to assert any positive sense of self. Morrison's imaginative employment of the primer convincingly suggests the debilitating effects of such white influence on black Americans. But because Naylor's text depicts an Afro-American community virtually free from the presence and direct influence of whites, it fails to recognize the *denigrative* impulses that fuel Morrison's art. In short, while Naylor can correctly interpret Morrison's text as a sustained investigation of the lives of black women (as a novel, in other words, whose theme is demoralized black female beauty), she apparently cannot see, and therefore misreads, its revisionary impulses vis-à-vis the primer.

Thus, despite its obvious indebtedness to *The Bluest Eye*—an indebtedness whose most suggestive manifestations I will further discuss below—*The Women of Brewster Place* is clearly not interested in tackling what Naylor herself believes is the major theme of her precursor's novel: racism's effects on Afro-American women. In fact, Naylor clearly and purposefully avoids the subject, not in an unconscious act of defensive self-promotion or Bloomian misprision, but, I think, in order to examine (or, perhaps more accurately, to posit) *intra*racial origins of Afro-American women's pain as a corollary to Morrison's more deeply investigated depiction of its *inter*racial sources. Reading Naylor's novel as an ancillary text to *The Bluest Eye* might successfully explain its otherwise troubling silence where white culpability is concerned and its equally troubling extirpation of the racially energized tropes that it borrows from Morrison. I am suggesting, then, that *The Women of Brewster Place* is fully comprehensible only when it is read *intertextually*, with Morrison's text assuming a precursorial or pretextual relationship to the subsequent novel. For in fascinating, but distinct, ways, Naylor's art as represented in her first novel is as fueled by her deconstruction ("taking apart") and refiguration of *The Bluest Eye* as that novel is itself propelled by its dissection of its own prefatory primer.

First, however, it is perhaps necessary to distinguish fully between Bloom's views of misreading and my own as they pertain to a cooperative, noncompetitive textual system of black women's creativity. For Bloom, tropological refiguration and textual misreading of precursor texts by subsequent writers represent defensive, heroic attempts to establish priority over canonized writers. There are, however, other possible explanations for tropological refiguration. It is certainly difficult to imagine that Naylor's revisions are intended as heroic corrections of Morrison when the weight of historical evidence emphatically insists upon the accuracy of the older writer's assessment of white culpability in the continuing tragedies of Afro-Americans. Her refigurative gestures might best be explained, I think, as investigations of intraracial sources of Afro-American women's pain in the context of what Donald Gibson calls the "pressures" of a particular historical moment.

Gibson's discussion in *The Politics of Literary Expression* of the mimetic impulses of Afro-American writers offers a provocative juxtaposition to Bloom's theories. For Gibson argues that "black writers have produced literature that reflects their situations as social beings existing within a particular historical framework and subject to the pressures of a special nature resulting therefrom."[13] Instead of an anxiety of self-promotion, Gibson speaks of the pressures on Afro-American writers to depict (one would assume *accurately*) the social realities of their people "within a particular historical framework." Social conditions, according to Gibson, are the primary determinants of the scope and focus of individual Afro-American texts. While I do not agree uncategorically with Gibson's assessments,[14] I do believe that the most fruitful means of comprehending noncompetitive revision in Afro-American expressive systems in general, and in the texts I am examining in particular, is by examining the social and historical differences between the contexts in which the various figures are being used. When I refer to Naylor's novel as an ancillary text to *The Bluest Eye*, I mean not only that much of its content is derived from Morrison's novel, but, more importantly, that a full understanding of *The Women of Brewster Place*'s refigurative gestures is possible only when the reader is cognizant of the differences between the social conditions in which the texts were composed.

It is evident just from the writers' presentations of white presence in the respective communities depicted in the novels that they are discussing decidedly different times. Despite these differences, however, Naylor chooses to repeat several of Morrison's figures. For example, her discussion of the history of Brewster Place in the prefatory section entitled "Dawn" clearly is a revision of Morrison's description of the

Breedlove family and household. Both texts explicitly contrast the socio-economic mobility of white former inhabitants with the state of virtual imprisonment of the current black residents. Morrison accounts for the Breedlove's inhabitance of a dilapidated storefront in the following way:

> The Breedloves did not live in a storefront because they were having temporary difficulty adjusting to the cutbacks at the plant. They lived there because they were poor and black, and they stayed there because they believed they were ugly.

In *The Women of Brewster Place*, blacks are also, in effect, confined to urban ghetto space:

> They [black Brewster dwellers] clung to the street with a desperate acceptance that whatever was here was better than the starving southern climates they had fled from. Brewster Place knew that unlike its other [white] children, the few who would leave forever were the exception rather than the rule, since they came because they had no choice and would remain for the same reason.

Unlike the non-black immigrants in both texts—unlike the Hungarian baker in *The Bluest Eye* who was "modestly famous for his brioche and poppy-seed rolls" and the "gypsies [who] used it [the Breedlove home] as a base of operations," and, in Naylor's text, the similarly "dark haired and mellow-skinned" people who had brought to Brewster Place "the pungent smells of strong cheeses and smoked meats"—the blacks who populate the subsequently abandoned space of the American ghetto are permanently bound there. In both texts, then, Afro-Americans are, despite their journeys north from what Naylor calls "starving southern climates," unable to partake of putatively superior opportunities for economic advancement.

The Women of Brewster Place presents the confinement to ghetto space of the Breedlove family as a reality for an entire Afro-American community. However, Naylor's refigurations are, to be sure, repetition with a difference. Unlike the black community in *The Bluest Eye*, all of whose residents suffer because of pressures to live in accord with white standards, Brewster Place is a physically and legislatively isolated urban island which is, for the most part, untouched by a direct white influence. Consequently, while Morrison's novel criticizes white-controlled institutional forces for their roles in causing the development of negative Afro-American self-images, Naylor's work looks elsewhere for the sources of black women's pain. An examination of the section of *The Women of Brewster Place* entitled "Cora Lee" offers evidence not only about where Naylor locates that source, but also about the nature of historically determined tropological refiguration.

IV

"Cora Lee" represents the clearest example of Naylor's reuse and refiguration of the deconstructed parts of *The Bluest Eye*. In this story,
Naylor's eradication of the interracial import of figures which she borrows from Morrison is fully evident and offers perhaps the best means
of conceptualizing the nature and precise motivation of such acts. The
story's initial paragraphs which discuss a young girl's overabundant love
of dolls appear, when considered in relation to Morrison's depiction of
Claudia's negative reaction to dolls, to represent perhaps the signal moment of critical revision in the Afro-American woman's narrative tradition. The text tells us of Cora Lee:

> Her new baby doll. They [the parents] placed the soft plastic and pink flannel
> in the little girl's lap, and she turned her moon-shaped eyes toward them in
> awed gratitude. It was so perfect and so small. She trailed her fingertips
> along the smooth brown forehead and down into the bottom curve of the
> upturned nose. She gently lifted the dimpled arms and legs and then rever-
> ently placed them back. Slowly kissing the set painted mouth, she inhaled its
> new aroma while stroking the silken curled head and full cheeks. She circled
> her arms around the motionless body and squeezed, while with tightly closed
> eyes she waited breathlessly for the first trembling vibrations of its low,
> gravelly "Mama" to radiate through her breast.

This reaction to Christmas gifts of dolls is directly and intentionally
antithetical to Claudia's response to white dolls:

> The . . . dolls, which were supposed to bring me great pleasure, succeeded
> in doing quite the opposite. When I took it to bed, its hard, unyielding limbs
> resisted my flesh—the tapered fingertips on those dimpled hands scratched.
> If, in sleep, I turned, the bone-cold head collided with my own. It was a most
> uncomfortable, patently aggressive sleeping companion. To hold it was no
> more rewarding. The starched gauze or lace on the cotton dress irritated any
> embrace.

The (white) doll is for Claudia, nothing short of a formidable foe—
unyielding, uncomfortable, unrewarding—to which she is clearly unable
to respond positively. Her inability to regard the doll positively demonstrates, it seems to me, Claudia's general rejection of sex-role stereotyping—she apparently has no natural attraction to sugar, spice, or
everything typically thought of as nice for young girls—just as her subsequent dissection of these dolls suggests her conscious repudiation of
white myths of superiority. The (brown) doll in "Cora Lee," however, is
a dimpled figure to which Cora attends with a near-religious devotion
and reverence; its plastic form yields not only pleasant, plastic aromas,
but also gratifyingly responsive voice—"the first trembling vibrations of
its low, gravelly 'Mama.'"

Cora's exuberant reaction to the doll's voice contrasts dramatically with Claudia's almost scientific investigation of the source of her doll's voice:

> the thing made one sound—a sound they [the adults] said was the sweet and plaintive cry "Mama," but which sounded to me like the bleat of a dying lamb, or, more precisely, our ice-box door opening on rusty hinges in July. Remove the cold and stupid eyeball, it would bleat still, "Ahhhhh," take off the head, shake out the sawdust, crack the back against the brass bed rail, it would bleat still. The gauze back would split, and *I could see the disk with six holes, the secret of the sound. A mere metal roundness* (my emphasis).

Unlike Cora Lee, who believes that the doll's voice is unquestionably a response to the affectionate and reverent nature of her embrace, Claudia—for whom the plastic figure's voice signifies death (the bleatings of dying lambs) and dilapidation (her refrigerator's door opening on rusty hinges)—learns that her doll's voice is a mechanical response to pressure. Claudia discovers upon further investigation "the secret of the sound," the source, if you will, of plastic voice: "A mere, metal roundness."

Naylor's revisionary gestures are further observable in her refiguration of Claudia's destruction of dolls. Because Claudia's de(con)struction yields sufficient information about the source of her doll's voice, she believes that further dissection may offer answers as to the source of the myth of white superiority. Like Claudia, Cora destroys dolls that are to her undesirable. But while Claudia's de(con)struction results directly from feelings of racial pride and from a desire or need for knowledge, Cora's destruction of dolls is a function of her inability or unwillingness to mature—of her determined avoidance of knowledge. The text informs us:

> she spent all of her time with her dolls—and they had to be baby dolls. She told [her parents] this with a silent rebellion the year they had decided she was now old enough for a teenaged Barbie doll; they had even sacrificed for an expensive set of foreign figurines with porcelain faces and real silk and lace mantillas, saris, and kimonos. The following week they found the dolls under her bed with the heads smashed in and the arms twisted out of the sockets.

Cora Lee destroys the dolls intended for an increasingly mature child in an effort to maintain a willful ignorance of the world and of herself. She has no interest in dolls against which she can measure signs of her own increasing physical maturity, or even in gaining raimentary knowledge of foreign cultures. Rather, quite unlike Claudia, Cora is interested in baby dolls as cuddly, helpless figures which she can think of as possessing an unvarying need for her attention and whose static natures are a perfect complement to her own inability to mature.

While their presentations of young girls' responses to dolls are, at the very least, antithetical, I would argue that Naylor is not seeking to call into question the accuracy of Morrison's depiction of the destruction efforts of white standards. Rather, Naylor's refigurations represent her submitting of her precursor's figure to the pressures of a different historical moment. Morrison's discussions of her motivations for writing *The Bluest Eye* not only serve to substantiate Gibson's claim that black writers "have produced literature that reflects their situations as social beings," but also offer information which aids our understanding of her specific figuration of the doll trope. In a cover story of *Newsweek* devoted to her, Morrison says of *The Bluest Eye*'s genesis: "It was 1967 and the slogan 'Black is beautiful' was in the air. I loved it, but something was missing."[15] Her essay "The Making of *The Black Book*" offers a clear elaboration of what she felt was "missing" in the slogan:

> the phrase evaded the issue and our plight by being a reaction to a white idea, which means it was a white idea turned inside out, and a white idea turned inside out is still a white idea. The concept of physical beauty as a virtue is one of the dumbest, most pernicious and destructive ideas of the Western world, and we should have nothing to do with it. Physical beauty has nothing to do with our past, present or future.[16]

The phrase "Black is beautiful" clearly is not, in several respects, black enough for Morrison. That is, it accepts white evaluative notions of worth—not the superiority of Caucasian beauty, but the "Western" belief that physical beauty, as determined by whatever subjective standards, connotes human worth—and, for Morrison, exposes its advocates' continued submission to white authority. What is missing in the slogan for Morrison, then, is a *denigrative* component that would allow Afro-Americans to promote black pride in accord with Black cultural truths, with something that "has . . . to do with our past, present or future." The doll trope in *The Bluest Eye*, then, serves as Morrison's means to criticize the white institutional tendency to promote a single standard of beauty, and to invalidate the idea that physical beauty connotes intrinsic human value.

When Naylor employs the doll trope in *The Women of Brewster Place*, the greatest problems in the Afro-American community are of a different nature. These problems concern not the beauty of blackness, but, some have argued, the self-destruction of the black underclass. Michele Wallace succinctly characterizes the "profound crisis" in the Afro-American community as its "accelerating rates of high school dropouts, imprisonment, teenage births, unemployment, [and] impoverished female-headed families."[17] Naylor's manipulation of the doll trope reflects her testing of the figure under the historical conditions Wallace describes in an overtly revisionary gesture. This revisionary gesture stands not as a competitive correction of the precursor's meaning, but as an erudite acknowledgment of the fact that few tropological configurations are indisputably "true" or "correct" in perpetuity.

Naylor's interest in exploring what Wallace calls the Afro-American community's "profound crisis" is observable in the subsequent pages of the story "Cora Lee." The title character, who is unable to appreciate her parents' gifts of dolls that befit her movement toward physical maturity, is also incapable later in her life of caring responsibly for her own growing children. Her immaturity occasions her childish conceptualization of the male phallus as—in her mother's euphemistic phrase—"the thing that felt good in the dark." She takes little thought of the economic and psychological consequences for her children of her perpetually bringing infants into the world. Cora Lee remains, despite the undeniably horrendous family life she has created for her children, magically attracted to infants who, like her dolls, depend solely upon her for sustenance. While she attends "religiously" to her infant children, because of her own emotional stagnation she has not the slightest notion of how to care for or nurture children when they are no longer babies. Her older children are for her simply incomprehensible nuisances who interrupt her soap opera viewing and destroy furniture and clothes. They are, in her candid (and much-expressed) view, "little dumb asses."

Cora apparently has no idea of her own culpability in her children's repugnant behavior—truancy, destruction of property, digging in garbage for sweets. Her ignorance of the fact that their scholastic weaknesses result largely from her failure to provide adequate inspiration or discipline is observable in her response to their insistence that they have no homework and, consequently, should be permitted to play outdoors: "'Awful strange,' she muttered darkly. 'No one ever has any homework. When I was in school, we always got homework.'"

Despite such unsettling beginnings, "Cora Lee" traces its protagonist's ultimate movement toward what Naylor calls "hopeful echoes of order and peace." Such a transformation is encouraged, somewhat ironically, by Kiswana Browne, the novel's resident dreamer, and by a black production of *A Midsummer Night's Dream*, Shakespeare's masterful exploration of the ambiguities of the space between reality and dream. Cora Lee ultimately moves from an almost total incomprehension of her non-infant children and of her role as mother to what is, for her, a rather profound knowledge of maternal responsibilities. On what the text refers to as "a night of wonders," Cora resolves to create a supportive academic environment for her children:

> School would be over in a few weeks, but all this truant nonsense had to stop. She would get up and walk them there personally if she had to—and summer school. How long had the teachers been saying that they needed summer school? And she would check homework—every night. And P.T.A. Sonya wouldn't be little forever—she'd have no more excuses for missing those meetings in the evening. Junior high; high school; college—none of them stayed little forever. And then on to good jobs in insurance companies and the post office, even doctors and lawyers. Yes, that's what would happen to her babies.

But, unlike the heavily textured Shakespeare comedy that Cora Lee and her family attend in which, in the words of the critic Anne Barton, a "new social order . . . has emerged from the ordeal of the wood,"[18] the protagonist's patterns of parenthood will not change appreciably. Despite the "hopeful echoes" resonating through her apartment, Cora nevertheless sleeps with the anonymous "shadow" lover "who had let himself in with his key" and, apparently—if we can trust Mattie's dream as accounted in the section "The Block Party" in which Cora Lee appears pregnant—begins again the cycle of pregnancy, infant adoration, and post-infant neglect which has characterized her adult life.

Such a reading of "Cora Lee" is made possible not only by the elevated, totally unrealistic (considering the narrator's comments about a severely limited black social mobility) nature of the mother's plans for her children—"even doctors or lawyers"—but also by her reaction to the presence of the shadow. Because of the physical and psychological abuse she suffers at the hands of her older children's fathers, Cora has learned to view her subsequent sexual partners as shadows, men "who came in the dark and showed her the thing that felt good in the dark, and often left before the children awakened." Upon seeing her latest sexual partner in bed at the close of a day of self-discovery, she "turned and firmly folded her evening like gold and lavender gauze deep within the creases of her dreams, and let her clothes drop to the floor." The title character's slovenly disrobing contrasts directly with her neat folding of her children's ragged clothing (and her figurative folding of her evening) and suggests, it would appear, her own return to a neglectful mode of parenthood.

"Cora Lee" not only contains within its pages evidence of reuse of Morrison's text which aids our comprehension of the nature of Naylor's "taking apart" of *The Bluest Eye*, but also offers the means of locating what appears to me to be the dominant theme of *The Women of Brewster Place*. "Cora Lee" is, like most of the other narrative sections, an exploration of unfulfilled and (within the context of the world its author creates) unachievable dreams of Afro-American women. Naylor's novel does not examine the societal forces which are responsible for the unfulfilling nature of many black women's lives in as systematic and illuminating a fashion as Morrison's novel. What it does offer, however, is the author's explorations of her characters' *own culpability* in the tragedies of their lives. The primary thematic differences between Naylor's and Morrison's novels can perhaps be briefly summarized in the following way: *The Bluest Eye* portrays the ramifications of the imposition of myth upon a people; *The Women of Brewster Place*, by contrast, describes the myriad problems for Afro-Americans (particularly women) who refuse to abandon unachievable dreams.

In a review of *The Women of Brewster Place*, Judith Brazburg argues that "The Two" and "The Block Party," the concluding sections of the novel, "address the question from Langston Hughes' poem, 'What happened to a dream deferred?' which is posed on the prefatory pages of the novel."[19] In fact, however, each of the novel's sections details the deferred dream of Afro-American women. These dreams are evident in textual information from Etta Mae Johnson's desperate need for social respectability that "stuff[ed] up her senses" to the point that she totally misreads the intentions of a visiting minister and Kiswana Browne's mother's characterization of her daughter as one who "constantly live[s] in a fantasy world—always going to extremes—turning butterflies into eagles," to Mattie Michael's dream of female community that concludes the novel. Naylor's most successfully rendered depiction of the consequences of disappointed dreams occur in "Lucielia Louise Turner." This section offers not only profound insight into Naylor's precise intentions where the novel's major theme is concerned, but also the author's subtle refigurations of both Morrison and Zora Neale Hurston.

V

Naylor's explorations of the consequences of deferred Afro-American women's dreams directs us intertextually not only to Hughes' poem, but also to Hurston's assertions with respect to women and dreams in the opening pages of *Their Eyes Were Watching God.* In contrast to men who, according to Hurston, wait passively for—and only occasionally achieve—their desires:

> women forget all those things they don't want to remember, and remember everything they don't want to forget. The dream is the truth. Then they act and do things accordingly.[20]

According to Hurston, women possess a greater capacity than men to actively pursue their desires. This greater capacity results from an ability to filter from consciousness an awareness of any matters that would hamper the dream's pursuit. It is this ability that allows Janie to ignore her initial misgivings about Joe Starks, for example, and to endure decades of mistreatment at his hands, hoping all the while either that he would be metamorphosed into her dream of an ideal man, or, when the evidence of this dream's unattainability becomes so overwhelming that it cannot be conveniently forgotten, that some other man can successfully fulfill this role.

In his essay "Zora Neale Hurston and the Nature of Female Perception," Lloyd Brown employs Simone de Beauvoir's discussions in *The Second Sex* of the female "realm of imagination" to analyze the consequences of female dream, and self-deception in *Their Eyes Were Watching God.* He says:

> de Beauvoir argues . . . [that] dreams are the women's means of compensating for a sense of subordination (immanence) through the "realm of imagination," and as such they are a form of transcendence, the "ultimate effort—sometimes ridiculous, often pathetic—of imprisoned women to transform her prison into

a heaven of glory, her servitude into sovereign liberty." Hurston's own narrative actually centers on the essential ambiguities which de Beauvoir attributes here to the woman as dreamer, with dreams as both triumphant transcendence and pathetic flight into imagination.[21]

In my chapter on *Their Eyes Were Watching God*, I stated my objections to Brown's reading of Tea Cake's and Janie's relationship. But Brown's discussion of the essential ambiguities involved in the transcendent female dream is remarkably astute. I would, however, take his assertion a step further. With respect to its negative consequences, not only does the female flight into imagination represent at times a "pathetic" attempt to transform a painful experience, but it also serves to compel women to commit plainly injurious acts of self-deception. Even after her recognition of her prodigious shortcomings, Janie still refuses to be governed by what she learns is the truth:

> "Maybe he ain't nothin'," she cautioned herself, "but he is something in my mouth. He's got tuh be else Ah ain't got nothin' tuh live for. Ah'll lie and say he is. If Ah don't, life won't be nothin' but uh store and uh house."

Her instinctive removal to the realm of imagination permits her transformation of the dream—Starks as bee man—to a lie about actuality—the insistence, despite a wealth of empirical evidence to the contrary, that she maintain her former image of her husband as a means of preserving any semblance of self-worth.

The text of *Their Eyes Were Watching God* makes it abundantly clear that sincere feelings of self-worth are impossible under such conditions of self-deception, and that only actual transcendence permits the subordinated female to discern her own human virtues. Janie's transcendence begins when she finds Tea Cake, the man who most closely resembles her dream of an ideal mate. In "Lucielia Louise Turner," the section of *The Women of Brewster Place* in which Naylor most expertly depicts the Afro-American woman dreamer's tragedy and subsequent self-affirmation, the beleaguered female's transcendence is made possible by the efforts of a female "kissin'-friend," Mattie Michael.

"Lucielia Louise Turner" traces, among other things, its title character's efforts to maintain her dream-draped image of her lover whose "deep musky scent . . . brought back the ghosts of the Tennessee soil of her childhood." Eugene is like Joe Starks in that he coerces his lover's submission to his authority, a submission which results directly in her abortion of the fetus of a baby she desperately wants, and indirectly in the death of their two-year-old daughter.

The utter failure of Ciel's actions to produce their desired ends—Eugene's willingness to remain in the relationship—becomes obvious when he announces that he is leaving her and their daughter Serena for putative employment on the docks of Maine. This announcement, coupled with his refusal to allow mother and daughter to accompany him and his confusion about the location of Newport, shatters the image that Ciel has held of her mate as effectively as Starks' slap destroys Janie's illusions about her second husband:

> She looked at Eugene, and the poison of reality began to spread through her body like gangrene. It drew his scent out of her nostrils and scraped the veil from her eyes, and he stood before her just as he really was—a tall, skinny black man with arrogance and selfishness twisting his mouth into a strange shape.

As in *Their Eyes Were Watching God*, the pollinated female perception gives way to what Naylor terms "the poison of reality"—the recognition of the male's self-interested, manipulative control that results in a woman's fruitless endurance of pain. Ciel's recognition of Eugene's inadequacies is followed by a period of "brief mourning for the loss of something denied to her" and an "overpowering need to be near someone who loved her." But her awakening is accompanied by an even more painful reality—the screams and subsequent death of her electrocuted daughter Serena.

"Lucielia Louise Turner" offers a provocative juxtaposition of two vastly different scenes of ritualistic cleansing: Ciel's failed attempts to completely clean a pot of cooked rice, and Mattie Michael's successful exorcism of pain from the grieving body of a woman she had helped to raise. The first such instance is occasioned by Eugene's statement, "I lost my job today," which signals, in Ciel's mind, the end of the tenuous peace that had existed in her apartment since his return. Upon hearing the announcement, Ciel, standing at the sink cleaning rice, transforms her culinary efforts into a (somewhat sadistic) rite of purification:

> The water was turning cloudy in the rice pot, and the force of the stream from the faucet caused scummy bubbles to rise to the surface. These broke and sprayed tiny starchy particles onto the dirty surface. Each bubble that broke seemed to increase the volume of the dogged whispers she had been ignoring for the last few months. She poured the dirty water off the rice to destroy and silence them, then watched with a malicious joy as they disappeared down the drain.

In this doubly symbolic rite, Ciel equates "scummy bubbles" with the repressed and "dogged whispers" of discord that were again entering the relationship. By sadistically drowning the whisper-containing bubbles, by silencing, in other words, the voice of reality, she displays a preference for illusion, silence, and dream and an unwillingness to confront directly the implications of the voice's message. Like Janie, Ciel fights stubbornly to maintain her image of her mate. Confronted by the ultimate failure of her purification rite, Ciel realizes that some sacrifice on her part is required in order to satiate Eugene, to whom she turns in "silent acquiesc[ence]" and asks, "All right, Eugene, what do you want me to do?" In an effort to maintain her relationship with this undependable, egregiously self-centered man, Ciel resolves to be governed by his will, even though such a resolve will result in her abortion of the fetus that grows inside her.

Ciel's refusal or inability to rid herself of her dream vision of Eugene leads to her particularly profound sense of self-division both during and after the abortion. Naylor tells us that during the abortion, for example:

> Ciel was not listening [to the droning voice of the abortionist]. It was important that she keep herself completely isolated from these surroundings. All the activities of the past week of her life were balled up and jammed on the right side of her brain, as if belonging to some other woman. And when she had endured this one last thing for her, she would push it up there, too, and then one day give it all to her—Ciel wanted no part of it.
>
> The next few days, Ciel found it difficult to connect herself up again with her own world. Everything seemed to have taken on new textures and colors. . . . There was a disturbing split second between someone talking to her and the words penetrating sufficiently to elicit a response.

Ciel's affective split or double consciousness is motivated, as were her efforts to silence the whispers of the scummy bubbles, by her desire to prevent reality from impinging upon her desperately held dreams about Eugene and, ultimately, herself. Such dreams concern, then, not only her lover's character, but also self-protective illusions about herself necessitated by her submission to the control of this shallow man. In effect, Ciel piles lie upon lie in an effort to forestall her own recognition of the fact that her life with Eugene, in Janie's apt phrase, "ain't nothin'." As a result of her refusal to confront the stark reality of her life, Ciel splits into two selves. One self plans and endures the physical and emotional pain of abortion "as if [the activities] belong[ed] to some other woman." This other woman, Ciel's other self, will eventually have to come to terms with these acts.

When Serena dies, Ciel is forced to confront not only the pain of her loss of a child, but also her own self-destructive acts—her inability to perceive Eugene correctly and thereby prevent the abortion of a fetus. No longer able to assign the blame for her undesirable actions to her other, future self, she is overwhelmed by an intense grief whose pain she had long deferred. The intensity of her grief propels her past pain and to the nadir of emotional insensibility. The text tells us of Ciel's failure to cry when Serena dies that others believed was a sign of "some special sort of grief": "Ciel was not grieving for Serena. She was simply tired of hurting. And she was forced to slowly give up the life that God had refused to take from her."

Mattie Michael, the title character of the novel's first section—whose maternal instincts where Ciel is concerned result from pre-Brewster days—recognizes intuitively her surrogate daughter's condition. In a heroic display of personal fortitude, Mattie forcefully intervenes:

> "Merciful Father, no!" she bellowed. There was no prayer, no bended knee or sackcloth supplication in those words, but a blasphemous fireball that shot

forth and went smashing against the gates of heaven, raging and kicking, demanding to be heard. "No! No! No!"

The deeply religious Mattie voices a resounding "no" to Ciel's impending death, a cry with heaven-shaking reverberations. It is not her words or voice that save Ciel from a premature, grief-stricken demise, however, but, rather, her actions—her painful but somehow soothing rocking and embrace. "Propelled," as Naylor says, by Ciel's almost inaudible moans, Mattie's resuscitating motion transports her younger friend through history so that she is able to observe the timelessness of her loss:

> Mattie rocked her out of that bed, out of that room, into a blue vastness just underneath the sun and above time. She rocked her over Aegean seas so clean they shone like crystal, so clear the fresh blood of sacrificed babies torn from their mother's arms and given to Neptune could be seen like pink froth on the water. She rocked her on and on, past Dachau, where soul-gutted Jewish mothers swept their children's entrails off laboratory floors. They flew past the spilled brains of Senegalese infants whose mothers had dashed them on the wooden sides of slave ships. And she rocked on.

Mattie's rocking allows Ciel to connect the pain of her own maternal losses with an apparently timeless—and, in a sense, equally gainless—history of maternal pain. Mattie's rocking "above time" offers Ciel—dying because of an emptiness caused by the loss of children and illusions—a recognition of her connection with women throughout history, a sense, in other words, of membership in a timeless community of women united by common suffering.

Ciel's imaginative flight does not end, however, with such insights. Mattie rocks Ciel from visions of the general—perceptions of the timelessness of her pain—to the specific—a direct confrontation with her illusions about life and about herself which rendered her incapable of preventing her personal tragedies. These illusions, in fact, had made her a hesitant participant in her tragedies' unfolding:

> [Mattie] rocked her into her childhood and let her see her murdered dreams. And she rocked her back, back into the womb, to the nadir of her hurt, and they found it—a slight silver splinter, embedded just below the surface of the skin. And Mattie rocked and pulled—and the splinter gave way, but its roots were deep, gigantic, ragged, and they tore up flesh with bits of fat and muscle tissue clinging to them. They left a hole, which was already starting to pus over, but Mattie was satisfied. It would heal.

The removal of the symbolic splinter leads to Ciel's ability to observe clearly the terrible consequences of the splinter's lengthy presence. These consequences include her inability to confront the origins of her repressed anguish—her unnamed "murdered dreams"—and her creation of self-protective illusions which encourage her continual victimization.

The salvation of Ciel is not accomplished solely by means of Mattie's allowing her to perceive timeless maternal pain and destructive personal illusions. Its ultimate achievement requires a communal act that is the section's second rite of purification. Ciel's vomiting after the splinter is uprooted is described as possessing spiritually purgative qualities: "The bile that had formed a tight knot in Ciel's stomach began to rise and gagged her as it passed her throat. . . . After a while she heaved only air, but the body did not seem to want to stop. It was exorcising the evilness of pain." This exorcism of the evilness of pain represents one aspect of a rite of purification; its completion involves Mattie's bathing of the young woman who has regressed to a state of physical helplessness akin to that of an infant:

> And slowly she bathed her. She took the soap, and, using only her hands, she washed Ciel's hair and the back of her neck. She raised her arms and cleaned the armpits, soaping well the downy brown hair there. She let the soap slip between the girl's breasts, and she washed each one separately, cupping it in her hands. She took each leg and even cleaned under the toenail. Making Ciel rise and kneel in the tub, she cleaned the crack of her behind, soaped her pubic hair, and gently washed the crease in her vagina—slowly, reverently, as if handling a newborn.

Mattie's and Ciel's are complementary acts of purification—the cleansing of the outside and the inside of the female respectively. Theirs is a wordless antiphonal rite in which Ciel's moans inspire Mattie's life-sustaining rocking, a rite which concludes with Ciel's crying "cold and good" tears. These tears provide the final stage of purification for Ciel's heretofore dying self which the text now describes as her "freshly wet, glistening body, baptized now." Inside and outside, previously disjointed because Ciel's maintenance of a willing ignorance about the reality of her life, perform as an interactive, complementary system set in motion by the affectionate rocking and bathing of Mattie and supported by Ciel's cleansing of her spiritual self and her will to live.

This scene provides, it seems to me, an explanation of the failures of similarly salvific gestures in *The Bluest Eye*. More precisely, it helps us to comprehend the failure of Claudia's and Frieda's efforts to save Pecola's incestuous seed. The MacTeer girls attempt, through an ama-teurish bit of conjure (the burial of money and garden seeds, and the incantation of "magic words") to save Pecola's baby which the rest of the community wants dead. The adult narrator Claudia attributes their effort's failure to nature's general unresponsiveness to humanity, and not to any incantatory shortcomings on their part. However, if read in terms of Naylor's scene, Claudia's and Frieda's efforts seem, despite the girls' obvious sincerity, hopelessly inadequate. For in the face of Pecola's intense self-hatred and the disdain of an entire community where Pecola and her pregnancy are concerned, discursive acts such as the MacTeer girls' incantations of putative (but, curiously, unspoken in the novel) "right words" cannot avoid being anything but insufficient. What is re-quired, as Naylor's text suggests, is the bonding of women, or what Ntozake Shange calls in *for colored girls'* final scene of an achieved female community—which, not coincidentally, is directly preceded by a male's murder of children—"a layin on of [female] hands."[22] This communal laying on of hands results in the liberation of the female self and "the holiness of myself released." Ciel's baptized and reborn self, like the holy and released female community in Shange's choreopoem, can courageously confront the problems inherent in being a black woman in America.[23]

VI

However profitable individual acts of sisterly love such as those described in the final pages of "Lucielia Louise Turner" prove, they do not have the power to alter significantly the deleterious conditions for Brewster Place's female as a group. *The Women of Brewster Place's* penultimate story, "The Two," makes this point abundantly clear. In this story, Naylor's revision of Morrison achieves its most profound and unsettling configurations. Such repetition takes form, for example, in aspects of characterization such as Ben's daughter's physical deformity and his surrogate daughter Lorraine's physical carriage which refigure, from *The Bluest Eye*, Polly Breedlove's rusty nail-inspired limp and her offspring Pecola's carriage which, according to Claudia, resembled a "pleated wing." In fact, it appears that Naylor conflates in the figure of Lorraine many of the manifest weaknesses of the characters of Morrison's novel. If, as I have argued, Pecola serves as scapegoat in a community's rites of purgation, then Lorraine's ultimate status in *The Women of Brewster Place* includes, in different instances, both purgative scapegoat and brutalized martyr whose demise apparently serves to unify a (female) community.

But while the sacrifice of Pecola—despite its obviously reprehensible motivation and outcome—does unite, in a sense, Lorain's black citizens, the decidedly feminist Afro-American women's community that forms in the final story of Naylor's novel, "The Block Party," is not represented as an actual narrative event at all but, rather, as merely the dream of Mattie Michael. In a novel where the products of the female "realm of imagination" have proven disastrous, the author's representation of what feminist texts such as Shange's choreopoem suggest are the most nurturing environment for women as a female character's dream calls into question Naylor's views of the possibilities—or perhaps even the uncategorical desirability—of such exclusively women's communities.

The major incidents from *The Bluest Eye* that Naylor refigures in "The Two" are Pecola's schoolyard encounter with a gang of boys and her rape by her father. As I have argued, Morrison's description of Pecola's taunters who, "like a necklace of semiprecious stones . . . surrounded her," is inextricably related to their employment of Pecola as scapegoat upon whom they project the evilness of the shadow of blackness. But in Naylor's refiguration, the group of male taunters that confronts Lorraine is threatened not by her undeniable blackness as in Pecola's case, but, rather, by her homosexual orientation which places her, C. C. Baker's gang fears, "beyond the length of [phallic] power."

Though many of her uses of Morrison's figures effectively bracket race, Naylor's description of Lorraine's expedition into black male gang territory is charged with an acute understanding of white racism's culpability in the creation of C. C. Baker and his gang of urban thugs. She says of Lorraine:

> She had stepped into the thin strip of earth [the alley near the wall] that they had claimed as their own. Bound by the last building on Brewster and a brick wall, they reigned in that unlit alley like dwarfed warrior-kings. Born with the appendages of power, circumcised by the guillotine, and baptised with the steam from a million nonreflective mirrors, these young men wouldn't be called upon to . . . scatter their iron seed from a B-52 into the wound of the earth, point a finger to move a nation, or stick a pole into the moon—and they knew it. They only had that three-hundred-foot alley to serve them as stateroom, armored tank, and executioner's chamber. So Lorraine found herself, on her knees, surrounded by the most dangerous species in existence—human males with an erection to validate in a world that was only six feet wide.

In a country which has, throughout its history, consistently rewarded "manly" displays of courage and machismo, the attitudes of C. C. Baker's gang seem, no matter how repugnant, almost relentlessly logical. Indeed, male psychological abusiveness and murderous potentials that are suggested in the other texts of Naylor's novel—Sam Michael's vicious beating of his daughter Mattie; Eugene's psychological abuse of Ciel; the fractured jaws, loosened teeth and permanent scars suffered by Cora Lee at the hands of men frustrated by the natural time demands of children—effectively prefigure the abhorrent display of misogyny and homophobia involved in the gang's brutalization of Lorraine. While the Afro-American literary tradition is replete with delineations of sexual violence directed at women, Naylor's description of the brutal gang rape of Lorraine is without question one of the most unsettling. As an intertext of *The Bluest Eye*, the scene combines, as I have stated, Cholly's rape of Pecola with Bad Bay and friends' verbal abuse and encircling of the young protagonist. Both Pecola's verbal victimization by the young boys and, later, her rape, are accompanied by her silence—her wordless "cover[ing] her eyes with her hands" in the circle of male scorn and her voiceless response to Cholly's sexual abuse. The text informs the reader about her wordless response to her father's sexual abuse: "the only sound she made [was] a hollow suck of air in the back of her throat."

Naylor's depiction of Lorraine's victimization also focuses on her silence. But unlike Pecola, who appears not to possess the proper vocabulary to respond to such abuse, Lorraine does attempt to verbalize a response—a plea to the boys' humanity. Throughout the rape, she was:

trying to form the one word that had been clawing inside of her—"Please."
It squeezed through her paralyzed vocal cords and fell lifelessly at their feet.
Lorraine clamped her eyes shut and, using all of her strength within her,
willed it to rise again.

"Please."

The sixth boy took a dirty paper bag lying on the ground and stuffed it
into her mouth. She felt a weight drop on her spread body. Then she opened
her eyes and they screamed and screamed into the face above hers—the face
that was pushing this terrible pain inside of her body. The screams tried to
break through her corneas out into the air, but the tough rubbery flesh sent
them vibrating back into her brain, first shaking lifeless the cells that nurtured
her memory.

Her appeal to her attackers' humanity proved fruitless. Lorraine's voice
has no life, no effect in the barbarous male circle formed to exhibit phallic
power.

As a consequence of the profound mental chaos that follows her rape,
she attacks the male figure who moved "in perfect unison with the sawing
pain that kept moving inside of her." In an attempt to stop the pain,
Lorraine kills Ben, Brewster Pace's janitor who had served as a father
figure for the otherwise painfully isolated woman. During an argument
with her lover Theresa, Lorraine, who believes that her homosexuality
does not represent a sense of difference significant enough to permanently isolate her from the larger Afro-American community, speaks of
herself as someone "who just wants to be a human being—a lousy human
being, who's somebody's daughter or somebody's friend or even somebody's enemy." She tells Theresa that she is able to achieve such feelings
only in Ben's basement apartment:

> they [the world at large, Brewster residents in particular] make me feel like
> a freak out there, and you try to make me feel like one in here. That (sic)
> only place I've found some peace, Tee, is in that damp old basement, where
> I'm not different.

The alliance between Lorraine and Ben is based primarily on their
feelings of difference, absence, and loss. Ben's northern journey to Brewster is motivated, at least in part, by his inability to protect his infirm
daughter from sexual exploitation at the hands of her white employer.
Lorraine travels to Brewster largely because of her fear of difference
and because of the pain of her father's violent reaction to her homosexuality. Each character fulfills for the other the role of absent family so they
no longer feel they are "livin' in a world with no address."

Lorraine achieves a positive sense of self with the assistance of Ben,
which leads to what Theresa views as "a firmness in her spirit that hadn't
been there before." Her insane lashing out at Ben, then, appears to
reflect simply the chaotic and deeply disturbed nature of Lorraine's psyche. But if it is correct to view Lorraine's victimization as exemplary of
the Afro-American woman's plight in a male-dominated world (as textual
evidence I will cite below seems to indicate), then it seems also possible

to regard Ben, the novel's only fully sketched male character, as in some respects representative of the Afro-American male. For though Ben's sensitivity where Lorraine is concerned is genuine and commendable, he is no more able in a northern urban environment to protect his surrogate daughter from sexual abuse than he was to defend his own offspring from the deep South's landowner's sexual exploitation. In fact, his wife frames her view of Ben's inadequacies in terms remarkably similar to the narrator's discussion of C. C. Baker and his gang's impressions of manhood. When Ben laments being rendered unable by the power dynamics of his relationship to Mr. Clyde either to avenge his daughter's suffering or to force it to cease—frustratedly saying, "If I was half a man I woulda—" his wife:

> came across the porch and sneered into his face. "If you was half a man, you coulda given me more babies and we woulda had some help workin' this land instead of half-grown woman we gotta carry the load for. And if you was even quarter a man, we wouldn't be a bunch of miserable sharecroppers on someone else's land—but we is, Ben."

His wife measures Ben's masculine and human worth by his abilities as a provider—both of babies and of moderately good economic stability—and finds him seriously lacking. He is not, in Elvira's economically pragmatic perception, "'even quarter a man.'"

He responds to her castigation by abusing alcohol and silently desiring to murder her:

> if he drank enough every day he could bear the touch of Elvira's body in the bed beside him at night and not have his sleep stolen by the image of her lying there with her head caved in or her chest ripped apart by shotgun shells.

Ben's murderous impulses are impeded only by "the gram of truth in her words [that] was heavy enough to weigh his hands down in his pockets." Apparently, then, he has accepted a purely materialistic conceptualization of manhood to which his situation as deep South sharecropper denies access. His self-defensive reaction to his wife's questioning of his masculinity—though suppressed—is, I would argue, not essentially different in kind from the gang's murderous exhibitions of phallic power. For if, as Naylor seems to suggest, the male response to unachievable dreams is violence—and violence, at least in *The Women of Brewster Place*, directed against women—then Ben's murder by his surrogate daughter seems not to be an arbitrary act where the author's explorations of male abuse of women is concerned.

In her refigurative conflations of *The Bluest Eye*'s primary scenes of male abuse of Pecola, Naylor depicts the encircling adolescent male gang as rapists and the (surrogate) father as a protective figure who asks, when he sees Lorraine—limping and bloodied—coming toward him: "My God, child, what happened to you?" While, as a narrative event, Lorraine's murder of Ben reflects the utterly chaotic nature of her mental faculties after the rape, it also serves to demonstrate, as part of the expertly wrought symbolic patterns of "The Two," the author's precise control of her material. Put simply, Naylor "kills" Ben because, despite his sensitivity to Lorraine's and his own daughter's circumstances, the urge for violence that is his response to his wife's castigations is of a kind with the reaction of the gang members to their inadequacies. When the text says of Ben's drunken movements near the wall after Lorraine is raped, "Side to side. Side to side. Almost in perfect unison with the sawing pain that kept moving inside of her," it insists that the reader view Ben as part of a continuum of male violence against women of which the actions of the gang are the reprehensible extreme. And though Ben is sensitively sketched by Naylor to a point that his true human failings— his alcoholism, inability to free himself from a restrictive concept of masculinity, and resultant violent urges—are comprehensible, the text fails ultimately to excuse these violent impulses. The manner of Ben's death can, thus, be viewed as a form of (authorial) retribution: Ben dies by having his skull crushed—one of the methods he envisions employing to murder his verbally abusive wife.

In both Naylor's and Morrison's first novels, a sense of societal order is formed as a result of sexually abusive acts. In *The Bluest Eye*, that order is a function of a black community's perceptions that with Pecola's demise it has purged itself of the shadow of blackness. On the other hand, Lorraine's victimization of *The Women of Brewster Place* occasions the development—because of a shared abhorrence regarding the brutal rape—of a sense of community among heretofore largely isolated women. For reasons that will be explored in the following section, however, this achieved woman's community is not depicted as an actual narrative event, but, rather, as the dream of the novel's most prominent character, Mattie Michael.

VII

The women of *Brewster Place*'s final story, "The Block Party," presents further evidence of Naylor's command of her material. It is a control that is, ironically, best demonstrated by the apparent failure of the totalizing gestures of this section. In her essay on *Their Eyes Were Watching God*, Barbara Johnson says of the textual unity in narrative forms: "However rich, healthy or lucid fragmentation and division may be, narrative seems to have trouble resting content with it, as though a story could not recognize its own end as anything other than a moment of totalization."[24] Naylor's novel, however, clearly recognizes the richness of its narrative fragmentation, a recognition that is exhibited in the intentional failure of its moment of totalization.

On the surface, "The Block Party" suggests that a new order results from the utter chaos surrounding the brutal rape of Lorraine. It is an order based on the female protagonists' comprehension of their interconnectedness. Ciel's return to the neighborhood, for example, is motivated by a dream that suggests her indistinguishability from Lorraine (whom she has never met). The dream was, according to Ciel:

> "one of those crazy things that get all mixed up in your head. Something about that wall and Ben. *And there was a woman who was supposed to be me,* I guess. She didn't look exactly like me, but *inside I felt it was me.*
> . . . "And she had on a green dress with like black trimming, and there were red designs or red flowers or something on the front." Ciel's eyes began to cloud. *"And something bad had happened to me by the wall—I mean to her—something bad had happened to her.* And Ben was in it somehow." She stared at the wall and shuddered (my emphasis).

Images of Lorraine have entered the unconscious thoughts of all of Brewster's females, causing the dreams of both mothers and daughters to be haunted by the image "of the tall yellow woman in the bloody green and black dress." The protagonists of the individual sections of *The Women of Brewster Place* form, in response to Cora's assertion that a week of rain has failed to wash Lorraine's blood from the wall, a determined and harmonious group working hysterically to tear down the structure. These women:

> flung themselves against the wall, chipping away at it with knives, plastic forks, spiked shoe heels, and even bare hands; the water [from a thunderstorm] pouring under their chins, and plastering their blouses and dresses against their breasts and into the cracks of their hips. The bricks piled up behind them and were snatched and relayed out of Brewster Place past overturned tables, scattered coins, and crushed wads of dollar bills. They came back with chairs and barbeque grills and smashed them into the wall.

Naylor's description of the wall's destruction concludes with a baptizing rain which, much like the symbolically reborn Ciel's tears, serves to demonstrate a sense of harmony between nature and woman, between outside and inside: "Suddenly, the rain exploded around their feet in a fresh downpour, and the cold waters beat on the tops of their heads— almost in perfect unison with the beating of their hearts." As opposed to the text's earlier depiction of harmony between inside and outside— the simultaneity of Ben's drunken movements and Lorraine's throbbing pain (whose phrasing—"Almost in perfect unison"—is repeated in the passage cited above)—the coincidence of rain beat and heartbeat suggests a valuable coalescence of heretofore divided entities. While the coincidence of Ben's movements and Lorraine's pain reflects—as narrative events—the utter chaos of the victim's mind, the harmonious rhythms that follow the destruction of the wall signal an achievement of female unity. Such unity has to do not only with the individual self and her relationship with nature, but also with the development of a community of women.

There is evidence in this section of a conscious refiguration of female-authored precursor texts. Like both *Their Eyes Were Watching God* and *The Bluest Eye*, the female unity described in Naylor's text is intricately related to double-voiced strategies of narration. *The Women of Brewster Place*'s depictions of female unity are elements of the dream of Mattie Michael, the primary agent of female coalescence in the novel. Not only does she act to save Ciel's life, but she serves as a supportive friend for Brewster Place's other females. She provides for Etta Mae Johnson after her ill-fated encounter with Reverend Woods "the light and the love and the comfort" to allow her to transcend her pain. Further, she gently chides Cora Lee about her "full load" of children, and, along with Etta Mae, defends Lorraine against Sophie's attacks.

Thus, her dream of female unity seems an imaginative extension of her efforts throughout the text. In this dream, she imbues all of the female protagonists, with the exception of Kiswana Browne,[25] with her desires for unity. Mattie's vision and voice control the final section of the novel and provide the work with a closing hopeful note: the possible coming to fruition of Mattie's dream of a supportive female community. But considering the novel's generally pejorative representation of the products of the female realm of imagination, it is difficult to rest content with such a positive reading of Mattie's dream. Such a reading proves especially difficult if, as textual evidence cited above suggests, Naylor's text does indeed possess a resolute authorial consistency with respect to its symbolic patterns. It seems to me that, like the text's other depictions of the products of the female imagination, Mattie's dream has similarly divisive consequences, not for an individual female, but for the entire novel.

Naylor's failure to represent achieved female community as an actual narrative event adds to the novel's overall narrative disjunctiveness. Instead of serving to unite the text's individual stories, Mattie's dream increases *The Women of Brewster Place*'s sense of disjunction by offering a vision that is directly antithetical to the omniscient narrator's presentation of female unity. In other words, Mattie's dream provides the narrative with an unresolved double voicedness. Because its presentation of female community is not offered as an actual narrative event, Mattie's dream is perhaps most profitably understood as an illusion that serves to perpetuate the text's content and formal disjunctions in much the same way that the self-deceptive dreams of Naylor's characters prolong their personally injurious self-divisions. Neither, then, do the women of Brewster Place or their individual texts ultimately achieve genuine coalescence.

Rather than provide the novel with a concluding sense of unity, Mattie's dream exposes—and even multiplies—the novel's various disjunctions. Without further exploration, Naylor's novel could best be characterized as an unachieved dream of wholeness, as a work that intentionally undercuts its own totalizing moment. But if we return briefly to *The Women of Brewster Place*'s male ancestral text, the generically enigmatic *Cane*, we can, by investigating Naylor's technical indebtedness to Toomer, begin to comprehend the reasons for her novel's various disjunctions.

VIII

In her essay "Untroubled Voice: Call and Response to *Cane*," Barbara Bowen argues that despite its unconventional form, Toomer's is a masterfully unified text whose unity is observable only when the literary critic regards it in terms of Afro-American expressive culture. Bowen says:

> *Cane* displays a restlessness with conventional forms. . . . [Toomer] sense[s] that the Anglo-American tradition cannot contain what he has to say . . .
> [W]hat distinguishes Toomer's work is that he is as demanding of his form as the Anglo-American novelists are of theirs. Toomer pushes the form of call and response as hard as Joyce pushes the form of the novel. And *Cane*'s most successful moments come when Toomer opens up for us what it means to turn the call-and-response pattern into a literary form.[26]

Bowen's essay seeks to explain, among other things, the problems inherent in attempting to assign to *Cane* a traditional or "conventional" Western generic designation. *Cane* is a work informed by the expressive principles—particularly call and response—of Black culture. Toomer's work is, if Bowen is correct, a *denigrated text* par excellence, a genuine Black book. In fact, Toomer's own discussion of his work offers ways in which to connect Bowen's analysis of call and response in *Cane* to my own discussion of Hurston's employment of the verbal behavior as narrative strategy in *Their Eyes Were Watching God*.

Toomer says of the generic diversity and narrative organization of the text: "*Cane*'s design is a circle [which moves] from simple forms to complex ones, and back to simpler forms."[27] If, as Bowen persuasively demonstrates, *Cane* represents its author's attempt to turn call and response into a literary form, then the critic should be able to observe antiphonal textual interaction occurring both intratextually and intertextually. Such textual antiphony is perhaps best demonstrated by the texts that conclude *Cane*'s first section, "Portrait in Georgia" and "Blood-Burning Moon."

In "Blood-Burning Moon," the text's oft-repeated song, the haunting

> Red nigger moon. Sinner!
> Blood-burning moon. Sinner!
> Come out that fact'ry door,

is the black woman's improvisational riff sung as a protective response
to the frightening omen of the full moon. As they are situated in the
text, at the conclusion of each of the story's three sections, these lyrics
operate as an ominous refrain, adding to Toomer's depiction of the inevitability of racial violence in the post-Reconstruction South a foreboding
of doom. The narrative provides numerous other foreshadowings. For
example, the story opens with a foreboding description of the fast-ap-
proaching dusk:

> Up from the skeleton stone walls, up from the rotting floor boards and the
> solid hand-hewn beams of oak of the pre-war cotton factory, [dusk] came. Up
> from the dusk the full moon came. Glowing like a fired pine-knot, it illumined
> the great door and soft showered the Negro shanties aligned along the single
> street of factory town. The full moon in the great door was an omen.

Just as ominous as the full moon proves for the story's characters are
the images of death and fire that foreshadow the racially motivated
lynching of Tom Burwell in the story's conclusion. These images are
themselves effectively prefigured in the text that directly precedes
"Blood-Burning Moon," the poem "Portrait in Georgia." This poem,
which impressionistically describes a white woman's beauty in terms of
a lynched, burned black body, reads as follows:

> Hair—braided chestnut,
> coiled like a lyncher's rope,
> Eyes—fagots,
> Lips—old scars, or the first red blisters
> Breath—the last sweet scent of cane,
> And her slim body, white as the ash
> of black flesh after flame.

In terms of an intertextual relation between Toomerian poem and
short story, I believe—with Bowen—that "Portrait in Georgia" serves as
much as an extra-textual "omen" of the tragedies that unfold in "Blood-
Burning Moon" as the moon, the refrain improvised in response to the
moon's full and blood-red presence, and the foreboding imagery such as
that which appears in the story's opening paragraph serve as intratextual omens. Thus, antecedent imagist poem, improvised folk song and
experimental short story—which have been traditionally ascribed varying degrees of artistic sophistication—interact and provide a powerful
conceptualization of deep South lynching. These pieces form, as it were,
a circle of texts, calling and responding to one another in a clearly Afro-
American expressive culturally informed manner. Both poem and story
explore lynching's sexually related motivations. The poem does so in
reference to a white Southern woman's beauty, a beauty whose alleged
inspection has apparently precipitated the lynching of a black man. In
the story, on the other hand, the racially motivated violence is a conse-

quence of its black female protagonist's physical desirability to both the easily-provoked Tom Burwell and to the son of a former slaveowner who bemoans the end of America's peculiar institution.

Toomer's multi-generic text can be thickly described in terms of the general cultural world view that informs the call and response pattern. That world view insists, as Geneva Smitherman suggests in a passage cited in chapter 1 of this study:

> The universe is hierarchical in nature. . . . Though the universe is hierarchical, all modes of existence are necessary for the sustenance of its balance and rhythm. . . . Thus we have a paradigm for the way in which "opposites" function. That is, "opposites" constitute interdependent, interacting forces which are necessary for producing a given reality.

In Toomer's text, improvisational vernacular song and "high" literary genre "interact" and provide *Cane* with its black and brilliant "chaotic" wholeness. By employing discursive "opposites" that constitute the range of expressive options available to the Afro-American literary artist (what Toomer himself calls "simple" and "complex" forms) and infusing even the most complex forms with antiphonal potentials, Toomer is able to faithfully and artistically represent the Afro-American folk spirit that had seemed to him "so beautiful" during his brief period of immersion in Afro-American culture.

Toomer's text arises largely out of what was, for him, a startling development in his attempt to resolve double consciousness. In a letter to *The Liberator*, he says:

> I have strived for a spiritual fusion analogous to the fact of racial intermingling. Without denying a single element in me, with no desire to subdue one to the other, I have sought to let them function as complements. I have tried to let them live in harmony. Within the last two or three years, however, my growing need for artist expression has pulled me deeper and deeper into the Negro group. And as my powers of receptivity increased, I found myself loving it in a way that I could never love the other. A visit to Georgia last fall was the starting point of almost everything of worth that I have done. I heard the folk-songs come from the lips of Negro peasants. I saw the rich dusk beauty that I had heard many false accents about, and of which til then, I was somewhat skeptical. And a deep part of my nature, a part that I had repressed, sprang suddenly to life and responded to them.[28]

This passage does not represent, of course, the final moment of Toomer's attempt to resolve his double consciousness. Ultimately, as critics of his work well know, he again represses the black elements of his "nature" and self which had provided him with the creative impetus to compose *Cane*, easily one of the signal achievements in the Afro-American literary tradition. But *Cane* represented for Toomer not only a celebration of the "very rich and sad and joyous and beautiful" Afro-American folk spirit, but also an attempt to preserve it in the face of what he perceived as its wholesale rejection by Afro-Americans. In an unpublished autobiography, he says:

> But I learned that the Negroes of the town objected to them [Black folk-songs and spirituals]. They called them "shouting." They had victrolas and player-pianos. So, I realized with deep regret, that the spirituals, meeting ridicule, would be certain to die out. With Negroes also the trend was towards the small town and then towards the city—and industry and commerce and machines. The folk-spirit was walking in to die on the modern desert. That spirit was so beautiful. Its death was so tragic. Just this seemed to sum life for me. And this was the feeling I put into "Cane." "Cane" was a swan-song. It was a song of an end.

For Toomer, writing here to express his confusion about "why people have expected me to write a second and a third and a fourth book like 'Cane'", his text documents the death of the Afro-American folk spirit. According to the author, early-twentieth-century black migration to cities and increasing contact with the by-products of modernity serve to separate the Afro-American permanently from the communal principles of his or her culture. *Cane*, then, is Toomer's lament for the modern Afro-American's cultural disconnectedness.

Hence, the sense of generic "chaos" that his friend Waldo Frank perceived in Toomer's text[29] could be viewed as the author's means of providing his work with an apparent unity of form and content. *Cane*'s apparently chaotic form seems to complement its textual depiction of a people increasingly separated from its soul—from itself. In his delineation of characters such as: the male suitors of Karintha and Fern, who prove unable to appreciate their intense spirituality; Esther, who concocts elaborate fantasies as antidotes for an emotionally barren life; and northern men and women who, because they lack highly developed sensibilities, cannot establish intimate relationships, Toomer creates an Afro-American panorama of individuals almost completely isolated from one another by the effects of modernity.

As we have seen, however, *Cane* does indeed possess a subtle artistic unity. This textual unity is fully discernible only in terms of Afro-American expressive practices—practices infused with the communal folk spirit whose death Toomer prematurely proclaims in his autobiographical statement. In fact, Toomer's view of his text notwithstanding, *Cane* does not, finally, suggest the death of the Afro-American folk spirit but, rather, its remarkably vibrant (expressive) durability. Just as Toomer's prediction of the demise of the Afro-American spiritual proves erroneous (ironically, the folk songs that the author so admired endure largely because they were preserved by means of "modern" recording devices), so, too, is his assessment of his text ultimately incorrect.

Darwin Turner offers in his introduction to *Cane* a profitable way to assess the Toomerian view of his acclaimed work: "No matter what it may have been for him, *Cane* still sings to readers, not the swan song of an era that was dying, but the morning hymn of the Renaissance that was beginning." In its achievement—despite its apparent disjunctiveness—of expressive unity, Toomer's text stands up as a distinguished example of the resilience of an Afro-American folk spirit that privileges coalescence.

IX

The Women of Brewster Place's primary inheritance from its male precursorial text is technical in nature. More specifically, it has to do with how most provocatively to depict the disunity of Afro-Americans while, at the same time, acknowledging and faithfully representing Black cultural impulses that insist on unity. There is, to be sure, sufficient evidence of refiguration of the content of Toomer's text such as Naylor's employment of the image of a bastard community that I discussed earlier in the chapter. But perhaps the clearest such example, and one even more illuminating where the unity of Naylor's text is concerned, is the employment in the novel's initial section, "Mattie Michael," of *Cane*'s central trope. Upon her arrival in the walled-in community of Brewster, Mattie smells a scent strongly reminiscent of the almost-forgotten aromas of her Tennessee childhood:

> For a moment it smelled like freshly cut sugar cane, and she took in short, rapid breaths of air to try to capture the scent again. But it was gone. And it couldn't have been anyway. There was no sugar cane on Brewster.

Naylor's introduction of cane is accomplished in terms of the memory of her protagonist, as if the author wants to evoke in the reader her memory of Toomer's text. The scent awakens in Mattie specific recollections of people and events in her past: "Sugar cane and summer and Papa and Basil and Butch." But what this scene awakens in the informed reader of Afro-American literature is *Cane*'s central trope. And while Mattie's conclusion that the scent she smells could not be cane possesses a clear and literal meaning, it also contains for that informed reader, an equally apparent implication having to do with Toomer's figuration of the cane trope. In the essay "Journey Toward Black Art: Jean Toomer's *Cane*," Houston Baker argues: "Throughout Part One there is an evocation of a land of sugar cane whose ecstacy and pain are rooted in a communal soil."[30] For Baker, Toomer employs cane as a symbol of Afro-American deep South communal impulses. If Baker is correct, then Mattie's statement suggests that the northern climate that Brewster typifies does not foster such communal inclinations.

When read in the light of such information, Mattie's subsequent efforts can profitably be viewed as her attempt to establish in the urban North the patterns of unity and communalism that had existed when the black American population was located primarily in the agrarian South. And like the failure of the MacTeer sisters' attempts to save Pecola's baby, Mattie's labors are ultimately unsuccessful because the northern environment proves "unyielding" to such efforts. The divisive effects of modernity cannot be undone, even by the strenuous efforts of Mattie, whose rescue of Ciel suggests that she possesses the communal inclinations and incantatory powers of her deep South forebears. *The Women of Brewster Place* evokes and refigures *Cane* in order to demonstrate canonical precedence for its imaginative exploration of the difficulties of (comm)unity in an intrinsically divisive setting. Like Toomer, Naylor seems to believe that the Afro-American folk spirit has met its demise in the urban desert of modernity.

In her *New York Times Book Review* statement, as we have seen, Naylor suggests that readers of *The Bluest Eye* "can see plainly what [narrative] strategies failed." When we are aware of *Cane*'s specific refigurations in Naylor's text, it becomes clear that what the younger female novelist views as faulty about Morrison's novel is the ultimate coalescence of its distinct narrative voices. For Naylor, such coalescence runs contrary not only to the text's myriad depictions of Afro-American division (including Pecola's pain-inspired schizophrenia), but also to her female precursor's clear understanding of the almost indefeasible obstacles to Afro-American unity. Morrison's resolution of her text's double voicedness is, for Naylor, a thematically unwarranted authorial imposition of a totalizing gesture onto a richly fragmented narrative strategy. This unjustified resolution represents, for Naylor, an authorial dream of wholeness which, like Mattie's dream, is not sufficiently grounded in the textual reality that precedes it.

Certainly the "correctness" of Naylor's apparent reading of *The Bluest Eye*'s narrative strategies is not incontestable. What is not debatable, however, is the fact that both authors perceive almost insurmountable obstacles to Afro-American coalescence in the modern North. Of the texts we have examined to this point, only *Their Eyes Were Watching God* can, apparently because of its deep South and timeless setting, present female resolution of division as possible. In the final novel to be treated in this study, Alice Walker's *The Color Purple*, the author delineates a female's (and, in fact, an entire Afro-American community's) achievement of unity. In addition to sharing with Hurston's novel a deep South setting, *The Color Purple* also serves as a provocative delineation of an Afro-American woman's defeat of divisive patriarchal forces that demand women's silence and subservience.

Notes

1. Clifford Geertz, *Local Knowledge* (New York: Basic Books, 1983), p. 102.
2. It is possible to suggest that the structure and conclusion of *The Women of Brewster Place* refigure and parody most directly Shange's important choreopoem. While *for colored girls* offers the stories of seven spatially divided female characters who suffer in an oppressively patriarchal Afro-America and ultimately concludes with the joyous songs of a unified black female community, Naylor's "novel in seven stories" ends with what is literally a dream of female (comm)unity. But Mattie's dream, as I will discuss at length later in this essay, suggests, unlike the conclusion of Shange's choreopoem, the utter difficulty of achieving female nexus in an American society that is not radically transformed in terms of its debilitating racism and sexism. Read intertextually, Naylor's text offers a bold criticism of the utopian resolution of *for colored girls*.
3. Elaine Showalter, "Feminist Criticism in the Wilderness," *The New Feminist Criticism*, Showalter, ed. (New York: Pantheon, 1985), p. 265. Subsequent references to this essay appear in the text in parentheses.
4. Sandra Gilbert, "What Do Feminist Critics Want?" *The New Feminist Criticism*, p. 32.
5. Gloria Naylor, *The Women of Brewster Place* (New York: Penguin, 1983), p. 1. All subsequent references to this novel appear in the text in parentheses.
6. Jean Toomer, *Cane*, 1923 (New York: Liveright, 1975), p. 39.
7. "Famous First Words," *New York Times Book Review*, June 2, 1985, p. 52.
8. It would generally be extremely problematic to argue that a literary artist is consciously employing deconstructionist theories either in her own texts or in her interpretations of the works of others. But Naylor did spend two years in New Haven earning an M.A. at Yale, the indisputable hotbed of deconstruction in America, and her comments—and, as I will demonstrate, her first novel—suggest that she absorbed a good deal of its theoretical suppositions.
9. Jonathan Culler, *On Deconstruction* (Ithaca: Cornell University Press, 1982), p. 249. Subsequent references to this study appear in the text in parentheses.
10. Harold Bloom, *A Map of Misreading* (New York: Oxford University Press, 1975), p. 3.
11. Toni Morrison, *The Bluest Eye* (New York: Washington Square Press, 1970), p. 157. Subsequent references to this novel are hereafter marked by page numbers in parentheses in the text.
12. "Famous First Words," p. 52.
13. Donald Gibson, *The Politics of Literary Expression* (Westport, Conn.: Greenwood Press, 1981), p. 4.
14. In an age when so many critics discuss literature's discursive properties and exclude the mimetic qualities of literature from their analyses, Gibson's "social theory of literature" is refreshing. But in disputing theories of literature which insist "that literature has a nature and character exclusively its own," Gibson overlooks intertextual relations between works of expressive art which have as much to do with individual authors' attempts to establish themselves as writers as they do with their efforts to re-create their social realities in an imaginative way. For Gibson, every authorial impulse has a strictly social origin, an assessment which, it seems to me, fails to account fully for revisionary gestures of the sort that the study examines.

15. Jean Strouse, "Black Magic," *Newsweek*, March 30, 1981, p. 56.
16. Toni Morrison, "Behind the Making of *The Black Book*," *Black World*, February 1974, p. 89.
17. Michele Wallace, "Blues for Mr. Spielberg," *Village Voice* (1986), 31(11):24.
18. Anne Barton, Introduction to *A Midsummer Night's Dream, The Riverside Shakespeare*, G. Blakemore Evans, textual ed. (Boston: Houghton Mifflin, 1974), p. 219.
19. Judith Branzburg, "Seven Women and a Wall," *Callaloo* (1984), 7(3):118.
20. Zora Neale Hurston, *Their Eyes Were Watching God*, 1937 (Urbana: University of Illinois Press, 1978), p. 9. All subsequent references to this novel appear in the text in parentheses.
21. Lloyd Brown, "Zora Neale Hurston and the Nature of Female Perception," *Obsidian* (1978), 4(3):39–40.
22. Ntozake Shange, *for colored girls who have considered suicide when the rainbow is enuf* (New York: Bantam, 1977), p. 66.
23. For a similar scene of salvific bathing of a symbolically reborn Afro-American female protagonist—a scene with clear intertextual connections to both Shange and Naylor—see Paule Marshall, *Praisesong for the Widow* (New York: Dutton, 1983), pp. 217–24.
24. Barbara Johnson, "Metaphor, Metonymy and Voice in *Their Eyes Were Watching God*," *Black Literature and Literary Theory*, Henry Louis Gates, Jr., ed. (New York: Methuen, 1984), p. 213.
25. Naylor subtly suggests that Kiswana Browne and, more specifically, Browne's story, do not "belong" in *The Women of Brewster Place*. Not only does her story fail to conform to the general patterns of the novel's other stories, but Kiswana also never succeeds in becoming a part of the female community that Mattie Michael envisions in "The Block Party."
26. Barbara Bowen, "Untroubled Voice: Call and Reponse in *Cane*," *Black Literature and Literary Theory*, p. 196.
27. Quoted by Charles T. Davis, "Jean Toomer and the South: Region and Race as Elements within a Literary Imagination," *Studies in the Literary Imagination* (1974), 7(2):32.
28. Quoted by Darwin Turner, Introduction to *Cane* (New York: Liveright, 1975), p. xvi. Subsequent references to this introduction appear in the text in parentheses.
29. Waldo Frank, "Foreword" to *Cane* (New York: Boni and Liveright, 1923), p. x.
30. Houston A. Baker, Jr., *Singers of Daybreak* (Washington, D.C.: Howard University Press, 1974), p. 61.

◆◆◆◆◆◆◆◆◆◆◆◆◆◆

Reading Rape

LAURA E. TANNER

While the relationship between the violence of a culture and its representational counterpart in art is probed in many literary and artistic works, few deal with the issue with the immediacy of Marcel Duchamp's room-size art work, "Etant Donnés: 1 la chute d'eau, 2 le gaz d'éclairage." "Etant Donnés" occupies one small room of the Philadelphia Museum of Art; the viewer's entrance into the room is marked by the absence of light, and the looming presence of an actual wooden door that appears to have been taken out of a garden wall and set down in the museum intact. While the door will not open, closer examination reveals that it contains two small holes through which it is possible to peer past the door itself, through the gap in a brick wall set about three feet behind the door, and into the world beyond. The backdrop of the scene that meets the viewer is artificially natural, a glitzy combination of fake trees, glittering lights, and mechanical waterfall that seems a poor imitation of an actual landscape. The glance of the viewer, however, is directed not toward that artificial backdrop but onto a life-size model of a woman's naked body, a body splayed out relentlessly before the viewer's eyes, a body that announces as its most prominent feature a hairless vagina that is cut into the woman like a wound. The woman lies as if abandoned after an act of violation, her legs spread painfully wide in a tangle of dark brush and autumn leaves. The peepholes in Duchamp's wooden door succeed in aligning the viewer's eyes with the glaring wound of the woman's sex; subtle techniques of focus that may be contradicted in a painting are replaced here by a physical alignment, a concrete limitation of sight, that is as effective as a strong pair of hands that jerk the viewer's head into position and hold it there. Having chosen to look, the viewer is held captive by the artwork, locked into the position of a voyeur without prelude or conscious choice. The degradation of the experience is heightened by the naked woman's forced participation in her own objectification. The victim, face obscured behind a wave of blonde hair, holds in her outstretched hand a gas lamp as if to illuminate every crack, crevice, and wound of the body that the viewer approaches as text. The violence to which the naked woman's body bears testimony is reenacted in the guise of art; the viewer becomes a violator whose gaze perpetuates the violence of a crime that reduces woman to object.

I

In deliberately blurring the boundaries between art and life, aesthetic and actual violence, Duchamp's study points to the way in which the conventions of art may both create and license the desire for violence. Art invites the audience's participation in its created worlds while offering that audience the comfort of aesthetic distance; that distance allows the reader or viewer to accept the work's invitation to titillation without appearing to become implicated in its trafficking with violence. Duchamp's work, in effect, upsets the fragile justification of aesthetic convention by undercutting the viewer's sense of the distinction between *studying* a scene of artistic violence and *participating* in an act of literal violation. "Etant Donnés" is shocking, not because it transgresses the boundaries that separate violence from the artistic *representation* of violence but because it forces its viewers to recognize that transgression.

In Faulkner's *Sanctuary*, on the other hand, the reader's presence as not only an observer but a participant in the novel's violence is obscured by a literary screen that assures the reader of his or her distance from the act of violence even as it affords an entry into that violence. Faulkner exploits the conventions of literature to lure the reader past the boundaries of the printed page into the barn where Temple is raped. As *Sanctuary* pressures the reader not only to perceive the rape from the perspective of the violator but to assume the position of that violator, to anticipate, to plan, and to execute—in the arena of the imagination— the crime of rape, the novel continues to assert the purely literary nature of the violence enacted in the reader's mind.

The sensational crime around which *Sanctuary* revolves is never described in the novel. While the back cover of one Vintage paperback edition advertises that the novel's protagonist is "raped in a peculiarly horrible manner," the novel itself continually fails to satisfy the appetite for lurid description that it—and its advertisement—creates. By withholding any direct representation of the rape upon which it focuses, *Sanctuary* shifts the burden of creation away from Faulkner and toward the reader; while Faulkner invokes the conventions of high literature to authorize *Sanctuary* as a work of art rather than a piece of popular fiction, the novel relies upon its readers to create the scandalous story of violation that it only suggests. The reader's access to Popeye's horrendous act of violence is limited to a series of adumbrated narrative descriptions and a montage of speculations by the novel's characters; the novel itself provides no authorized version of the rape. With each tauntingly inadequate representation of the violence, each symbolic allusion to the crime, each purely imaginary conjecture of the rape by the novel's characters, the act itself becomes more visibly absent; the rape becomes a gaping hole in the text that the reader must fill in. In *The Act of Reading*, Wolfgang Iser describes such narrative gaps as "structured blanks." "Communication in literature," Iser states, "is a process set in motion and regulated, not by a given code, but by a mutually restrictive and magnifying interaction between the explicit and the implicit, between revelation and concealment. . . . Hence, the structured blanks of the text stimulate the process of ideation to be performed by the reader on terms set by the text."[1] Such blanks function as invitations to the reader to participate not only in the viewing but in the making of the novelistic universe; the gap in the narrative "turns into a propellant for the reader's imagination, making him supply what has been withheld."[2] In *Sanctuary*, the narrative's withholding of the representation of Popeye's crime shifts the burden of creation away from Faulkner and toward the reader. The novel's refusal to write the rape jolts the reader into becoming the author of the crime.[3]

It is the reader who first articulates the possibility of rape in *Sanctuary*. The narrative's continual allusions to the danger that threatens Temple's sense of well-being are ambiguous and incomplete. Denied access to information that Temple herself possesses, the reader must name the threat that plagues the novel's protagonist. Even as Temple is about to communicate to Gowan (and the reader) the source and substance of her fear, her narrative is temporarily suspended; her recounting of her conversation with Ruby is interrupted by a crucial ellipsis that frustrates the reader's desire to pinpoint the exact nature of Temple's suspicions: "'Gowan, I'm scared. She said for me not to—You've been drinking again; you haven't even washed the blood—She says for us to go away from here. . . . . . .'"[4] The revelation that Temple appears about to deliver is immediately interrupted by her observation about Gowan's drinking. As a result, it is the reader who must fill in the gap marked by the narrative ellipsis. The reason for Temple's fear is never explicitly articulated; while the possibility of violence is suggested, the threat of rape is acknowledged by the reader alone.

While Temple's initial expression of her fear conceals more than it reveals, the anxious response that portrayal generates in the reader is kept alive through narrative ambiguity. Temple's elliptical comments feed the reader's suspicions of the threatened crime without actually confirming them. Her disjointed sentences, ambiguous pronouns, and logical inversions create referential puzzles that the reader must take apart and reconstruct if Temple's remarks are to make sense: "'There are so many of them,' she said in a wailing tone, watching the cigarette crush slowly in her fingers. 'But maybe, with so many of them. . . . . . .' The woman had gone back to the stove." Temple's comments appear as a type of idiosyncratic shorthand that bodies forth a more complete system of thought; in supplying the referential system for Temple's remarks, the reader remakes those remarks in accordance with his or her own assumptions. The narrative puzzle is never "solved"; instead, its pieces are reformed into diverse configurations that conform to the narrative patterns created by individual readers. The truncated nature of Temple's comments licenses the reader's imaginative foray into violence and sex by serving as an apparent narrative anchor for those explorations. In fact, however, Faulkner plays upon the ambiguity of the narrative's comments to transfer the responsibility for the creation of the novel's lurid plot to the reader.

The reader's active role in the construction of meaning blurs the conventional line between a novel and its audience, encouraging the reader's entrance into the fictional text. Temple's fragmented sentences and abrupt shifts of focus often emerge as if in response to an invisible commentator/reader who articulates her fears of violence. Having asked Ruby Lamar for a ride into town, for example, Temple suddenly breaks into a frantic speech that is supposedly directed at Ruby and her infant child. In fact, however, the monologue appears to be part of a dialogue begun somewhere outside the text; it opens with a response to what seems to be a missing question: "'I'm not afraid,' Temple said. 'Things like that don't happen. Do they? They're just like other people. You're just like other people. With a little baby. . . . What a cute little bu-ba-a-by,' she wailed, lifting the child to her face; 'if bad man hurts Temple, us'll tell the governor's soldiers, wont us?'." Temple's unsolicited assertion—"I'm not afraid"—lacks apparent textual motivation, just as the demonstrative pronoun she employs—"Things like *that*" (emphasis mine)—lacks a visible referent. Her comments appear to be a response to an extra-textual observation, a reply to the unvoiced concern of a reader who speaks from outside the novelistic world. Because the novel's characters fail to voice the threat of violence that haunts Temple, it is the reader who supplies the missing referent for her ambiguous words. While Temple's comments emerge as if in response to the reader's questions, they continue to conceal as much as they reveal. Her ominous reference to the unspoken fate that she fears—"Things like that don't happen. Do they?"—fuels the reader's imaginary fears even as it refuses to confirm the substance of those fears. The ambiguous imaging of the narrative assures, once again, that the only violence made explicit in the novel is a violence born of the reader's imagination; it is the reader's fearful anticipation of that violence that lends the rape imaginative form and brings it to life.

The early warnings of the rape that rumble through the novel without ever assuming articulate form tease the reader into a state of protracted sensitivity; in that state, the slightest movement, the least reported sound, triggers an avalanche of imaginative violences. Before the rape ever occurs, Faulkner plays upon the reader's understanding of literary conventions to ensnare the overeager reader in the web of his or her own expectations. As Iser points out, the function of the break between chapters in a novel "is not separation so much as a tacit invitation to find the missing link";[5] at the beginning of chapter II, Faulkner invokes the convention of the chapter break to deliver such a "tacit invitation." He exploits the reader's expectation of the rape and understanding of the possibility of "off-screen" intra-chapter action to lure the reader into believing that the rape has already occurred: "Temple waked lying in a tight ball, with narrow bars of sunlight falling across her face like the tines of a golden fork, and while the stiffened blood trickled and tingled through her cramped muscles she lay gazing quietly up at the ceiling." In this description, the sun becomes a weapon that rakes its tines across Temple's body to produce the trickling blood and cramped muscles that the reader—his or her anticipation heightened—automatically associates with rape. Faulkner plays upon the artificiality of metaphor to invoke the signs of rape in an alternative context. The narrative provides the raw materials of violent description, while the reader's heightened antici-pation of the event constructs those materials into a representation of violence. Temple's physical discomfort, however, is soon traced to its undramatic origin in her cramped sleeping quarters; the rape to which the narrative seems to have alluded has occurred only in the reader's imagination.

Denied an explicit account of the novel's violence, the reader is tempted and frustrated, tempted and frustrated, until the process of reading begins to assume the rhythm of desire itself. The reader's ab-sorption of warnings about the imminence of Temple's rape translates into an eagerness to peruse the spectacle that has been promised; his or her sensitivity to the subtle conventions of fiction is exploited by a narra-tive trap that invites the reader—if only momentarily—to envision and even create the promised violence. With the continued reiteration of hints and clues about the crime, however, the reader's horrified response to the projected rape may fade into a kind of numbed expectation. Through the sheer act of repetition, the novel's protracted inexplicit references to the rape rob the crime of its shock value; the reader's sympathy for the victim and the indignation inspired by the mere thought of the violent act become tinged with an impatience bred of familiarity. The desire for narrative closure turns the violent event that would pro-vide that closure into a mere literary device as the reader is pressured into not only anticipating but impatiently awaiting the promised violence.

Like the reader, the little man who attempts to protect Temple from the advances of Goodwin and Popeye is also reduced to a state of dulled immunity to the impending rape. Throughout the first part of the novel, the physical postures of Temple's protector, Tommy, chart her increasing vulnerability and the reader's building agitation. Initially, Tommy reacts to Temple's impending violation with an indignation so violent that it overwhelms his own body: Tommy "began to think about Temple again. He would feel his feet scouring on the floor and his whole body writhing in an acute discomfort. 'They ought to let that gal alone,' he whispered to Goodwin. 'They ought to quit pesterin her.'" The "acute discomfort" that Tommy experiences as his "whole body writh[es]" not only points toward Temple's rape but metaphorically enacts it; his tortured empathy becomes a means of channeling his own unacknowledged and illicit desire. As the narrative progresses in its path toward the violence that both Tommy and the reader recognize as inevitable, the ineffectual protesting of Temple's protector generates a tension born as much of repressed desire as of moral frustration: "'Durn them fellers,' Tommy whispered, 'durn them fellers.' He could hear them on the front porch and his body began again to writhe slowly in an acute unhappiness. 'Durn them fellers.'" Tommy's distress echoes the discomfort of a reader forced to squirm in his or her seat while awaiting with frustrating slowness the inevitability of the rape that is to follow. Like the reader, Tommy follows Popeye's path back and forth, toward and away from Temple, unable to intervene as either protector or violator: "The third time he smelled Popeye's cigarette. Ef he'll jest keep that up, he said. And Lee too, he said, rocking from side to side in a dull excruciating agony. And Lee too." The "scouring feet" and "writhing" body that characterized Tommy's initial response to Temple's situation give way to what is now described as a "dull, excruciating agony." While that agony, like the other physical signs of his discomfort, is born of feeling for Temple, it is now a feeling tinged with resignation. The reader's pain, like Tommy's agony, is replaced by a "dulled" perception of the inevitability of Temple's violation.

As the prolonged anticipation of violence is finally confirmed, Faulkner downplays the reader's voyeuristic interest by emphasizing the apparently self-contained literary status of the rape. He uses the artifice of literary device—in this case, blatant symbolism—both to pique the reader's desire to view the forbidden act and to license that desire by clothing it in literary terms. As Popeye moves toward the cringing Temple, his approach is described as a type of symbolic and almost ritualistic dance in which the movement of his gun is clearly associated with the aggressive penis: "He leaned out the door, the pistol behind him, against his flank, wisping thinly along his leg. He turned and looked at her. He waggled the pistol slightly and put it back in his coat, then he walked toward her." Faulkner's choice of verbs exposes the discrepancy between literal vehicle and symbolic import; while the word "waggled" appears inappropriate for a gun, it is very appropriate for the symbolic counterpart of that gun. The mismatch of Faulkner's terms emphasizes the *process* through which violence is translated into literature and encourages the reader to reenact that process in reverse, to trace the path from symbol to sign, from sign to signified. The reader participates in the creation of the rape scene by stripping away the layers of aesthetic mediation to unearth the crime beneath.

Like the symbolic imaging of Popeye's approach, the cryptic description of the violence that follows denies the reader a concrete representation that would take the place of the reader's own hazy formulations of the rape:

> She could hear silence in a thick rustling as he moved toward her through it, thrusting it aside, and she began to say Something is going to happen to me. She was saying it to the old man with the yellow clots for eyes. "Something is happening to me!" she screamed at him, sitting in his chair in the sunlight, his hands crossed on top of the stick. "I told you it was!" she screamed, voiding the words like hot silent bubbles into the bright silence about them until he turned his head and the two phlegm-clots above her where she lay tossing and thrashing on the rough, sunny boards. "I told you! I told you all the time!"

In this long-awaited "representation" of violence, the natural consequences of the rape are overshadowed by the function of the episode as a literary device; Temple's rape is communicated only as a *linguistic* event. The act is signified by a subtle motion of language, a shift of tense that marks the realization of narrative foreshadowing but not the demarcation of any visualizable incident. Temple's predictive remark, "Something is going to happen to me," is replaced by "Something is happening to me!"; in the infinitesimal space between the two phrases the rape is located but never defined, alluded to but never enacted. This confirmation of the reader's expectations of violence is less a resolution of tension than another invitation to narrative play that ends only in frustration. Like the old blind man who "witnesses" the rape, the reader is brought close to the scene only to be denied sensory access to it.

In fact, the old man "with the yellow clots for eyes" acts in many ways as the reader's double in the rape scene. Although he is close enough to the rape to reach out and touch Temple's writhing body, the old man remains "sitting in his chair in the sunlight, his hands crossed" in the posture of inaction. His handicaps appear to make his presence in the scene unproblematic; his blindness and deafness not only excuse his passive response but make intervention a sheer impossibility. The fundamental distance that separates the old man from the act that occurs in his presence affords him a unique status; he is exempted from the normal human responsibility for intervention. The reader, too, is present in the scene; while the old man "observes" the act blindly, the reader watches the violence unfold before his/her eyes, protected from the charge of voyeurism by an abstract representation that emphasizes the noninterventionist dynamics of the reading process. Temple's desperate accusation—"'Something is happening to me!'"—is directed at the old man who sits passively by as the rape unfolds; the *reader*, however, is clearly implicated by the remark as well. It is the reader, after all, who alone has been the recipient of Temple's frequent warnings of impending violence, the reader, as well as the old man who sits silently, passively watching without intervening. Even as the reader's imagination provides the details of a violence that the narrative has withheld, the hysterical young woman who is about to be raped screams out desperately: "I told you it was! . . . I told you all the time!"

Not surprisingly, then, in the metaphorical description of the rape that Faulkner *does* provide, it is the voyeur who perpetrates the ultimate crime. Faulkner's only description of the rape scene casts the violence as a struggle not between Temple and Popeye, but between Temple and the old man with the phlegm-clotted eyes. During the rape, Temple screams desperately as a foreign body hovers over her own; it is not into Popeye's unresponsive eyes that she stares, however, but at "the two phlegm-clots above her where she lay tossing and thrashing on the rough, sunny boards." It is into the old man's blind eyes that Temple, at least in a metaphorical sense, looks as she thrashes on the boards; it is the old man, the voyeur, the reader, who assumes the posture of the rapist while Popeye himself stands on the sidelines, impotent.

At Miss Reba's, the endless parade of visitors through Temple's room reflects the desire of the novel's characters to look upon Temple's body—the object of rape—and to reconstruct through her presence the elusive details of that violence. Temple becomes an object of curiosity not only to Snopes (who is caught "peeping through the keyhole" of her door) and Benbow but to the reader as well. Her account of the rape, however, merely replaces the reader's fictional inventions with her own fantastic imaginings. As she weaves a story of rape that is actually a narrative of her own fantasies, Temple shocks Benbow into the realization that "she was recounting the experience with actual pride, a sort of naive and impersonal vanity, as though she were making it up." Temple's relationship to her own experience of violation is defined by a detachment and a fascination not unlike that which governs the reader's literary experience of the rape. Like the naked woman in Duchamp's sculpture, she participates in her own objectification, offering herself up to the gaze of others as she peers at herself. Temple's account of the rape stimulates Benbow's own masturbatory fantasy, just as her lovemaking with Red arouses Popeye as he lingers panting and whinnying at the side of the bed. The light that Temple shines on her own experience thus implicates her, as well as the novel's characters and readers, in the pattern of obsessive looking that Faulkner establishes in the novel.

While both Temple and Benbow offer fantasy renditions of the novel's violence, it is not until the trial scene that the reader is offered any concrete information about the details of the rape. The information that is provided does not take the form of an eye witness account or a straightforward recreation of the event; instead, the reader is offered yet another incomplete revelation, an invitation to speculation about an object that the reader must imaginatively place at the scene of Temple's rape: "The district attorney faced the jury. 'I offer as evidence this object which was found at the scene of the crime.' He held in his hand a corn-cob. It appeared to have been dipped in dark brownish paint." The District

Attorney's definitive proclamation of the corn-cob's relevance obscures the speculative nature of the reader's conclusions about the object. While the prosecutor invokes the testimony of a chemist and gynecologist to support his conclusions, the reader's access to those testimonies is blocked by the narrative's refusal to represent them; in the same way, the reader's access to the "evidence" that the prosecutor introduces is limited by the narrative's evasive description of the corn-cob. Although it seems clear that the stain on the cob is actually dried blood, the narrative insists on describing it as "dark brownish paint." Faulkner chooses the figure rather than the direct description because by indirect reference the reader is made to interpret the appearance of the cob, to transform paint into human blood; he or she has thus not read about a bloodied cob but has imaginatively created one. Having bloodied that cob, the reader has no difficulty in envisioning its function as the rape weapon; the narrative's failure to provide logical connections and accurate representations encourages the reader actively to construct the District Attorney's case. This technique of requiring the reader to image the violence, making the reader do his work for him, is characteristic of Faulkner's approach throughout *Sanctuary*.

It is this same approach that the prosecutor utilizes to convict Goodwin in the trial itself. The District Attorney's deliberate omission of details about the rape transfers the responsibility for imaging the event to the jury. The trial, then, serves as a reenactment of the reading process in which prosecutor and jury dramatize the interactive dynamics that govern the relationship between *Sanctuary* and its readers. The trial is sketched as a dialogue between the prosecutor—who provides only the barest of details—and the courtroom voyeurs who imaginatively participate in the construction of the rape scene:

> The District Attorney bowed toward the Bench. He turned to the witness and held her eyes again.
> "Where were you on Sunday morning, May twelfth?"
> "I was in the crib."
> The room sighed, its collective breath hissing in the musty silence.

The "hissing" of the room's "collective breath" articulates the audience's voyeuristic fascination with the drama that the District Attorney promises to reenact. Temple's simple statement—"I was in the crib"—licenses imaginative speculation about the crime. It is in the imagination of "the room" that Temple is raped, for the District Attorney is careful never to solicit Temple's explicit testimony. Instead, he proves the imaginative impetus for the jury's construction of the event:

> The District Attorney returned. . . . [H]e caught [Temple's] gaze and held it and lifted the stained corncob before her eyes. The room sighed, a long hissing breath.
> "Did you ever see this before?"
> "Yes."

The District Attorney turned away. "Your Honor and gentlemen, you have listened to this horrible, this unbelievable story which this young girl has told; you have seen the evidence and heard the doctor's testimony: I shall no longer subject this ruined, defenseless child to the agony of—."

In fact, the "horrible . . . unbelievable story" that Temple has related has been no story at all. The District Attorney's questioning places Temple and Goodwin in the crib, confirms that Temple has seen the corn-cob . . . and goes no further. The anxious prosecutor interrupts Temple's testimony in mid-sentence on three separate occasions; at every point in her interrogation when she attempts to respond with more than a simple phrase, to fill in the story with details of her own, his "Wait" or "Just a minute" cuts off her narrative. It is the audience, the jury, that the District Attorney invites to fill in the ellipses of Temple's story, just as it is the reader whom Faulkner encourages to fill in the structured blanks of the narrative.

The dynamics of reading violence that underlie both the reader's and the jury's experience of Temple's rape are encapsulated in a casual conversation between out-of-town observers of the trial:

"They're going to let him get away with it, are they?" a drummer said. "With that corn cob? What kind of folks have you got here? What does it take to make you folks mad?"

"He wouldn't a never got to trial, in my town," a second said.

"To jail, even," a third said. "Who was she?"

"College girl. Good looker. Didn't you see her?"

"I saw her. She was some baby. Jeez. I wouldn't have used no cob."

The drummers' distance from the act allows them not only to deplore the rapist but to recreate the rape, not only to denigrate the method but to replace it with one of their own imagination. The self-righteous moralizing of these bystanders invites their imagination of the rape; in order to be appropriately horrified by the act they must reenact it mentally. In doing so, they create fictions of violence, casting *themselves* in the part of the rapist whose actions they so vehemently denounce.

For the reader, as for the drummer, the experience of Temple's rape is an imaginative one. Instead of obscuring the artifice inherent in fictional representation, Faulkner capitalizes on that artifice; the obvious literary quality of his representation invites the reader's creative voyeurism while offering the safety of a purely aesthetic manipulation. Reading appears to offer the opportunity for voyeuristic perception without actual participation; the distance between reader and text seemingly affords the opportunity to enter imaginatively—and with impunity—into fictional universes of violence and sex. By emphasizing the literary quality of this rape, Faulkner invokes the distance of reading as a screen that obscures the reader's awareness of his or her own participation in the scene of violence. Although the knowing anticipation of another's rape lies dangerously close to an indulgence in voyeuristic pleasure, intellectual participation in a purely literary violence may appear to involve a manipulation of symbols rather than sexuality, of literary conventions rather than living bodies. While Duchamp's "Etant Donnés" blurs the boundaries that separate violence from the artistic representation of violence, Faulkner's *Sanctuary* exploits the reader's assumption of such boundaries even as it invites that reader to transgress them. Like the outraged drummers who go on to use Temple's rape as a springboard for a crime of their own creation—"I wouldn't have used no cob"—the reader, too, conspires in an act of imaginative assault that implicates that reader in the novel's violence not merely as a voyeur but as a violator.

II

In "Visual Pleasure and Narrative Cinema," Laura Mulvey explores the way in which the "unconscious of patriarchal society" has structured film form.[6] Applying the theories of Freud and Lacan to the conventional cinematic situation, Mulvey traces the spectator's visual pleasure to its origin in two "structures of looking." Scopophilia, the first aspect of viewing that Mulvey discusses, is defined by a voyeuristic dynamic in which the erotic identity of the viewing subject is clearly separated from the object (usually a woman) on the screen; the viewer derives pleasure from objectifying the screen persona and subjecting that persona to the power of the controlling gaze. The second and seemingly contradictory aspect of viewing allows the spectator to identify with the object on the screen (usually a male hero); through what Mulvey describes as "the spectator's fascination with and recognition of his life," the viewer participates vicariously in the screen protagonist's exploits.[7] The process of identification with the screen hero depends upon the viewer's ability to transcend the barrier of the screen by entering imaginatively into the cinematic world. The voyeuristic outlook associated with scopophilia, on the other hand, is authorized by the sense of distance that governs the viewer's experience as he or she watches the large screen from the comfort and anonymity of the darkened auditorium. Because these processes of identification and objectification rely upon differing manipulations of the perceived distance between the audience and the cinematic world it observes, Mulvey describes them as the two "contradictory aspects" of viewing.

As *Sanctuary* reveals, however, these "structures of looking" only appear to contradict one another; in fact, the processes often occur simultaneously and function symbiotically. The processes of cinematic viewing that Mulvey describes operate in much the same way that the dynamics of reading operate in *Sanctuary*. While Faulkner's exaggeration of literary conventions distances the reader from the violence in the text, the structured blanks of the novel subtly undermine that distance by encouraging the reader's imaginative participation in that violence. In both Faulkner's novel and the films that Mulvey discusses, the viewer/ reader's reluctance to participate imaginatively in an artistic universe of sex and violence is defused by conventions of reading and viewing—be they the reiteration of literary symbols in the novel or the literal separation of audience and screen in the theater—that emphasize the distance separating that viewer/reader from the on-screen or intratextual acts. Despite their contradictory origins, both voyeuristic viewing and imaginative identification "pursue aims in indifference to perceptual reality, creating the imagised, eroticized concept of the world that forms the perception of the subject and makes a mockery of empirical objectivity."[8]

In *Sanctuary,* the "empirical objectivity" of rape disappears altogether to be replaced by an imaginative construct created by the reader and endorsed by the text; within the frame of that construct, the reader identifies with (imaginatively becomes) the violator while the victim remains an object of imaginative manipulation, her body merely the text on which the crime is written. The reader who responds uncritically to the novel's structured blanks thus silently embraces the possibility of rape without pain, of violation without its attendant dehumanization. The juxtaposition of representations of rape in *Sanctuary* and *The Women of Brewster Place* brings the assumptions about violence implicit in both into relief. While *Sanctuary* exploits the processes of identification and objectification that Mulvey cites as central to the patriarchal gaze, Gloria Naylor's representation disrupts those processes to overturn the "imagised, eroticized" response to rape seemingly authorized by literary convention.

The rape scene in *The Women of Brewster Place* occurs in "The Two," one of the seven short stories that make up the novel. The story explores the relationship between Theresa and Lorraine, two lesbians who move into the run-down complex of apartments that make up "Brewster Place." Lorraine's decision to return home through the shortcut of an alley late one night leads her into an ambush in which the anger of seven teenage boys erupts into violence:

> Lorraine saw a pair of suede sneakers flying down behind the face in front of hers and they hit the cement with a dead thump. . . . [C.C. and the boys] had been hiding up on the wall, watching her come up that back street, and they had waited. The face pushed itself so close to hers that she could look into the flared nostrils and smell the decomposing food in its teeth. . . .
>
> [C.C.] slammed his kneecap into her spine and her body arched up, causing his nails to cut into the side of her mouth to stifle her cry. He pushed her arched body down onto the cement. Two of the boys pinned her arms, two wrenched open her legs, while C.C. knelt between them and pushed up her dress and tore at the top of her pantyhose. Lorraine's body was twisting in convulsions of fear that they mistook for resistance, and C.C. brought his fist down into her stomach.
>
> "Better lay the fuck still, cunt, or I'll rip open your guts."

The impact of his fist forced air into her constricted throat, and she worked her sore mouth, trying to form the one word that had been clawing inside of her—"Please." It squeezed through her paralyzed vocal cords and fell life-lessly at their feet. Lorraine clamped her eyes shut and, using all of the strength left within her, willed it to rise again.

"Please."

The sixth boy took a dirty paper bag lying on the ground and stuffed it into her mouth. She felt a weight drop on her spread body. Then she opened her eyes and they screamed and screamed into the face above hers—the face that was pushing this tearing pain inside of her body.[9]

In Naylor's representation of rape, the victim ceases to be an erotic object subjected to the control of the reader's gaze. Instead, that gaze, like Lorraine's, is directed outward; it is the violator upon whom the reader focuses, the violator's body that becomes detached and objectified before the reader's eyes as it is reduced to "a pair of suede sneakers," a "face" with "decomposing food in its teeth." As the look of the audience ceases to perpetuate the victimizing stance of the rapists, the subject/object locations of violator and victim are reversed. Although the reader's gaze is directed at a body that is, in Mulvey's terms, "stylised and fragmented by close-ups," the body that is dissected by that gaze is the body of the violator and not his victim.

The limitations of narrative render any disruption of the violator/spectator affiliation difficult to achieve; while sadism, in Mulvey's words, "demands a story," pain destroys narrative, shatters referential realities, and challenges the very power of language.[10] The attempt to translate violence into narrative, therefore, very easily lapses into a choreography of bodily positions and angles of assault that serves as a transcription of the violator's story. In the case of rape, where a violator frequently co-opts not only the victim's physical form but her power of speech, the external manifestations that make up a visual narrative of violence are anything but objective. To provide an "external" perspective on rape is to represent the story that the violator has created, to ignore the resis-tance of the victim whose body has been appropriated within the rapist's rhythms and whose enforced silence disguises the enormity of her pain. In *The Accused,* a 1988 film in which Jody Foster gives an Oscar-winning performance as a rape victim, the problematics of transforming the vic-tim's experience into visualizable form are addressed, at least in part, through the use of flashback; the rape on which the film centers is repre-sented only at the end of the film, *after* the viewer has followed the trail of the victim's humiliation and pain. Because the victim's story cannot be told in the representation itself, it is told first; in the representation that follows, that story lingers in the viewer's mind, qualifying the vic-tim's inability to express herself and providing, in essence, a counter-text to the story of violation that the camera provides.[11]

While Naylor's novel portrays the victim's silence in its narrative of rape, it, too, probes beneath the surface of the violator's story to reveal the struggle beneath that enforced silence. Naylor represents Lorraine's silence not as a passive absence of speech but as a desperate struggle to regain the voice stolen from her through violence. "Power and violence," in Hannah Arendt's words, "are opposites; where the one rules absolutely, the other is absent."[12] The nicety of the polite word of social discourse that Lorraine frantically attempts to articulate—"please"—emphasizes the brute terrorism of the boys' act of rape and exposes the desperate means by which they rule. "Woman," Mulvey observes, "stands in patriarchal culture as signifier for the male other, bound by a symbolic order in which man can live out his phantasies and obsessions through linguistic control by imposing them on the silent image of woman still tied to her place as bearer of meaning, not maker of meaning."[13] In Naylor's description of Lorraine's rape "the silent image of woman" is haunted by the power of a thousand suppressed screams; that image comes to testify not to the woman's feeble acquiescence to male signification but to the brute force of the violence required to "tie" the woman to her place as "bearer of meaning."

While the distance that defines the experience of reading is exaggerated by Faulkner's constant invocation of literary conventions in *Sanctuary*, the illusion of distance is constantly undermined in Naylor's representation of rape. Rather than watching a distant action unfold from the anonymity of the darkened theater or reading about an illicit act from the safety of an armchair, Naylor's audience is thrust into the middle of a rape the representation of which subverts the very "sense of separation" upon which voyeurism depends. The "imagised, eroticized concept of the world that . . . makes a mockery of empirical objectivity" is here replaced by the discomforting proximity of two human faces locked in violent struggle and defined not by eroticism but by the pain inflicted by one and borne by the other:

> Then she opened her eyes and they screamed and screamed into the face above hers—the face that was pushing this tearing pain inside of her body. The screams tried to break through her corneas out into the air, but the tough rubbery flesh sent them vibrating back into her brain, first shaking lifeless the cells that nurtured her memory. Then the cells went that contained her powers of taste and smell. The last that were screamed to death were those that supplied her with the ability to love—or hate.

The gaze that in Mulvey reduces woman to erotic object is here centered within that woman herself and projected outward. The reader is locked into the victim's body, positioned *behind* Lorraine's corneas along with the screams that try to break out into the air. By manipulating the reader's placement within the scene of violence, Naylor subverts the objectifying power of the gaze; as the gaze is trapped within the erotic object, the necessary distance between the voyeur and the object of voyeuristic pleasure is collapsed. The detachment process that authorizes the process of imaginative identification with the rapist is withdrawn, forcing the reader within the confines of the *victim's* world.

Situated within the margins of the violator's story of rape, the reader is able to read beneath the bodily configurations that make up its text, to experience the world-destroying violence[14] required to appropriate the victim's body as a sign of the violator's power. Lurking beneath the image of woman as passive signifier is the fact of a body turned traitor against the consciousness that no longer rules it, a body made, by sheer virtue of physiology, to encircle and in a sense embrace its violator. In Naylor's representation, Lorraine's pain and not the rapist's body becomes the agent of violation, the force of her own destruction: "The screams tried to break through her corneas out into the air, but the tough rubbery flesh sent them vibrating back into her brain, first shaking lifeless the cells that nurtured her memory." Lorraine's inability to express her own pain forces her to absorb not only the shock of bodily violation but the sudden rupture of her mental and psychological autonomy. As the body of the victim is forced to tell the rapist's story, that body turns against Lorraine's consciousness and begins to destroy itself, cell by cell. In all physical pain, Elaine Scarry observes, "suicide and murder converge, for one feels acted upon, annihilated, by inside and outside alike."[15] Naylor succeeds in communicating the victim's experience of rape exactly because her representation documents not only the violation of Lorraine's body from without but the resulting assault on her consciousness from within.

In order to capture the victim's pain in words, to contain it within a narrative unable to account for its intangibility, Naylor turns referentiality against itself. In her representation of violence, the victim's pain is defined only through negation, her agony experienced only in the reader's imagination:

> Lorraine was no longer conscious of the pain in her spine or stomach. She couldn't feel the skin that was rubbing off of her arms from being pressed against the rough cement. What was left of her mind was centered around the pounding motion that was ripping her insides apart. She couldn't tell when they changed places and the second weight, then the third and fourth, dropped on her—it was all one continuous hacksawing of torment that kept her eyes screaming the only word she was fated to utter again and again for the rest of her life. Please.
>
> Her thighs and stomach had become so slimy from her blood and their semen that the two boys didn't want to touch her, so they turned her over, propped her head and shoulders against the wall, and took her from behind. When they had finished and stopped holding her up, her body fell over like an unstrung puppet. She didn't feel her split rectum or the patches in her skull where her hair had been torn off by grating against the bricks. Lorraine lay in that alley only screaming at the moving pain inside of her that refused to come to rest.

Recognizing that pain defies representation, Naylor invokes a referential system that focuses on the bodily manifestations of pain—skinned arms, a split rectum, a bloody skull—only to reject it as ineffective. Lorraine, we are told, "was no longer conscious of the pain in her spine or stomach. She couldn't feel the skin that was rubbing off of her arms. . . . She couldn't tell when they changed places. . . . She didn't feel her split rectum or the patches in her skull where her hair had been torn off." Naylor piles pain upon pain—each one an experience of agony that the reader may compare to his or her own experience—only to define the total of all these experiences as insignificant, incomparable to the "pounding motion that was ripping [Lorraine's] insides apart." Naylor, like Faulkner, brings the reader to the edge of experience only to abandon him or her to the power of the imagination: in this case, however the structured blanks that the novel asks the reader to fill in demand the imaginative construction of the victim's pain rather than the violator's pleasure.

If Faulkner's reader is gendered male/violator, the reader of *The Women of Brewster Place* is gendered female and victim; Naylor's novel, then, effectively upsets Mulvey's model of patriarchal viewing. The freedom to navigate through the text of *Sanctuary* lends the reader the power of authoring his or her own crime. Like the violator who appropriates the victim's body to conform to the demands of his own violent script, Faulkner's reader treats Temple as an object of imaginative manipulation that may be safely invoked, altered, or destroyed to suit a particular scenario. That reader, then, possesses the autonomy of the rapist, the freedom to create a story of violence that the bodies of others are forced to substantiate. In *Against Our Will*, Susan Brownmiller describes the way in which the phenomenon of rape strips not only rape victims but all women of their freedom to act as autonomous persons. The ever-present vulnerability of women's bodies makes the possibility of rape a constant threat; by virtue of their physiology, women may be forced into a position of curtailed activity and psychological vulnerability that Brownmiller likens to enslavement. Describing rape as "man's basic weapon of force against woman, the principal agent of his will and her fear,"[16] Brownmiller observes: "A world without rapists would be a world in which women moved freely without fear of men. That *some* men rape provides a sufficient threat to keep all women in a constant state of intimidation, forever conscious of the knowledge that the biological tool must be held in awe for it may turn to weapon with sudden swiftness borne of harmful intent."[17] The very possibility of rape serves as a cultural dividing line that enforces a hierarchy of autonomy in which the male, free to think, imagine, and act without fear of sexual violation, is always in a position of power. The very act of navigating through the texts of Faulkner and Naylor situates the uncritical reader on different levels within that cultural hierarchy.[18] While the experience of reading rape in *Sanctuary* is one of moving freely throughout the text, *The Women of Brewster Place* strips the reader of that freedom, pinning him or her to the victim's body and communicating an experience of rape that genders the reader—whatever sex he or she may be—female.

As Naylor disentangles the reader from the victim's consciousness at the end of her representation, the radical dynamics of a female-gendered reader are thrown into relief by the momentary reintroduction of a distanced perspective on violence: "Lorraine lay pushed up against the wall on the cold ground with her eyes staring straight up into the sky. When the sun began to warm the air and the horizon brightened, she still lay there, her mouth crammed with paper bag, her dress pushed up under her breasts, her bloody pantyhose hanging from her thighs." In this one sentence, Naylor pushes the reader back into the safety of a world of artistic mediation and restores the reader's freedom to navigate safely through the details of the text. Under the pressure of the reader's controlling gaze, Lorraine is immediately reduced to the status of an object—part mouth, part breasts, part thighs—subject to the viewer's scrutiny. In the last sentence of the chapter, as in this culminating description of the rape, Naylor deliberately jerks the reader back into the distanced perspective that authorizes scopophilia; the final image that she leaves us with is an image not of Lorraine's pain but of "a tall yellow woman in a bloody green and black dress, scraping at the air, crying, 'Please. Please.'" This sudden shift of perspective unveils the connection between the scopophilic gaze and the objectifying force of violence. The power of the gaze to master and control is forced to its inevitable culmination as the body that was the object of erotic pleasure becomes the object of violence. While Freud associated scopophilia with the idea of "taking other people as objects,"[19] the same process of objectification underlies violence, in which violators "dehumanize their intended victims and look on them not as people but as inanimate objects."[20] By framing her own representation of rape with an "objective" description that promotes the violator's story of rape, Naylor exposes not only the connection between violation and objectification but the ease with which the reader may be persuaded to accept both. As the object of the reader's gaze is suddenly shifted, that reader is thrust into an understanding of the way in which his or her own look may perpetuate the violence of rape.

In that violence, the erotic object is not only transformed into the object of violence but is made to testify to the suitability of the object status projected upon it. Co-opted by the rapist's story, the victim's body—violated, damaged and discarded—is introduced as authorization for the very brutality that has destroyed it. The sudden interjection of an "objective" perspective into Naylor's representation traces the process of authorization as the narrative pulls back from the subtext of the victim's pain to focus the reader's gaze on the "object" status of the victim's body. Empowered by the distanced dynamics of a gaze that authorizes not only scopophilia but its inevitable culmination in violence, the reader who responds uncritically to the violator's story of rape comes to see the victim not as a human being, not as an object of violence, but as *the object* itself.

The "objective" picture of a battered woman scraping at the air in a bloody green and black dress is shocking exactly because it seems to have so little to do with the woman whose pain the reader has just experienced. Having recognized Lorraine as a human being who becomes a victim of violence, the reader recoils from the unfamiliar picture of a creature who seems less human than animal, less subject than object. As Naylor's representation retreats for even a moment to the distanced perspective that operates throughout *Sanctuary*, the objectifying pressure of the reader's gaze allows the reader to see not the brutality of the act of violation but the brute-like characteristics of its victim. To see Lorraine scraping at the air in her bloody garment is to see not only the horror of what happened to her but the horror that *is* her. The violation of her personhood that is initiated with the rapist's objectifying look becomes a self-fulfilling prophecy borne out by the literal destruction of her body; rape reduces its victim to the status of an animal and then flaunts as authorization the very body that it has mutilated. Insofar as the reader's gaze perpetuates the process of objectification, the reader, too, becomes a violator.

Naylor's temporary restoration of the objectifying gaze only emphasizes the extent to which *her* representation of violence subverts the conventional dynamics of the reading and viewing process. By denying the reader from the freedom to observe the victim of violence from behind the wall of aesthetic convention, to manipulate that victim as an object of imaginative play, Naylor disrupts the connection between violator and viewer that Mulvey emphasizes in her discussion of cinematic convention. If *Sanctuary* perpetuates the distanced dynamics that Duchamp exposes in "Etant Donnés," Naylor explodes those dynamics. Inviting the viewer to enter the world of violence that lurks just beyond the wall of art, Naylor traps the reader behind that wall. As the reader's gaze is centered within the victim's body, the reader, like the naked woman displayed in Duchamp's art work, is stripped of the safety of aesthetic distance and the freedom of artistic response. In Naylor's representation of rape, the power of the gaze is turned against itself; the aesthetic observer is forced to watch powerlessly as the violator steps up to the wall to stare with detached pleasure at an exhibit in which the reader, as well as the victim of violence, is on display.

Notes

1. *The Act of Reading: A Theory of Aesthetic Response* (Baltimore: Johns Hopkins University Press, 1978), pp. 111–12.
2. Iser, p. 194.
3. For a different use of Iser's theories of reading, see Terry Heller, "Terror and Empathy in Faulkner's *Sanctuary*," (*Arizona Quarterly* 40 1984), pp. 344–64.
4. William Faulkner, *Sanctuary* (New York: Vintage, 1987), p. 51.
5. Iser, p. 197.
6. *Screen* 16, No. 3 (1975), 6.
7. Mulvey, p. 10.
8. Mulvey, p. 10.
9. Gloria Naylor, *The Women of Brewster Place* (New York: Penguin, 1983), p. 170.
10. Mulvey, p. 14. For a discussion of pain and language, see Elaine Scarry, *The Body in Pain: The Making and Unmaking of the World* (New York: Oxford University Press, 1985).
11. Despite this radical pre-telling of the rape story, the camera's ultimate representation of the rape is, in fact, intricately bound to the rhythms of the male violators. At one point in the act of violation, for example, the camera shifts to a bottle that bounces with increasing fury on the pinball machine on which the victim is raped until, at the moment of the violator's climax, the bottle smashes to the floor.
12. Hannah Arendt, *On Violence* (New York: Harcourt, 1970), p. 56.
13. Mulvey, p. 7.
14. The notion of pain and violence as "world-destroying" is taken from Scarry, pp. 4–29.
15. Scarry, p. 53.
16. *Against Our Will: Men, Women and Rape* (New York: Bantam, 1976), p. 5.
17. Brownmiller, p. 229.
18. I use the term "uncritical reader" to account for the fact that not all readers—male or female—will be swept up by the novel's formal mechanisms of captivation.
19. Mulvey, p. 8.
20. Michael N. Nagler, *America Without Violence* (Covela, Calif.: Island, 1982), p. 12.

♦♦♦♦♦♦♦♦♦♦♦♦♦♦

Stealing B(l)ack Voices: The Myth of the Black Matriarchy and *The Women of Brewster Place*

CELESTE FRASER

It would appear that books, like genetic parents, beget books and the sheer proliferation of the work, if nothing else, inscribes an impression point at which the makers and patrons the traditional canon of American literature and the very structure of the values that decides the permissible must now stop and rethink their work.

Reading against the canon, intruding into it a configuration of symbolic values with which critics and audiences must contend, the work of the black women's writing community not only redefines tradition, but also disarms it by suggesting that the term itself is a critical fable intended to encode and circumscribe an inner and licit circle of texts.

—Hortense J. Spillers[1]

Myth is a *value*, truth is no guarantee for it, nothing prevents it from being a perpetual alibi.

—Roland Barthes[2]

Winning the American Book Award for *The Women of Brewster Place*, Gloria Naylor added force to the impression currently being made by the black women's writing community upon both the literary establishment and the reading public of the United States. In her effort to "sit down and write something I hadn't read about . . . that was all about me—the Black woman in America," Naylor opposed yet another fictional force that seeks to describe and define African-American women.[3] The proliferation of fictional self-images generated by the black women's writing community in the 1980s coincides with the resuscitation of the tandem myths of the traditional family and the black matriarchy. Just as what Spillers calls the "critical fable" of a literary tradition establishes "an inner and licit circle of texts," the political fable of the "traditional American family" circumscribes an "inner and licit"—or, in the parlance of sociological studies and government reports—a "legitimate" circle of citizens. The role played by fiction in constructing the fable of tradition suggests a more than rhetorical relationship between the "books" and the babies produced by black women as writers and as "genetic parents." "The Black woman in America" serves as a textual terrain where the literary fictions of black women writers clash against the fictions with which recent Republican administrations would legitimate both the racialization and the feminization of poverty.[4]

THE BÊTE NOIR

Daniel Patrick Moynihan introduced the myth of the black matriarchy into government policy in 1964 with a report to the Department of Labor entitled *The Negro Family: The Case for National Action,* since known as the notorious "Moynihan Report." Through the mediation of then presidential assistant Bill Moyers, Lyndon Johnson delivered a policy speech based on the Report in 1965. In 1986 and again in 1989, Moyers himself rejuvenated the trope for television with the production of his own "documentary" and a follow-up: *The Vanishing Black Family—Crisis in Black America.*[5] Both Moyers and Moynihan isolate an imaginary "Black America" remote from impact by an implicit "White America." This distinction evades the issue of racism in the impoverishment of African Americans by locating the cause of poverty within the structure of the black family and de-emphasizes poverty as a phenomenon affecting society as a whole. Narrowing the discussion of poverty to one of "the Negro family" creates a closed economy in which the blame for economic oppression falls within the oppressed community. This tunnel vision leads to the conclusion that the amelioration of poverty requires a strengthening of moral rather than economic values. As sociologist Patricia Collins points out, Moynihan and Moyers rely on this conclusion in order to assert that "appropriate values and their accompanying behavioral outcomes produce economic success, while deviant values produce behaviors that incur economic penalties."[6]

For Moynihan, the "deviant values" distinguishing impoverished African-American families from "traditional" American families promote "disorganization"—the "matriarchal structure"—of "the Negro family."[7] William Ryan observes that "illegitimacy looms large in the Moynihan report, in the text and in the illustrations . . . [I]llegitimacy . . . shines through the report as the prime index of family breakdown."[8]Moynihan relies upon the concept of "illegitimacy" to explain poverty. He voices the sexist assumption that views the birth of a child to a single woman as inherently undesirable in a pithy aphorism: "Negro children without fathers flounder and fail."[9] The only hope for these children and their mothers according to Moynihan lies in the reassertion of patriarchal authority within the Negro family. Moyers later develops that conclusion by suggesting "not that male power be enhanced but, rather, that female power be attenuated."[10] The sexist foundation of this prescription creates a paradox: the strength necessitated for the survival of African-American women weakens their families. In promoting the "traditional family" as a substitute for the survival skills developed by women struggling against poverty, Moynihan and Moyers prescribe silence and passivity in the hope that women might then acquire husbands who can provide economic support. The Moynihan Report and Moyers' documentary trap the African-American woman in a double bind by posing her strength as the weakness of her family and the undoing of her race. If she attempts to challenge this image, the formulation captures that challenge as proof positive of the black woman's debilitating strength. In proposing dependence upon men as the solution to poverty, the makers of the myth of the black matriarchy would silence black women and speak in their place.

The substitution of myth for the voices of real black women enacts a symbolic impoverishment, an element Roland Barthes identifies as essential to mythmaking. Myth "does not suppress [the personal history of the mythified object], it only impoverishes it; it puts it at a distance, it holds it at one's own disposal."[11] The mythmaker manipulates the personal history of the mythified object in order to further the mythmaker's own agenda, while retaining the recognizable outlines of that history. *"[M]yth hides nothing:* its function is to distort, not to make disappear."[12] The myth of the black matriarchy retains the image of the African-American woman as a kind of ventriloquist's dummy through whom the mythmakers speak. Barthes elaborates:

> [M]yth is a speech stolen and restored. Only speech which is restored is no longer quite that which is stolen: when it was brought back, it was not put exactly in its place. It is this brief act of larceny, this moment taken for surreptitious faking, which gives mythical speech its benumbed look.[13]

Moynihan's mythifying of "the Black woman in America" enacts a symbolic robbery of the speech of African-American women. This robbery deprives the image of all variation, replacing the diversity of African-American women with a monolithic mute.

The symbolic impoverishment of black women corresponds closely to the disproportionate economic impoverishment among African-American female heads of households. Margaret Burnham, a contributor to *The Nation*'s 1989 special issue, "Scapegoating the Black Family," points out, in arguments favoring the "dismantling of domestic social programs" the "most acute condemnation is reserved for the black teenage A.F.D.C. mothers, who are unable to make a case for themselves or to represent much of a political threat."[14] A racist and politically dishonest representation of both black women and impoverished families legitimizes efforts to obliterate social services. According to Marian Wright Edelman, director of the Children's Defense Fund, such program cuts further a "primary goal of the federal government in the 1980s": "[T]o provide a ready supply of low-wage labor to employers and to ensure that the welfare system does not offer an alternative to jobs at below-poverty wages."[15] Edelman analyzes the economic condition of these easy targets for mythification as indicative of economic trends with far-reaching implications:

> [I]n some important respects, trends for blacks foreshadow trends for whites, or are exaggerated representations of broader problems in our society, as

blacks are often hurt earlier and more profoundly by social and economic program changes that injure all poor and working-class Americans.[16]

African-American women have a two-tiered relationship to the economic policies of the Republican agenda. Materially, given the high proportional poverty rate among blacks, the widening gulf between rich and poor pushes African-American women farthest first from financial well-being. Symbolically, the image of the black woman serves to legitimate economic policies with impact beyond that group.

Sociologist Charles Murray, in his book advertised as "the [Reagan] Administration's new 'bible,'" constructs just such a legitimation. In *Losing Ground: American Social Policy 1950–1980*, Murray's nominal critique of the programs initiated in the War on Poverty provides a convoluted rationalization for examining the African-American community and poverty as equivalent phenomena.[17] Murray reinscribes the picture of the black economy as distinct from the dominant society by blaming "black male joblessness" on a "ghetto lifestyle."[18] But Murray's solution for the African-American community ultimately clears a path for changes in federal policy extending far beyond that community:

> The proposed program, our final and most ambitious thought experiment, consists of scrapping the entire federal income-support structure for working-aged persons, including A.F.D.C., Medicaid, Food Stamps, Unemployment Insurance, Workers' Compensation, subsidized housing, disability insurance, and the rest. It would leave the working-aged person with no recourse whatsoever except the job market, family members, friends, and public or private locally funded sources. It is the Alexandrian solution: cut the knot for there is no way to untie it.[19]

Despite the impact of these measures upon all impoverished and many middle-class people, the vast majority of whom are not African-American, Murray relies upon a racist lens to focus his argument in a section labeled "PART II: Being Poor, Being Black: 1950–1980." Murray rhetorically divides and conquers the family when he places African-American women and children in a chapter labeled "The Family" and African-American men in a chapter labeled "Crime." "The Family" chapter's two subheadings, "Illegitimate Births" and "Female Householder, No Husband Present," identify the cause of the family's "fall": the single African-American female. In "concentrat[ing] on two indicators that almost everybody agrees are important evidence of problems with the family: illegitimate births, and families headed by a single female," Murray employs the same formula identified by Collins in the Moynihan Report and the Moyers documentary.[20] "[R]acial difference . . . explain[s] class disadvantage," she notes, "while gender deviancy . . . account[s] for racial difference."[21] However, Murray significantly revises Moynihan's and Moyers' theses. The menace of the black matriarchy does not primarily lie in the emasculation of the black male—who appears in the family only as an absence and in the streets only as a criminal—but in the immoral fecundity of the black female which drains federal funds.

To support this argument, Murray presents a brief history of Aid to Families with Dependent Children (A.F.D.C.), the program most commonly associated with welfare. Murray purports that the original purpose of A.F.D.C. was to allow the State to step in as a missing husband in order to support poor widows with children, but the program took a disastrous turn.

> A.F.D.C. evolved into the *bête noir* of the social welfare system. By the fifties it had become embarrassingly, outrageously clear that most of these women were not widows. Many of them had never been married. Worst of all, they didn't stop having babies after the first lapse. They kept having more. This had not been part of the plan.

> The most flagrantly unrepentant seemed to be mostly black, too. The statistics might show that whites have always been the largest single group of A.F.D.C. recipients, but the stereotype that enraged the critics was the family of four, five, six, and more children reared at government expense, and somehow the stories always seemed to talk about black families.[22]

Not asking readers to pardon his French, Murray constructs a procreative "black beast" who menaces as the ultimate—the "most flagrantly unrepentant"—of female sinners. His history becomes a morality play in which the "black beast" represents the "lapse" into darkness of the widow who, once remarried to the State, continues to consort with mortal lovers. Murray hints at the importance of this welfare myth as "story" not statistical fact, but rather than refute this "stereotype" he perpetuates it in order to prove that the marriage between the State and the widow has turned into an illicit partnership with a faithless black beast who churns out babies for welfare checks.

While the "evolution" of A.F.D.C. depicted by Murray suggests an inevitable development given the structure of federal support, this evolution bears little resemblance to the most significant actual change in the system. The social program Aid to Dependent Children (A.D.C.) became A.F.D.C. in 1962, in the decade *after* Murray locates the shift in aid recipients. African-American women for the most part could not even receive federal aid before the 1962 change eradicated the eligibility distinction between the "deserving" and the "undeserving" poor that assigned them to the latter category on the basis of race. Murray observes this shift in the composition of people receiving benefits "for white widows to unwed mothers and women of color"[23] poetically, as he figures the menacing black beast metaphorically for women he considers to have darker skin and more dubious morals. In order to legitimize the dismantling of welfare, Murray replaces the historical range of A.F.D.C. recipients with his own creation: a black female monster.

THE EBONY PHOENIX

The moral of the stories constructed by Murray, Moynihan, and Moyers—that the State has an interest in breaking the power of the black matriarchy—profoundly impacts the material conditions of the lives of many African-American women. To disarm these fables, Gloria Naylor employs the "Afro-American strategy of Signifyin[g],' characterized by Henry Louis Gates, Jr., as "a rhetorical practice that is not engaged in the game of information giving . . . [but] turns on the play of a chain of signifiers, and not on some supposedly transcendental signified."[24] Rather than claim to represent the world the mythmakers falsify, Naylor's characters inhabit, in order to revise from within, the mythical world detailed by the myth of the black matriarchy. The women living in Brewster Place speak through individual short stories, loosely structured as a novel because, in Naylor's words,

. . . one character couldn't be *the* Black woman in America. So I had seven different women, all in different circumstances, encompassing the complexity of our lives, the richness of our diversity, from skin color on down to religious, political, and sexual preference.[25]

In contrast to the monolithic image of the mythical black matriarch, Naylor refuses to portray one uniform image of the black woman or the black family: This strategy allows Naylor the freedom to discuss African-American women without confining their image to the shape of her discussion.

From the opening phrase, *The Women of Brewster Place* invades the terrain of the myth of the black matriarchy as Naylor enacts a "double-voiced representation in art [utilizing] . . . [r]epetition, with a signal difference."[26] Naylor repeats claims for illegitimate children as the cause of poverty, but she shifts the stigma of illegitimacy from the illicit sexuality of single black women to the illicit partnership between government and commerce that created the ghetto: "Brewster Place was the bastard child of several clandestine meetings between the alderman of the sixth district and the managing director of Unico Realty Company."[27] To legitimate the "consummation of their respective desires," the establishment powers of the city declared their intention to "help make space for all their patriotic boys who were on their way home from the Great War." In the time of Naylor's telling, however, Brewster is space not for male military heroes but for "colored daughters [who] milled like determined spirits among its decay, trying to make it a home." Naylor materializes the closed economy in which the government would place African-American poverty as the brick wall erected by the city legislature making Brewster Place a dead-end street. The wall serves a double function in both isolating the women and marking them as "different in their smells, foods, and codes from the rest of the town." Naylor characterizes this difference not in the dehumanizing terms of the "black beast" but in the supernatural image of an "ebony phoenix" who will rise from the ashes of utter destruction.

Naylor not only reveals the complicity of the establishment powers in the construction of the ghetto, she parodies the welfare myth presented as legitimation for ghetto conditions by those powers. In the story "Cora Lee," Naylor plays on the convention in Shakespearean comedy identified by Northrop Frye: a romp into the forest temporarily topples conventions in order to expose social hierarchies, but these hierarchies remain in place within the society beyond the forest, to which the characters must return.[28] Naylor borrows the forest from a production of Shakespeare to expose the conventional myth of the welfare mother as (literally) *A Mid-Summer Night's Dream.*

The story begins with a reading direction lifted from the play:

> True, I talk of dreams,
> Which are the children of an idle brain
> Begot of nothing but vain fantasy.

This fragment instructs readers to approach "Cora Lee" as "nothing but vain fantasy." Naylor brilliantly maneuvers this passage from Shakespeare in order to shift the accusations of laziness and relentless reproductivity away from A.F.D.C. mothers to the makers of the welfare myth whose "idle brains" themselves "begot" the fantastic "children" of Cora Lee. Reminiscent of Murray's description of the *bête noir*, Cora Lee's "babies just seemed to keep coming—always welcome until they changed" into demanding youngsters. Cora Lee's desire for babies serves as the tautological *reductio ad absurdum* for the faulty causality posited by Murray in which welfare mothers procreate for profit: she has babies for the sole pleasure of having babies.

Cora Lee's story negates the salvation the Moynihan Report promises with the return of the absent father, because the men "who had promised to marry [Cora Lee] and take her off Welfare" deliver only violence. "A pot of burnt rice would mean a fractured jaw, or a wet bathroom floor a loose tooth. . . ." In the place of a permanent partner we find black men in the image sociologist Elliot Liebow observed in his 1967 anthropological study *Tally's Corner: A Study of Negro Streetcorner Men.* "The adult male, if not simply characterized as 'absent'," Liebow writes, "is a somewhat shadowy figure who drifts in and out of the lives of the family members."[29] When the fathers-in-residence of her older children leave, Cora Lee makes love with "only the shadows—who came in the night and showed her the thing that felt good in the dark." The shadows "would sometimes bring new babies" but at least "didn't give you fractured jaws or bruised eyes." Moynihan and Murray's idyllic image of the nuclear family relies upon the repression of the potential for domestic violence in order to present marriage as always and everywhere preferable to mothering alone.

When black middle-class activist Kiswana Browne invites Cora Lee to an all-black production of A Mid-Summer Night's Dream, she proffers tradition in its literary essence as a panacea for Cora Lee's inadequate mothering. In accepting Kiswana's invitation, Cora Lee accepts the equation of great books and good citizens championed by former Secretary of Education William Bennett and director of the National Endowment for the Humanities, Lynne Cheney, among others.[30] Naylor parodies this simplistic equation by having Cora Lee imagine that through exposure to "Shakespeare and all that" her children would "do better in school and stop being so bad."

In preparation for the play, Cora Lee costumes her children in rare respectability after a burst of housekeeping in which she fit the children and house alike to the drama of the traditional family. "She lined up the scoured faces, carefully parted hair, and oiled arms and legs on the couch, and forbid them to move." At the theater, Cora Lee monitors the behavior of her children in the mainly white audience in order to "show these people that they were used to things like this." Their directed behavior parallels that of the actors who awed Cora Lee because "she had never heard black people use such fine-sounding words and they really seemed to know what they were talking about." Naylor does not question the ability of African Americans to succeed as doctors, lawyers, or Shakespearean actors; rather she questions the roles assigned to African Americans in the received white dramas labeled Tradition. The narration of Cora Lee's vision of "what would happen to her babies" as she planned to "check homework," attend P.T.A., and set up her children in "good jobs," progresses synchronically with the action of Bottom's dream as the play approaches the last act. Significantly, Bottom awakens in the last act estranged from the queen of the faeries, and is once again merely a Mechanical giving an inadequate performance before nobility amused at his expense.

In subsequent stories, the reader finds Cora Lee pregnant again and the children still in disarray, belying critic Charles Johnson's rosy conclusion that "by the story's end, Cora has changed, found a light she'd lost."[31] Cora Lee returns home not to "light" but to "the shadow, who had let himself in with his key." The return of the "shadow" creates new meaning for Puck's epilogue, reproduced in part in the text:

> If we shadows have offended,
> Think but this and all is mended:
> That you have but slumber'd here,
> While these visions did appear.
> And this weak and idle theme,
> No more yielding but a dream . . .

By stopping here, Naylor reassures those would find the traffic of shadows through Cora Lee's bedroom offensive: they need only wake up. She insists that the "weak and idle theme" presenting a lazy, procreative welfare mother who keeps her children from the salvation of acculturation into white patriarchal society is "no more yielding but a dream."

Michael C. Cooke lists *The Women of Brewster Place* as an Afro-American novel that "experiment[s] technically with kinship along feminist lines."[32] As an alternative to unquestioned acceptance of an ideal patriarchal family, Naylor offers a federation among the women of the street, headed by Mattie—an incarnation of the Mat(tie)riarch deplored by Moynihan. Naylor widens the circle of permissible family in her representation of what Dorothy Height calls the "black tradition of the extended family [which] grew out of the primary need to survive, an urgency that for the most part made gender largely irrelevant."[33] This relationship finds poignant expression when Mattie serves as a spiritual substitute for the husband Etta Mae, Mattie's girlhood friend, failed to obtain. After an unsuccessful attempt to seduce a visiting minister into marriage, "Etta laughed softly to herself as she climbed the steps toward the light and the love and the comfort that awaited her" in Mattie's house.

Opposing the strength of the female-headed household to the picture of that household as a sign of family breakdown, Naylor risks perpetuating the erasure of the black male under the label "absent father." Despite Naylor's assertion that she "bent over backwards not to have a negative message come through about the men," Charles Johnson asserts that "except for the old sot Ben, nearly every black male in this book resembles the Negro Beast stereotype described so many years ago by white racists as the brutal, stupid creatures of violent sexual appetites."[34] However, Naylor carefully separates the acts of individual black men from the patriarchal system in which those men might participate. The metaphorical portrayal of Mattie's single sexual encounter with Butch Fuller as eating sugar cane runs counter to the community's view of Fuller as a "low-down ditch dog." Against the over-determined sweetness of the portrayal of sex as the ingestion of sugar, Naylor opposes the violence of a system that restricts sexuality outside marriage by stigmatizing single motherhood. Mattie's father beats her to extract the name of her child's father:

> Mattie's body contracted in a painful spasm each time the stick smashed down on her legs and back, and she curled into a tight knot, trying to protect her stomach. He would repeat his question with each blow from the stick, and her continued silence caused the blows to come faster and harder.

As the beating of the daughter by her father suggests, male violence in *The Women of Brewster Place* occurs not in connection with sexual appetites but with attempts to subject black women to patriarchal authority.

Naylor directly addresses the proposition that black men need only assert themselves as patriarchs to overcome poverty in her story "Luciella Louise Turner." The argument for marriage as the family ideal (commonly phrased "for the children's sake") is refuted in the desperate attempts by Mattie's adopted daughter Luciella (Ciel) to hold on to her husband Eugene; attempts producing first an unwanted, sacrificial abortion and later the accidental death of their toddler, Serena. As if following advice from the Moynihan Report, Eugene asserts patriarchal power by expelling Mattie from their apartment and denying her offer to watch his child. "She can stay right here," Eugene br[eaks] in. "If she needs ice cream, I can buy it for her." Rather than providing security for his child, however, Eugene's commands leave Serena unattended during an argument in which Ciel attempts to keep him from leaving her. While the lovers dispute in another room, Naylor manipulates the emotions of her readers as she draws us with the child behind a roach walking toward a wall socket. The scene breaks one moment before certain disaster: "Picking up the fork, Serena finally managed to fit the thin flattened prongs into the electric socket." The readers' horror grows with Ciel's increasing awareness of her self-degradation as she implores: "'Eugene, please.' She [listened] with growing horror to herself quietly begging." Ciel shifts her thirst for love from her husband to her daughter too late. Naylor punctuates the moment at which Ciel decides to accept the legitimacy of the female-headed household with her daughter's death:

> Ciel began to feel the overpowering need to be near someone who loved her. I'll get Serena and we'll go visit Mattie now, she thought in a daze.
>
> Then they heard the scream from the kitchen.

The substitution of the scream for the pleading "please" that marks Ciel's decision to let Eugene go emphasizes the function of the female-centered household as a survival method rather than an immoral, or even unequivocally feminist, choice.

Ciel's collapse after Serena's death allows her to receive her adopted mother's spiritual legacy. Mattie nurses Ciel back to health through a ritual "baptism" into maternal history and female-centered survival:

> [Mattie] sat on the edge of the bed and enfolded the tissue-thin body in her huge ebony arms. And she rocked . . . She rocked her over the Aegean seas so clean they shone like crystal, so clear the fresh blood of sacrificed babies torn from their mother's arms and given to Neptune could be seen like pink froth on the water. She rocked on and on, past Dachau, where soul-gutted Jewish mothers swept their children's entrails off laboratory floors. They flew past the spilled brains of Senegalese infants whose mothers dashed them on the wooden sides of slave ships. And she rocked on.

Mattie rocks Ciel as a mother rocks a child, carrying her over the grief of mothers bereft of their children due to massive, institutionalized violence. The strength of motherhood rests not in any essential or mythological characteristic of black women, but in the necessity of overcoming violence. As black writer/historian (and former welfare recipient) Barbara Omolade puts it: "black families headed by women reflect the strength and difficulty of black life in the 1980s."[35]

Mattie's wordless rocking gives Ciel the strength not to support her pain, but to expel it. Her body "was exorcising the evilness of pain," through retching. Ciel mouths her weakness and her strength; she marks her need for a husband with the word "please," her pain with a scream, and her expulsion of pain with retching. The discussion of black women's mouths in *Tally's Corner* illuminates the threat that female speech—which can expose and expel as well as submit to oppression—poses to male authority within the African-American community. Prohibited from fulfilling patriarchal expectations by socioeconomic conditions, the "streetcorner man"

> . . .avoids the "why" of [his female partner's] nagging behavior and complains of the "how." He does not deny the legitimacy of her exhortations but objects to their insistent repetition and the unrelieved constancy of it all.[36]

Perceived as the remainder of, rather than the partner in, the economic hardship of the black man in white society, the mouth of the black woman becomes a target for violence. One man derisively refers to his wife as "The Mouth" and another recounts his action to a light-skinned lover who called him names associated with his darker skin: "I put my fist in her mouth."[37] The myth of the black matriarchy stops the mouth of the black woman by stealing her voice, and serves the white patriarchy by attempting to silence black women on a national scale. In the gesture of writing a novel, Naylor not only reclaims the voices of black women stolen by the myth, but inscribes the motif of the violent stopping of mouths into the stories those voices tell. Naylor transforms the "nagging behavior" lamented by the men in *Tally's Corner* into the "insistent repetition" of violent attempts to silence black women, with the "signal difference" of containing those attempts within the narrative voice of a black woman writing.

The double-enunciation of a black woman writer "speaking the silencing" of black women culminates in the narration of the gang-rape of Lorraine in "The Two." The title of the story refers to a middle-class lesbian couple, Lorraine and her lover Theresa, who flee more affluent neighborhoods only to discover in Brewster Place the same homophobia they had hoped to escape. "The Two"—a female-female household—represents a departure from the patriarchal structure that neither Murray, Moyers, nor Moynihan even consider. The gang-rape signifies an attempt to force "The Two" back into a patriarchal power structure. As Barbara Christian observes, Lorraine becomes "an accessible scapegoat"[38] for the racism and powerlessness in the community as experienced by "the most dangerous species in existence—human males with an erection to validate in a world that was only six feet wide." Those "six feet," reminiscent of a grave, dramatize the closed economy of oppression within the wall around "Black America," literalized as the wall at the dead end of Brewster Place. This wall blocks the young black men from access to full patriarchal power by conferring on them the status of "dwarfed warrior-kings" with "appendages of power, circumcised with a guillotine." The young men do not rebel against the social forces that built the constricting wall, but rather resort to terror against black women to assert themselves as patriarchs.

The gang rapes Lorraine against the same dead-end wall that limits their own power, emphasizing the misdirection of such "resistance" trapped within the enclosure of the African-American community. The attack on Lorraine, in Christian's explication, represents "an attack on all women, not only because lesbians *are* women, but because lesbian stereotyping exposes society's fear of women's independence of men."[39] The penis of gang-bang leader C.C. incarnates the phallic power promoted as part of the ideal of the traditional family. C.C. violently imposes patriarchy on Lorraine by announcing his intention to "slap that bitch in her face and teach her a lesson." This lesson links voice and gender transgression as C.C. first threatens to "stick [his] fist in [her] cunt-eatin' mouth!" and later, as a prelude to rape, rubs his penis in her face saying, "See, that's what you need."

Naylor's graphic depiction of this attack denies the rape any connection with sexuality. She thus starkly negates the potential for prurient pleasure in the reader and for the rationalization of violence in the mythology of black male sexuality. This act of violence again targets the black woman's voice, silencing her through sexual terror: "He slammed his kneecap into her spine and her body arched up, causing his nails to cut into the side of her mouth to stifle her cry." Naylor frustrates the rapists' attempt to impose a fiction of their own power upon Lorraine's body by disrupting the external representation of violence.[40]

The narrative moves from a depiction of the rapists' action and a description of Lorraine's body to an internal account of Lorraine's experience of pain. With the first blow she received from C.C., Lorraine emitted the word "Please," linking her experience of violence to Ceil's attempt to retain her husband. The narration moves inside her as she "clamped her eyes shut" and pushed the word "please" out a second time. Rape serves as a method to stifle the black woman's voice, forcing her into a script of submission. The boys then stop her mouth/voice with a paper bag and begin penetration. The narration works to reverse the action of penetration by moving from the "tearing pain inside her body" outward: "screams tried to break through her corneas into the air." The stifling of those screams "screamed to death" Lorraine's ability to think and feel. The rape serves as a negation of her experience, leaving "what was left of her mind centered around the pounding motion that was ripping her insides apart." Naylor narrates the final actions in negative terms: "She *couldn't feel* the skin that was rubbing off her arms"; "She *couldn't tell* when they changed places"; "She *didn't feel* her split rectum or the patches in her skull. . . ." Denied a voice to expel her pain, Lorraine retreats into a realm where she can no longer feel. The negation of voice effectively negates experience.

Naylor completes the circle of resistance trapped in the closed economy of oppression with a reversed gender dynamic in Lorraine's murder of her friend Ben. Ben tells Lorraine earlier in the novel: "You remind me lots of my little girl" (his daughter), who also suffered repeated rape. The sexual exploitation of Ben's daughter by a white neighbor re-emphasizes the inaccessibility of white patriarchal power to the impoverished black man. This exploitation takes place down South, where Ben cannot earn enough money to support his family. His wife blames Ben personally for their troubles, rather than the sharecropping system through which her white neighbor wields power over her husband.

> If you was half a man, you coulda given me more babies and we woulda had some help workin' this land instead of a half-grown woman we gotta carry the load for. And if you was even a quarter of a man, we wouldn't be a bunch of miserable sharecroppers on someone else's land—but we is, Ben.

Ben internalizes his wife's blame and drinks alcohol to dull his sense of inadequate manhood. Naylor links the inebriation of the "old sot" Ben directly to the closed circle of oppression, as his drunkenness serves as the plot mechanism that allows for his death. Lorraine's act of murder resonates symbolically: she hits Ben on the mouth with a brick. The bricks from the wall erected by the city provide the currency of violence in the closed economy of oppression, circulating from the gang that silenced Lorraine, to Lorraine's hands, providing the tool to smash Ben's mouth. By positioning Mattie at her window during this sequence, a distant witness too late for Ben's murder and Lorraine's rape, Naylor deflates the destructive strength attributed to the mythical matriarch. Mattie can only follow behind the violence engendered by the economic and symbolic circumscription of the African-American community, nursing or burying the victims.

The final story, "The Block Party," replaces the Moynihan and Murray myths of the black matriarchy with the dreams of the women who live on Brewster Place. Mattie, the putative matriarch herself, dreams of the destruction of the myth that "created" her. Rain bursts into Mattie's nightmare, dispersing the block party initiated by Kiswana and designed to bring the neighborhood together in confrontation with the landlord. One of Cora Lee's children discovers blood on the bricks, presumably residue from the attack on Lorraine. Cora "yanked the brick out," calling to Mattie to join her in tearing down the wall, while "[a]ll of the men and children now stood huddled in doorways." Mattie starts a chain, in which the brick "was passed by the women from hand to hand, table to table, until the brick flew out of Brewster Place and went spinning out onto the avenue." All seven of Naylor's women throw the resistance to oppression they circulated among themselves out into the dominant society, breaking the flow of that society past Brewster Place as "[c]ars were screeching and sliding around the flying bricks." When Cora Lee asks Theresa to join the rest of the women with the words "Please. Please," Theresa demands: "Now, you go back up there and bring some more [bricks], but don't ever say that again—to anyone!" In throwing the bricks, Theresa throws away the word "please" and discards the script of submission imposed upon African-American women.

In Mattie's dream, the seven women of Brewster Place unite to tear down the wall that the city legislature built. In Naylor's novel, they speak together to tear down the definition of the African-American family erected by Murray, Moyers, and Moynihan. Mattie awakens from this dream, but the epilogue tells us that the dreams of "the colored daughters of Brewster . . . ebb and flow, ebb and flow, but never disappear." Gloria Naylor's stories telling "all about me—the Black woman in America" feed the tide of African-American women's fiction which threatens to submerge the mythical black matriarch. While the fictional images of African-American women conceived by black women writers cannot eradicate the material impoverishment of black women, their articulation provides a security against continued silencing. Naylor registers a profound protest against the robbery of the voice of African-American women attempted by makers of the myth of the black matriarchy who would use her to legitimize the robbery of funds from the nation's poor.

Notes

1. Hortense J. Spillers, "Afterword," *Conjuring: black women, fiction, and literary tradition*, eds. Marjorie Pryse and Hortense J. Spillers (Bloomington: Indiana University Press, 1985), 250–51.
2. Roland Barthes, *Mythologies*, trans. Annette Lavers (New York: Hill & Wang, 1972), 123.
3. "The Women of Brewster Place," *Ebony* 41 (March 1989)1: 126.
4. See Margaret B. Wilkerson and Jewell Handy Gresham, "The Racialization of Poverty: Sexual Politics of Welfare," *The Nation* 24/31 (July 1989), 126. "The feminization of poverty is real, but the racialization of poverty is at its heart. To discuss one without the other is to play a mirror game with reality."
5. Jewell Handy Gresham, "The Politics of the Black Family," *The Nation* 24/31 (July 1989), 117–18.
6. Patricia Collins, "A Comparison of Two Works on Black Family Life," *Signs: A Journal of Women in Culture and Society* 14 (Summer 1989)4: 876.

7. Daniel Patrick Moynihan, *The Negro Family: The Case for National Action* (Westport, Conn.: Greenwood Press, Publishers Reprint, 1981), 30. In a more recent work, *Family and Nation* (New York: Harcourt, Brace, Jovanovich, 1987), 145, Moynihan extends his critique of "illegitmacy" from African-American women to all women as he notes: ". . .by the mid-1980s, it was clear that family disorganization had become a general feature of the American population and not just an aspect of a frequently stigmatized and appropriately sensitive minority community." This generalization has chilling implications given his prescription—a strengthened patriarchy—to redress such "disorganization" in family life.

8. William Ryan, "Savage Discovery—The Moynihan Report," in *The Black Family: Essays and Studies*, ed. Robert Staples (Belmont, Calif.: Wadsworth Publishing Company, Inc., 1971), 59.

9. Moynihan, *Negro Family*, 35.

10. Collins, "Two Works," 881.

11. Barthes, *Mythologies*, 118.

12. *Ibid.*, 121.

13. *Ibid.*, 125.

14. Margaret Burnham, "The Great Society Didn't Fail," *The Nation* 24/31 (July 1989), 124.

15. Marian Wright Edelman, *Families in Peril: An Agenda for Social Change* (Cambridge: Harvard University Press, 1987), 82.

16. *Ibid.*, 24.

17. Charles Murray, *Losing Ground: American Social Policy 1950–1980* (New York: Basic Books, Inc., 1984). See pp. 54–55, where Murray essentializes poverty as a racial characteristic, arguing that "a black-white difference murkily reflects a difference between poor and not-poor, not a racially grounded difference."

18. *Ibid.*, 81.

19. *Ibid.*, 227–8.

20. *Ibid.*, 125.

21. Collins, "Two Works," 882.

22. Murray, *Losing Ground*, 18.

23. Wilkerson and Gresham, "Racialization of Poverty," 128.

24. Henry Louis Gates, Jr., *The Signifying Monkey: A Theory of African American Literary Criticism* (New York: Oxford University Press, 1988), 52.

25. "The Women of Brewster Place," 123.

26. Gates, *Signifying Monkey*, 51.

27. Gloria Naylor, *The Women of Brewster Place* (New York: Penguin Books, 1988), 2.

28. Northrop Frye, *A Natural Perspective: The Development of Shakespearean Comedy and Romance* (New York: Columbia University Press, 1965), 141.

29. Elliot Liebow, *Tally's Corner: A Study of Negro Streetcorner Men* (Boston: Little, Brown, & Co., 1967), 5–6.

30. Cheney and Bennett make this equation to oppose the entrance into the classroom curricula of literature by writers others than canonized white men. Both have represented the classroom as the site of salvation for the West, which must be sealed against black and female voices if not against black and female students. Cheney feels that "too many colleges are neglecting the achievements of Western culture [while] requiring ethnic courses" (*New York Times*, 23 Sept. 1988, A-16). Bennett worried aloud about Stanford's curriculum: "But how are we supposed to protect the West if we set about

systematically robbing ourselves of opportunities to know and study it?" (*New York Times*, 19 April 1988), A-18.

31. Charles Johnson, *Being and Race: Black Writing Since 1970* (Bloomington: Indiana University Press, 1988), 110.

32. Michael C. Cooke, *Afro-American Literature in the Twentieth Century: The Achievement of Intimacy* (New Haven: Yale University Press, 1984), 111.

33. Dorothy Height, "Self-Help: A Black Tradition," *The Nation* 24/31 (July 1989), 137.

34. Gloria Naylor and Toni Morrison, "A Conversation," *Southern Review* 21 (1985)34: 579; Johnson, *Being and Race*, 111.

35. Quoted in Wilkerson and Gresham, "Racialization of Poverty," 130.

36. Liebow, *Tally's Corner*, 128.

37. *Ibid.*, 183.

38. Barbara Christian, *Black Feminist Criticism: Perspectives on Black Women Writers* (New York: Pergamon Press, Inc., 1985), 196.

39. *Ibid.*, 196.

40. Elaine Scarry, *The Body in Pain* (New York: Oxford University Press, 1985), 18. "In torture, it is part of the obsessive display of agency that permits one person's body to be translated into another person's voice, that allows real human pain to be translated into a regime's fiction of power."

◆◆◆◆◆◆◆◆◆◆◆◆◆◆

Naylor's Geography: Community, Class and Patriarchy in *The Women of Brewster Place* and *Linden Hills*

BARBARA CHRISTIAN

1

Like Toni Morrison, Gloria Naylor is intrigued by the effect of place on character. Perhaps Afro-American writers have been particularly interested in setting, because displacement, first from Africa and then through migrations from South to North, has been so much a part of our history. Because of the consistency of forced displacement in our collective experience, we know how critical where we are is to the character of our social creations, of how place helps to tell us a great deal about who we are and who we can become. Perhaps place is even more critical to Afro-American women writers. For women within the Afro-American community have functioned both inside and outside the home, have been conservers of tradition (if only because we are mothers), while we have had to respond to the *nuances* of a changed environment. How we negotiate the relationship between the past, as it has helped to form us, and the present, as we must experience it, is often a grave dilemma for us.

The setting of *Linden Hills*, Naylor's second novel, makes it clear that she is creating a geographical fictional world like, say, Faulkner's Yoknapatawpha county. Her first novel is set in Brewster Place, her second in Linden Hills. Brewster Place and Linden Hills are geographically in the same area; both are inhabited by blacks, and in both novels, characters refer to each of these places as proximate neighborhoods, though quite different in their orientation. Linden Hills is a posh upper-middle-class settlement, Brewster Place the last stop on the road to the bottom in American society, where you live when you can't live anywhere else. The outside world perceives Linden Hills as a symbol of black achievement while Brewster Place is seen as a manifestation of failure. Ironically, through her two novels' respective characters and structure, Naylor portrays Brewster Place as a black community (though flawed and vulnerable) held together primarily by women, while Linden Hills is characterized as a group of houses that never becomes a community, a showplace precariously kept in place by the machinations of one wealthy black patriarchal family.

A single writer's juxtaposition of two Afro-American neighborhoods, different in values, separated by class distinctions, yet located in the same geographical area, is an unusual one in Afro-American literature. Afro-American writers have tended to portray black communities as distinct from white society. There have, of course, been novels about upper-middle-class Afro-Americans such as the works of early 20th-century writer Jessie Fauset, or more recently Andrea Lee's *Sarah Phillips* (1984). But when contrasts in class are discussed in these novels, they are usually in relation to the white world. There have been many novels about urban ghetto blacks such as *The Street* by 1940s writer Ann Petry. Again class distinctions are usually presented in relation to white society. There have been novels about small-town blacks such as Toni Morrison's *The Bluest Eye* (1970), which indicate through their variety of characters that class distinctions among blacks do exist. But these characters are presented in relatively few situations. And there have been works about rural Southern blacks such as Alice Walker's *The Third Life of Grange Copeland* (1970) and *The Color Purple* (1982). But in these novels, the primary points of contrast in terms of class is decidedly the white world that tragically imposes its values on black people as a race.

Most Afro-American writers have tended to focus either on middle-class blacks or poor blacks and have tended to feature their protagonists as belonging to a black community which is distinct, if only because of the threat of a racist white society. When class distinctions are commented on, as they are, for example, in Zora Neale Hurston's portrayal of Jody Stark in *Their Eyes Were Watching God* (1936), Paule Marshall's portrayal of Jay Johnson in *Praisesong for the Widow* (1982), and Toni Morrison's portrayal of Macon Dead in *Song of Solomon* (1977), they are located in the conflict between that one character and others, and on the price he pays for social mobility, or sometimes, as in Grier Brown of Shange's *Betsey Browne* (1984) in that character's allegiance to his less fortunate brethren. Even when the novel is decidedly about class distinctions as in Morrison's *Tar Baby* (1980), conflict is gauged by individuals, in this case, the upper mobile Jadine and the underclass, Son. Neither are presented as having viable communities to which they belong. Marshall's monumental *Chosen Place, Timeless People* (1969) does present a black world in which class distinctions are extensively explored, but this society is emphatically Caribbean.

Gloria Naylor's two novels, when looked at as the developing opus of a single writer, are unique in that together they offer us a graphic depictment of Afro-American groups, physically close, yet so distant because of their class differences. However, as my overview of recent Afro-American women novels indicates, Naylor's novels have been preceded in recent years by an increasing concern among these writers, Morrison in *Song of Solomon* (1977) and *Tar Baby* (1980), Marshall in *Praisesong for the Widow* (1982), Andrea Lee in *Sarah Phillips* (1984), and Shange in *Betsey Browne* on the issue of a distinct Afro-American middle class and on the implications of such a dimension in the Afro-American worldview. As such, Naylor both participates in this concern of other Afro-American women writers, even as she extends their analysis.

2

In the geographical world Naylor is creating, Brewster Place and Linden Hills coexist, and persons from each place have attitudes about the other. So touched by the revolutionary fervor of the 1960s, Melanie Browne of Linden Hills changes her name to Kiswana and goes down to live with "the people" in Brewster Place, much as some whites in the sixties went to live in black communities. The people of Brewster Place wonder what this privileged black woman is doing living in their midst, even as Melanie's family in Linden Hills is hurt, for they have made sacrifices so that she would never have to be associated with the kind of people who live in Brewster Place. The class distinctions between the people of Brewster Place and Linden Hills are clearly perceived by each group and make for a great distance between them even as they both are black.

That is not to say that Gloria Naylor is unconcerned with race as a determining factor in her geographical world. It is precisely the fact that Naylor's two neighborhoods *are* black which causes them to so clearly perceive their difference. Importantly, Naylor locates their similarities and differences in a historical process. Both Brewster Place and Linden Hills have been created by racism, or more precisely, as a result of the effects of racism on their founders. Linden Hills is literally carved out of a seemingly worthless soil by ex-slave Luther Nedeed, who in the 1820s has the secret dream of developing "an ebony jewel," a community of successful blacks who could stave off the racism of America and exhibit through their fine houses that members of the race can be powerful. In contrast, Brewster Place is "the bastard child of claudestine meetings" between local white politicians, at first to satisfy expected protests from the Irish community over the undeserved dismissal of their too honest police chief. Later Brewster Place becomes the neighborhood of successive waves of European immigrants, unwanted Americans who finally become, over time, the black poor.

The origin of communities and their historical development are critical to the structure of Naylor's novels as they are to Marshall's and Morrison's. These two writers, Marshall particularly in *Browngirl, Brownstones*, Morrison particularly in *Sula*, begin their narrative, not with the introduction of their characters, but with the history of their characters' natal communities. In many ways, Naylor's recounting of the immigrant waves which precede the coming of blacks to Brewster Place echoes Marshall's rendition of the history of the Brooklyn brownstones. And Naylor's chronicle of the history of Linden Hills is similar to Morrison's tale of the Bottom on the top, for both communities are originated by ex-slaves in the 19th century. The differences between these authors' respective treatments, however, is instructive, for Marshall's West Indian immigrants see their brownstones as places they can eventually own, as a step up, while Naylor's blacks of Brewster Place are at a dead end. Morrison's ex-slave earns his "bottom" as payment from his ex-master and is cheated in the process, for he is given the worse land in the area. But Naylor's Nedeed carefully *chooses* his site, outwitting everyone who sees his plateau as having no value.

Although Naylor's characterizes one neighborhood as held together by women and the other as controlled by a family, she stresses that both are started by men for the purpose of consolidating power. The intentions of these men are evident in the geographical choices they make. Nedeed's choice of "a V-shaped section of land," "the northern face of a worthless plateau," indicates his direction. Not only is his site so clearly visible; even more important, its V-shape allows his land to be both self-enclosed yet situated in the world. And since Nedeed lives on the lowest level of "the hills," he stands as a sentry to his private development. The shape of Brewster Place too is self-enclosed, for a wall is put up, separating it from other neighborhoods and making it a dead-end. Ironically, what is positive in one context is negative in another, depending on who has power. For black Nedeed uses his enclosed V-shape to select those who will be allowed to live near him, while the people of Brewster Place have a wall imposed on them by white city officials who want them separated from more "respectable" folk.

Although the wealthy Luther Nedeed appears to have power and the residents of Brewster Place do not, they are both immeasurably affected by their race, if only because they are separated from other Americans. The physical separation of Brewster Place and Linden Hills from the surrounding areas—one imposed, the other chosen—is itself symbolic of Afro-Americans' dilemma in the United States. Race and class distinctions are intertwined in Naylor's geography, for in attempting to transcend the racial separations on streets like Brewster Place, her middle class separates itself from less fortunate blacks. They shut themselves in, so that they might not be shut out from the possibility of achieving power in white America. And as Naylor's narrative in *Linden Hills* suggests, they also separate themselves from each other and are not able to become a community.

In keeping with the contours of this geography, Naylor uses quite different forms in her two novels, forms that demonstrate the relationship between the shapes of her two neighborhoods and the ways in which power relations affect them. Because women usually have little access to power in the larger society, it is not surprising that black women, doubly affected by their racial and gender status, are the central characters in poverty-stricken Brewster Place, while the apparently powerful Luther Nedeed is the kernel character in Linden Hills. Yet, in dramatizing the stories of the women in Brewster Place, who seem to be in control but are not, and in analyzing the precarious position of Luther Nedeed, Naylor shows the inaccuracy of such terms as *matriarch* or *patriarch* as they apply to Afro-Americans.

The Women of Brewster Place begins with an introduction about the history of that street, which is followed by a series of stories, each about a particular woman who lives there. The novel concludes with Mattie Michaels' dream-story about a block party in which all the women appear, as well as a coda which announces the death of the street. Created by city officials, it is destroyed by them. Although each of their narratives could be called a short story, the novel consists of the interrelationship of the stories, as a pattern evolves, not only because the characters all live in Brewster Place but also because they are connected to one another. With the exception of the lesbians in "The Two" (a point to which I will return), Naylor emphasizes the distinctiveness of each story by naming it after the specific woman on whom she is focussing, even as she might include that woman in another's story. By using this form, one that heightens the individuality of her characters so that they are not merely seen as faceless "female heads of households," while stressing their interrelationships, Naylor establishes Brewster Place as a community in spite of its history of transients—a community with its own mores, strengths, and weaknesses. Even when that specific Brewster Place is destroyed, its characteristics remain, for most of its inhabitants must move to a similar street. Brewster Place, then, stands for both itself and other places like it.

Linden Hills also begins with the history of this place, which is really the history of the Nedeed men for they *are* Linden Hills. That history is followed by sections, headed not by names but by dates, December 19th to the 24th, this in spite of the many residents of Linden Hills we meet in the course of the novel. Ostensibly the story line is the winding of Lester, a recalcitrant Linden Hills resident, and Willie, his street friend from nearby, poor Putney Wayne, through the affluent neighborhood of Linden Hills as they do odd jobs to make some money for the holidays, which ironically commemorate giving.

Although we meet many Linden Hills people, at the center of the story is Luther Nedeed himself, for he has power over the individuals who live in this settlement. His story includes within it the story of his wife, and the wives of the Nedeed men who precede him. For his story is all of their stories, the present Mrs. Nedeed, the story of all the Mrs. Nedeeds that preceded her except that this Mr. and Mrs. Nedeed will be the last of their kind. What Naylor presents is the hidden history and herstory that has made Linden Hills possible, at least as it now exists. Hence, in contrast to *Brewster Place*, the process of time, rather than the character of distinct personalities, is the formal structural element of Linden Hills.

What is interesting to me is how many layers of stories Naylor attempts to weave together in Linden Hills, layers that finally do not hold together. For although the persons focussed on in stories within the story overlap, they never connect with each other. Like *The Women of Brewster Place*, *Linden Hills* does conclude with a scene in which all the residents appear, a scene which signals the end of this place as we have known it. But while the residents of Brewster Place are getting together to have a block party, the residents of Linden Hills unilaterally ignore the burning down of the Nedeeds' house by putting out their lights. Hence, the wall that separates Brewster Place from the outer world becomes their mark of community as well as their stigma, while the houses of Linden Hills are critical to the concluding section of that novel precisely because they are the measuring stick of these people's wealth as well as their unwillingness to interact with one another. Only Lester and Willie, outcasts from Linden Hills, are "hand anchored to hand" in those last days of the year.

3

While Linden Hills destroys itself from within, Brewster Place is ostensibly destroyed from without. But Naylor's stories of the women there, usually characterized as strong, matriarchal, enduring by media, scholarship, government policy, emphasize their powerlessness. Most of her central women characters, Mattie Michaels, Etta Mae Johnson, Luciela Louise Turner, Cora Lee, live in Brewster Place because they must. Their possibility for controlling their own lives has been blocked by societal mores about women's sexuality and their individual responses to these restrictions. So, although poverty is a condition that they all share, they have been condemned to that state because of society's view of them as women, and their response to that view.

These four women, Mattie Michaels, Etta Mae Johnson, Lucielia Louise Turner, and Cora Lee, are presented as sets of counterpoint, so that Naylor can demonstrate how individual personality is not the determining factor that brings them to this street. Both Mattie Michaels and Etta Mae Johnson come from the same Southern community. But while Mattie is a sweet girl, domestic in her orientation, Etta Mae Johnson is rebellious, yearning for adventure. Still both women are wounded by the fact that they *are* women. Mattie Michaels is "ruined" by a single sexual encounter; her pregnancy results in her estrangement from her doting, then enraged, father who feels she has betrayed him. Mattie makes up for that loss by doting on her son Basil, only to receive from God what she prayed for, "a little boy who would always need her." The son's betrayal of his aging mother depletes her savings and precipitates the necessity for her move to Brewster Place. Etta Mae, too, is estranged from her community. Whites force her to leave because she is too uppity. She lives, however, primarily through hitching her wagon to a "rising black star," to a succession of men; she too never discovers that she can live through herself. Naylor's comment on the effect of sexism and racism on her is so astute:

> Even if someone had bothered to stop and tell her that the universe had expanded for her just an inch, she wouldn't know how to shine alone.[1]

Although they have had opportunities to avoid a dead-end street like Brewster Place, both Mattie and Etta Mae end up there because of their concept of themselves as women. Mattie sacrifices herself to her son. Etta Mae will not put up with the nonsense that men bring with them, but neither is she able to see that she can make up her own life. As a result the sweet Mattie and the adventurous Etta Mae arrive at a certain period in their lives without sufficient economic or psychological resources.

Both these middle-aged women live through others; but that is also true of the younger Lucielia and Cora Lee. Their lives complement Mattie's and Etta Mae's. For Lucielia will do practically anything to maintain her relationship with her husband, while Cora Lee is obsessed with having babies. Their stories are counterpoint to each other in that Lucielia's relationship with her husband is damaged because she does get pregnant while Cora Lee does not care about men except to get pregnant. Lucielia's husband sees her womanhood as a trap: "With two kids and you on my back, I ain't never gonna have nothing." Children for him are a liability since he is a poor man. When Ceil aborts her second child only to lose her first while she is pleading with her husband to stay with her, she almost loses all sense of herself. On the other hand, encouraged by adults in her childhood to desire baby dolls, Cora Lee wants nothing more than to take care of babies. No longer concerned with her children when they naturally grow beyond babyhood, Cora Lee lives in a fantasy world, interrupted only by the growing demands of the human beings she has birthed.

Because of their lack of economic resources, these four women *must* live in Brewster Place. However Kiswana Browne and "the two" choose to live there for different reasons. Kiswana feels repressed, both communally and sexually, in her natal home, Linden Hills. She sees her sojourn in Brewster Place as bonding with her true people, black people. As well, her interaction with her mother, the major event in her story, demonstrates quite clearly that Kiswana sees Linden Hills' morality as hypocritical and narrow-minded. Her prim mother characterizes African sculpture, the heritage Kiswana proudly displays, as obscene, too blatantly sexual. Yet these two women have much in common in that they both enjoy their sensuality, the younger quite openly (at least in Brewster Place), the older more covertly. Naylor's use of their adornment of their feet, a part of the female body that is usually hidden and which is not considered particularly sexual is an indication of their own pleasure in themselves. But finally it is Mrs. Browne's willingness to visit Kiswana in Brewster Place, the fact that she is concerned about her daughter's welfare despite their disagreements, that is an indication of the strength of their bond. Like the daughter in Carolyn Rodgers' poem, "The Bridge That Is My Back," Kiswana understands that "irregardless" *her* mother is there for her.

Kiswana's meeting with her mother is an amplification of a major chord sounded throughout this novel, for Brewster Place women mother one another. Perhaps these women are sometimes labeled "matriarchs" because together they are able to endure so much. There is no question that their stories in this novel are interconnected because of the caring bond they assume for one another, a bond that does not, however, preclude disagreements, falling-outs, even ineffectiveness.

So although Mattie's mother is ineffectual in her dealings with her father, it is she who, through threatened violence, prevents him from beating the pregnant girl to a pulp. And it is a stranger, Miss Eva, who mothers Mattie and her son, giving them a secure and happy home. Miss Eva may, as she says, be partial to men, but in the novel it is Mattie she treats like kin. The same attitude is evident in Mattie's friendship with Etta Mae Johnson. First mothered by Billy Holiday's music which articulates her spirit for her, Etta may believe that men are her means to success. But it is to Mattie she perennially returns for renewal. Just as Kiswana is mothered, she also mothers. She takes Cora Lee and her children to see Shakespeare in the park, and it is on that occasion that this lover of babies begins to think about possibilities for her children who are no longer babies. Ciel as well mothers her child Serena and in turn is mothered by Mattie. In one of the most moving scenes in the novel, Mattie bathes the numb grief-stricken Ciel, bringing her from death into life as she reawakens her senses in a ritual of shared womanhood much like Rosalee's bathing of Avey Johnson in Marshall's *Praisesong for the Widow*, a ritual still practiced in voodoo and derived from African religions.

Women mothering other women is consistent throughout this novel as they hold each other in survival. Such mothering, though, does not extend to "the two," the lesbians who for most Brewster Place residents do not even have specific names. The community of women in Brewster Place cannot approach even the thought of sexual love between woman, partly because so many of them have had such close relations with each other. As always, Mattie puts the community's fears into words. When Etta Mae says how different Lorraine and Theresa's love must be from the love so many of them share, Mattie responds:

> Maybe it's not so different . . . maybe that's why some women get so riled up about it 'cause they know deep down it's not so different after all . . . it kinda gives you a funny feeling when you think about it that way, though.[2]

Unlike Celie and Shug in *The Color Purple,* Lorraine has no community and very much wants one. It is her tragedy that she believes because she is black, she is in the same boat as the other residents of Brewster Place. She learns too late that the effects of racism on this black community exacerbates the homophobia so rampant in the outer world. Although she is killed by men, the women of Brewster Place too share the blame for her death. They do not mother her; instead, they reject her.

Ben, the wino who had lost his crippled daughter, is the only one who befriends Lorraine. Ironically, it is Ben who Lorraine kills in her frenzied effort to defend herself from her attackers. Ben is the first black resident of Brewster Place, and his death at the wall is a sign of Brewster Place's death as a community, of its inability to hold together much longer. Even as the women in the final scene of the novel chip away at the wall that imprisons them, we are aware that this is someone's dream, for such an act would be the prelude to a community rebellion, a step that these nurturing restricted women cannot take if they are to survive as they have. Before such a route can be explored, Brewster Place is condemned by politicians, forcing its people to disperse. As nurturing as Brewster Place "Afric women" may be, the community cannot withstand the power of those in high places. So Brewster Place residents are displaced again, just as they had been before. They are as powerless as they were when they first came to Brewster Place.

4

While Brewster Place is a community of transients, Linden Hills is a secure settlement with a long history. And unlike the people of Brewster Place, Luther Nedeed has access to people with power. In fact, because of careful planning and sacrifice, his family becomes one of those with power, at least in relation to Linden Hills. The Nedeed men caress, cultivate their dream of an ebony jewel community as if it were a woman they are wooing. Naylor's use of a V-shaped piece of land suggests the female body even as Nedeed's house situated at the entry suggests the male who wishes to take possession. The land is, for succeeding generations of Nedeed men, their love. They carefully select the families who are allowed to live on it. For *their* people:

> are to reflect the Nedeeds in a hundred facets and then the Nedeeds could take these splintered mirrors and form a *mirage of power* to torment a world that dared to think them stupid—or worse totally impotent.[3]

But even the Nedeeds, gods that they are, cannot live forever. It is necessary that they have heirs in order to continue to cultivate their dream. Wives then are necessary to their plan, the choice of a wife critical. Naylor gives us the outlines of a developing patriarchy in her description of the way the pursuit of power affects the relations between men and women. In order to serve the dream, the women must be malleable (grateful to be the wife of a Nedeed); they must look like a prize, hence their light skin, but not be demanding beauties. They must bear a son as close in nature as possible to their father, and of course the life of a Nedeed's wife must be submerged in the life of her husband.

It is this flaw in their century old plan, critical to the development and maintenance of Linden Hills, which generates the novel. For the present Mrs. Nedeed does not give birth to a Nedeed boy that resembles his paternal ancestors. Nature triumphs over planning, for this son harkens back to his maternal ancestors, as the too-long submerged blood of the Nedeed women finally manifests itself. Unwilling to believe that this could happen, that his father's genes could be superseded by his mother's, Luther Nedeed convinces himself that his wife has been unfaithful, for he will not recognize even his own mother's face in his son's features.

At the very core of patriarchal myth, as Naylor presents it, is the idea that the son must duplicate the father, and that he must be separated from the mother. In an attempt to restore order in the world he has created, Nedeed imprisons his wife and child in the cellar, causing the death of his motherlike son, hence ending the heretofore unbroken line of descent. He also precipitates his wife's discovery of the Nedeed women who preceded her, the final blow to his kingdom. In refusing to accept a variation in the pattern his father had decreed, Luther Nedeed destroys all that his forebears had set in motion.

But of course it is not only this individual Nedeed that causes the destruction of this artificial world; for years Linden Hills has been rotting from the inside as Nature refuses to succumb indefinitely to even his family's iron will. The imprisoned Mrs. Nedeed remembers *her* real name because she discovers the records left by her predecessors, letters, recipes, photographs—as the mothers cry out to be heard, to be reckoned with, to exist. As Willa Prescott Nedeed relives the herstory so carefully exhumed from the Nedeeds' official records, we realize how the experiences of the women are a serious threat to the men's kingdom.

Naylor's rendition of this herstory emphasizes one element—that once these women had produced one male, once they had carried out their function for patriarchy, they are isolated from life until they no longer exist. They however leave some record of their presence, their lives, in their own individual feminine forms. Through letters to herself, the first Mrs. Nedeed, the slave Luuwana Packerville, tells us how she is silenced to death; through her recipes, Evelyn Creton demonstrates how she had eaten herself to death, and through the family photograph album, Patricia Maguire graphically displays that she is gradually disappearing. In an act of defiance, in the last photo of the album she scrawls the word "me" in the place where her face should be.

None of these women can fight back effectively, for at first they do not know what is being done to them. When they do begin to discover that *they* are not wrong, that they are being erased not because they have lost their charm, or do not fix the right meals, it is too late. Since she has been systematically isolated from the world, no one questions the absence of the present Mrs. Nedeed, for no one knows her well enough to realize that she has not gone away for the holidays. By emphasizing the Nedeed women's ignorance of their own herstory, Naylor shows how the repression of women's herstory is necessary to the maintenance of patriarchy, and why it is that History is so exclusively male.

Naylor does not present Willa Prescott Nedeed's meditation on her dead child and on the herstory she discovers in a straight line. Rather she juxtaposes it to her presentation of other Linden Hills residents who also must erase essential parts of themselves if they are to stay in this jewel neighborhood. Most of these characters are men: the lawyer, Wynston Alcott; the businessmen, Xavier Donnell and Maxwell Symth; the Rev. Hollis; the historian Braithwaite; and one woman, Laurel. Each of their lives has been damaged by the pursuit of wealth and power that Nedeed embodies, though some do not even know it. They distort their natural inclinations, introducing death into their lives, even as the Nedeeds, who make their money as funeral parlor directors, have distorted their families in order to create Linden Hills.

Naylor shows us the different currencies in which these characters pay for their ascent to Linden Hills—usually it is their deepest natural pleasures that they give up in order to "make it." So Wynston Alcott gives up his lover David and marries, for homosexuality is not allowed in Linden Hills. Xavier Donnell gives up his idea of marrying Roxanne, a black woman who lives in Linden Hills, because she is so much herself, she might drain him of the energy necessary to reach the top. Maxwell Symth becomes totally artificial. Everything—his diet, his clothes, the temperature in his house, sexuality—is regulated so as to eliminate any funk. The pressures of his fraudulent job leaves Rev. Hollis without the wife he loves and he becomes an alcoholic. Laurel puts everything into becoming a successful businesswomen, sacrificing her relationship with her friends, her love of music and swimming, even her concern for the grandmother who brought her up. Her relationship with her husband is described as an ascent up "two staircases, that weren't strictly parellel," and whose steps "slanted until even one free hand could not touch the other's." She finally breaks into a million pieces.

Important among Linden Hills folk is Braithwaite, the historian who separates himself from life, in order to chronicle the comings and goings of the Nedeeds. His view of historiography is that of detachment and disinvolvement for only then he thinks can he be objective. He believes that he cannot participate in life if he is to observe it. As a result he does not get to know history's cunning passages—the letters, recipes, the photographs of the Mrs. Nedeeds—since only interest and concern could lead him to them. Through this character, Naylor critiques the intellectual version of Linden Hills where official history-making and an obsession with objectivity means that men like Braithwaite are not concerned with human life.

What Braithwaite does not know and does not wish to know are the very things that cause destruction of Linden Hills. On Dec. 24th the final day of the book, Nedeed insists on carrying out the family tradition of decorating the tree. He pays those Linden Hills handymen, Lester and Willie, to help him, for his family is supposedly away. By refusing to vary tradition one iota, Nedeed continues to effect his own downfall. He must have the homemade ornaments his family has always used. The closed door is left open so that Willa Nedeed Prescott can ascend, her dead child in hand, the *net* and *veil* of her predecessors encircling her, to make her own order. The final struggle between Luther and Willa will unite them and their child in a circle of fire: "They breathed as one, moved as one and one body lurched against the fireplace."

Nedeed is not only destroyed by his suppression of his mothers, he is destroyed as well by the Linden Hills residents whom he presumed to create. In an act that reveals their hatred for him as their controller as well as the disinvolvement he has always demanded of them, his neighbors let him and his house burn down. Only Willie from Putney Wayne is willing to try to save the Nedeeds who after all are only flesh and blood to him. Finally as if asserting *her* order, Nature immediately reclaims the Nedeed house. The lake, which served as the barrier between the Nedeeds and the world, pulls the century-old house into itself in one single stroke. The Nedeed tradition is extinguished forever.

I think it is important that Willie, the poet from Putney Wayne, and Lester, a descendent of Grammy Tilson, the only one who did not bend to the first Luther Nedeed's will, are the witnesses to this story of Linden Hills. Too, Naylor may be signaling through Willie's importance in the novel, as well as the story of Wayne Ave. residents, Ruth and Norm, that Putney Wayne, a working class neighborhood, may be the setting of her next novel. If it is, these Putney Wayne characters have learned much about the folly of trying to be a god and that those who place wealth above human beings cannot create a community that endures.

5

In *The Women of Brewster Place* and *Linden Hills*, Gloria Naylor's portrayal of her two neighborhoods demonstrates the effects of class distinctions on the Afro-American community and how these distinctions are gender-oriented. As well, when read together, her two novels present "solutions" idealized during the last decade by important powerless American groups, solutions which are characterized by Naylor, finally, as ineffectual routes to empowerment.

By creating a tapestry of nurturing women in her first novel, Naylor emphasizes how female values derived from mothering—nurturing, communality, concern with human feeling—are central to Brewster Place's survival. Published in 1982, *The Women of Brewster Place* was preceded by a decade of American feminist writing which responded to patriarchal society's devaluation of women by revalorizing female values.[4] In reaction to the Western patriarchal emphasis on the individual, on the splitting of human beings into mind and body, and on competition, conquest and power, these writers saw the necessity of honoring female values. If women were to become empowered, it was necessary for them to perceive their own primacy, their centrality to their society, as well as to analyze how dangerous patriarchal values were to a harmonious social order.

Because of their origins and history, Afro-American women could lay claim to a viable tradition in which they had been strong central persons in their families and communities, not solely because of their relationship to men, but because they themselves had bonded together to ensure survival of their children, their communities, the race. Partly because of the matricentric orientation of African peoples from which they were descended, partly because of the nature of American slavery, Afro-American women had had to bond with each other in order to survive. Afro-Americans as a race could not have survived without the "female values" of communality, sharing and nurturing.

At the same time, the centrality of Afro-American women in their communities was in such great contrast to the American norm of woman's subordination in the nuclear family that they were denigrated both in black and white society. The Afro-American mother was punished and maligned for being too strong, too central in her family, for being a "matriarch," a vortex of attitudes which culminated in white American government policy such as the Moynihan Report and in black cultural nationalist rhetoric of the 1960s.

Afro-American women writers of the 1970s responded to black and white society's denigration of the black mother and of female values by showing how such a position was sexist, was based on a false definition of woman as ineffectual, secondary, weak. Marshall in *Browngirl, Brownstones* and Morrison in *Sula* present women who are strong, who believe in their own primacy, and who are effective in some ways. But these writers also presented another view—that Afro-American women who internalize the dominant society's definition of women are courting self-destruction. So Morrison's Pauline and Breedline, Pecola in *The*

Bluest Eye, and Walker's Margaret and Mem Copeland in *The Third Life of Grange Copeland* are destroyed by their inability to resist society's false definitions of man and woman. It is important to note as well that these novels demonstrate not only how these specific women fall prey to sexist ideology but also that they do partly because black communities themselves are sexist. Thus Morrison in *Sula* and Walker in *Meridian* critique motherhood as the black community's primary definition of woman.

Naylor's rendition of her women's lives in the community of Brewster Place indicates that she is intensely knowledgeable of the literature of her sisters and that the thought of Afro-American women during the seventies is one means by which she both celebrates and critiques women-centered communities.

The obvious characteristic that her women share, with the exception of Kiswana and the two, is that they *must* live in streets like Brewster Place, that is that they are displaced persons. Naylor is not the first Afro-American woman writer to present a black community which is *where* it is because of socioeconomic factors. Marshall's Barbadian-American community in *Browngirl, Brownstones* is in Brooklyn because Barbados offers them little opportunity for advancement; Morrison's southern folk in *The Bluest Eye* migrate to Lorain, Ohio, because they need jobs. Each of these communities is attempting to forge a new tradition based on the old but related to the new circumstances in which they find themselves. But while they still have some belief in being able to improve their lives, the women who live in Brewster Place are caught in a cycle of never-ending displacement. Thus Brewster Place has got a tradition of mores long before Mattie Michaels or Etta Mae Johnson ever get there. Naylor, then, presents a small urban community of black women who are outcasts precisely because they are poor black women, a type of community that has been a part of black life in the United States for many generations. While the urban Selina of *Browngirl, Brownstones* and the small-town Claudia of *The Bluest Eye* can look back at their story of growing up as an education, the women of Brewster Place are in a static landscape. They were here yesterday and unless there is some catastrophic change in society, they will be here tomorrow.

The culture of sharing and nurturing in Brewster Place is based on a black tradition in this country that harkens back to slavery. Important contemporary novels written by Afro-Americans have presented women characters who are mutually supportive of one another. Margaret Walker's *Jubilee* (1966) reminds us that it was such values that allowed the ordinary slave to survive. Paule Marshall's *Browngirl, Brownstones* provides us with vivid scenes of Silla and her women friends around the kitchen table as they defend themselves against their men as well as white society. Toni Morrison gives us a lyrical account of Southern women like her Aunt Jimmy in *The Bluest Eye* who created communities in their own image, as well as a stunning description of the Peace's matrifocal house in *Sula*. In these novels, as in *The Women of Brewster Place*, women share common concerns such as the raising of children and like Brewster Place, these women-centered communities are defenses against sexism and racism, in other words against the abuses that are inflicted on black women. But while these women may be independent, it is an independence forged from the necessity of having to fend off attack; in fact, some of them would prefer not to have such independence since they have not chosen it. And in all of these novels, the women do not or cannot change their condition, so much as they cope with it as best they can.

So neither the feistiness of Eva Peace nor the persistence of Silla Boyce prevents the destruction of the Bottom nor the tearing down of the Brooklyn brownstones. What does occur in these novels is that someone understands something about her relationship to her community. But Naylor is not only concerned with this relationship. While stressing through the form of her novel that her women have strong bonds with each other, she emphasizes as well that these relationships do not substantively change their lives. Her novel ends not with Nel missing Sula nor with Selina understanding her mother, but with the movement of these women to yet another such street, where they no doubt will relive this pattern as "Brewster Place still waits to die."

By presenting a community in which strong women bonds do not break the cycle of powerlessness in which so many poor black women are imprisoned, Naylor points to a theoretical dilemma with which feminist thinkers have been wrestling. For while the values of nurturing and communality are central to a just society, they often preclude the type of behavior necessary to achieve power in this world, behavior such as competitiveness, extreme individualism, the desire to conquer. How does one break the cycle of powerlessness without giving up the values of caring so necessary to the achievement of a just society? Doesn't powerlessness itself breed internalization of self-destructive societal values? How does one achieve the primacy of self without becoming ego-centered. Further, since the values of these women are necessary to their survival, wouldn't they change if their socio-economic conditions changed? Isn't it the very fact that these women do cope through these values that precludes their destruction of the wall which entraps them? How does one fight power without taking on the values of those who have power?

Two elements in the novel suggest other avenues. One is Mattie's dream at the end of the story in which the women learn that they have participated in the destruction of Lorraine, one of their sisters, and can redeem themselves only if they protest her death—in other words that their internalization of societal values helps to keep them powerless. Having learned this, the anger of the women erupts against their real enemy, the wall that shuts them in. But Mattie awakens from this dream to a gloriously sunny day on which the community is to have a block party, an event which will take the pain away, at least for a short time, of Brewster Place's inhabitants.

The other element in the novel is Naylor's portrayal of the character Kiswana. Although she is presented as lacking the grit and humor of the other women who have endured more and lived more deeply, she is nevertheless the only one who attempts to help the community see itself as a political force—that it can fight the landlords and demand its rights. Still she can leave Brewster Place when she wishes. She does not risk survival, as the others would, if they rebelled; nor has she yet been worn down by the unceasing cycle of displacement that the others have experienced. And she has a sense of how power operates *precisely* because she comes from Linden Hills, a place which she leaves *precisely* because it is so focussed on money and power.

Naylor's inclusion of Kiswana as a pivotal character in *The Women of Brewster Place* indicates the great distance between women who *must* live in women-centered communities and those who have the option to live in them. For Kiswana's choice to live in Brewster Place is already a sign that, in relation to the other women, she has some privilege in the society. She is an "exception," while they are the majority. And her privilege comes from the fact that she was raised in a wealthy community.

Kiswana is, in fact, the link between Naylor's first novel and her second, *Linden Hills*, in which the pursuit of money and power is a central issue. Given the nature of the power in this society, many powerless groups have experienced the ineffectiveness of sharing and nurturing communities as a means to liberation. They therefore have often idealized another solution in their search for autonomy, that of taking on the values of the powerful. In *Linden Hills*, Naylor analyzes the effects of the drive for power, a drive that originally emanates from Nedeed's desire to elevate black people's status in America.

Just as *The Women of Brewster Place* was preceded by a decade of writing about female values, *Linden Hills*, published in 1985, was preceded by a decade that marked the rise of a more distinctly visible black middle class than had ever existed before in this country.[5] This period was, as well, a time when the goal of women was often portrayed as "making it" in the system. Recent media events such *Newsweek's* article on the Black Underclass and ABC's program on the Women's Movement emphasize this orientation. What these analyses often omit, however, is that the rise of the money/power solution among powerless groups in the 1970s has much to do with the character of Afro-American and women's mass movements of the '60s and early '70s when political goals were difficult to achieve, not because they were not vigorously fought for but because of the system's successful resistence to meaningful change. In the '70s, the emphasis on material gain that characterized so much media presentation of these groups' desires is actually a return to an old strategy which has never worked. But since so few of us are aware of our history, it is not surprising that the swing from mass political movements to an emphasis on individual gain as a route to empowerment would occur.

In critiquing the solution of money and status as a means to empowerment, Naylor stresses that it too is part of Afro-American tradition. Unlike Morrison's Macon Dead of *Song of Solomon* who begins his rise in the 1920s, Luther Nedeed's plan originated in the 1820s when slavery was very much alive. By charting the Nedeed generations, she reminds us that a black upper middle class has existed for some time, and that the drive to liberate the race through the creation of an elite group is not unique to the 1970s. Also, in portraying the original Nedeed plan, Naylor points up an abiding element of this "solution," for in choosing those who will be allowed to become a part of this class, Nedeed recognizes that they must deny their history of shared oppression, lest they see structural changes, rather than a duplication of the existing structure, as their goal.

What also distinguishes Naylor's presentation of the black upper middle class is her analysis of its patriarchal position. All the Nedeed men clearly grasp the fact that the subordination of the female to the male is an essential element in becoming a powerful people in America. The first Nedeed buys his wife, a slave, and never frees her and successive Nedeed men imprison their wives through isolating them. As well, the subordination of female to male is, in Naylor's narrative, interwoven with the Nedeed's emphasis on a fixed hierarchy as a necessary characteristic of their domain. So what level one lives on in the "hills" is a sure indication of one's status, and absolutely adhered to traditions determine even the Nedeed men's behavior, as they attempt, through the control of community mores, to obliterate change.

In selecting her essential elements of a developing patriarchy, Naylor has learned more from contemporary Afro-American women's literature, for it has provided her with clues about the dangers to which the creation of a black elite might lead. So Linden Hills is not so much hill as plateau, in much the same way that in *Sula* Morrison's Bottom is actually the top. One means by which the powerless are kept powerless is through the distortion of words, of naming, that is imposed on them. Like Morrison, Naylor emphasizes then how language, in this case the language of one of the powerless, is distorted to camouflage truth. And like Morrison, Naylor also uses dates to name her chapters, as if the march of time is the determining factor in her narrative. Naylor's dates are not only ironic in that they are the days of giving and of peace; they also emphasize the Christian and therefore Western orientation of Linden Hills. So while Morrison's chapters emphasize that time for the folk is not so much chronology as it is significant action, Naylor's chapters are a means by which we discover the tension between Nedeed's Western patriarchal orientation toward time and the difficulties such rigidity imposes on even his most willing residents. As has been true of so many monarchs, his inability to change is one major cause of his downfall in those last days of the year.

Naylor also revises Morrison by having Luther Nedeed, her ex-slave, become financially successful, because he, unlike Morrison's nameless exslave, excludes from his settlement those blacks who refer to a collective history. While Morrison's Bottom, then, is a distinctly Afro-American community with a distinct Afro-American culture, Linden Hills residents reject black culture. It is no wonder that Luther Nedeed sees that his ancestors' plan has failed. For though Linden Hills residents have money and status, they are no longer black. They have lost their identity, the identity which was the source of Linden Hills' origins. They therefore cannot create a community, and worse they hate their controller, Nedeed himself, who has so conditioned them as to be interested only in individual gain. By placing the pursuit of money and power above all else, the Nedeeds fragment the black community and destroy the goal for which they have sacrificed family feeling, love, fraternity, pleasure, the very qualities that make life worth living, qualities which are central to liberation and enpowerment.

Ironically, not only have Linden Hills residents lost their identity, neither have they gained power. Nedeed perceives how his showplace is threatened by the proliferation of Brewster Place, those who have been excluded from money and status. To the larger world, Linden Hills' image is affected by Brewster Place's image, just as the status of the black upper middle class today is affected by the fact that during the '70s there was a corresponding rise in poor blacks, particularly poor black women. The creation of an elite class has not empowered the race, nor has it resulted in the existence of a group of blacks unaffected by racism. The distance between Linden Hills and Brewster Place, then, is not as great as it might appear to be, and Nedeed is not so much a patriarch as a manager, who must hold to rules that are actually determined by whites.

Naylor recalls, as well, Marshall's depiction of her Barbadian-American community in *Browngirl, Brownstones* by demonstrating their desire for property and status as a bulwark against failure. But while Marshall's Silla belongs to a distinct woman-community and passes on some of its values to her daughter, Selina, the Nedeed women are isolated from other women as all traces of female values or of a distinct woman community are erased from Linden Hills. Like Marshall's Avey in *Praise Song*, the Nedeed women lose their identity and sense of community. But while Avey is able to retrieve her true name because of her experience with her maternal ancestors, the Nedeed women are cut off from their own herstory and have no daughters to whom they can bequeath their own personal experience. By emphasizing these women's ignorance of their herstory as well as their sons' separation from them, Naylor revises Marshall's emphasis in all of her novels, of the continuity of community values, of "female values," among New World Blacks. Naylor suggests then that such values can be obliterated by the predominant class distinctions inherent in the urge to develop a patriarchy.

In many ways, the Nedeed women more resemble Jadine of Morrison's *Tar Baby* in that they themselves believe in the primacy of material success and place little value on the ancient women—properties of sharing and nurturing. But Jadine does sense, through her obsession with the African woman in the yellow dress and her dream in Eloe of her maternal ancestors, that she may be giving up something of incalculable value. However the Nedeed women, as well as Laurel, the successful businesswoman of Linden Hills, do not sense this until it is much too late. Like the tragic mulattoes of the nineteenth- and early twentieth-century literature, they are trapped by their own adherence to class values which demean them as women without their even being aware of it. Unlike Hurston's Janie Stark, who too experiences the trap of ladydom, they find, too late, the language to give a name to their condition. Nor given the lack of a community, which has got a tradition of pleasure as an important value, do they encounter a woman friend, as Walker's Celie does, who might enable them to challenge the Nedeed patriarchy.

What is also interesting about Naylor's account of Linden Hills as opposed to recent Afro-American women's literature is her presentation of central male characters. In her development of Nedeed's character, she not only gives us their attempt to develop their patriarchy but their failure as well. That failure is due to their inability to create a community, which Naylor suggests must be the source of any route Afro-Americans take to empowerment. A community does not exist if it is rigidly controlled nor can it exist without a shared history or without shared values. But Naylor also presents male characters who experience the restrictions of Nedeed's vision. Like Son in Morrison's *Tar Baby*, Willie in *Linden Hills* values fraternity above money, but significantly unlike Morrison's refugee, Willie is still a viable part of a working class community, Putney Wayne. While her first novel focusses on women friendships, *Linden Hills* emphasizes the friendship between men, Willie and Lester. And in contrast to one other such friendship in contemporary Afro-American women's fiction, the friendship between Morrison's Milkman and Guitar in *Song of Solomon*, Naylor's Willie and Lester are not opposed to each other's values. In so tenderly portraying the relationship of these two, Naylor may be suggesting that genuine friendship between men who share similar values, as well as friendship between women, is critical to the Afro-American community's search for empowerment.

Like Kiswana, who is the transitional character between *The Women of Brewster Place* and *Linden Hills,* Willie may be the transitional figure between Linden Hills and Naylor's next novel. Like Kiswana he is interested in and knowledgeable about the history and literature of Afro-Americans. But he is also educated in one respect that she is not. He comes from a living working class Afro-American community with a deep cultural past that is as old as Linden Hills. Through his friendship with Lester, he learns about Linden Hills from the inside and thus knows that the solution of the creation of an elite class fragments and destroys the community. As a person intensely involved in the direction of his folk's future then, he is not as likely, as have some upper-mobile working class men, to repeat Nedeed's error.

What he and others like him can do to empower their communities is not solved for us in either of these novels. For Naylor does not so much give us solutions as she uses her knowledge of Afro-American women's literature to show how complex the condition of powerless groups are. She may be the first Afro-American women writer to have such access to her tradition. And the complexity of her two novels indicate how valuable such knowledge can be. In doing her own black feminist reading of her literary tradition so as to dramatize the convoluted hierarchy of class, race and gender distinctions in America today, she has begun to create a geographical world in her fiction, as varied and complex as the structure of our society.

Notes

1. Gloria Naylor, *The Women of Brewster Place* Penguin Contemporary American Fiction Series (New York, 1982), p. 60.
2. *Ibid.,* p. 141.
3. Gloria Naylor, *Linden Hills* Tucknor and Fields (New York, 1985), p. 141.
4. Marilyn French's *Beyond Power* and bell hooks' *Feminist Theory: From Margin to Center* both summarize this orientation and suggest theoretical dilemmas that result from it.
5. William Wilson's *The Declining Significance of Race* and Thomas Sowell's *Ethnic America* discuss this phenomenon from different points of view.

◆◆◆◆◆◆◆◆◆◆◆◆◆◆

Dream, Deferral, and Closure
in *The Women of Brewster Place*

JILL L. MATUS

After presenting a loose community of six stories, each focusing on a particular character, Gloria Naylor constructs a seventh, ostensibly designed to draw discrete elements together, to "round off" the collection. As its name suggests, "The Block Party" is a vision of community effort, everyone's story. We discover after a first reading, however, that the narrative of the party is in fact Mattie's dream vision, from which she awakens perspiring in her bed. The "real" party for which Etta is rousing her has yet to take place, and we never get to hear how it turns out. Authorial sleight of hand in offering Mattie's dream as reality is quite deliberate, since the narrative counts on the reader's credulity and encourages the reader to take as narrative "presence" the "elsewhere" of dream, thereby calling into question the apparently choric and unifying status of the last chapter. The displacement of reality into dream defers closure, even though the chapter appears shaped to make an end. Far from having had it, the last words remind us that we are still "gonna have a party."

The inconclusive last chapter opens into an epilogue that too teases the reader with the sense of an ending by appearing to be talking about the death of the street, Brewster Place. The epilogue itself is not unexpected, since the novel opens with a prologue describing the birth of the street. So why not a last word on how it died? Again, expectations are subverted and closure is subtly deferred. Although the epilogue begins with a meditation on how a street dies and tells us that Brewster Place is waiting to die, *waiting* is a present participle that never becomes past. "Dawn" (the prologue) is coupled neither with death nor darkness, but with "dusk," a condition whose half-light underscores the half-life of the street. Despite the fact that in the epilogue Brewster Place is abandoned, its daughters still get up elsewhere and go about their daily activities. In a reiteration of the domestic routines that are always carefully attended to in the novel—the making of soup, the hanging of laundry, the diapering of babies—, Brewster's death is forestalled and postponed. More importantly, the narrator emphasizes that the dreams of Brewster's inhabitants are what keep them alive. *"They get up and pin those dreams to wet laundry hung out to dry, they're mixed with a pinch of salt and thrown into pots of soup, and they're diapered around babies. They ebb and flow, ebb and flow, but never disappear."* They refers initially to the "colored daughters" but thereafter repeatedly to the dreams. The end of the novel raises questions about the relation of dreams to the persistence of life, since the capacity of Brewster's women to dream on is identified as their capacity to live on. The street continues to exist marginally, on the edge of death; it is the "end of the line" for most of its inhabitants. Like the street, the novel hovers, moving toward the end of its line, but deferring. What prolongs both the text and the lives of Brewster's inhabitants is dream; in the same way that Mattie's dream of destruction postpones the end of the novel, the narrator's last words identify dream as that which affirms and perpetuates the life of the street.

If the epilogue recalls the prologue, so the final emphasis on dreams postponed yet persistent recalls the poem by Langston Hughes with which Naylor begins the book: *"What happens to a dream deferred?"* In a catalog of similies, Hughes evokes the fate of dreams unfulfilled: They dry up like raisins in the sun, fester like sores, stink like rotten meat, crust over like syrupy sweets. They become burdensome, or possibly explosive. The poem suggests that to defer one's dreams, desires, hopes is life-denying. Images of shriveling, putrefaction, and hardening dominate the poem. Despair and destruction are the alternatives to decay. My interest here is to look at the way in which Naylor rethinks the poem in her novel's attention to dreams and desires and deferral, and then to consider the implications of her vision in terms of the novel's sensitivity to history and social context.

Naylor's desire to write the experience of black American women was born from an impatience with the critical establishment's assumptions that black writers should provide "definitive" reflections of black experience. The emphasis on the definitive, she argues, denies the vast complexity of Afro-American experience. In a conversation with Toni Morrison, she speaks of her struggle to realize the dream of writing the lives of black women without falsification and sentimentality, making visible those whom society keeps invisible (Naylor "Conversation"). She dedicates the novel to those who "gave me the dream, believed in it . . . nurtured it . . . applauded it."

Naylor talks also of how she came to see the bound copy of her completed book as a tombstone. She experienced a sense of loss in taking leave of the characters and making an end, which is the reason that the published book seems to her a marker of death. A book unwritten is desire unbounded, yet the very drive to write the experience eventually produces a tombstone. Desire fulfilled, which is the satisfaction of seeing the book in print, is the death of desire, since, in Lacanian terms, desire depends on lack, want, and propulsion toward the object of satisfaction. What Naylor says sustains her is the birth of a new book, a new desire. But one could argue that this desire is not new. It is rather a continu-

ation, since the focus of her next book *(Linden Hills)* is bequeathed by
Brewster Place itself; you can see Linden Hills from Kiswana's window.
Similarly, Naylor's recent novel *Mama Day* focuses on a minor, off-stage
character in *Linden Hills*. In this sense, then, the bound copy of *The
Women of Brewster Place* is a false grave, for it has demonstrated powers
of generation and perpetuation that defy its definition as a finished work.
The poles of dream (the wish to write the lives of black women) and
death (the finished novel as tombstone) apply to Naylor's experience as
a writer as much as they inform the focus and technique of her writing.

The dream of the last chapter is a way of deferring closure, but this
deferral is not evidence of the author's self-indulgent reluctance to make
an end. Rather, it is an enactment of the novel's revision of Hughes's
poem. Yet the substance of the dream itself and the significance of the
dreamer raise some further questions. Why is the anger and frustration
that the women feel after the rape of Lorraine displaced into dream?
There are many readers who feel cheated and betrayed to discover that
the apocalyptic destruction of Brewster's wall never takes place. Are we
to take it that Ciel never really returns from San Francisco and Cora is
not taking an interest in the community effort to raise funds for tenants'
rights? All that the dream has promised is undercut, it seems. And yet,
the placement of explosion and destruction in the realm of fantasy or
dream that is a "false" ending marks Naylor's suggestion that there are
many ways to dream and alternative interpretations of what happens to
the dream deferred.

If there is a central character in a novel that so avoids definition and
homogeneity, she is Mattie. Mattie's is the first story, and from it we
understand that she knows what it is to love and to suffer loss, paternal
abuse, betrayal, and dispossession. Although men like Eugene do not
like her—she speaks the truth as she sees it—, she is received and respected by most others. Cora singles her out as the only one around who
doesn't feel it necessary to do jury duty on other people's lives. She
refuses to join in the community condemnation of Lorraine and Theresa's
lesbian relationship, preferring to mind her own business and open her
mind to the kinds of love that women can bear for other women. After
the catastrophic death of Ciel's daughter, she is mentor and nurturer.
Mattie's moving ritual of bathing and cleansing Ciel draws on common-
sensical folkloric wisdom and links her to the tradition of black women
who have nursed their sisters through grief and suffering. As the community's best voice and sharpest eye, she is well-qualified to express the
unconscious urgings of the community and dream the collective dream.

It is a dream that draws heavily on what Northrop Frye, in *Anatomy
of Criticism*, calls demonic imagery. The chapter begins with a description of the continuous rain that follows the death of Ben. Stultifying and
confining, the rain prevents the inhabitants of Brewster's community
from meeting to talk about the tragedy; instead they are faced with

clogged gutters, debris, trapped odors in their apartments, and listless children. Men stay away from home, become aggressive, and drink too much. In their separate spaces the women dream of a tall yellow woman in a bloody green and black dress—Lorraine. Mattie's dream expresses the communal guilt, complicity, and anger that the women of Brewster Place feel about Lorraine. Ciel is present in Mattie's dream because she herself has dreamed about the ghastly rape and mutilation with such identification and urgency that she obeys the impulse to return to Brewster Place: "'And she had on a green dress with like black trimming, and there were red designs or red flowers or something on the front.' Ciel's eyes began to cloud. 'And something bad had happened to me by the wall—I mean her—something bad had happened to her.'" The presence of Ciel in Mattie's dream expresses the elder woman's wish that Ciel be returned to her and the desire that Ciel's wounds and flight be redeemed. Mattie's son Basil, who has also fled from Brewster Place, is contrastingly absent. He is beyond hope, and Mattie does not dream of his return. For many of the women who have lived there, Brewster Place is an anchor as well as a confinement and a burden; it is the social network that, like a web, both sustains and entraps. Mattie's dream scripts important changes for Ciel: She works for an insurance company (good pay, independence, and status above the domestic), is ready to start another family, and is now connected to a good man. Ciel hesitantly acknowledges that he is not black. Middle-class status and a white husband offer one alternative in the vision of escape from Brewster Place; the novel does not criticize Ciel's choices so much as suggest, by implication, the difficulty of envisioning alternatives to Brewster's black world of poverty, insecurity, and male inadequacy. Yet Ciel's dream identifies her with Lorraine, whom she has never met and of whose rape she knows nothing. It is a sign that she is tied to Brewster Place, carries it within her, and shares its tragedies.

Every woman and small girl there has had disturbing dreams about Lorraine. Cora attributes her weird dreams to the fact that she is pregnant, and Ciel dismisses the dream that has summoned her back as "crazy." Beyond what the women know cognitively, the dreams unite them and provide a context of sharing and connection. It is interesting that Mattie and Etta conceal from Ciel the significance of her dream. Mattie becomes intent on basting her ribs, and Etta responds that she is trying to figure out what number she can play off the dream. "Now I know snakes is 436 and a blue Cadillac is 224, but I gotta look in my book to see what a wall is." Rather than explore the eerie significance of Ciel's link to Brewster, Etta clouds the felt truth with the hocus pocus of superstition. Freud's remarks on the abuse of dream interpretation are apposite here: "The final abuse of dream interpretation was reached in our days with attempts to discover from dreams the numbers fated to be drawn in the game of lotto." Within Mattie's dream, which the reader initially assumes to be part of the progressive narrative temporality, Etta is "interpreting" Ciel's dream in a way which the reader is implicitly counseled to avoid. How then are we to interpret Mattie's dream?

Everyone in the community knows that this block party is significant and important because it is a way of moving forward after the terrible tragedy of Lorraine and Ben. As it begins to rain, the women continue desperately to solicit community involvement. A man who is going to buy a sandwich turns away; it is more important that he stay and eat the sandwich than that he pay for it. As the rain comes down, hopes for a community effort are scotched and frustration reaches an intolerable level. The dream of the collective party explodes in a nightmarish destruction. Poking at a blood-stained brick with a popsicle stick, Cora says, "'Blood ain't got no right still being here.'" Like the blood that runs down the palace walls in Blake's "London," this reminder of Ben and Lorraine blights the block party. Tearing at the very bricks of Brewster's walls is an act of resistance against the conditions that prevail within it. The more strongly each woman feels about her past in Brewster Place, the more determinedly the bricks are hurled. Ciel, for example, is not unwilling to cast the first brick and urges the rational Kiswana to join this "destruction of the temple." Kiswana cannot see the blood; there is only rain. "Does it matter?" asks Ciel. "Does it really matter?" Frustrated with perpetual pregnancy and the burdens of poverty and single parenting, Cora joins in readily, and Theresa, about to quit Brewster Place in a cab, vents her pain at the fate of her lover and her fury with the submissiveness that breeds victimization. The women have different reasons, each her own story, but they unite in hurling bricks and breaking down boundaries. The dismal, incessant rain becomes cleansing, and the water is described as beating down in unison with the beating of the women's hearts. Despite the inclination toward overwriting here, Naylor captures the cathartic and purgative aspects of resistance and aggression. Demonic imagery, which accompanies the venting of desire that exceeds known limits, becomes apocalyptic. As the dream ends, we are left to wonder what sort of register the "actual" block party would occupy. The sun is shining when Mattie gets up: It is as if she has done the work of collective destruction in her dream, and now a sunny party can take place. But perhaps the mode of the party about to take place will be neither demonic nor apocalyptic. The close of the novel turns away from the intensity of the dream, and the satisfaction of violent protest, insisting rather on prolonged yearning and dreaming amid conditions which do not magically transform. The collective dream of the last chapter constitutes a "symbolic act" which, as Frederic Jameson puts it, enables "real social contradictions, insurmountable in their own terms, [to] find a purely formal resolution in the aesthetic realm."

The final chapter and epilogue mediate between violent disruption and persistent yearning by offering first a cathartic dream of resistance and then an affirmation of quiet, sustaining, personal dreams. Two stories in particular—"The Two" and "Cora Lee"—prepare for the final chapter's mediation. In "The Two" Naylor considers the tragedy of Lorraine's rape and the deadly eruption of her deferred self-assertion, which results in Ben's death. By considering the violent release that follows deferral, the story enacts on a personal level what "The Block Party" attempts to redeem through community action. The story of Lorraine and Theresa, two lesbians who move to Brewster Place, is more than a powerful and disturbing portrayal of prejudice and sexism. It would have been just that if Naylor had concluded with the brutal rape of Lorraine by a vicious teenage gang, but the story is carefully structured around the relationship of Lorraine and Ben, the "harmless old wino" and the first black person to have settled in Brewster Place. Ben is the most fully realized male character in Brewster Place—there because he is old and broken and has nowhere else to run to. He drinks to displace the poisonous melody of his personal song, which tells of his collusion long ago in his lame daughter's prostitution. Ben is the father who has betrayed and lost his daughter; Lorraine is the daughter who has been banished by an unaccepting father.

Rejected because she is a lesbian, Lorraine nevertheless continues to send her father a birthday card every year. Because these have always been returned unopened, she has stopped putting her return address on them so that she can imagine that one day he may open one. Naylor uses the symmetry in the stories of Ben and Lorraine predictably, to develop the bond of sympathy between them. The banished daughter and the bereft and guilty father connect. Ben's daughter is lame, and Lorraine's "inner limp," which defines her as a victim, is the quality in her that reminds him of his daughter. Although she lives with Theresa, she feels guilty and ashamed of their relationship. Unwilling to confront hostility, Lorraine defers by changing location. The couple has moved from one district to another, giving up Theresa's apartment in Linden Hills because of Lorraine's sensitivity about what "they" will think. Brewster Place, as the end of the line, is no freer of prejudice against lesbians than anywhere else. After Lorraine has been mutilated and assaulted because she is a "dyke," she crawls toward Ben, who sways drunkenly on an overturned garbage can. We expect that she will ask for and receive help, but Ben becomes her unwitting target, the object of her desire now to fight back. Ironically, Lorraine murders the "father" who has been kind to her. Man and father must pay, and who more fittingly than the father who has failed his own daughter? Although there is something contrived about the ironies with which the story ends, the reader is left feeling the horror and tragedy of the situation. Ben's daughter is not redeemed by Lorraine's submissiveness turned savageness; Ben's death avenges neither the machismo of C.C.'s gang nor Lorraine's repressed anger towards her father. Rather, the text suggests that accumulated hurts and betrayals breed a store of violence which erupts on displaced targets. Deferral and displacement proliferate the tragedies, which is perhaps the reason that "The Block Party" only dreams its desire for violent protest and destruction.

An alternative to explosion and destruction is postponement and persistence, sustained by the endurance of dreams. But when are dreams or hopes vain and delusional, and when are they life-affirming? "Cora Lee" is important in exploring the ambiguities of dream and setting up a polarity between dream as vain fantasy and sustaining or transforming power. A quotation from *A Midsummer Night's Dream* opens the story: "True, I talk of dreams, / Which are the children of an idle brain / Begot of nothing but fantasy." Cora, who as a small child desired no other toys than a new baby doll every year, becomes a woman who reproduces her dream and finds herself with a large, demanding family. Unable to cope with the children those babies have become, she nevertheless continues to satisfy her desire for the sweet, soft, vulnerable newborn. Cora is a portrait of obsessive and arrested desire: The inability to absorb the baby as developing, needy child is part of her blocking of realities that are impinging and uncomfortable. As caretaker of a small baby she regresses into a world that reflects a comforted, comforting sense of self. The image of herself as mother—the power, the sensuous pleasure, and the closely circumscribed world of the mother-child dyad—marks the end of her desire. Cora's dream projects a static world in which the mother-infant relationship must never be ruptured—hence the necessity for infinite replacement of the newborn baby. Cora's attentiveness to the infant and disregard for anything outside this circle are strongly contrasted. Her other children exist for her as frozen portraits of their baby days. Concerns about their schooling, rotting teeth, truancy, and slovenliness are easily drowned by the anodyne of soap operas, and it is with a sense of pique and puzzlement that Cora finds herself accountable for a multitude of young, growing lives. Cora's men are now marginalized as shadows. She tried living with one of the fathers, but when a pot of burnt rice translates into a fractured jaw, singleness is preferable, even though it spells abject poverty. Men come and go; once one promised to marry her, but he never returned from a trip to the corner store to buy milk. So Cora lives on welfare and accommodates the shadows in her bed for the brief sensuous pleasure and the sperm they provide. When Cora recalls the fathers of some of her children, her knowledge is vague, a series of generalizations and stereotypes. For example, her child Dorian has a head "like a rock," which makes him like his father: "'All those West Indians got hard heads.' Well, I guess he was West Indian, she thought, he had some kind of accent." The antithesis is Kiswana, who is so concerned about ethnic specificity and the recovery of her African roots that she fails to recognize her commonality with her mother. Cora becomes one of Kiswana's challenges. Kiswana is going to change Cora's life and open her eyes, and starts by inviting her to a black production of Shakespeare's *Dream*—Kiswana's boyfriend Abshu Ben-Jamal has a grant from the city.

The visit to the play looks like a breakthrough, and in some ways it is. Cora's abdication of responsibility is briefly redressed, and the experience at the theatre puts her in touch with the needs of her older children. She resolves to check their homework every night, join the P.T.A., and see that they get to summer school. She dreams of good jobs for them "in insurance companies and the post office," homes in Linden Hills—a simple catalog of middle-class aspiration. When her son asks her whether Shakespeare is black, she replies, "Not yet," remembering guiltily how she has beaten him for writing rhymes on the bathroom walls. No Shakespeare can be nurtured in the environment she provides for her children. The dreams that *Dream* provokes reflect a simple faith that education will secure for her children a larger piece of the pie than Cora herself has ever been entitled to command.

But one trip to the park to see Shakespeare is not going to resolve magically life's confusing demands. What awes Cora are the fine-sounding words which she doesn't understand and the sparkling splendor of the costumes. Her fantasies for her son and daughter are also clearly untutored by any feminist consciousness: She envisions for her daughter the role of the fairy queen and thinks about her son as a potential black Shakespeare. Even though her dreams show the absorption of cultural and gender stereotypes, the breakthrough, Naylor suggests, is that Cora is sparked to imagine and dream at all. The evening has been a "night of wonders," but it gets folded like "gold and lavender gauze deep within the creases of her dreams." Cora's story explores the ambiguities of the dream: Is it vain fantasy, escape, and magic; inspirational; delusional? When she appears in Mattie's dream vision in "The Block Party," she is pregnant again, impatiently cajoling her children, bemoaning the fact that Sonya has passed out of babyhood and started to walk. Yet she is there at the block party and interested in the collection of funds to secure a lawyer for renters' rights. Although slight, changes are detectable. It is also Cora who discovers the bloodied brick and tears it from the wall. Despite her exhaustion, she participates in the symbolic purgation of Brewster Place.

Further reasons for Naylor's negotiation between persistent yearning and violent protest are to be found in the novel's reflection of history and moment. Despite its heavy dependency on general images of birth and arrested development, the prologue provides markers that locate Brewster temporally and geographically. Its conception was a political act around the time of "The Great War":

> Brewster Place was the bastard child of several clandestine meetings between the alderman of the sixth district and the managing director of Unico Realty Company. The latter needed to remove the police chief. . . . the alderman

> *wanted the realty company to build their new shopping center on his cousin's property.* . . .

Years later, after the Second World War, Irish and Italian immigrant mothers hope that their sons will settle there when they return from combat. Then one year before the Supreme Court decision in *Brown v. Topeka Board of Education* (1954), the first "brown-skinned" man comes to live in Brewster. In the fifties, we learn, Brewster's inhabitants are largely Mediterranean immigrants. Reflecting demographic trends, the neighborhood becomes increasingly black through the sixties and seventies.[1] In casual details about the characters, Naylor's novel mirrors the social transformation of Afro-America. Naylor chooses a slum neighborhood—possibly an area of Boston, since there is mention of the Irish immigrant community, Eugene has a job at the docks, and Newport is close by. Mattie chides Etta Mae about having run from St. Louis and Chicago; now Etta Mae wants [to] leave "here" and go to New York. Naylor apparently wants to contrast the big Northern city and the South, from which many of the older characters (Mattie, Etta Mae, and Ben) have fled. Although Brewster Place is a hair's breadth from poverty, it is still clearly preferable to the starving South.[2]

Not only does Langston Hughes's poem speak generally about the nature of deferral and dreams unsatisfied, but in the historical context that Naylor evokes it also calls attention implicitly to the sixties' dream of racial equality and the "I have a dream" speech of Martin Luther King, Jr. In her historical account of the impact of black women on race and sex in America, Paula Giddings writes about the hopes generated by King's dream in the context of a growing despair:

> If hopes were buoyed when 250,000 people marched on Washington to dream Martin Luther King's eloquent dream, they were dashed by the Birmingham bombing less than a month later. . . . The dream of racial harmony, the belief that America had a genuine moral conscience that just needed awakening, was cracking around the edges. It would turn to dust by the end of the summer of '64.

Dashed, cracking, and *dust* link Giddings' history rhetorically to Hughes's poem. In both cases the failure of the dream is foregrounded. Giddings, however, is preceded by King himself in acknowledging the nightmare of disappointment during the years that followed his "I have a dream" speech. In a sermon preached on Christmas Eve of 1967, Dr. King spoke of the nightmare his earlier dream had become:

> In 1963, on a sweltering August afternoon, we stood in Washington, D.C., and talked to the nation about many things. Toward the end of that afternoon, I tried to talk to the nation about a dream that I had had, and I must confess to you today that not long after talking about that dream I started seeing it turn into a nightmare. . . . It was when four beautiful, unoffending, innocent Negro girls were murdered in a church in Birmingham, Alabama. I watched that dream turn to a nightmare as I moved through the ghettos of the nation

and saw my black brothers and sisters perishing on a lonely island of poverty in the midst of a vast ocean of prosperity, and saw the nation doing nothing to grapple with the Negroes' problem of poverty. I saw that dream turn into a nightmare as I watched my black brothers and sisters in the midst of anger and understandable outrage, in the midst of their hurt, in the midst of their disappointment, turn to misguided riots to try to solve that problem.

But King's sermon goes further: After acknowledging the nightmare and invoking (like Giddings and Hughes) the rhetoric of disappointment and disaster, he finds (like Naylor) sustenance in deferral and persistence and then proceeds to a rousing vision of arrival. The sermon's movement is thus from disappointment, through a recognition of deferral and persistence, to a reiteration of vision and hope:

Yes, I am personally the victim of deferred dreams, of blasted hopes, but in spite of that I close today by saying I still have a dream, because, you know, you can't give up in life. If you lose hope, somehow you lose that vitality that keeps life moving, you lose that courage to be, that quality that helps you to go on in spite of all. And so today I still have a dream.

The remainder of the sermon goes on to celebrate the resurrection of the dream—"I still have a dream" is repeated some eight times in the next paragraph. Naylor's novel is not exhortatory or rousing in the same way; her response to the fracture of the collective dream is an affirmation of persistence rather than a song of culmination and apocalypse. King's sermon culminates in the language of apocalypse, a register which, as I have already suggested, Naylor's epilogue avoids: "I still have a dream today that one day every valley shall be exalted and every mountain and hill will be made low. . . , and the glory of the Lord shall be revealed. . . ." Hughes's poem and King's sermon can thus be seen as two poles between which Naylor steers. The novel recognizes the precise political and social consequences of the cracked dream in the community it deals with, but asserts the vitality and life that persist even when faith in a particular dream has been disrupted. Although remarkably similar to Dr. King's sermon in the recognition of blasted hopes and dreams deferred, *The Women of Brewster Place* does not reassert its faith in the dream of harmony and equality: It stops short of apocalypse in its affirmation of persistence. Further, Naylor suggests that the shape and content of the dream should be capable of flexibility and may change in response to changing needs and times. What the women of Brewster Place dream is not so important as that they dream.

Naylor's emphasis on persistence and continuity as important in themselves recalls Alice Walker's concerns in *Meridian*, a novel which also opens with an epigraph that addresses itself to dreams and their destruction. In the course of the novel the character Meridian deals specifically with the aims of the Civil Rights Movement and how she will live them in the aftermath of revolutionary hopefulness. Meridian's commitment to living among the people, registering voters of the South is not so much an indication of the Movement's lost dreams as an enactment at a personal level of the continuity of struggle. Interestingly, Meridian's quarrel with Christianity is that it is a religion of martyrs. Walker explains Meridian's thinking in an interview with Claudia Tate: "Just before the crucifixion, according to Meridian, Jesus should have left town." Instead of dying, sacrificing themselves, Christ (and King) should have taken off to continue elsewhere. Meridian's recurrent nightmare is that she is a character in a novel whose ending depends on her death. In fact, she persists and "survives" the narrative's closing; this is one protagonist who escapes the traditional formula's equivalence of ending and death. In a similar way, *The Women of Brewster Place* turns from the grand and explosive ending to affirm endurance and persistence in the face of unfulfilled dreams.

Brewster's women live within the failure of the sixties' dreams, and there is no doubt a dimension of the novel that reflects on the shortfall. But its reflection is subtle, achieved through the novel's concern with specific women and an individualized neighborhood and the way in which fiction, with its attention focused on the particular, can be made to reveal the play of large historical determinants and forces. There is an attempt on Naylor's part to invoke the wide context of Brewster's particular moment in time and to blend this with her focus on the individual dreams and psychologies of the women in the stories. Perhaps because her emphasis is on the timeless nature of dreams and the private mythology of each "ebony phoenix," the specifics of history are not foregrounded. Even though the link between the neighborhood and the particular social, economic, and political realities of the sixties is muted rather than emphatic, defining characteristics are discernible. In Brewster Place there is no upward mobility; and by conventional evaluation there are no stable family structures. Brewster is a place for women who have no realistic expectations of revising their marginality, most of whom have "come down" in the world. The exception is Kiswana, from Linden Hills, who is deliberately downwardly mobile. Naylor's next work, *Linden Hills*, is an extended treatment of this black neighborhood, infernal and purgatorial, whose inhabitants have sold their souls for a piece of the American pie. Similarly, Paule Marshall's *Praisesong for the Widow* exposes the self-betrayal that takes place in the pursuit of the black bourgeois dream: Avey Johnson's nausea in response to the peach parfait on her world cruise tells us that she can no longer swallow her comfortable middleclass self. *The Women of Brewster Place*, however, focuses on the women and neighborhood that never get to taste the disappointment of having "made it."

As presented, Brewster Place is largely a community of women; men are mostly absent or itinerant, drifting in and out of their women's lives, and leaving behind them pregnancies and unpaid bills. It would be simple to make a case for the unflattering portrayal of men in this novel; in fact Naylor was concerned that her work would be seen as deliberately slighting of men:

> . . . there was something that I was very self-conscious about with my first novel; I bent over backwards not to have a negative message come through about the men. My emotional energy was spent in creating a woman's world, telling her side of it because I knew it hadn't been done enough in literature. But I worried about whether or not the problems that were being caused by the men in the women's lives would be interpreted as some bitter statement I had to make about black men.

Bearing in mind the kind of hostile criticism that Alice Walker's *The Color Purple* evoked, one can understand Naylor's concern, since male sins in her novel are not insignificant. Mattie is a resident of Brewster partly because of the failings of the men in her life: the shiftless Butch, who is sexually irresistible; her father, whose outraged assault on her prompts his wife to pull a gun on him; and her son, whom she has spoiled to the extent that he one day jumps bail on her money, costing her her home and sending her to Brewster Place. There is also the damning portrait of a minister on the make in Etta Mae's story, the abandonment of Ciel by Eugene, and the scathing presentation of the young male rapists in "The Two."

"The enemy wasn't Black men," Joyce Lander contends, "'but oppressive forces in the larger society,'" and Naylor's presentation of men implies agreement. But while she is aware that there is nothing enviable about the pressures, incapacities, and frustrations men absorb in a system they can neither beat nor truly join, her interest lies in evoking the lives of women, not men. Their aggression, part-time presence, avoidance of commitment, and sense of dislocation renders them alien and other in the community of Brewster Place. Basil and Eugene are forever on the run; other men in the stories (Kiswana's boyfriend Abshu, Cora Lee's shadowy lovers) are narrative ciphers. Mostly marginal and spectral in Brewster Place, the men reflect the nightmarish world they inhabit by appearing as if they were characters in a dream.

Although *Brewster Place* is a novel about women and concentrates on exploring the experiences of women, it does not enlist a dogmatic feminist ideology. There is little of *The Color Purple*'s celebration and rejoicing in the discovery of self, sexuality, and creativity in the face of male abuse and repression. Celie is encouraged to trade her razor—she wants to slit Albert's throat—for a needle, the implement of her autonomy and creativity. If *The Color Purple* mediates a feminist solution to the problems of the oppressed Celie, Naylor's novel is far more tentative about celebrating the efficacy of female friendship, lesbian relationships, and self-affirmation through sisterhood. There are important moments of friendship and supportive connection, but there are no radical transformations; Naylor does not, as Walker does, draw on feminist ideology as an agent of transcendence. Naylor calls attention to the particular problems of black women without suggesting that such problems are gender issues alone. When she says that she hopes the novel does not make a bitter statement about the men, she is, I think, voicing a concern that the problems she addresses will be oversimplified if they are seen only in terms of male-female relationships.

"The Block Party" is a crucial chapter of the book because it explores the attempts to experience a version of community and neighborhood. People know each other in Brewster Place, and as imperfect and damaging as their involvement with each other may be, they still represent a community. As the title suggests, this is a novel about women and place. Brewster Place names the women, houses them, and defines their underprivileged status. Although they come to it by very different routes, Brewster is a reality that they are "obliged to share." *Obliged* comes from the political, social, and economic realities of post-sixties' America—a world in which the women are largely disentitled. *Share* directs emphasis to what they have in common: They are women, they are black, and they are almost invariably poor. Among the women there is both commonality and difference: *"Like an ebony phoenix, each in her own time and with her own season had a story."*

Naylor's novel does not offer itself as a definitive treatment of black women or community, but it reflects a reality that a great many black women share; it is at the same time an indictment of oppressive social forces and a celebration of courage and persistence. By considering the nature of personal and collective dreams within a context of specific social, political, and economic determinants, Naylor inscribes an ideology that affirms deferral; the capacity to defer and to dream is endorsed as life-availing. Like Martin Luther King, Naylor resists a history that seeks to impose closure on black American dreams, recording also in her deferred ending a reluctance to see "community" as a static or finished work. There are countless slum streets like Brewster; streets will continue to be condemned and to die, but there will be other streets to whose decay the women of Brewster will cling. The image of the ebony phoenix developed in the introduction to the novel is instructive: The women rise, as from the ashes, and continue to live. Although the idea of miraculous transformation associated with the phoenix is undercut by the starkness of slum and the perpetuation of poverty, the notion of regeneration also associated with the phoenix is supported by the quiet persistence of women who continue to dream on. While acknowledging the shriveling, death-bound images of Hughes's poem, Naylor invests with value the essence of deferral—it resists finality.

Notes

1. As W. Lawrence Hogue points out, "After 1950 a new phenomenon of Afro-American social reality appeared: large urban black populations." Until the 1950s the majority of blacks lived in the South, but industrial expansion in the North caused a shift in the labor force and mass migration out of the rural areas.
2. The novel here endorses statistics showing that, on average, the bottom of the urban-industrial ladder is higher than the bottom of the Southern agricultural ladder, despite the fact that black unemployment rates doubled those of whites in the early 1960s.

◆◆◆◆◆◆◆◆◆◆◆◆◆◆

Reading in Black and White:
Space and Race in *Linden Hills*

LUKE BOUVIER

Where is Linden Hills? At first glance, it seems almost ludicrous to ask such a question, since the obsessive structuring and delimiting of space in Gloria Naylor's *Linden Hills* would appear to leave no room for ambiguity. The obvious answer is that Linden Hills was founded in 1820 by Luther Nedeed on the worthless northern face of a plateau that Nedeed had bought upon coming north to Wayne County. The V-shaped land, originally bordered on top by the white farmer Putney Wayne's fields, sloped sharply down a rocky facing covered with briar bush and linden trees, curved through the town cemetery, and ended in a sharp point in front of an apple orchard owned by another white man named Patterson. Nedeed built a cabin at the very bottom of the land, and realizing that the land was worthless for farming, he began an undertaker's business. He also built shacks up on the hill and began renting them out to poor blacks who worked in the local sawmills or tar pit. Through five generations of Nedeeds, Linden Hills eventually grew and prospered and has since become a wealthy, middle-class black community. The inhabitants are spatially situated along eight curved roads descending from First Crescent Drive through Fifth Crescent Drive, continuing down three more roads named Tupelo Drive, and ending in the home of Luther Nedeed, the fifth in a line of Luther Nedeeds, who presides over the community and still runs the undertaker's business started by his great-great grandfather.

Linden Hills is *the* black space par excellence, or at least the realization of Luther Nedeed's vision of what a black space should be. As the land value of Linden Hills increased, old Luther Nedeed's son decided to protect the community from the encroaching white community by offering thousand-year-and-a-day leases to the poor blacks living there, provided that they passed the plots on to their children, to another black family, or failing this, back to the Nedeed family itself. The integrity of the "blackness" of Linden Hills thus assured, the Nedeeds set out to create a showcase black community, one that would succeed on white terms, that would be "a wad of spit—a beautiful, black wad of spit right in the white eye of America." To show up the white racists who had attempted to force the blacks out of Linden Hills and take over the now-valuable land, Nedeed had to create "a jewel—an ebony jewel that reflected the soul of Wayne County but reflected it black." Nedeed thus founded the Tupelo Realty Corporation and began financing and building private developments in Linden Hills, as well as carefully selecting who would live in them. Only those who were willing to forget the "black" past of slavery and failure and to buy into the vision of a "black" material progress could be a part of Linden Hills; everyone else was either forced out by Nedeed or denied a mortgage by the Tupelo Realty Corporation. Linden Hills thus has become a model black success story: "making it into Linden Hills meant 'making it'"; blacks everywhere send in applications to Nedeed's real estate office, hoping for the chance to move to one of the curved drives with the possibility of one day moving down the hill toward Nedeed's house and the most exclusive properties on Tupelo Drive.

Linden Hills thus appears to be a stable, highly demarcated, black space, with respect both to the internal division of space (and prestige) among its black inhabitants and to the surrounding "white" Wayne County. From the very beginning of the novel, however, this spatial/racial delimitation finds itself radically disrupted and put into question by a persistent dispute over boundaries. It seems that no one in Wayne County can agree on the exact location of Linden Hills, and that this dispute has raged among everyone associated with Wayne County ever since old Luther Nedeed began using the name "Linden Hills" for his land. At first, "Linden Hills" was always "elsewhere"; nobody would live in the shacks that Nedeed had built on Tupelo Drive, and the blacks living farther up the hill always insisted that they lived "*up* from Linden Hills." Likewise, the white farmer Putney Wayne denied any association with "Linden Hills": "That was coon town and he didn't have a blade of grass there; he was *across* from Linden Hills." Gradually, though, as time effected a reversal of values in Wayne County, making "Linden Hills" a desirable name and "Tupelo Drive" even more desirable, everyone in the county tried to lay claim to living in the *real* "Linden Hills" in order to differentiate themselves from everyone else in the county, both black *and* white. The Tupelo Drive residents insisted on keeping the name "Tupelo Drive" for their three roads, instead of renaming them as Crescent Drives as the city commissioner wanted to do. They also put up a bronze plaque at the entrance of Tupelo Drive with the words "LINDEN HILLS" engraved in Roman type, which caused the residents on First through Fifth Crescent drives to put up their own, wooden, "WELCOME TO LINDEN HILLS" sign behind the marble banister separating First Crescent Drive from the Putney Wayne neighborhood. The poor blacks in Putney Wayne were also addressing their mail "LINDEN HILLS," since Linden Road ran up the hill, crossed Wayne Avenue, and then continued on through their neighborhood, too. In any case, only blacks lived in both areas, so why shouldn't they be allowed to call their land "Linden Hills"? Even the whites living on the other side of the plateau could not resist telling outsiders that they too lived in "Linden Hills"—"the *real* Linden Hills."

What is fundamentally at stake here is the legitimacy of a particular conception of language and race that is disrupted by this instability of boundaries. The five generations of Luther Nedeeds all try to establish and maintain Linden Hills as a space of absolute difference, of absolute blackness. In attempting simply to reverse the poles of the black/white binary opposition by valorizing "black" instead of "white," the Nedeeds remain within the same problematic as the white racists they are supposedly defying, for they both continue to naturalize and essentialize the rhetorical figure of race. "Linden Hills" vs. "the outside" is purely a trope, a linguistic construct emblematizing the racial trope of "black" vs. "white." The novel subverts a naturalized, essentialized understanding of such linguistic oppositions not through an erasure of these differences, but rather by evidencing the complicated historical interaction of the terms of the oppositions. The age-old boundary dispute thus serves first and foremost to suspend the certainty of reference of the terms "Linden Hills," "Wayne County," "black," and "white" and to inscribe them as unstable differential terms in a complex, dynamic history of signification, rather than as essential names eternally linked with some unchanging, natural reality. It is precisely this historical dimension that the five generations of Nedeeds attempt to suppress, thus transforming Linden Hills into a profoundly dislocated and dislocating space.

The logic of the Nedeeds is one of unchanging essences, stable significations, and the absolute suppression of all internal, contestatory forces. The Nedeeds conceived of Linden Hills as a timeless space outside of history, or rather, as the space of a family history the Nedeeds would make, which would speak of black achievement. "You step outside Linden Hills and you've stepped into history," that is, into the history of black suffering and "failure," as those in Linden Hills see it. The Nedeed history of Linden Hills is a timeless anti-history where little changes. All the Nedeed patriarchs are named Luther, and all have the exact same dark black face, giving the Nedeed clan an aura of permanent, essential, black authority over the community. They give out leases of a thousand years and a day, a period so long as to be virtually an eternity. All of the roads of Linden Hills come from nowhere and lead nowhere, except to/from Nedeed's house at the bottom of the hill, suggesting a space without past or future, where Nedeed acts as the master of signification and guarantor of meaning. It is not surprising, then, that the Nedeeds so thoroughly embrace the process of commodification, for the logic of commodity capitalism dovetails neatly with the logic of Linden Hills.

The commodity by its very form conceals its own past.[1] With the production and exchange of commodities, that is, of anything that is produced for exchange, labor appears as an objective property of its own products: as their value. The individual producers of commodities enter into real social relations with each other, but these only take the form of the relationship between the values of their commodities on the market. The reality of social labor is thus concealed behind the values of commodities, while human relations, properties, and actions are transformed by the commodity form into the relations, properties, and actions of human-produced things. This process of commodity fetishism, or reification, causes the commodity to take on a "phantom objectivity": it appears as an essential object with an inherent, natural value, strictly following only the rationality of the market and revealing no trace of its fundamental nature as a relation between people. The individual producer's labor is abstracted into the exchange value of the commodity and thus becomes alienated from him or her as the seemingly natural value of the object; as pure exchange value, playing the role of general equivalent among commodity values, money emerges as the most fetishized commodity. Such fetishism is at work whenever capital is seen as a source of profit, for the category of capital obscures the productive potentialities of social labor that it commands and from which it extracts surplus value. Capital thus presents the mystifying appearance of an ability to produce interest or profit as an inherent quality, concealing by its very form and function the links with its past, that is, with the human labor that created it and makes it "grow."

In Linden Hills, the Nedeeds are the prime exploiters and capital accumulators of the community. Their money comes from the rents extracted from the poor blacks originally living in Linden Hills, and later from the mortgage payments to the Tupelo Realty Corporation. In addition, they also make money from burying the dead of Linden Hills. This undertaker's business, seen in the light of commodity fetishism, emerges as a powerful figure of the Nedeeds' exploitation of the Linden Hills community. The Nedeeds from the outset conceive of Linden Hills as a fetishized commodity from which they can make money—through rents and through burials. For them, it is the land that essentially appears to produce money and to have value: the second Luther Nedeed thinks of his father and sees "his words engraved in the scarred landscape of the county" as "the sun, the twentieth century, and the value of his hard, sod hill creep upward as slowly and concretely as the last laugh from a dead man's grave." The words of the father engraved on the land recalling the Nedeeds' essentializing conception of signification, the Nedeeds here effect a similar essentialization necessary for the process of fetishization. The burial business perfectly emblematizes this process, for the commodified land appears as the essential source of value and profit, while at the same time, the real producers of value—the people—are killed and concealed within the commodity in what must appear to the fetishizing sensibilities of the Nedeeds as a perverse form of "capital reinvestment."

Like the Nedeeds' essentializing understanding of the signifying binary oppositions that define the space of Linden Hills, their essentializing embrace of commodities also functions to suppress a certain historical dimension. As remarked above, the Nedeeds attempt to impose a pure, black space apart from history, outside of the tradition of "black failure," but also outside of the concrete, historical reality of the black/white opposition as a dynamic signifying practice. The Nedeeds are concerned most of all with the accumulation of money, that memoryless commodity of commodities, which allows them to forget about where the money came from and to build their vision of a community of "black" material progress: "Luther Nedeed didn't care where Linden Hills thought he had gotten his money, but he spent several years deciding where it should go." Nedeed carefully weeds out those "who had rooted themselves in the beliefs that Africa could be more than a word; slavery hadn't run its course; there was salvation in Jesus and salve in the blues," in short, those "who would dream of a true black power that spread beyond the Nedeeds." In place of this dangerous black heritage of "failure" the Nedeeds impose a (pseudo-) history of "black" material success, which is supposed to constitute "a community for their children to be proud of," so that "when they needed to journey back, it would be to the brick and marble" of Linden Hills. This vision of a successful, pure "black" space once again finds its essentialist illusions subverted, however. The "history" of Linden Hills does not constitute a sustaining black heritage of success, but rather an alienated and alienating process of advancing commodification. As the fifth and last Luther Nedeed realizes, something has gone wrong with the vision; Linden Hills has turned out to be a dislocated, alienated space of empty, rootless people, constantly moving down the hill, who finally aren't left with "enough humanity . . . to fill the rooms of a real home": "The shining surface of their careers, brass railings, and cars hurt his eyes because it only reflected the bright nothing that was inside of them."

What is worse, though, from Nedeed's point of view, is that the commodification process that seemed so compatible in its premises and its goals with his dream of a successful, pure black space has now turned out to undermine the absolute "blackness" of Linden Hills. "Linden Hills wasn't black; it was successful," muses Nedeed. Indeed, the commodification process ends up not fortifying a pure black space but rather revealing that the illusion of a pure, essential black can only be maintained by suppressing "external" white elements found within its borders, not by simply setting up a fixed boundary separating "black" from "white." The boundary dispute, which subverts an essential blackness or whiteness by undermining reference and revealing the unstable signifying history of the differential terms "black" and "white," also reveals that "black" and "white" as a signifying pair are deferred and displaced onto each other. This functioning of these two signifiers subverts any possibility of a pure "black" or "white" by undermining the crucial internal/external opposition, for "Linden Hills" and "Wayne County," as the emblematic terms of the black/white opposition, are tangled in a problematic relationship where "Linden Hills" is a part of "Wayne County" as well as being apart from it, and vice versa. The illusion of an essential black space can thus only be maintained by suppressing the specter of this internal white other, a task for which the Nedeeds marshal all the resources of the commodity culture that they adopt. In particular, the Nedeeds link the black/white opposition to the repressive potency of the producer/exploiter opposition and superimpose them most effectively on the male/female opposition in order to smother and conceal this internal whiteness.

The Nedeed wives are pale-skinned octoroon women completely subordinate to their dark-skinned husbands. Each is known only as "Mrs. Nedeed," thus maintaining at the level of the name the Nedeeds' appearance as an unchanging, essentially black ground of signification for the community. They are producers of both food and future Luther Nedeeds, but caught up in the essentializing logic of commodities, these products are taken and alienated from them by their husbands, who remain blind to the mother/producer's role and claim their sons as their own, as Nedeeds, as incarnations of essential blackness. Indeed, the original Luther Nedeed reputedly sold his octoroon wife and six children to get the money to move North and buy the land for Linden Hills, the very founding of the community thus based on the commodifying exchange of his pale wife and children for money that bears no traces of its sordid history. The original Luther Nedeed later takes on another octoroon bride, whom he buys out of slavery, but as we later learn, he never manumits her and in fact keeps her as his own, legal slave.

What is becoming clear is that by adopting the producer/exploiter opposition and using it forcefully to assure the blackness of Linden Hills, the Nedeeds and the community they control are paradoxically becoming more and more white beneath an increasingly thinner facade of blackness. To support their ethic of a new black space of material progress, the Nedeeds increasingly imitate the repressive technique of the exploiting white racists they are supposedly defying. Besides the slave-trading incident above, they also run guns to the confederacy for money during the Civil War and crush or commodify beyond recognition any elements of the "dangerous" black heritage, such as the word "Tupelo," which, as the name of the city where Nedeed sold his wife and children and later took his new bride into a new slavery, finds itself appropriated as the name for Nedeed's exploitative realty agency and for the most exclusive section of Linden Hills. Eventually, Nedeed even joins forces with the racist Wayne County Citizens' Alliance to stop the construction of government subsidized low-income housing in Putney Wayne, which would house mostly poor blacks and would also lower the property values in Linden Hills. The fifth Luther Nedeed realizes that the black space of Linden Hills has been compromised somehow, for "Wayne County had watched his wedge of earth become practically invisible—indistinguishable from their own pathetic souls," and it has been living in peace with Linden Hills for the past twenty years.

Linden Hills has thus reached the point where what is "black" is really only a thinly disguised/displaced/deferred "white." Even the name "Linden Hills" only defers and displaces the other name for the linden tree—the lime tree, which recalls the white lime tombstones in the town cemetery that cuts through Linden Hills. The "last laugh from a dead man's grave" thus takes on a new, ominous, mocking meaning for Luther Nedeed, for both blacks *and* whites are promiscuously buried together in that cemetery, the very land betraying his essential black space as its repressed past comes back tainted white. The survival of the community now depends on Nedeed cynically struggling to assert a mastery of signification, of boundaries, of women in order to maintain the facade of blackness, but the boundaries have somehow already broken down, and whiteness has insidiously, "treacherously" entered the community. Nedeed himself completes the revelation of the Linden Hills hypocrisy by breaking with his fathers and marrying not an octoroon woman but rather a darker-skinned woman, whom he nevertheless treats just as tyrannically as his fathers treated their pale wives. His wife, however, gives him a son who looks just like him, but it turns out to be white, "a ghostly presence that mocked everything his fathers had built." The internal/external opposition and the commodity fetishism of the Nedeeds both come undone, as the supposedly "excluded," alienated whiteness of the Nedeed wives finally returns to challenge the basic premises of Linden Hills. This whiteness returns through Luther and his fathers, whom the Nedeed wives are finally claiming as their own creations, thus challenging the fetishizing understanding the Nedeeds have of themselves as essential, autonomous, inherently black individuals. Luther, however, refuses to recognize this possibility and blindly struggles to reassert the old essentialized dichotomies, claiming that the child cannot be his and that his wife must have betrayed him. He forces them both down into the old morgue in the basement of the house and locks them in, scapegoating his wife for the insurgent whiteness of the community and hoping to eliminate it by burying it with her and her son in a desperate, forceful reaffirming gesture of fetishism that recalls the functioning of Nedeed's undertaker's business examined above.

The assault on the foundations of Linden Hills is already too far advanced, however; the repressed margins—women, producers, a true black historical consciousness—reemerge during the six days before Christmas that constitute the balance of the novel in order to bring down the edifice of Linden Hills by revealing its untenable contradictions. During these six days, a poor young black poet named Willie Mason journeys down Linden Hills with his friend, Lester Tilson, doing odd jobs for the residents in order to make some money for Christmas presents. The two, like Dante and Virgil, move down the circular drives one by one and witness the profound alienation, rootlessness, and displaced blackness of this modern-day inferno.[2]

Willie represents the ideal figure for exposing and subverting the essentialist illusions of the community as they are manifested in the boundary and signification problems, the ravages of commodification, and the suppression of women. He is a liminal figure, living on Wayne Avenue, the problematic boundary between Linden Hills and Putney Wayne, which as a neighborhood of poor blacks represents the heritage of black "failure" from which the Nedeeds want to distinguish themselves. He is also twenty years old, no longer a boy but not yet a man. His name takes on particular importance for the signification problems associated with naming, for he has been given the nickname "White" because he is "so black that the kids said if he turned just a shade darker, there was nothing he could do but start going the other way." His nickname thus appears as a figure of linguistic disjunction, blocking any essential, natural conception of names, because it suspends its "normal" referential function and points back toward itself as language with the power of constructing or instituting difference, rather than simply reporting an essential pre-existing difference. In the same way, his last name, "Mason," defers and displaces its binary opposite, for Willie eventually helps to *destroy* the bases of Linden Hills. In addition, Willie in a certain sense appears on the borderline between masculine and feminine; he is defensive and somewhat secretive about his poetry because it seems "queer" and makes him look like a "sissy," and he usually lies about having wrapped his own presents because it looks "like something a woman would do." Later on, when thinking about Nedeed's wife and Linden Hills, and his ominous sense of foreboding, he thinks to himself, "Christ, now he really was turning into a woman—he sounded like somebody's superstitious old aunt." Finally, Willie is a producer—both a worker in Linden Hills and a composer of poems who memorizes them all and refuses to write them down. He thus avoids a certain alienation from his poetic creations, refusing to part with them and run the risk of a certain commodification, while at the same time, he incarnates an oral black literary tradition linked with the authentic black heritage that Nedeed wants to suppress.

Willie's passage through Linden Hills takes on the dimensions of the trajectory of a search for a name—the name of Luther Nedeed's wife. This name has the potential to subvert the Nedeed clan because it would introduce an internal pole of difference that would undermine the full, essential presence and blackness of the name "Nedeed." As Willie makes his way down the hill with Lester, becoming increasingly obsessed with the mystery surrounding this strangely absent name, Nedeed's wife proceeds on a journey of her own toward this name, unearthing the personal effects of the past Nedeed wives, which were stored away and forgotten in the basement morgue where she is now a prisoner. One by one, she discovers the name and history of each of these women through a bible, a set of cookbooks, and a family photo album, constituting in sum a history of despair and madness, of a gradual loss of identity for each wife. Nedeed's wife resurrects this buried history, though, and turns it against the Nedeed men. The history of "failure" of these marginalized octoroon women reveals the names of the past wives—Luwana Packerville, Evelyn Creton, and Priscilla McGuire—and thus introduces a resurgent element of difference, both between each Luther Nedeed and his wife and between each Luther Nedeed and the other Luther Nedeeds. This formerly suppressed history of signification of the name "Luther Nedeed" in a differential relationship with the names of the Nedeed wives and the other "Luther Nedeeds" constitutes a sort of "internal" counterpart to the threat to Linden Hills posed by the problems raised by the "external" boundary dispute, understood as a problematic history of signification.

Willie, too, discovers a history of black "failure" associated with the absence of names. The homosexual relationship between David and Winston, two young black men in Linden Hills, is broken up by Nedeed, who forces Winston to marry by threatening anonymously to ruin his career at his prestigious law firm by revealing his homosexuality. As Winston points out, the lack of a name for their relationship undercuts its ability to survive: "'Don't you see what I'm up against? How am I going to live with you when they haven't even made up the right words for what we are to each other?'" Likewise, the "successful" corporate executive, Laurel Dumont, eventually commits suicide in despair over the emptiness of her life because she can't find that place "they ain't got no name for yet, where you supposed to be at home," as her grandmother, Roberta Johnson tells her. Most importantly, Luther Nedeed's white son remains without a name for the first five years of his life, and eventually dies in the basement morgue, as Nedeed had hoped. This white son had presented Nedeed with an insoluble quandary, because to name him "Luther Nedeed" and accept him as his own would be virtually to contradict the very premises on which the Nedeed family and Linden Hills were constructed, while any other name would introduce an intolerable element of difference into the family history. Nedeed thus had no choice but to bury him along with the damning evidence of his white face as the "treacherous" products of his wife's alleged adultery, in order to make a last, desperate attempt to maintain the illusion of an internal black purity.

Nevertheless, the deferral and displacement of the signifying pairs "black"/"white" and "Linden Hills"/"Wayne County," which undermine the internal/external opposition, proliferate throughout the novel in the guise of disruptive, contestatory "external" elements within supposedly pure entities, which can no longer contain and suppress their internal "others." Lester's grandmother, Mamie Tilson, who stands up to Luther Nedeed and refuses to let him coerce her off her land in Linden Hills, is described as "that one flaw" that Nedeed will bury "deep in the middle of his jewel" so that "no one would know the difference." "Somewhere inside of her must be a deep flaw or she wouldn't have been capable of such treachery," Nedeed thinks about his wife, who along with her white son constitutes the disruptive flaw in the Nedeed family. On the rhetorical level, the narration of *Linden Hills* makes extensive use of free indirect discourse, which is basically the rendering of the thoughts and feelings of characters in the voice of the narrator. This type of narration presents itself as an internally dialogized form, where the boundaries between the "autonomous" narrator and characters break down; a single set of words becomes a scene of struggle where the narrator can confront and argue with the perspectives of the characters, and vice versa, producing varying degrees of irony and parody. In *Linden Hills*, the use of free indirect discourse undermines any "pure black" or "pure white" narration, since the discourse of both blacks and whites is presented this way, and it also dispels any notion of an objective, totalizing historical narrative that would remain distant and disinterested from the facts that it would simply report. Finally, the story of Luther's wife discovering the identities of the past Mrs. Nedeeds as well as her own identity in the basement morgue is isolated typographically in a different typeface from the rest of the novel, constituting a rupturing text that interpolates itself periodically into the body of the main text, further undermining any concept of a pure, unified, masterful narrative of Linden Hills.

The poetry Willie has memorized constitutes one more disturbing "external" element inside Linden Hills. At Winston's wedding reception, David as best man reads the Whitman poem ("Whoever you are, holding me now in hand"), revealing for Willie the relationship between Winston and David and the hypocrisy of the wedding. Likewise, at a wake for Lycentia Parker, Willie recalls to himself the words of the Wallace Stevens poem "Cuisine Bourgeoise," which gives meaning for him to the scene of hypocritical mourning and mindless commodity consumption that he witnesses unseen from upstairs in the Parker house. The food the mourners eat is metonymically linked with the Nedeed wives, who produce food as one of their prime activities. The mindless consumption of the food as a fetishized commodity represents in a certain sense the devouring of the Nedeed wives and emblematizes the futile attempt to bury and exclude their whiteness, which the mourners accomplish by paradoxically reincorporating that whiteness into themselves as food and thereby unwittingly subverting the internal/external and black/white oppositions. Willie glimpses the meaning of this scene through a process of involuntary memory triggered by it, which brings back to him the line of "Cuisine Bourgeoise": "These days of disinheritance, we feast on human heads. . . ." Likewise, at the home of the Linden Hills historian, Daniel

Braithwaite, after Laurel Dumont's suicide, Willie undermines his amoral, totalizing historical project by recalling to himself the T. S. Eliot poem "Gerontion," and in particular, the line "After such knowledge, what forgiveness?" All three of these poems appear in italics, set off from the main body of the text, and rupturing it in the same way that the narrative of Luther's wife does.

The last poem in the novel is one that Willie is trying to compose to make sense of his Linden Hills experiences. Having memorized 665 poems to date, this one will be number 666, the biblical sign of the beast, and thus promises to make sense of the inverted inferno of Luther Nedeed, who lives in house number 999. Willie's path of understanding here recalls that of Luwana Packerville, the first Mrs. Nedeed, who, having made 665 cuts on her body to represent the times she has been called on to speak over the course of a year, records as the next entry in her bible/diary, "There can be no God." After much anguish, Willie finally arrives at the first line of his poem, "There is a man in a house at the bottom of a hill. And his wife has no name," and immediately triggers in the narrative of Luther's wife the discovery of her own name and identity as the last in a line of Mrs. Nedeeds: Willa Prescott Nedeed. This name constitutes the final blow to the reign of the Nedeeds, both through its disruptive power within the line of Luther Nedeeds and through its articulation at the level of the signifier ("Willa"—"Willie") with the disruptive powers associated with Willie. Willa reasserts her identity and image and seizes the power of naming from Luther by naming their son "Sinclair" just before she emerges from the basement on Christmas Eve. This name signifies both the "clear sin" of the boy's color and its suppressed etymological meaning of "sinus clarus," where "sinus" can mean in Latin "the interior, inmost part, heart, or bosom," in short, that place "where you supposed to be at home," which Laurel fails to find but Willa recovers.

Thus Willie finds himself with Lester on Christmas Eve at Nedeed's house to help Nedeed trim his tree for pay, having made the entire journey through Linden Hills toward the name of Nedeed's wife. In a melodramatic twist, Willie accidentally knocks open the bolt to the cellar door just as Willa is heading up the cellar steps, and unwittingly triggers the final collapse of the Nedeed family and Linden Hills. Carrying the body of the dead Sinclair wrapped in an old lace bridal veil, Willa forcefully emerges to begin cleaning the house and to reclaim her legitimate role within the Nedeed family. As Willie, Lester, and Nedeed finish trimming the tree in the den, Willa appears in the doorway and announces, "Luther, . . . your son is dead," returning from her underground grave to confront Nedeed with *his* white son and the insoluble contradictions of Linden Hills and the Nedeed family as the last laugh from a dead *woman's* grave. In the struggle that ensues, the Christmas tree crashes to the floor, its lighted candles setting the house on fire as Lester forces

Willie to flee the scene. The burning house sheds light over all of Linden Hills, revealing the resurgent whiteness at the very foundation of the community, as Willie and Lester realize that this scene taking place before their eyes is no longer "governed by the rules of . . . black and white." The house burns to the ground with the Nedeeds embraced in a single struggling mass inside, while the entire community watches it and lets it burn, denying the very evidence before their eyes—a final act of hypocrisy and suppression that is certainly the only possible response worthy of Luther Nedeed and his community.

Notes

1. The notion of commodity fetishism is first introduced by Marx in *Capital*, Vol. 1, Ch. 1, Section 4, "The Fetishism of Commodities and the Secret Thereof," and is later elaborated in Lukács, "The Phenomenon of Reification," pp. 83–110.
2. For an analysis of *Linden Hills* as a modern rewriting of Dante's *Inferno*, see Ward, "Gloria Naylor's *Linden Hills:* A Modern *Inferno*."

♦♦♦♦♦♦♦♦♦♦♦♦♦♦

The Woman in the Cave

MARGARET HOMANS

In Gloria Naylor's novel *Linden Hills*, a grim fantasy of wealthy black suburbia with open acknowledgments to Dante's *Inferno* as well as to a series of classical and Christian underworlds, a lower hell opens below the lowest circle Dante imagined: the former morgue in a basement where Luther Nedeed, the novel's Lucifer, imprisons his wife and their five-year-old son, without food or medicine, to "turn her into a wife": that is, to punish her for bearing a child who does not resemble his father as exactly as Nedeed himself replicates his forefathers. Attempting to efface his wife as three generations of previous Luther Nedeeds had effaced their wives, Nedeed embodies a crime neither considered nor punished by Dante: the crime of making (or attempting to make) women into disposable machines for replicating men. At the end of the novel, Willa Nedeed succeeds in giving miraculous birth to herself and to a revolutionary intention: "the amber germ of truth she went to sleep with [the truth that she does exist, that she has her own name, and that she can walk up out of the basement] conceived and reconceived itself, splitting and multiplying to take over every atom attached to her being."[1] Her son is already dead, and she too will die by the end of the novel, but Willa Nedeed's story of resistance and rebirth resonates not only with classical and later Western accounts of the successful effacement of women but also with feminist critiques of and resistance to such effacement. This essay will read *Linden Hills* together with Luce Irigaray's *Speculum of the Other Woman*, a work of political and cultural theory that relies on the conventions of fiction to critique androcentric myths of reproduction such as that of Plato's cave and to reconceive such myths in a way that illuminates and is illuminated by Naylor's vision. Both Irigaray and Naylor are centrally preoccupied with their relation to a predominantly male literary and philosophical heritage, a line whose members have been as concerned as Luther Nedeed to maintain patrilineal continuities. And both Irigaray and Naylor tell the story not told by Plato, Virgil, or Dante, the story of the woman in the cave.

It has been noted often how many of the *topoi*, plots, and traditions of the European literary canon depend upon and perpetuate the exclusion of women and especially of mothers, both literally, in the exclusion of most writing by women, and figuratively, in the construction of an androcentric epistemology. From Genesis and *Paradise Lost* to *Frankenstein* and *The Double Helix*, as Christine Froula and Mary Jacobus have argued, heterosexual procreation and maternity are replaced by the asexual reproduction of fathers on their own.[2] Characteristically, this substitution turns on the privileging of the disembodied over the bodily, in terms both of the product and the mode of production. In recent years, the substitution of male for female models of creation has extended to works of criticism and theory—even to works of this kind that subscribe to feminist goals. Tania Modleski writes that, for Jonathan Culler, "each stage of feminist criticism renders increasingly problematic the idea of 'women's experience.' By calling this notion into question, Culler manages to clear a space for male feminist interpretations of literary texts," by substituting, as the subject of feminist criticism, for the category of experience—the woman reader—the "'hypothesis'" of the man reading as a woman. She cites Culler's citing of Freud's idea, in *Moses and Monotheism*, that patriarchy relies on the privileging of the hypothetical over the sensible, which is to say paternity over maternity, and then she applies Culler's critique of this notion to Culler himself: "If the privileging of the hypothetical and the invisible is indeed related to a patriarchal world view, then it follows that Culler himself is being patriarchal just at the point when he seems to be most feminist—when he arrogates to himself and to other male critics the ability to read as women by 'hypothesizing' women readers."[3]

It is clear enough, in these instances, to see where the problem lies, but proposing a workable alternative is often more difficult. Feminist criticism works to critique the androcentric erasure of women, and yet, as Modleski is aware, simply reversing the process to reinstitute "woman" as experiential subject is too simple an answer, because, as Peggy Kamuf points out, such a project may "remain caught as a reflection of the same form of nineteenth-century humanism from which we have inherited our pervasively androcentric modes of thought,"[4] and because the women whose stories could be revived were, after all, women whose lives were constructed within patriarchy, their creativity limited, for example, to maternity. Naylor's and Irigaray's narratives of the woman in the cave are driven by their critiques of the canonical erasure of women. But at the same time, both authors are sensitive to the possible limitations of simply reinscribing the story of the lost or effaced woman. Neither claims to have access to essential or prediscursive "woman": although each tells a story covered up by the male fictions she follows, and although the story of the woman in the cave told from her point of view differs from the indications of that story in the classical authors, that woman is clearly from the start a construction of androcentric culture. These works, then, perform two important tasks: they imagine the restoration and revaluation of lost women's experiences; at the same time, by tracing with such rigorous honesty the narratives of these restorations, they explore not only the powers but also the limits of feminist revisionism.

* * *

One instance of the canonical replacement of female by male creation, of the kind that provides the starting point for both Naylor and Irigaray, emerges in Virgil's *Aeneid*, beginning with the death of Aeneas's wife Creusa. As he escapes the burning ruins of Troy, Aeneas has Creusa "follow at a distance" while the future founder of Rome carries his father Anchises on his shoulders and takes his son by the hand. When Anchises orders his son to run, Creusa gets lost and dies.[5] That her death is the result of semideliberate collaboration between father and son is suggested by the fact that her death is necessary both for the founding of Rome and for the motivation of the poem. Aeneas must be unmarried in order that his quest can be figured as a quest for a new wife. And as M. Owen Lee points out, "Creusa cannot be a part of the group that is mean to symbolize *pietas*": *pius*, Aeneas's most important epithet, can apply only to a man's relation to his father, his son, his gods, and his civilization, not to his marriage.[6] Moreover, Virgil chooses the moment of Creusa's death to signal his patrilineal literary inheritance, by replicating, in his account of Aeneas's meeting with Creusa's ghost, Homer's description of the ghost of Odysseus's mother Antikleia:

> Three times
> I tried to throw my arms around her neck;
> three times the Shade I grasped in vain escaped
> my hands—like fleet winds, most like a winged dream.[7]

Intangible through death, the ghosts of two mothers enable the spiritual embrace of two male artists.

These ghosts provide profoundly sad and even textually disturbing encounters for their heroes. Creusa's ghost, though she teaches Aeneas to go on without her, brings Book II to its close, as if temporarily arresting the will to go forward. More strikingly, Antikleia threatens to end prematurely Odysseus's narrative of his adventures. His visit to the land of the dead, as he narrates it in Book XI, begins with the curious detail that, although he sees his mother's ghost right away, he must keep her at a distance until he has first received from the ghost of Tiresias directions for his future. When he does speak with her in the scene that includes their failed embrace, her effect is nearly to derail the up to then unstoppable machine of Odysseus's narrative. The memory of this meeting leads to the catalogue of the ghosts of famous women—his mother puts strong women on his mind, so to speak—which seems to halt his narrative impulse: "'But how name all the women I beheld there, / daughters and wives of kings?' . . . Then he fell silent."

What is so disturbing about these ghostly women, both to the hero and to the very procedure of the narrative? Whatever it is, it does not trouble the third appearance of these lines, in Aeneas's meeting with the ghost of his father in the underworld in Book VI:

> Three times
> he tried to throw his arms around Anchises'
> neck; and three times the Shade escaped from that
> vain clasp—like light winds, or most like swift dreams.

Though *pius* Aeneas sheds the requisite tears at this encounter, the failed embrace leads to an assurance of spiritual presence that more than compensates for the absence of the father's body. Anchises is at his best as a spirit: a drag on the plot while alive, in Elysium he is an expansive host and a virtuosic tour guide. While an immaterial mother is a troubling contradiction in terms, spirit is the appropriate condition of fathers. Rather than arresting the onward flow of narrative, as the ghosts of the women do, the failure to embrace Anchises' ghost leads directly to what Aeneas has descended to see. Immediately following this passage, over his father's ghostly shoulder "Aeneas . . . can see" Virgil's assembly line for reincarnation, the mechanism for turning old souls into new beings, the hero's assurance that the future, and especially the successive generations of his sons, will come to pass.

As Anchises describes the machinery of metempsychosis, he aligns the good with the immaterial and the bad with the body in such a way as to confirm the prestige of a ghostly father:

> Fiery energy
> is in these seeds, their source is heavenly;
> but they are dulled by harmful bodies, blunted
> by their own earthly limbs.

Suffering through the "cycle of the ages . . . annuls the ancient stain / and leaves the power of ether pure in us." After that the shades are given new bodies, but that part of the story is elided. This is how the reproduction not only of men but of patriarchy works. In place of the bodily contact of mothers and fathers, this myth of creation exhibits a son and his disembodied father (like Adam and God) watching from a distance as a reproduction machine does its antiseptic work, without the help of any mothers or any bodies.[8]

After demonstrating the process of reincarnation, Anchises proudly shows Aeneas the souls of future Romans. As such names as Silvius Aeneas and Julius Caesar (after Aeneas's son Iulus) suggest, Aeneas can, like Luther Nedeed, expect to be replicated in his descendants.[9] This tour ends on a somber note, however, with a glimpse of Marcellus, the nephew of the sonless Augustus and a young man of extraordinary promise who was to have been his uncle's heir and successor, had he not died at twenty. Indeed, the poem returns obsessively to tales and images of sons who die before their fathers, often in their presence: Priam and Polites, Daedalus and Icarus, Mezentius and Lausus, Evander and Pallas, and Aeneas's fear of harm to Iulus. Such fears are inevitable in a poem pivoting on a myth of reproduction that embodies so fundamental a lie: an exclusively spiritual theory of reproduction, one that represses the mother's part and holds that reproduction can go on without her body. The anxiety that there may be no way to generate more sons is the price paid for killing off all the mothers.

Finding Anchises as a ghost makes explicit the positive implications of negating Creusa, establishing the priority of spiritual over material creation. The scene of Creusa's ghost leads us to think that Lavinia will be her bodied equivalent, but the scene with Anchises' ghost assures us that Lavinia too is merely part of the replication machine: the future has already been determined spiritually, where it counts, before Lavinia comes so tenuously on the scene. Where do women come from, anyway? Though Aeneas meets Dido and other women in less prestigious parts of the underworld, none of the refurbished souls in Elysium is a woman's.

The underworld in the *Aeneid*, like the land of the dead in the *Odyssey*, is regulated by Minos, who had the labyrinth built to contain the Minotaur and whose story is mentioned, in the context of the story of Daedalus and Icarus, at the start of Book VI. Minos makes a fitting ruler for the *Aeneid*'s male-run replica machine, for his labyrinth makes explicit certain aspects of the Virgilian underworld. An artificial underground cavern that is also a world of death, Minos's labyrinth betrays the fears of female sexuality, the repression of which seems to motivate the underworld machinery of the *Aeneid*. Into the labyrinth goes the Minotaur, the monstrous child who shows us what lawgivers think of such lawless female lusts as his mother Pasiphaë's, and out of it come Theseus and Ariadne, a perfectly male-dominated couple that restores the hierarchy Pasiphaë disturbs. (Just like Creusa, Ariadne will be left behind to die.)

The story of the Minotaur's adulterous, bestial origin appears, however, to be a cover story, concealing Minos's fear of his own sexuality by blaming it on his wife, by calling her desires bestial. Minos could very well be the Minotaur's father, and the bull genes his own, since Minos's parents were Europa and Zeus in the guise of a bull. And the myth begins with an overt displacement of male guilt that betrays the insistence of Minos's bullish origins. The beautiful bull had been sent by Poseidon to Minos for Minos to sacrifice; Minos's (narcissistic?) desire to keep the bull instead led Poseidon to punish Minos by imposing on Pasiphaë her monstrous lust. The story that the Minotaur was fathered not by Minos but by an actual bull may exist to explain male fears not only of sexuality but also of the distinctive feature of sexual reproduction: the unpredictability of the result. The Minotaur's hybrid body—half human, half bull—provides undeniable proof that mother and father, two sets of genes, contribute to the new being. While the souls of the future sons of Rome replicate Aeneas's piety and heroism, and for now show no trace of female bodily taint, the Minotaur, with his irreducible bodiliness and his insatiable maw, the inverse of those pious sons, betrays the doubleness and the physicality of his beginnings. He resembles his mother and his father, but above all he is something new. While the main feature of the descendants of Aeneas is their predictability and their predetermination, the Minotaur is a sport, that which is repressed in those ghostly sons of Rome.[10]

This unpredictability is exactly what Luther Nedeed abhors in the son he rejects and locks up underground. The child has "the same squat bowlegs, the same protruding eyes and puffed lips" as his father and three generations of fathers before him, but in color he resembles neither his mother nor his father: he is "a white son . . . a ghostly presence that mocked everything his fathers had built." Just as bad, the child also resembles his mother's mother. Up to the present, each Mrs. Nedeed has been a mere carrier for the next Luther, her own contribution rigorously excluded from the result: "It seemed that when old Luther died in 1879, he hadn't died at all, especially when they spoke to his son and especially when they glanced at those puffed eyelids and around those bottomless eyes"; by the third generation "it surprised no one when the baby was male and had the father's complexion, protruding eyes, and first name— by now it had come to be expected." But Willa's child, the fourth generation, is not an exact duplicate but a new creation. Concluding that his wife is guilty of adultery (much as Minos concludes about Pasiphaë), Nedeed punishes both mother and son by imprisoning them in a location equivalent to that of Virgil's underworld, until she learns its art of perfect duplication.

The basement makes a promising scene for the reformation of Mrs. Nedeed into a replication machine, because it was originally the first Luther Nedeed's morgue. In that room are the remnants of actual machinery, chemicals, and cosmetics for, in a literalizing parody of Virgil's underworld, turning the dead into renewed images of themselves. The room also literalizes the Virgilian repression of mothers, for stacked in it, dusty and ignored, are trunks full of the memorabilia of generations of Mrs. Nedeeds, waiting to be discovered by Willa. In his own morgue, the present Luther Nedeed takes pleasure in forming a human being to fit his desire: "With the proper touch, you could work miracles. . . . it took gentleness and care to turn what was under your hands into a woman." Like Frankenstein in the movie version (and, more remotely, like Milton's God), Nedeed makes people in his laboratory with the help only of a male assistant, substituting the art of two men for natural maternity. Nedeed hideously parodies this patrilineal art when, by subjecting his son to the renovated old embalming room, he perfects his son to death. Already a "ghostly presence" because of his pale skin, the boy in dying enacts the Virgilian fear that comes from the repressed knowledge that paternal self-duplication is impossible. Refusal to acknowledge the mother's part means that fathers reproducing alone produce only ghosts. The boy is, curiously, both a hybrid, like the Minotaur, proof of the mother's participation, and a ghost, a representation of the consequences of trying to repress the mother.

The basement morgue is carved out below and subtends another and larger underworld that is likewise a sort of replica machine. The fortune and real estate holdings that make the reproduction of an heir so urgent ("there must always be Nedeeds") were built on the first Nedeed's undertaking business, and each successive Nedeed has been a king of the dead, embalming his former tenants and burying them in the cemetery next to his house. Pointing down toward that end are the three steep slopes of Linden Hills, the Dantean pit where the Nedeeds have built a series of palatial houses that they lease (not sell) to wealthy blacks. The streets are "eight curving circular drives," corresponding roughly to Dante's circles of hell.[11] Like Dante's hell, Linden Hills contains Virgilian features: the first place the two poet-protagonists stop on their descent, the home of one of them (Lester, the Virgil character), is decorated all in green, recalling the green pastorals in Virgil and in Dante where the ancient poets live; and the lowest part, Tupelo Drive, is entered through brick pillars that correspond to the walls around Dis in Virgil and in Dante. There are also some purely Dantean features, such as the steepness of the topography ("the hill seemed to slope for about three hundred feet and then fall into an abyss"), which makes it "almost impossible to turn around once you enter Tupelo Drive." The figure of Luther next to a lake of ice at the very bottom is a parody and inversion of God very like Dante's Lucifer, with whom Nedeed shares the negativity, darkness, and circumscription of his world: having built his cabin, the first Nedeed "sat there every day for exactly seven days—his thick, puffed lids raising, lowering, and narrowing over eyes that seemed to be measuring precisely the depth and length of light that the sun allowed his wedge of their world." And it is a Beatrice figure, the poets' friend Ruth Anderson, who proposes their descent (to earn money for Christmas by doing odd jobs) and sends them aid at crucial points; Willie, the Dante figure, "was just sorry that she hadn't asked him to go into hell for her so he could really prove himself."

Like Dante's hell, Linden Hills is an inverted world: as Lester remarks, "up means down in the Hills." With the evil Nedeed himself living at the very bottom, the embodiment of black wealth, power, and success, the aspiration of all who move into the upper circles of the neighborhood is to move into a house lower down. The closer down to Nedeed people live, the more soulless and spiritually dead they are, till they literalize that condition in Nedeed's mortuary and graveyard. The neighborhood as a whole has become a machine for turning out phantoms, with Nedeed turning the crank. During the six days of de-creation covered by the present time of the novel, Nedeed presides over a funeral, provokes and then silently observes one suicide, and arranges the soul-destroying marriage of a homosexual man whom he knows will end as another suicide. Moreover, recalling the conspicuous infertility of the *Aeneid*, the narrative details the childlessness, through accident or choice, of each family or individual in Linden Hills.

Although in the *Aeneid* the purified souls travel upwards, eventually to gain new bodies, seemingly the inverse of Naylor's Dantean vision of bodies traveling downward, losing their souls, the pessimistic tone that ends Anchises' tour of the future sons of Rome is akin to the mood of Naylor's tale, and the very end of Virgil's Book VI confirms that pessimism. There are two gates through which dreams leave the underworld, and Aeneas leaves by the gate of ivory, the gate for false dreams. Thereafter (as many have noted) Aeneas acts not as an individual but as an institution, since by the beginning of Book VII he has cast off all his personal ties: wife, father, lover, and finally his nurse. We might account for his surprising exit through the gate of false dreams by noting that Aeneas himself is now a phantom produced by the underworld, not bodiless but soulless, and not unlike the blacks at the bottom of Nedeed's pit.

No part of the Nedeeds' fantastic, inverted structure, their machine for separating body from soul, would be possible without the subordination of each successive Mrs. Nedeed—spirit, identity, and womb—to the patrilineal project. Were it not for the exact duplication of the first Luther Nedeed in four generations of his sons, the unity of ambition necessary for their gradual building of Linden Hills would have been diluted with other intentions. Moreover, slavery multiplies the condition of the wife: the novel suggests that what whites do to blacks, (some) black men have done to black women. The first Luther Nedeed "financed gunrunners to the Confederacy" and is said to have "sold his octoroon wife and six children for the money that he used to come North and obtain the hilly land." In the pages that separate one book of her Bible from another, the next Mrs. Nedeed, Luwana Packerville, records her discovery that she is still a slave: purchased by her husband, she thought, so as to be set free, she still literally belongs to him and will belong to her son after him. But most of the documents Willa discovers in the basement are a record simply of effacement and silencing. Gradually excluded from domestic life by her identical husband and son, the enslaved Mrs. Nedeed finally ceases to speak, carves the record of her silence into her skin, and, in the end, writes in her Bible, "There can be no God." The next Mrs. Nedeed, Evelyn Croton, tries to affirm her existence by baking and cooking vast quantities of food. Defeated, evidently, she starves and then poisons herself; her last grocery order is for vanilla ice cream and prussic acid. The last Mrs. Nedeed before Willa, Priscilla McGuire, leaves behind photographs recording her early happiness in herself and her child, yet in later photos a shadow covers and then obliterates her face: "She was no longer recording the growth of a child; the only thing growing in these pictures was her absence." The presence of absence is also a feature of the representation of Willa Nedeed: during her imprisonment Nedeed brings to a party a store-bought cake that gives the lie to his claim that his wife is at home, baking. Eating this cake is "tasting her absence."

An absence that is present, tangible, is a ghost: these enslaved women fuel the machine for making middle-class black people into phantoms, and then they themselves become part of the production. Plato's cave, too, is a machine for producing phantomlike replicas, and according to Irigaray's reading of it, this replication depends (as in Virgil and in Naylor's revisionary underworld) on the appropriation and repression of women's bodies.[12] But I shall begin not with Irigaray but with Derrida's reading of Plato's cave, as mediated through his reading of Mallarmé's *Mimique*, in the "Double Session" section of *Dissemination*, a work that predates Irigaray's discussion of Plato by four years and that both assists and is subject to her critique of Plato.

"Presence" denotes, for Derrida, that which deconstruction seeks tirelessly to show has never existed. Although he sometimes masculinizes this term, as when he identifies the target of deconstruction as "phallogocentrism," in *Dissemination* he calls presence a "mother-form [*forme-mère*]."[13] Through the ambiguous term *hymen*, which signifies both the bar to marriage and marriage, both desire and fulfillment, Mallarmé's *Mimique* purports to do away with that "mother-form" of presence, by doing away with the difference between present and future. A curious idea: the hymen does away with the mother. But it is no coincidence that presence is eliminated as a "mother-form," as is clear from the context: this demonstration emerges from discussion of a story about a man who kills his wife. *Mimique* is Mallarmé's reading of a book about a book about a mime performance by and about a Pierrot who murders his Columbine for what he views as her unfaithfulness with Harlequin, that is, her violation of his patriarchal authority over her in marriage. Unfortunate as this story is, Derrida's use of it echoes the story itself: his argument, like the Pierrot's honor, depends on Columbine's death, and moreover on his substituting, for her "presence," a body part—the hymen—detached from its place and transformed into what Gayatri Spivak (aiming to take Derrida off the hook) calls the "denaturalized and non-empirical" figure for his own intellectual project.[14]

The key to Mallarmé's story, and to Derrida's as well, is that Pierrot kills Columbine by tickling her feet until she dies of "the ultimate spasm." Because Pierrot only tickled her to death, Derrida claims, a crime was not committed, or as he puts it, "no act [was] committed as a crime," because it was indistinguishable from pleasure. For Derrida, this ambiguity amounts to a perfect example of hymen: violation and violence occur, yet the body's boundaries remain intact. And this supposed lack of an originary event demonstrates that all language is only the copying of copies without originals, in contrast to Plato's view that there is an ultimate truth to which all representations finally refer.

But is it really so difficult to tell the difference between one kind of spasm and another? Dismissing Columbine's death as a textual joke can only be possible from the point of view of the male reader, or a reader whose misogyny takes the form of overly hypothetical or figural reading.[15] A woman reader, or a reader whose feminism takes the form of taking things literally, finds it hard to laugh.[16] Such a reader notes the redoubling of Columbine's death in the murder that is represented and in the transformation of her murder into the proof of the absence of all origins, the ground and condition of representation itself. Only by discounting her bodily experience is it possible for Derrida to say that there is no origin, and as Derrida's text unfolds, that is true of the bodily experiences of pregnancy and childbirth as well. The appropriation and effacement of Columbine's body subtends the rolling out of copies of copies, and of an argument about copies, in a way that makes the maternal body disposable, in much the same way that the ghostly Mrs. Nedeeds—or the ghost of Creusa—subtend the production of replica-phantoms in Linden Hills and in Virgil's underworld.

Derrida explicates the betweenness of the hymen not only through the supposed ambiguity of Columbine's death but also by equating it with the world that can be spelled *entre* and mean "between" or *antre* and mean "cave"—Plato's cave, of course, which is also the *hystera*, or "womb." For example, "the hymen remains suspended *entre*, outside and inside the *antre.* . . . nothing is more perverse than this rending penetration that leaves a virgin womb intact." The hymen can, in this scheme, be both the barrier or entrance to the womb and the womb itself because it is folded; like "invagination," the term supposedly demonstrates that the inside is only the outside folded in on itself.[17] As we might expect of this cave that reshapes and represses the female body, there are ghosts in it, too. Just as making copies of copies—and proving that that is all there is—depends on the ghostliness of a woman, so too the copies themselves are ghosts (as in the doubling of ghostly women and the production of ghosts in Virgil and Naylor). Combining two modes of asexual reproduction in describing the relation between *Mimique* and the texts on which it is based, Derrida writes: "*Mimique* is also haunted by the ghost or grafted onto the arborescence of another text." In his white make-up, Mallarmé's Pierrot looks like a ghost, who seems to originate and write his story on the blank page of his face but who is really the ghost-effect of the series of textual foldings that has produced him. Derrida describes the copy that is "mimicry imitating nothing" as "a ghost that is the phantom of no flesh, wandering about without a past, without any death, birth, or presence." To discover the ghostliness of a literary figure is for Derrida a welcome demystification. But, as we shall see, for Irigaray the ghost means the impoverishment of the system of human production, its reduction to a replica machine.

Irigaray condemns what Derrida applauds. From the perspective of Derrida's reading of Plato, the difference is between Plato's celebration of forms and his derogation of copies on the one hand, and, on the other, Derrida's celebration of copies as copies. But from the perspective of Irigaray's reading, Derrida and Plato are more similar than they are different. Whether the copies of copies refer back to an original truth, as in Plato, or whether they do not, as in Derrida, the operation of making replicas demands the elimination of a woman and of the particularity of women's bodily experience and the substitution of figures more fully under male control, as in the pretense of ambiguity surrounding the death of Columbine and the subsequent apotheosis of the "denaturalized" human. Like Derrida, and perhaps in order to argue with him, Irigaray focuses her reading of Plato's cave on the pun between *entre* and *antre*, but to different effect. While Derrida critiques Plato by affirming the discovery that there is no difference between inside and between—the discovery he makes by means of the double meaning of the hymen as *antre* and *entre*—Irigaray critiques Plato and Derrida for doing precisely the same thing: for making the *entre* over into the *antre*, for obliterating the distinction that is the distinctiveness of women's bodies. In a characteristic gesture, Derrida shows how the two terms of an apparent opposition merge with each other, in the name of undoing the kind of hierarchized opposition of which the pair "male/female" is the most egregious example. And yet, for Irigaray, Derrida's gesture in this case has the opposite effect: not of undoing the subordination of female to male but of reinstituting it.[18]

"Plato's *Hystera*," the final section of Irigaray's *Speculum of the Other Woman*, begins by noting that Plato's myth rearranges the female body it both represents and represses. Because Plato stages his myth of the creation of reality in a cave, he implies that the womb is a metaphor for his cave, rather than the other way around; or, as Irigaray puts it, "the womb has been played with, made metaphor and mockery of by men."[19] The positioning of the men in the cave—chained so that they cannot see its entrance and origin, but only a wall on which appear the shadows of objects held up before a fire behind them—reflects the double meaning of *hystera* as both "womb" and "the latest" or "last" and causes the men to mistake back for front, first for last, origin for end. This reversal is the premise of all representation: that the cave's beginning (or *hystera*) "is never susceptible of representation" means that it "produces, facilitates, permits all representations." Representation, that is, would be neither necessary nor possible if a direct view of the origin were possible. Moreover, Plato has arranged the cave so that down is up: the invisible opening leads up where it ought to lead down. And these physical reversals are paralleled by epistemological ones. First, like Milton's

God addressing Eve as she gazes at her reflection, Plato claims that what the men see, the sensible, is actually unreal, whereas what they cannot (yet) see, the hypothetical or intelligible, is real. Second, this privileging of the hypothetical over the sensible depends on a reversal of that very logic, since it requires that the myth of the cave (presumably itself a shadow) be taken for truth and that the knowledge that the cave is an imitation of the womb be repressed.

Repressing, like Virgil, his recollection that the cave is only a figure for and displacement of the womb, and that any creation story must begin there, Plato takes the liberty of further rearranging it. Having turned the backs of the men on the origin of the cave, he takes the path leading to the outside and relocates it inside the cave, as the path running behind the men and in front of the fire, the path on which other men walk holding up the statues that cast the shadows projected on the opposite wall. "*The forgotten path.* . . . A repetition, representation, figuration re-enacted within the cave of that passage which we are told leads in and out of it. Of the path *in between* [*entre*] . . . that links . . . the sun, the fire, the light, the 'objects,' and the cave [*antre*]." As a result, "when the passage is forgotten, by the very fact of its being re-enacted *in* the cave [*antre*], it will found, subtend, sustain the hardening of all dichotomies, categorical differences." For not only has the vagina or passage been forgotten, the hymen too has been relocated and rebuilt inside the cave as the *teikhion*, or "little wall," running along the path, that conceals the bodies of the walking men. In contrast to the ambiguous, permeable hymen, "always already half open," this wall inside the cave is opaque, rigid, impermeable, and it is never crossed. The hymen seems also to have been relocated in the cave in the form of the projection wall, another hard, blank surface, "the *silent virginity* of the back of the cave." Because of the transposition of the path and these substitutions of hard membrane for soft, betweenness is eliminated and oppositions harden between inside and outside, sun and shade, above and below, true and false, "all oppositions that assume the *leap* from a worse to a better. An ascent . . . Vertical. Phallic even?" For example, like Freud theorizing that "the little girl is therefore a little man,"[20] the men imagine the passage is a "penis . . . *inside out.*" Without the passage between, "all divergencies will finally be proportions, functions, relations that can be referred back to *sameness.*"

This reduction of betweenness to opposition that is sameness is enacted also at the level of rhetoric. As when Plato takes his own myth for truth, his metaphors—and perhaps all metaphors—tend to erase difference. Metaphor is "that transport, displacement of the fact that passage, neck, transition have been obliterated," and it "is reinscribed in a matrix of resemblance, family likeness." "Family likeness" of the sort desired by Anchises and Nedeed for the generations of their sons? "Reinscribed in a matrix," or mother, metaphor underwrites the reproduction of sameness just as the mother does: "The maternal, the feminine serve (only) to keep up the reproduction-production of doubles, copies, fakes, while any hint of their material elements, of the womb, is turned into scenery to make the show more realistic."[21] Moreover, betweenness is eliminated too in Platonic "dialogue": "The 'we' and the 'I replied' would have no other strategic aim than to disguise and sustain at one and the same time the priority or the apriorism of sameness." Implicating the re-arrangement of the *hystera*/cave (the collapse of the difference between *entre* and *antre*) in the form of "dialogue" itself, Irigaray writes that Plato's conception of language depends upon a "truth that *decides* in advance how conversation [*entretien*], interventions, will develop. These 'inters' are dictated by a specular genealogy, by a process of images, reflections, reduplications which are rated in terms of their conformity . . . to the true that is meant to be uncovered."

Looking back at *Dissemination* from the point of view of Irigaray's reading of Plato, we could now observe that Columbine is turned into a replica machine just like the one Plato makes of the *hystera*, through the obfuscatory reading of her death as demonstrating that all representa-tions are copies with no originals. Just as Derrida's demonstration that all representations are copies without originals depends on not register-ing the difference between one kind of spasm and another, Plato's cave as a machine for producing sameness depends on violating the integrity of the female body and confusing the locations of its parts.

Plato's cave, Irigaray argues, as her tracing of the myth continues, not only depends on violence done to a woman's body but is also so constituted as to produce only ghosts. (Here she and Derrida agree, disagreeing only, but thoroughly, on their evaluation of this arrange-ment.) The "prestigious fake[s]" produced inside the cave, when the men carry their objects between the fire and the wall, are "phantoms" and "specters," because the relocated hymen-wall is "impregnable": only ghosts can cross a rigid wall. Were it possible for men and things to cross over or through the wall, there would be no occasion for representation, the casting of shadows, no reason for the men and their objects not to appear directly before the prisoners. The rigidity of the wall makes representation as we know it possible by foreclosing all other ways across. Moreover, much as in Virgil's underworld and in Linden Hills, only ghosts, Irigaray maintains, are capable of leaving Plato's cave. Be-cause of the removal of the path, there is a barrier between the cave and the sun, just as rigid as the *teikhion* within the cave, which generates prestige for the ghostly Platonic "Idea" in much the same way that the *teikhion* necessitates the shadows: "How does one break clean through that opaque, watertight partition in order . . . to be torn away from the depths of that crypt? Unless one is a phantom? . . . A cave where/whence even men's bodies would appear to be merely illusory, breeding nothing but ghosts."

Part of the "dialectical trick" of pitting as opposites across this barrier the cave and the sun is the insistence that the former cave dwellers choose one version of truth over the other. Subjected to an "authoritarian pedagogy," they are forced to denigrate the evidence of their senses (their long experience of believing in the shadows) in favor of what they are only told is true, subjugating their own frame of reference to "*the discourse of a master* . . . the logos, the logic, of the philosophy tutor." Though reluctant to yield up or forget their origin in the cave, the men do gradually turn to the sun, choosing father over mother. But that choice was never a fair one, for they were already being indoctrinated through their experience of the man-handled cave, which wasn't the womb itself but already a metaphor for the womb, the womb "reproduced" by and as artifice. The place where the mother ought to have been was "haunted by magicians who would have you believe that (re)production can be executed by skillful imitators, working from the divine plans. . . . Engendering the real is [said to be] the father's task, engendering the fictive is [said to be] the task of the mother—that 'receptacle' for turning out more or less good copies of reality." And so this sublimated body—the body understood as an inferior copy turned out by an inferior copyist, the mother—is already a ghost: "This cave produces more ghosts than any other, even if they are sometimes clean, clear, even sunlit ghosts. Washed of their uterine contaminants and their graveyard corruption. White, like any self-respecting ghosts."

The whiteness of Plato's ghosts—Pierrot's ghostly face that Derrida finds a welcome demystification, or the "sunlit ghosts" that earn Irigaray's disapproval—returns us to Naylor. The privilege of whiteness in a world that knows father as sun and mother as lightless cave is also the privilege of racial supremacy. Nedeed seeks to replicate himself as his fathers have done for the sake of oppositional difference: the development of Linden Hills was intended by its founder as "a beautiful, black wad of spit right in the white eye of America." But, as Irigaray would have predicted, opposition has collapsed into sameness: "Linden Hills wasn't black; it was successful." As when Irigaray discovers that the Derridean undoing of oppositions can have the reverse of a liberating effect, the careers, habits, and tastes of the wealthy black inhabitants, so identical to those of the whites the first Nedeed set out to defy, unhelpfully undo the difference between black and white: "There was no torment in Linden Hills for the white god his fathers had shaken their fists at, because there was no white god, and there never had been. . . . The Almighty Divine is simply the *will* to possess. . . . How could it be any color when it stripped the skin, sex, and soul of any who offered themselves at its altar before it decided to bless?" Like the sameness created by the oppositional rigidity of the walls in and of Plato's cave, the rigid opposition of black and white that the history of slavery has made ineradicable can only produce sameness in the present: the privilege of whiteness. And just as only white ghosts can cross the barrier in Irigaray's cave, the process of moving down in Nedeed's world drains blacks of their color. Maxwell Smyth, the only character who is as much at home in Linden Hills as Nedeed, finds the accusation that "he was trying to be white totally bizarre. Being white was the furthest thing from his mind, since he spent every waking moment trying to be no color at all." What he does not realize is that, in the world of corporate America, the absence of color *is* whiteness, because neutrality is impossible where hierarchical thinking prevails.

As for the cave beneath the Dantean pit, the basement morgue containing Willa and her dead son, what leaves it, too, is pale and ghostly. As if she were exiting from Plato's cave, Willa must cross a rigid barrier (a door bolted with iron). She does so as a ghost, in the sense that she knows her husband cannot afford to let her live, and she carries her dead, white son wrapped in the gauzy white wedding veil of a long dead Mrs. Nedeed. But unlike Plato's ghosts, and unlike the colorless, soulless blacks of Linden Hills, she does not renounce her knowledge of or belief in what she learned in the cave; she does not renounce her mothers in favor of the father. Although, to return to Irigaray, the white male ghosts that leave Plato's cave are "educated" in being "cut off from any remaining empirical relation with the womb," this education is not the end of Irigaray's tale of the cave: despite the attempt to erase her, the mother is still there, for Willa and those like her to remember. The sun's privilege is premised on the assumption that it is the only source of heat and light, the fires in the cave only those "lit by the hand of man." But the disregarded interior of the earth has its own "burning, incendiary chambers," even if "all the flames have been pressed back into the core." "She herself knows nothing (of herself)," yet "if she were to shine, then the light would no longer, simply, belong to sameness." She is, Irigaray suggests, the source of a heat and light altogether different from, not opposite to, that of the sun.

To locate this maternal depth that does not look and function like Plato's cave, Irigaray turns, in the central sections of *Speculum*, to the figure of the mirrored cave.[22] Irigaray mocks the "subject [who] plays at multiplying himself" for obliging everything not himself to be "a faithful, polished mirror, empty of altering reflections. Immaculate of all auto-copies." As a way of defeating the binary thinking the cave has been appropriated to support, Irigaray proposes the counterimages of concave or convex mirrors, which reflect images that are "both like and unlike" and thus disconcert the opposition between true and false, original and copy. Like the flexibility of the hymen for which Plato has substituted the rigid wall, the concave mirror preserves the possibility of a difference more flexible not only than Plato's rigid oppositions, but also than Derrida's claim to show that true and false do not differ. The mirror shaped like a cave may moreover form an alternative cave to give the lie to

Plato's misrepresentations and to restore to those who have been misrepresented the power of negating those who misrepresent them.[23]

What Irigaray would not like to see hypostatized as her alternate myth of the cave is presented most vividly in a chapter that precedes the reading of Plato, titled "Any Theory of the 'Subject' Has Always Been Appropriated by the 'Masculine.'" At the start of this chapter, two sets of images for the relation between the sexes converge on the morphology of the cave. First is the image of woman as the ground on which male erections are built: "And even as man seeks to rise higher and higher—in his knowledge too—so the ground fractures more and more beneath his feet," and as a consequence he "must dig his foundations deeper, extend the underground passages which assured the edifice of his determination, further dig out the cellars upon which he raises the monument of his identification," and "he must resurface the earth with this floor of the ideal." Second, as I have already described, Irigaray introduces and mocks the notion of woman as mirror, "immaculate of all auto-copies"; and then she puts these figures together. As a result of "man's" project to possess the ground and appropriate all otherness, to make "the very place and space of being his own, he becomes a prisoner of effects of symmetry that know no limit. Everywhere he runs into the walls of his palace of mirrors, the floor of which is in any case beginning to crack and break up." And through or underneath his palace of (male-constructed?) mirrors, which is also the linear and logical syntax of androcentric language, are further (perhaps really female?) mirrors:

> But perhaps through this specular surface which sustains discourse is found not the void of nothingness but the dazzle of multifaceted speleology. A scintillating and incandescent concavity, of language also, that threatens to set fire to fetish-objects and gilded eyes. The recasting of their truth value is already at hand. We need only press on a little further into the depths, into that so-called dark cave which serves as hidden foundation to their speculations. For there where we expect to find the opaque and silent matrix of a logos immutable in the certainty of its own light, fires and mirrors are beginning to radiate, sapping the evidence of reason at its base! Not so much by anything stored in the cave—which would still be a claim based on the notion of the closed volume—but again and yet again by their indefinitely rekindled hearths.

The next sentence links what may be called the positive and negative aspects of this fabulous image: "But which 'subject' up till now has investigated the fact that a *concave mirror* concentrates the light and, specifically, that this is not wholly irrelevant to woman's sexuality?" The concentration of light refers chiefly to the use of the concave mirror as "burning glass, which enflames all that falls into its cup," as Archimedes is said to have used giant mirrors to burn the Roman fleet off Syracuse. In this sense, the book *Speculum* is a gigantic, man-made mirror, but with a curve put in it by its female author, that reflects Freud, Plato, and others back at themselves so that their own logic destroys them; and since a speculum is a dilator, too, then the eye that prospects (with a speculum-dilator) will be burned (by the speculum-mirror).[24] The nonir-relevance of the concave mirror to woman's sexuality refers with deliber-ate tentativeness to a more positive or even essential notion of women's sexual morphology. Irigaray protests the equation of "woman's sexuality with her reproductive organs," yet she also claims that there is a "secret of the caves. . . . intact. Elsewhere. Burning still."

I detail what I am reductively calling Irigaray's alternate myth of the cave at such length in part because of the fit between so many of its features and the topography and action of *Linden Hills*. Like "man" in Irigaray's formulation, the male Nedeeds are excavators, and something very like "the dazzle of multifaceted speleology" features centrally in the description of the male Nedeeds' oppositional project and its failure:

> These people [their tenants] were to reflect the Nedeeds in a hundred facets and then the Nedeeds could take those splintered mirrors and form a mirage of power to torment a world that dared think them stupid—or worse, totally impotent. But . . . how could these people ever reflect the Nedeeds? Linden Hills wasn't black; it was successful. The shining surface of their careers, brass railings, and cars hurt his eyes because it only reflected the bright nothing that was inside of them.

Linden Hills could have been a "burning glass," ferociously reflecting the glare of white prejudice back at itself, but it fails through its narcissism, its misuse of its mirrors. In Nedeed's view, this narcissism takes the form of his tenants' absorption in the shininess of expensive surfaces; but narcissism also flaws the Nedeeds' original conception of this defiant mirror, for they have wanted first of all a hundred-faceted mirror *of themselves*. And Nedeed's failure to transform his Dantean pit into an Irigarayan mirrored cave can finally be traced back to his patrilineal narcissism: the hideous crime of demanding that a wife be only a mirror and dehumanizing her when she fails. Nedeed fails to make an Irigarayan cave not simply because he is not a woman, but because of the perverse form his masculinity has taken.

There are also in the novel more conventional (flat, unfaceted) mirrors that serve positive ends, mirrors and aims that Irigaray might depre-cate. The mirror becomes one of the central figures for a saving self-knowledge, the absence of which means damnation. The one resident who holds out against the latest Nedeed's development scheme, Grandma Tilson (who also starts the rumor that the first Nedeed backed the Con-federacy), describes the condition of Linden Hills as "selling the mirror in your soul . . . that part of you that lets you know who you are" (Iri-garay too notes the convention of psyche as mirror). The most positive of all these mirrors is one that Willa Nedeed creates from the aluminum pot in which she catches the meager allowance of water Nedeed sends down the pipes each day. Water comes into the pot with a Jovian "sound of thunder," yet Willa invents the need for a mirror before she finds one:

like Irigaray's mirror, Willa's is ambiguously both a patriarchal artifact and a female creation. When she has finished reading the disappearance of the three Mrs. Nedeeds, she begins to feel for signs of her own existence, touching her face again and again to learn its contours, "trying to form a mirror between her fingers, the darkness, and memory. . . . if only she had a shiny surface." When she catches sight of the pot of water and holds it still beneath her, "No doubt remained—she was there." Recognition brings tears, which collect in the pot, from which she then drinks, feeling, for the first time, that "she could rebuild." The "shiny surface" enabling this salvific self-discovery directly answers the "shining surface of their careers," the destructive narcissism that induces the rest of Linden Hills to sell the mirror in their souls. Like Eve, Willa discovers herself as an image in water; but unlike Eve, she is not persuaded to derogate that visible identity in favor of the hypothetical law of the father.

For Irigaray, "self-knowledge" would be a poor substitute for the fiery power of the mirrored cave, for, to recall her title, "any theory of the 'subject' has always been appropriated by the 'masculine.'" That is, any "knowledge" of the "self" such as Willa achieves is always irremediably bound up with androcentric patterns of subjugating the other to the self. Indeed, *Speculum* shows how in Plato, too, water becomes a mirror, but in what is for Irigaray an entirely negative way as an instance of male self-absorption and appropriation of the female, the reverse of Willa's mirror. When the men come up out of Plato's cave, as Irigaray notes, before their unaccustomed eyes can look directly at things, humans, and the heavens, they first look at shadows and at the reflections of things in the water. For Irigaray, this view of water as merely yet another copy machine, with its emphasis on (frozen) surface over (liquid) depth, is another androcentric way of repressing the mother, "since by acting 'like' a mirror, water freezes access to the bottomless depths of the sea, to its night. Water serves as a reflecting screen and not as a reminder of the depths of the mother; it sends back the image of the sun, of men, of things, even of the prisoner-child."[25] While the frozen lake that surrounds Nedeed's house may be a version of this kind of mirror (while it is also the equivalent of the ice in the *Inferno*), contributing generally as it does to the imprisoning of one Mrs. Nedeed after another, little is made of its reflective properties. By contrast, the water in Willa's mirror is emphatically not only reflective but also liquid and living: it receives her tears, and she sustains life by sipping it. Unlike Plato's water-mirror repressing the mother, Willa's water-mirror gives life and power to a mother.

Linden Hills thus would seem to invert the terms of *Speculum:* the mirrored cave belongs to the man (and is misused by him), while the flat mirror belongs to and empowers the woman. Perhaps racial oppression puts Luther Nedeed in a position of marginality roughly equivalent to that of women in Irigaray's scheme and gives him the opportunity to perform their acts of criticism, an opportunity that he wastes. While Willa is recovering her face and her name (her will) in the cellar, Luther is upstairs in his "den," another sort of cave, absorbed in an apparently benign, miniaturized, literal (but, as we shall see, constitutively masculine) version of the "splintered mirrors" that have failed him on a larger scale. With the reluctant paid assistance of Lester and Willie, he is decorating his Christmas tree. Like everything else he has, the ornaments are handed down from father to son, precious antiques that he can hardly bear to have Lester and Willie handle. Each glittering object miniaturizes something real: there is, for example, "a gilded cornucopia" filled with "incredibly tiny glass-blown fruit and nuts"; an "embossed cardboard boat was an exact replica of the original. Tiny silver chains, strung from the deck to the stacks, had silk flags attached to them, and he fluffed out the cotton simulating smoke." This "cardboard paradise . . . mean[s] the world to him" quite literally: when his tenants and his wife fail to mirror him exactly, here at least is a shiny, unchanging world that is under his control. His favorite ornament is a "globe" that, as the god of this paradise, he rotates in his hand. And his tree is both emphatically reflective and the generator of its own light: metal snowflakes and stars, gilded and silvered cardboard, and a "mirrored diamond" reflect the light of candles placed among them and inside the globe. In the den lit otherwise only by a fireplace fire, this tree comes diabolically close to Irigaray's "dazzle of multifaceted speleology. A scintillating and incandescent concavity" where "fires and mirrors are beginning to radiate." Except that the cone-shaped tree is a mirrored convexity, and where Irigaray rhetorically asks if the concave mirror "is not wholly irrelevant to woman's sexuality" she goes on to ask, "Any more than is a man's sexuality to the convex mirror?"

Willa, meanwhile, is walking up from the cellar. The narrative of her resolution to do so focuses on what both Irigaray and Naylor call the "path," here the twelve concrete steps connecting the cellar to the kitchen above. As she reviews with painstaking detail the history of her life, in order to recover her identity, she thinks,

> Willa Nedeed was a good mother and a good wife. For six years, she could claim that identity without any reservations. But now Willa Nedeed sat on a cot in a basement, no longer anyone's mother or anyone's wife. So how did that happen? She stared at the concrete steps leading up to the kitchen door. It happened because she walked down into this basement. That was simple enough; that was clear. In a pair of canvas espadrilles, she walked down twelve concrete steps away from her home and into a room that was cold and damp. Willa had to squeeze her eyes tightly so she would see only those steps.

Forgetting this path has meant, up to now, as it does for the men in Plato's cave, accepting a master's inverted reality. Remembering it—as Irigaray too remembers it—means becoming able to overturn the master's law: "She was sitting there now, filthy, cold, and hungry, because she, Willa Prescott Nedeed, had walked down twelve concrete steps. And since that was the truth—the pure, irreducible truth—whenever she was good and ready, she could walk back up."[26]

Unlike Irigaray, Naylor never suggests that her novel's version of the cave was once originally maternal or female, later appropriated by men; Willa's prison is simply a male construct. But Naylor joins Irigaray in presenting her cave as the scene of discovering the truth about women's oppression, in contrast to the lies perpetrated overhead, and at the last she hints at an Irigarayan way at a link between the topography of the path and the woman's body. As Willa breathes in and out in sleep, her discovery of the reversibility of the path becomes linked to pathways in her own body: "she breathed out. Out, past cells that divided to form ovaries, wombs, and glands. Out, past the crumbling planetary matter that formed the concrete for that room. Out, toward the edge of the universe with its infinite possibility to make space for the volume of her breath." The allusion here to her maternal body leads to the passage I quoted at the beginning of this essay, where her newly discovered "truth . . . conceived and reconceived itself. . . . It was a birth." It is as though, momentarily, an Irigarayan woman came to inhabit the cave appropriated by man and to reshape it to her contours, restoring the "forgotten path" and substituting for his artificial replications her originating birth. It is also as if the Eumenides had decided to climb back up out of the earth, where Apollo and Athena (taking the side of the father) place them at the end of Aeschylus's trilogy, and resume their ancient life as Furies, fierce defenders of the mother's right and avengers of a matricide that the law has condoned.

By overdetermined coincidence, Willie, who has worried about Willa's absence and who by his name seems designated to be an extension of her will, unbolts the cellar door moments before she reaches it. The rigid barrier of sexual opposition, to recall Irigaray's terms, has been restored as a permeable hymen, a collaboration between a woman and a womanly man. Her eyes at first unfocused, just like those of the ghost-men exiting from Plato's cave, Willa cleans the kitchen (the novel does not pretend that she is fully sane; she is compared to "the wingless queen [of] a horde of army ants"), then walks toward the den, where her arrival is represented in a mirror: "There in the mirror next to the open kitchen door was a woman, her hair tangled and matted, her sunken cheeks streaked with dirt." This vision is so incredible that, also like the men coming out of Plato's cave, Willie "was . . . being forced to surrender faith in his eyes," and Luther, like Plato's philosopher, attempts to convert the boys from the evidence of their senses to his masterly logic: "'Gentlemen, thank you for your help. Your checks will be in the mail.'" The boys find themselves out-of-doors, unable to imagine what to do, while indoors Willa, Luther, and their dead son become a hideous parody of the Trinity, not unlike the three-headed figure of Lucifer revealed at the end of the *Inferno:* "they breathed as one, moved as one, and one body lurched against the fireplace. The trailing veil brushed an ember. . . . And now no path to the clutter by the door except through the lighted tree. They went hurling against it, the top smashed a side window, and the December wind howled in." When the fire is eventually put out, not "three bodies . . . but one massive bulk was covered and carried to the ambulance." Though she destroys herself in the process, Willa succeeds in appropriating the mirrored fires in Nedeed's den and turning them into Irigaray's "burning glass, which enflames all that falls into its cup." Unlike the ghosts exiting from Plato's cave that she otherwise resembles, she maintains her hold on the truths she discovered there and is not swayed from her knowledge that the master lies. She takes his desire to replicate himself using her body as mirror—that desire as it is figured in the convex mirrors in his den—and she makes that desire its own end.

Willa literally brings down the house of patriarchy. It is an act of negation almost as pure as that of *Speculum*, since it destroys her even as she destroys it. Although Willa's mirror promises the recovery of identity and self-knowledge and the establishment of a heroine, the novel is either unable or unwilling to fulfill that promise. Indeed, Irigaray might argue that it is because a woman's claiming identity in a mirror isn't revolutionary at all that Willa's revolt ends so quickly in suicide. Whatever the reason, it is striking that the novel institutes no counter-tradition of strong womanhood to oppose the destructive legacy of patriarchy. The dead Mrs. Nedeeds, the line of Willa's mothers-in-law, can expose the destructive truth, but they offer no hints for constructing a new one. The novel dimisses careers for black women in the upper echelons of white-run businesses even more urgently than it does for black men; the suicide Laurel Dumont is "the biggest woman at IBM," but she suffers far more than her similarly placed husband because she hasn't had time for children or a home. Laurel's grandmother Roberta, like Grandma Tilson, exemplifies the strong, maternal, traditional black woman who holds out against those soul-destroying "advances" that Linden Hills represents, and she invokes the music of Bessie Smith and Billie Holiday in an attempt to give Laurel the consoling sense of shared pain. But Grandma Tilson fails to stop Nedeed's development, and Roberta cannot save her granddaughter.

This feeling that the line of mothers is inefficacious against the fathers—or can at best only suicidally negate them—extends to literary lineage as well. The inverted topography of Linden Hills, as much as it derives from Dante, alludes also to Toni Morrison's *Sula*. That novel opens with a description of the "nigger joke" through which a piece of rocky, barren, hilltop land came to be the black neighborhood called "the Bottom": a white master tricks his former slave into accepting poor land instead of rich valley land by telling him, "'when God looks down, it's the bottom. That's why we call it so. It's the bottom of heaven—best land there is.'"[27] As in *Linden Hills*, racism locates the black neighborhood on land disdained by whites. But in contrast to Nedeed's sinister know-ingness, which makes the inversion of up and down in Linden Hills a moral indictment of its inhabitants, the gullibility of the freed slave in *Sula* gives his descendants the moral advantage of simple victimization. They remain poor, unlike the citizens of Linden Hills, and they remain authentically different from the whites. Their position seems to make possible something very like Irigaray's mimicry: the inhabitants of the Bottom literally "look down on the white folks. . . . It was lovely up in the Bottom." Just as the Nedeeds parody God's creation, the Bottom has a black god, but instead a benign one: "The creator and sovereign of this enormous house with the four sickle-pear trees in the front yard and the single elm in the back yard was Eva Peace, who sat in a wagon on the third floor directing the lives of her children, friends, strays, and a constant stream of boarders."

Naylor seems to correct Morrison by making explicit the problem Morrison might seem to resist acknowledging. Naylor inverts Morrison's inversion to show that mere inversion cannot sustain good effects. Luther Nedeed and the sterile and self-destroying Linden Hills, Naylor seems to argue with Morrison, not Eva Peace and the tree-lined Bottom, is what happens when black invert white categories; difference is not preserved. But Morrison had already admitted this: though her inverted topography seems to enable powerful forms of skepticism and to preserve difference in a way not possible in *Linden Hills*, Eva Peace gets her power through self-mutilation and, unable to save her daughter from burning to death, she is (like Roberta) ultimately no more efficacious as a god—and scarcely more benign—than Nedeed. Less spectacularly than the burning of the symbolic center of Linden Hills, the Bottom too is being unbuilt in the present time from which most of the narration of *Sula* is a flashback.

Whereas for Naylor a female tradition (whether in literary history or among her characters) is not sufficiently powerful to counteract the patrilineal power to erase women, her two heroes do benefit from patrilineage in the form of (primarily white) male literary history. While Bessie Smith and Billie Holiday are of no use to Laurel Dumont, Willie and Lester are empowered by their inheritance from both black and white male poets, Whitman, Eliot, and "the great slave poet, Jupiter Hammon," and Malcolm X as well. It is chiefly their unconscious impersonation of Virgil and Dante that pays off, not only in spectacularly educational adventure, but in poetry: toward the end of the novel Willie begins his own oral epic about his visit to the underworld, "'There is a man in a house at the bottom of a hill. And his wife has no name.'" Willie improves on Dante by acknowledging his homosocial impulses and by concerning himself with the victimized woman in his hell, but his epic may differ from Virgil's or Dante's only in degree, in that his poem like theirs depends on the absence of a woman.

In keeping with the negativity of Willa's incendiary act, Naylor does not represent herself as a black woman artist in her novel, even though it is she who most obviously both profits from and critiques the gaps in the white male heritage, and even though her narrator knows and represents the missing female history that is preserved as enticing mystery for the male poet. Even more strikingly, Irigaray's work is almost entirely restricted to argument with her philosophic fathers and proffers no stably positive image of female power. Though I have arranged the sequence of Irigaray's myth of the mirrored cave to foreground its most aggresive image, "Plato's *Hystera*" and *Speculum* as a whole end on a note approaching defeatism, when, completing its slow journey through Plato's myth, the text arrives abruptly at Plato's certainty that the prisoners would kill any one of their number who left and then returned, a murder (of someone already dead) that would rehearse not only the murder of the mother but also the prisoners' own self-destruction.

Yet these two works do not amount to absolute negation. Willa is at least fleetingly and memorably a heroine. *Speculum* allows for a positive construction not only of the mirrored cave but also of the figure of the *mystèrique*, a female figure conflating the medieval mystic and the modern hysteric who, like the mirrored cave, can, through Irigaray's deliberate and destabilizing ambiguities, be construed as supplying both/either an example of the terrible result of patriarchal practices and/or a positive image of women's (relatively) authentic speech. Moreover, whether Irigaray is defending the womb or Naylor is defending the identity of a character who is a mother, each is concerned to defend women's existence as an empirical fact.

Is it that it is impossible for even the most radical feminist thought to sustain pure negation, or is it rather that it is impossible for a U.S. feminist reader to tolerate it? I have reason to suspect my own reading. The dominant forms of feminist criticism in this country tend, like Willa Nedeed looking in her mirror, to view the recuperation of subjectivity in the form of female identity as the best defense against androcentrism. This focus on figures of individual women intensifies in essays that generalize about the project of feminist criticism, as if those figures presented a desired wholeness and coherence, the fullness and grand simplicity of what the writer wants to say about an intricate and often fragmentary subject. Recent examples include Susan Gubar's "Sapphistries," Patricia Joplin's "The Voice of the Shuttle Is Ours" (on Philomela), and Nancy K. Miller's "Arachnologies," each of which transforms a grand, ancient, and violated female figure into the type of a new project against violation. *The Madwoman in the Attic* would fall into this category, as would almost any work of feminist criticism focusing on female authors. Of French feminist works, the best known here tend to be those featuring figures that can be construed as heroines: Hélène Cixous's laughing Medusa, Irigaray's "lips [that] speak together," Wittig's *guérillères*. Jane Gallop points out about a recent volume of feminist psychoanalytic essays that "the heroine in this book is surely the mother."[28]

It may be that our attachment to such figures is a way of warding off our fear of what psychoanalytic critics would call "castration." Naomi Schor has recently argued that contemporary feminist critics practice what she calls "female fetishism": the fetish's function of representing both presence and absence (or the "oscillation between denial and recognition of castration") obscures the difference between and balances the negativity of critiquing women's oppression and the celebration of sexual difference.[29] Figures like the ones I have cited from recent critical works serve both to remind us of the history of women's oppression and to reveal the powerful strategies with which women have met that oppression. At issue, in the psychoanalytic terms Schor uses (and she is quite candid about the difficulty of turning such terms to feminist uses) are two phallocentric assumptions: that women are inherently lacking ("castrated") and that children's fantasies about their mothers' wholeness and power take the form of an imagined "phallic mother," assumptions that derive in turn from Freud's assumption that the child is a boy. Feminist critics, as daughters, may be seeking the early mother, that repository of illusions of power that offer imaginary compensation for loss and weakness. But the wound we seek to mend—in our mothers and ourselves— is different from the one envisaged by Freud: a feminist "fetishism" would be concerned to heal not the mother's "castration" but rather the effects on mothers and daughters of the father's rape.[30] What's the difference? While "castration" and "phallic mother" assume that the natural state of women is lack, identifying women's lack as an effect of violation assumes that plenitude and power might not be, for women, necessarily just illusions.

The narrators and the characters in *Linden Hills* and *Speculum* (if Irigaray's shadowy cave/woman, the negation of a negation, can be said to be a character) represent this duality of the absence and presence of power that is the result not of castration but of patriarchal rape. Hoping not to be misunderstood as essentializing woman in any way, I shall nominate, as my own feminist "fetish," Virgil's sibyl in her cave in Book VI of the *Aeneid*, as a figure for the sort of active negation that characterizes the narratives of *Speculum* and *Linden Hills*. The sibyl, like the narrators of both these works, knows her way around in the underworld and goes in and out of it at will, giving tours. She determines that Aeneas is fit to descend, smooths his path, and explains the topography, until Anchises supersedes her as guide in the scene I have already discussed.

Though, unlike Irigaray and Naylor, she is not overtly critical of the way the underworld is run by the father's law, she sees it in a more feminocentric way than do Aenes and Anchises. It is she who believes in the importance of Proserpina's golden bough as entry ticket, she who believes in "Hecate, the queen / of heaven and of hell" and such other ancient female powers as the Furies. Just as in Irigaray's version of Plato's cave, the stage props and backdrop of the underworld are largely female, even if it is now run by and for the fathers' law. She knows, better than any other figure, that the underworld amounts to the male appropriation of the female body, for like the underworld, the sibyl is herself—her body and her voice—routinely appropriated by the masculine. In asymmetrical contrast to the muse (the female figure by whom the male poet pretends to be inspired, nonetheless taking for himself the credit for poetry), the sibyl is possessed by Apollo, who speaks through her and takes the credit for her utterances. The androcentric literary tradition speaks through Irigaray and Naylor with considerably less authority, because of the ironic twist they introduce into their Apollos' messages, yet it remains true that they commit their ironies within the frame of the sibyl's traditional female role, as transmitter and explicator of male culture.

When Dante returns to the *Aeneid* for the prototype of his infernal journey, for the relationship between tourist and tour guide he draws most explicitly on the relatively minor figure of the poet Musaeus who briefly introduces Aeneas to Elysium, thus privileging the tradition of male poet as guide. But it is the sibyl who in her longest speech provides the most immediate prototype for Dante's *Inferno*, the sibyl whose voice is therefore appropriated to Virgil when he reappears guiding Dante. In this speech, in which she describes to Aeneas the torments of those being punished in Tartarus, she says that her knowledge came through Hecate, who guided her through lowest hell as the sibyl now takes Aeneas through the underworld's easier reaches. Where Dante has one male figure instruct another, the original tour guide and tourist were two women, so that it is not only the sibyl's voice but also her voice as it echoes Hecate's that Dante takes over for his Virgil. The sibyl concludes her verbal tour of hell with one final crime being punished there: beyond even the traitor "who sold his fatherland [*patriam*] for gold," "This one assailed / the chamber of his daughter and compelled / forbidden mating." Although the sibyl does not describe a topographical hierarchy as Dante will do, she emphasizes this crime by naming it last, and she emphasizes the crime against the daughter over the crime against the father(land). By contrast, presenting nothing lower than the traitors in the lowest circle of his hell, Dante silently omits the crime the sibyl privileges. It is likely not by accident that the sibyl emphasizes patriarchal rape, for that, we learn earlier, is her experience of Apollo:

> But she has not yet given way to Phoebus:
> she rages, savage, in her cavern, tries
> to drive the great god from her breast. So much
> the more, he tires out her raving mouth;
> he tames her wild heart, shapes by crushing force.

When Hecate tells it to the sibyl, and when the sibyl tells it to Aeneas, hell's lowest spot is reserved for the patriarchal control and violation of women's minds and bodies, the violation that the sibyl herself experiences without being able to protest it directly. Virgil does not make his sibyl a critic or an ironist, but he grants her this rhetorical revenge against her own rapist. This revenge may be so subtle that Dante can overlook it, but Irigaray and Naylor do not. Remembering and valuing the sibyl's account, Naylor and Irigaray reinstate this crime, not only as the bottom but as the defining feature of their hells. And like the sibyl, each narrator of this crime protests against the patriarchal violation and appropriation of her own voice even as she protests against the violent appropriation she narrates. I would not claim that the sibyl stands for feminist criticism, nor would I claim for her an authentic female voice somehow speaking between the lines of Virgil's text.[31] Indeed, precisely because Irigaray and Naylor are aware of their own narrations as constructed by, as well as subversive of, androcentric culture, the sibyl's role most aptly suggests the canniness of each one's narrator: a female figure, violated yet surviving, a subtle ironist who takes it as her task to expose to view the underworld of male domination, letting its horrors speak for themselves.

Notes

1. Gloria Naylor, *Linden Hills* (1985; New York: Penguin, 1986), p. 289.
2. Christine Froula, "When Eve Reads Milton: Undoing the Canonical Economy," *Critical Inquiry*, 10 (1983), 321–48; Mary Jacobus, "Is There a Woman in This Text?" *New Literary History*, 14 (1982), 117–41; reprinted in Mary Jacobus, *Reading Woman: Essays in Feminist Criticism* (New York: Columbia Univ. Press, 1986), pp. 83–109. In this paragraph I am briefly summarizing the opening section of my review essay, "Feminist Criticism and Theory: The Ghost of Creusa," *The Yale Journal of Criticism*, 1 (1987), 153–82. I am grateful to Lisa Cartwright for pointing out to me that reproductive technology—which can remove at least part of the process of reproduction from women's bodies and place it in the hands of (chiefly male) doctors—literalizes such myths of the elimination of the mother as Irigaray exposes in *Speculum*.
3. Tania Modleski, "Feminism and the Power of Interpretation: Some Critical Readings," in *Feminist Studies/Critical Studies*, ed. Teresa de Lauretis

(Bloomington: Indiana Univ. Press, 1986), pp. 132–33. Modleski is quoting from Jonathan Culler, *On Deconstruction: Theory and Criticism after Structuralism* (Ithaca: Cornell Univ. Press, 1982), chapter 1, section 2, "Reading as a Woman," pp. 43–64.

4. Peggy Kamuf, "Replacing Feminist Criticism," *Diacritics* 12 (Summer 1982), 44–45.

5. Virgil, *The Aeneid*, trans. Allen Mandelbaum (New York: Bantam Books, 1972), p. 52. Subsequent references to this work will be included in the text.

6. M. Owen Lee, *Fathers and Sons in Virgil's Aeneid: Tum Genitor Natum* (Albany, N.Y.: SUNY Press, 1979), p. 45.

7. Robert Fitzgerald translates as follows the corresponding passage in the *Odyssey* (New York: Doubleday, 1961), p. 191:

> I bit my lip,
> rising perplexed, with longing to embrace her,
> and tried three times, putting my arms around her,
> but she went sifting through my hands, impalpable
> as shadows are, and wavering like a dream.

8. It may seem questionable to propose this process as a myth of reproduction, but it presents itself as such in a poem in which reproduction of another kind is conspicuously missing. Aeneas is between the loss of one wife and the acquisition of another; he and Dido, making love first in a cave, conspicuously don't conceive a child; the cobbled together family at "little Troy" (Hector's widow Andromache has been married off to her brother-in-law Helenus) mourns the baby Astyanax but, in keeping with its nostalgic orientation, produces no new child.

9. Lee speculates, "Aeneas's soul (we may want to read from what follows) will take on new flesh as Romulus and eventually as Augustus."

10. Dorothy Dinnerstein uses the image of the Minotaur to focus on the human anxiety that all our "sexual arrangements" are monstrous and specifically on human fears of female sexuality. *The Mermaid and the Minotaur: Sexual Arrangements and Human Malaise* (New York: Harper and Row, 1976).

11. Catherine C. Ward has spelled out the correspondences between Dante's characters and geography and Naylor's, in "Gloria Naylor's *Linden Hills*: A Modern *Inferno*," *Contemporary Literature*, 28 (1987), 67–81.

12. Classical scholars tend to focus on the connections between Virgil's underworld and Plato's afterlife—where women are also devalued—in Book X of the *Republic;* my concern here is with the culturally more resonant "underworld" of Plato's cave, in Book V.

13. Jacques Derrida, *Dissemination*, trans. Barbara Johnson (Chicago: Univ. of Chicago Press, 1981), p. 210. Subsequent references to this work will be included in the text. "Presence" is again "matrix" in "Structure, Sign, and Play in the Discourse of the Human Sciences," in *Writing and Difference*, trans. Alan Bass (Chicago: Univ. of Chicago Press, 1978); by contrast, the essay ends by appropriating the language of childbirth to describe an explicitly nonmaternal "birth" that would undo that matrix.

14. Gayatri Spivak, "Displacement and the Discourse of Woman," in *Displacement: Derrida and After*, ed. Mark Krupnick (Bloomington: Indiana Univ. Press, 1983), p. 175. Spivak (in the same essay) and Frances Bartkowski (in "Feminism and Deconstruction," *Enclitic*, 4, No. 2 [1980], 70–77) have backed up Derrida's claim, elaborated elsewhere in *Dissemination*, that the term "dissemination" offers a model of writing less teleological and more

"feminine" than "insemination," a model closer to the fluidity associated with women's bodies than to the hardness associated with men's. Yet the word's etymology recalls the ancient, androcentric view that man supplies the seed to the female ground that merely nourishes it, the view Anchises echoes in his description of souls as heavenly seeds "dulled by harmful bodies." Thus etymology recuperates the male dominance the word would otherwise seem to dismantle. Moreover, dissemination occurs in relation to what Derrida pictures as the blank screen of the hymen, about which Derrida writes: "It is the hymen that desire dreams of piercing." Whose desire? the woman reader asks. "Dissemination" may have feminized the phallus, but here desire is again construed as the traditional phallic solid, with hymen defined from a phallocentric point of view. That the hymen becomes—for the moment— Derrida's icon of undecidability ("the hymen only takes place when it doesn't take place," as he riddlingly puts it) only reduplicates—and not so very playfully—the old picture of woman as puzzle and enigma: you are yourselves the problem, according to Freud.

15. See, again, Modleski.

16. This is the significant difficulty attributed by Wayne Booth to his wife in "Freedom of Interpretation: Bakhtin and the Challenge of Feminist Criticism," *Critical Inquiry*, 9 (1982), 45–76.

17. Moreover, Derrida claims *entre* and *antre* are etymologically linked: *antre* is a cave which is a cleft which is an interval which is in between. One such cave or cleft or in-between place, Derrida mentions, is "the sacred vale between the two flanks of the Parnassus, the dwelling-place of the Muses and the site of Poetry." The Muses may represent the surviving trace of the repressed memory of the mother's originary power with spoken language, and if that is so, this citation of the Muses as *antre/entre* constitutes yet another instance of Derrida's suppression of the maternal body and its special relation to language and his transformation of it into a figure more easily controlled. Like Derrida's version of hymen, the Muses represent the male appropriation of something perhaps originally and actively female and its transformation into a passive figuration that merely grounds androcentric fictions.

18. For a lucid account of Derrida's failure to avoid duplicating the sexism of the philosophical tradition he follows, see Michael Ryan, "The Politics of Deconstruction," in *Politics and Culture* (London: Macmillan, 1989).

19. Luce Irigaray, *Speculum of the Other Woman*, trans. Gillian C. Gill (Ithaca: Cornell Univ. Press, 1985), p. 263. Subsequent references to this work will be included in the text. The following review of what happens in "Plato's *Hystera*" is much indebted to Gillian Gill's "Introduction," written in 1982 to accompany her translation of *Speculum* but not published with it, owing to Irigaray's view that her work should stand alone, and to seminar papers by Lisa Cartwright and Serene Jones, Yale University, 1987.

20. From "Femininity," in *New Lectures on Psycho-analysis;* cited and discussed in *Speculum*, p. 25.

21. Domna Stanton criticizes Irigaray for using what Stanton calls the "maternal metaphor," on grounds that duplicate Irigaray's own critique of Plato's use of metaphor as a "matrix of resemblance." In Irigaray's own positive uses of the term, however, "mother" bears the relation of synecdoche or metonymy, not metaphor, to the category "women." See "Difference on Trial: A Critique of the Maternal Metaphor in Cixous, Irigaray, and Kristeva," in *The Poetics of Gender*, ed. Nancy K. Miller (New York: Columbia Univ. Press, 1986), pp. 157–82.

22. While describing Plato's cave, both Derrida and Irigaray follow Plato's practice elsewhere in the *Republic* of using mirroring as a synonym for the representational projection of shadows and creation of copies; on the tradition that art mirrors life, see M. H. Abrams, *The Mirror and the Lamp* (London: Oxford Univ. Press, 1953), pp. 30–35. Irigaray also follows Virginia Woolf's use of the mirror to figure women's historical relation to men: "Women have served all these centuries as looking-glasses possessing the magic and delicious power of reflecting the figure of man at twice its natural size." Woolf, *A Room of One's Own* (1929; New York: Harcourt Brace Jovanovich, 1957), p. 35. While Woolf's image seems to be of a slightly convex mirror, Irigaray privileges the concave; and while Woolf sees women's power in the possibility that they could take the mirror away—"if she begins to tell the truth, the figure in the looking-glass shrinks; . . . take it away and man may die"— Irigaray sees power, if still a negative power, in the act of mirroring itself.

23. In Irigaray's view, "mimicry [*mimetisme*]" is the best subversive strategy available to women given our embeddedness in androcentric culture. Irigaray explains that form of irony in this way: "One must assume the feminine role deliberately. Which means already to convert a form of subordination into an affirmation, and thus to begin to thwart it. . . . It means to resubmit herself . . . to ideas about herself, that are elaborated in/by a masculine logic, but so as to make 'visible,' by an effect of playful repetition, what was supposed to remain invisible." Irigaray, *This Sex Which Is Not One*, trans. Catherine Porter with Carolyn Burke (Ithaca: Cornell Univ. Press, 1985), p. 76. As Gillian Gill points out, concave mirroring is Irigaray's chief vehicle for mimicry, a practice best exemplified by the relation between *Speculum* and the works of such androcentric thinkers as Plato and Freud. Gillian C. Gill, "Introduction," and "The Burning Glass of Theory: Luce Irigaray in the Context of Franco-American Feminism," unpublished essay, Lexington, Mass., 1980.

24. It is never clear whether the entire structure of the mirrored cave is a male projection that women revise, or whether women "are" truly this kind of cave (rather than Plato's). Nor is it ever clear where the light comes from: whether from "incendiary chambers" of her own or, instead, from the sun (the light of sameness) or from the sunlike male gaze. Of course, such destabilizing of a reader's expectations for coherence and linear logic is part of the point; Irigaray points out about her book that a mere "reversal" or overturning would "amount to the same thing in the end."

25. In French, the puns on *glace*—meaning both "mirror" and "ice"—and on *mère/mer*—meaning "mother" and "ocean"—make this point more resonant; the section of *Speculum* titled *"Une Mère de Glace"* develops this point more fully.

26. Ward takes the Mrs. Nedeeds' positioning in the basement to mean that they are Dantean sinners just like the rest of the inhabitants of Naylor's hell (their crime would be treachery). She may be right, although I have been reading their location as the sign not of their own crimes but of their husbands'. At any rate, that Willa can reverse her descent into this lowest circle suggests that she is not down there for her crimes alone; or, to put it another way, it suggests that her criminality (and that of the other women) cannot be understood wholly in the terms of free *choice* that govern Dante's conception of hell.

27. Toni Morrison, *Sula* (New York: Knopf, 1974), p. 5.

28. Susan Gubar, "Sapphistries," *Signs*, 10 (1984), 43–62; Patricia Klindienst Joplin, "The Voice of the Shuttle Is Ours," *Stanford Literature Review*, 1

(1984), 25–53; Nancy K. Miller, "Arachnologies: The Woman, the Text, and the Critic," in *The Poetics of Gender*, ed. Nancy K. Miller (New York: Columbia Univ. Press, 1986), pp. 270–95; Sandra Gilbert and Susan Gubar, *The Madwoman in the Attic* (New Haven: Yale Univ. Press, 1979); Hélène Cixous, "The Laugh of the Medusa," trans. Keith Cohen and Paula Cohen, *Signs*, 1 (1976), 875–93; Luce Irigaray, "When Our Lips Speak Together," in *This Sex*, pp. 205–18; Monique Wittig, *Les Guérillères*, trans. David Le Vay (New York: Viking, 1971); Jane Gallop, "Reading the Mother Tongue: Psychoanalytic Feminist Criticism," *Critical Inquiry*, 13 (1987), 316.

29. Naomi Schor, "Female Fetishism: The Case of George Sand," in *The Female Body in Western Culture*, ed. Susan Rubin Suleiman (Cambridge, Mass.: Harvard Univ. Press, 1986), p. 368. Schor builds her argument on Sarah Kofman's *The Enigma of Woman*.

30. Christine Froula has proposed patriarchal rape as a paradigm for women's relation to patriarchal literary canons; see "The Daughter's Seduction: Sexual Violence and Literary History," *Signs*, 11 (1986), 621–44. For a related formulation, putting patriarchal rape at the center of women's experience of literature, see Joplin.

31. This claim for the authenticity of representations of women's voices in male-authored classical literature has, however, been made persuasively in two recent articles. See Joplin, and Christine Froula and Adrienne Munich, "Women, Literature and the Humanities: A Reply to Carolyn Lougee," *Women's Studies Quarterly*, 9, No. 2 (1981), 14–15. Froula and Munich write, "Might not Marcela's declaration of independence [in *Don Quixote*], even though fictional and male-authored, show 'woman thinking' as well as Christine de Pisan's historically true lament that she was not born a man?"

◆◆◆◆◆◆◆◆◆◆◆◆◆◆

Linden Hills: A Modern Inferno

CATHERINE C. WARD

Gloria Naylor's second novel, *Linden Hills*,[1] is a modern version of Dante's *Inferno* in which souls are damned not because they have offended God or have violated a religious system but because they have offended themselves. In their single-minded pursuit of upward mobility, the inhabitants of Linden Hills, a black, middle-class suburb, have turned away from their past and from their deepest sense of who they are. Naylor feels that the subject of who-we-are and what we are willing to give up of who-we-are to get where-we-want-to-go is a question of the highest seriousness—as serious as a Christian's concern over his salvation.

Naylor could not have chosen a more suitable framework for *Linden Hills* than Dante's *Inferno*. The Dantean model emphasizes the novel's serious moral tone and gives a universalizing mythic dimension to what otherwise might be considered a narrow subject, the price American blacks are paying for their economic and social "success."

An interest in Dante is a well-established tradition in American letters.[2] The *Divine Comedy* has been translated and edited by such diverse poets as Longfellow and John Ciardi, and it has been analyzed by American critics from James Russell Lowell to T. S. Eliot. Dantean echoes, allusions, and inversions occur in the works of novelists from Nathaniel Hawthorne to John Hawkes and of writers as various as F. Scott Fitzgerald, Amiri Baraka (Le Roi Jones), and Norman Mailer.[3] By basing the structure and the ethic of *Linden Hills* on the *Inferno*, Naylor places the novel at the heart of the American literary tradition; moreover, she forces all her readers, and not just the middle-class blacks who are the subject of *Linden Hills*, to apply to their own lives the hard questions the novel raises.

The novel also shows the influence of some of the best contemporary black writers without imitating any one of them. *Linden Hills* deals with men's oppression of women, a subject that Alice Walker has examined so forcefully in *The Third Life of Grange Copeland* and *The Color Purple*. Naylor's novel also emphasizes the important role a person's cultural history plays in his identity, a topic that has been explored by Paule Marshall in *Praisesong for the Widow* and by Toni Morrison in *Song of Solomon* and *Tar Baby*. Finally, the lyricism and imagery of *Linden Hills* recall the poetic style of both Morrison and the earlier Zora Neale

Hurston. Naylor is a fresh, daring voice in American letters; let us look at the Dantean materials she uses to shape her story; then let us listen to the tale itself.

Like Dante, Naylor believes that man is a rational being with the power of choice and that his choices matter. Naylor's Linden Hills, like Dante's Hell, represents not so much a place as a state: the consequences of man's choices. To dramatize this state Dante pictures Hell as a huge, funnel-shaped pit that lies beneath Jerusalem and is entered through the Dark Wood of confusion and ignorance. Ten concentric circles contain separate categories of sinners and two special groups of souls who are not fit for Heaven but still do not deserve the punishment of Hell. Just beneath Jerusalem but above Hell is a plateau occupied by the neutrals, those who have never made any clear moral choice. Beneath this plateau is the vestibule to Hell, Circle One, where virtuous, unbaptized pagans such as Virgil dwell. The sinners who occupy Hell itself are divided into two large classes: 1) those who have sinned because of an uncontrolled appetite, and 2) those who have sinned because of malice or the misuse of reason. In the first class are sinners guilty of lust, Circle Two; of gluttony, Circle Three; of avarice and prodigality, Circle Four; and of anger and melancholy, Circle Five. The second class of sinners is punished in lower Hell, a walled-off section, called the City of Dis, which is under the direct rule of Satan. In Circle Six are the heretics, whose intellectual pride has led them to prefer their own version of truth to God's.[4] In Circle Seven are men who committed acts of violence or bestiality: tyrants, marauders, suicides, spendthrifts, and blasphemers. In Circle Eight are the fraudulent, those who have perverted their intellects, such as seducers, hypocrites, or evil counselors. Beneath this circle is Circle Nine, where traitors are frozen in a lake. At the center is Satan himself, who constitutes Circle Ten. A gigantic figure, Satan is trapped in the frozen lake from the waist down. He had three faces, and from each mouth dangles the body of one of the arch-traitors: Judas, Brutus, and Cassius.

Naylor's tale is an allegory based on the physical and moral topography of Dante's *Inferno*. It covers four days in the life of a twenty-year-old black poet, Willie Mason, who lives in a poor neighborhood called Putney Wayne that lies above Linden Hills. Working temporarily as a handyman to earn money to buy Christmas presents, Willie passes through Linden Hills and, like Dante, analyzes the moral failures of the lost souls he encounters. By the time Willie escapes from the frozen lake at the bottom of Linden Hills and crosses to the safety of a nearby apple orchard, he has experienced a spiritual awakening. The "new" Willie has decided to give up his aimless drifting and to take charge of his life. He becomes, as his name implies, a decisive builder. He accepts responsibility for his life, he refuses to blame his problems on others or on fate, and he realizes that he can choose a middle way between the poverty of the ghetto and the depravity of Linden Hills.

Eight concentric drives cross Linden Hills. First Crescent Drive through Fifth Crescent Drive correspond to Circles One through Five in Dante's upper Hell.[5] Below upper Linden Hills lies a more exclusive section, the Tupelo Drive area, which corresponds to the City of Dis. At the center of Linden Hills is the house of Luther Nedeed, surrounded by a frozen lake.[6] Luther Nedeed is the fifth of his line; the original Luther Nedeed came from Tupelo, Mississippi, and founded the area in 1820.[7] The Luther Nedeeds are the Satans or anti-Christs of Linden Hills. Each one has been both an undertaker and a real estate developer and thus has been able to control the residents in death as well as in life. The novel traces two journeys. It follows Willie Mason's physical journey through Linden Hills and his growing awareness of the spiritual qualities that true success should have; and it traces Willa Nedeed, Luther's wife, as she discovers the history of the Nedeed women and, through their failures, learns what success should mean for a woman.[8]

In Linden Hills up is down; the most prestigious lots are those lower down the hill. To gain one of these lots, which are never sold but are leased for 1001 years,[9] each of the residents must give up something—a part of his soul, ties with his past, ties with his community, his spiritual values, even his sense of who he is. Like Dante's lost souls, the people of Linden Hills live on a circle that is appropriate to their "sins." Here most residents stay for the rest of their lives, locked in their wrong choices. Those who move usually move down, although at least one person, Ruth Anderson, has returned to Putney Wayne.

Two typical residents are Maxwell Smyth, who lives in upper Linden Hills, on Third Crescent Drive, and Laurel Dumont, whose home is lower down, off Tupelo Drive on the sixth circular road. Smyth and Dumont are male/female counterparts at different stages in their scramble down Linden Hills. Smyth is Naylor's version of a Dantean glutton; his excessive appetite is not for food, however, but for professional advancement in the white corporate world. So far Smyth has been able to satisfy his hunger for professional success: he is the highest ranking black executive at General Motors. But the price for such advancement has been high: Smyth has given up his racial identity. In order to make "his blackness . . . disappear," he adopts tricks like spelling his name "Smyth," getting straight A's, never appearing to sweat or get cold, avoiding sex and its "erratic rhythms and temperatures," and adopting a special diet and routine that allow him to control even his bowel habits so they become a five-minute ritual. Smyth is in "a race against the natural"—and he is "winning."

Laurel Dumont has already achieved the professional goals that Smyth craves. Laurel's name suggests her status; she has been a winner all her life. Smyth stifles his natural and physical impulses in order to conceal his racial identity, but Laurel cultivates her natural and physical talents while she starves herself emotionally. Laurel's mother died when the child was quite young, and when her father remarried, Laurel felt alienated from her stepmother. Consequently, the girl began spending summers in rural Georgia with her grandmother, Roberta Johnson. From the grandmother's tales of Brer Fox and Brer Bear, Laurel might have absorbed some of the old woman's practical wisdom and capacity for love. Instead, the girl concentrated her energies on improving her swimming skills in order to bring home trophies. Throughout her life Laurel cuts herself off from Roberta's world and remains trapped in a "private valley" where she "wrap[s] her soul around . . . trivial things." Laurel attains these "trivial things" in quick succession. After graduating Phi Beta Kappa from Berkeley, she works her way into a top executive position at IBM and marries a man predicted to become the next State's Attorney, but she remains emotionally detached from her husband and even from her deepest sense of herself. Laurel is an Amazon who mutilates her spirit in order to be both successful and free. She is what Smyth will become if he keeps on "moving down" in Linden Hills. When her husband of ten years decides to divorce her, she faces not just the emptiness of her life, but the emptiness of herself. Finally, a confrontation with Luther Nedeed makes Laurel realize that there is no inner core to her person, only a frightening void. When she kills herself by diving off the high dive into an empty pool, her faceless body symbolizes her spiritual state.

The novel starts just outside Linden Hills, when Willie meets his friend and fellow poet, Lester Tilson, in the schoolyard of Wayne Junior High. Lester, like Virgil, is Willie's companion and guide. Willie is in a Dantean Dark Wood, having dropped out of school after the eighth grade because he considered formal education a corrupting influence.[10] Lester, who finished high school but refused to attend college, writes his poems down; but Willie's poetic tradition is oral and therefore ephemeral. Like a modern *scop*, Willie composes poems in his head, memorizes them, and then recites them for pay. Willie's accomplishments are fragile, to say the least. The two poets greet each other under the three bronze plaques over the doors of the high school. The inscription on the plaques is a parody of the opening nine lines of the *Inferno:*

> I am the way out of the city of woe
> I am the way to a prosperous people
> I am the way from eternal sorrow
>
> Sacred justice moved my architect
> I was raised here by divine omnipotence
> Primordial love and ultimate intellect

Only the elements time cannot wear
Were made before me, and beyond time I stand
Abandon ignorance, ye who enter here.

In order to gain the wisdom that he needs, Willie has to "abandon ignorance" and pass through these doors, but the pathway is dangerous. Most of the people whom Willie meets in Linden Hills have misused their knowledge. Naylor is suggesting that, far from imparting wisdom or a true sense of one's cultural history, the schools are often the gateway to spiritual corruption.

Willie and Lester go from the schoolyard to visit Ruth Anderson, who, like Willie, also lives on Wayne Avenue, a poor street just outside Linden Hills. Ruth had once lived on Fifth Crescent Drive, but now, after a divorce and marriage to Norman, who suffers from periodic schizophrenia, Ruth lives in poverty so extreme that it's a "standing joke" even on Wayne Avenue. She and Norman have next to nothing: one sofa, one cheap kitchenette set, two towels and washcloths, three styrofoam cups. Two cups are for guests, and Ruth and Norman share the third. Ruth epitomizes the ultimate in human love, just as Dante's Beatrice symbolizes Divine Love. Ruth was not always content to live in such poverty. After four years of marriage to Norman, she realized that as long as she stayed with him she would never be able to have the children and the comfortable home she dreamt of. But as she packed to leave Norman, Ruth was immobilized by a painful pelvic infection. Fighting against his own personal demons, Norman struggled to bring Ruth some painkillers. Impressed by Norman's concern for her, Ruth stayed. Now she and Norman help each other to bear their pain. When Willie asks half-jokingly which partner rules the family, Norman answers, "'Love rules in this house,'" and Ruth agrees. Ruth, who tells Norman that she will follow him anywhere except back to Linden Hills, is the ideal wife of the Book of Ruth, who finds a second husband in an alien country. Lester fails to see Ruth's spiritual intensity. To him, she is simply an object he lusts after. But to Willie she is a dream and a source of inspiration. It is Ruth who suggests to Willie that he and Lester earn Christmas money by working at odd jobs in Linden Hills. Although Willie is afraid of going into Linden Hills, he enters to please Ruth. Later, Ruth sends Norman down to Fifth Crescent Drive because she is afraid Willie may be in trouble.[11]

Ruth is not quite real, nor is she meant to be. She is a symbol of the fullest expression of human love. But even though she is willing to sacrifice her life out of love for Norman, she will not sacrifice her spirit for him. Ruth knows who she is, where she comes from, and where she's going. She is no plaster saint, but a beautiful, joyous person—in sharp contrast to Laurel Dumont or the Nedeed women.

Once in Linden Hills, Willie and Lester stop at Lester's home on

First Crescent Drive.[12] Here, like the neutrals in the vestibule outside Circle One of the *Inferno*, live those who are neither good nor evil, the uncommitted who chase after banners and are stung by wasps and hornets that cause putrid, oozing sores. Into this category fall Lester's sister Roxanne[13] and their mother, and to some extent Lester himself. The trio is nasty and bickering. Lester mocks his mother's materialism and eagerness to be accepted by those "further down" in Linden Hills; Lester resents his mother because he believes that she pushed his overworked father to an early grave while the father tried unsuccessfully to earn enough money to keep his wife happy. Also, Lester considers Roxanne a hypocrite because, though she has given token support to Civil Rights issues, her true goal is to marry "well." Sarcastic and unloving with his mother and sister, in his own eyes Lester is morally superior because he refuses to go to college and supports himself by giving poetry readings and doing an occasional odd job. But he continues to live in comfort at home, while condemning the source of his physical comfort. The Tilson family members are tormented because they never make a clear choice, always afraid that if they do, they will miss something. Yet they have been warned by old grandmother Tilson that the price of living under the Nedeed domain is too high. When old Luther Nedeed tried to buy her land and then lease it back to her, Grandma Tilson ran him off her property. She warned her children and neighbors that they were in danger of losing the "mirror" in their souls, of forgetting what they "really want and believe." Like Roberta Johnson, Grandma Tilson is a voice from the past whose message goes unheeded. The three generations of Tilson women show a gradual degeneration of spirit. Grandma Tilson was her own woman, free and defiant. Lester's mother craves entrance into lower Linden Hills, but never gets there. Roxanne has not made her move yet, but she is clearly "headed on down."

Willie and Lester spend their first full day of work as busboys at the wedding of Winston Alcott of Second Crescent Drive, equivalent to Dante's circle of carnal sinners. Winston has been persuaded to end an eight-year relationship with his lover David because rumors of Winston's homosexuality threaten his legal career. As a reward to Winston for entering a doomed marriage, Luther Nedeed grants him a lease on the exclusive Tupelo Drive area. David and Winston are Naylor's version of Dante's Paolo and Francesca, the lovers who were tempted to passionate indulgence after reading an Arthurian romance. The medieval lovers are punished by being locked in an eternal embrace while they fly around in a perpetual whirlwind. In Naylor's version, David recites and parodies a Whitman poem as a means of announcing to Winston that their love affair will end if he goes through with the marriage. David's and Winston's punishment is not the eternal embrace of Paolo and Francesca, but a lifelong separation. David suffers in this circle because he loves a man who is unworthy of him, but Winston is headed for lower Hell, among the betrayers. Both are miserable. Willie is shocked when he surmises the relationship between David and Winston and Winston's rejection of it, but at first Willie is secretly "proud that someone black could afford" such a lavish reception. Later, however, Willie sees that beneath the glittering surface, the wedding guests are devoid of life and spontaneity. They are not living; they are watching themselves live.

At the Alcott wedding Willie meets Xavier Donnell from Third Crescent Drive, the circle of the gluttons. Xavier is in love with Roxanne Tilson, but he worries about whether she would be a "wise" choice as a wife. Xavier is as ambitious as Maxwell Smyth; he just hasn't learned all of Maxwell's tricks for hiding his blackness. When Xavier asks Maxwell's opinion about marrying Roxanne, Maxwell advises against it because Roxanne's family "has one foot in the ghetto and the other on a watermelon rind.'"[14]

Willie's and Lester's next task takes them to Fourth Crescent Drive and the home of Chester Parker, who is entertaining mourners the night before the funeral of his wife Lycentia. Here we find greedy indulgence of all kinds. The house is crowded with guests who keep the twelve chairs around Chester's dining room table filled. The scene is a depraved parody of the Last Supper as Parker's guests stuff themselves with food, especially with the white cake that Luther Nedeed brings. The mourners cut, chew, and swallow with abandon. As soon as one eater vacates a seat, another takes his place. This feeding frenzy is a paradigm of Linden Hills where new residents rush in to take over one of the leases as soon as it is available. The table is also a reflection of Chester's marriage. Lycentia is not yet buried, but Chester has hired Willie and Lester to steam off the wallpaper in her bedroom so that the room will be repapered and new furniture moved in during the funeral; thus all will be ready for Chester's next wife as soon as Lycentia is buried.

Lycentia is a dog-in-the-manger type. In life she spearheaded a group whose goal was to block a housing development in Putney Wayne in order to preserve the property values in Linden Hills. Lycentia called it keeping "those dirty niggers out." Luther Nedeed completes Lycentia's work by cutting a deal with a white racist organization. The parallel to the *Inferno* is clear. In Circle Four the sinners formed two groups, the avaricious and the prodigal, and waged war by pushing huge boulders against each other. Indulgence leads these sinners to form hostile gangs. Ironically, when the followers of Nedeed and Lycentia unite to obstruct housing for the people of Putney Wayne, they are really rejecting a part of themselves, their own past.

The next day these same mourners gather to hear the Reverend Michael T. Hollis conduct Lycentia's funeral. The Reverend lives at 000 Fifth Crescent Drive, the last house on the last circle in the upper section of Linden Hills. This drive parallels Circle Five in the *Inferno*, where the angry tear at each other and the melancholic bring forth a bubbly froth whenever they try to speak. Hollis is a lesser version of Nedeed, and the two quarrel at Lycentia's funeral.[15] Hollis is angry because he thinks that Nedeed is infringing on his territory by assuming an official role at the service. As the president of the Tupelo Drive Realty Company, Nedeed delivers a eulogy whenever a tenant dies. Hollis is also depressed. He has to lubricate himself with multiple shots of Scotch in order to deliver an old-style, emotional sermon. Years spent pursuing sensual pleasure and material possessions have isolated Hollis. He has an endless supply of women, closets full of expensive suits, and a couple of LTD's, but he has lost his wife and he has lost touch with his own feelings.

Two brick pillars mark the entrance of Tupelo Drive and the last three levels of Linden Hills,[16] where Laurel Dumont, Professor Daniel Braithwaite, and the Nedeed "family" live. When Willie witnesses Laurel Dumont's suicide, he sees her make the last of a series of wrong choices. The history of Laurel's decline lies in the string of residents that Willie has met so far and what they had to give up to get where they are. Her education fed a professional ambition that left no room for human love. She never forged any ties with her past or developed any close sense of her own identity.

Willie is sickened by Laurel's suicide, but the other witness, Daniel Braithwaite, remains analytically detached.[17] Braithwaite is a history scholar whose entire education has been paid for by Nedeed. Once Braithwaite received his Ph.D., he moved one street down from the Dumonts into a home given to him by Nedeed; here Braithwaite has lived for thirty years. With a clear view up and down Linden Hills and full access to the records of the Tupelo Drive Realty Company, he has written a twelve-volume history of the area. His goal is to be awarded a Nobel Prize. Braithwaite has abandoned ignorance, as the inscription over the door of Wayne Junior High admonishes, but his knowledge is sterile because it is irresponsible. This Daniel is no prophet. He leads no one. Since his wife's death, Braithwaite's house has remained tomblike, closed up. He killed the willow trees in his yard because they blocked his view of Linden Hills and the cemetery that encloses the Tupelo Drive section. Year in and year out, Braithwaite sits here recording the decay around him. He has no intention of stopping the corruption he observes, only of using it as a means of winning an honor. The fraudulent counselors in Dante's Circle Eight gave false counsel, but Braithwaite refuses to counsel at all. Appalled at Braithwaite's abandonment of the responsibility that his knowledge entails, Willie asks himself, "After such knowledge, what forgiveness?"[18] Braithwaite's negative example makes Willie resolve never to become the hired pen of any man or group. Willie leaves Braithwaite's house determined never to live in Linden Hills if it is "'the last place on earth.'"

During the four days that Willie has been working in Linden Hills, he has suffered from increasingly terrifying nightmares that reflect his daytime experiences.[19] He dreams first of a huge clock with snakes and spiders for hands, then of hands shooting out from rows of coffins and offering him specious gifts; finally he dreams of himself—a man with no face. The dreams trace the path of degradation that Willie has witnessed in Linden Hills and the temptations he has suffered and rejected. Twenty years old, Willie is not yet at midlife as Dante was, but he faces a crisis nevertheless. Time calls him to face his adulthood and to assume some direction as a man and an artist. Carrying a catalogue of his poetry in his head and reciting selections on demand is not enough. More serious work awaits him, but he fears that he will sell out for unworthy gains, or, worse yet, lose touch with himself. On Christmas Eve Willie sits alone on his window sill and takes stock of his journey so far. He decides that there is "no such thing as fate or predestination. . . . People . . . [make] their own fate." Willie makes up his mind to leave Putney Wayne, but not for Linden Hills. He will succeed in some other, as yet undefined, way. Before he can go on to life beyond Linden Hills, however, Willie and Lester have one more chore to complete, helping Luther Nedeed put up his family Christmas tree. Nedeed has agreed to match whatever they've earned all week if they will help him.

With great reluctance Willie goes, lured by the money. There he meets his female counterpart, Luther Nedeed's wife, Willa Prescott Nedeed. She has been making her own journey through time as she discovers the history of the Nedeed women. All of the Nedeed men except the last have married octoroon women, whose paleness of skin matched their paleness of spirit. Each wife bore her husband one black, froglike son, who was a physical and spiritual duplicate of the father— all except for Willa Prescott Nedeed, who is dark-skinned but bears a fair son. Nedeed considers the child a bastard, and to punish his wife he locks her and the six-year-old boy in the morgue-basement of their home with a limited supply of cereal and water. The son, who is Nedeed's but carries the light-skinned genes of his maternal ancestors, dies; but Willa survives and, dazed, roots through the papers and trunks in the base- ment that reveal to her the stories of the previous Nedeed women. Theirs is a tale of progressive depersonalization, as each husband became in turn more cruel and evil than his father. Willa suffers in this circle because she is a traitor. She has betrayed herself by willingly submerging her own identity in her husband's. She becomes his faceless tool and allows him to starve their son to death without really putting up a fight. Willa hopes that if she doesn't protest about Nedeed's murder of their son, Luther will allow her to come out of the basement and bear him another child. She is like Count Ugolino in Circle Nine of the *Inferno*, who, with his sons and grandsons, was imprisoned in a tower and starved. Unlike Ugolino, however, Willa ultimately finds salvation.

What saves Willa is what she learns about the previous Nedeed women from the homely records they have left behind in letters, diaries, cookbooks, and photographs. Naylor implies that the history of women is found not in books and official archives but in the oral wisdom of a Roberta Johnson or a Grandma Tilson and in the mundane records of women's daily lives. From the papers of Luwana Parkerville, Willa learns how enslavement by her husband causes Luwana to lose faith in God. Because Luwana's husband had bought her before he married her, she literally belongs to him. After he uses her to produce the male heir he requires, he totally ignores her. When Luther reads a newspaper account of a slave who kills his owner by poisoning his soup, he denies Luwana the one service she has been allowed to perform for her husband and son—cooking. Years pass; no one speaks to Luwana and she speaks to no one. But her total silence is not even noticed. In desperation she writes and answers letters to herself. A religious woman, Luwana eventually loses faith and decides, "'There can be no God.'"

Next Willa discovers the history of the second Nedeed wife, Evelyn Creton Nedeed. Evelyn tries to manipulate her world through food. First she bakes huge meals in order to win her husband's attention, if not his love. Then she grinds up various aphrodisiacs in the dishes she serves him. When neither device works, she starves herself to death by eating little and consuming large doses of laxatives. Wife number three, Priscilla McGuire Nedeed, is more sophisticated, more aware, and more exuberant than either of the previous wives. A series of photographs traces her deterioration from a laughing, free newlywed to a mother increasingly held down by her son, who casts a deeper and deeper shadow across her face. She changes from being an animated woman with a strong sense of her own identity to a fading and finally absent presence. In the last photos, she has cut out or blotted out her face and in the empty space has written *"me."* The three wives are Naylor's versions of the three arch-traitors whom Satan chews on in Circle Ten. Judas, Brutus, and Cassius have betrayed their lords or benefactors; the Nedeed women have betrayed themselves. Each has cooperated with her husband's denial of her value. Luwana is Luther's silent victim, who renounces God instead of renouncing her husband's treatment. Evelyn tries to earn her husband's love for a while, but finally gives up and destroys her own body. Priscilla is worse. Without a fight, she watches as the shadows of her husband and son blot out her soul.

Naylor has said that the treatment of the Nedeed women symbolizes the way that men have regarded women throughout history—as means of generation that have no value in themselves. As far as men are concerned, women have no history because they do not really exist. Now Naylor calls attention to that history.

For four days Willa's voice, "a long, thin wail," has risen from her basement prison and reverberated throughout Linden Hills. The cry is the lamentation of generations of women whose existence has been denied by men, and it is Willa's own "plea for lost time." At first Willie cannot hear Willa's plea; later it grows stronger and haunts him. To rid himself of nightmare images of Willa Nedeed, whom he has never met, Willie tries to capture her essence in a poem: "'There is a man in a house at the bottom of a hill. And his wife has no name.'" By the time Willa emerges from the basement, she has found the identity she had lost. Shocked by Priscilla's annihilation of her self, Willa staggers around the basement in a daze and glances down into a pan of water. There she sees the reflection of her soul, which Grandma Tilson had warned her children never to lose. When Willa sees the blurred outline of her dirty, emaciated face, she realizes for the first time that she really exists. At that moment she is reborn. She cries, then drinks the stale, rusty water and decides to rebuild her life.

Willa examines and evaluates herself for the first time. Like Willie, she decides that she is responsible for her life; she is stuck down in the cellar not because of her parents or Luther, but because of herself. Willa realizes that she has made wrong choices and is continuing to make them. Luther may have led her to the basement steps, but she had walked down herself and can walk back up whenever she is ready. This knowledge gives her "strength" and "power" but then leaves Willa exhausted, and she sleeps. In her sleep she recreates her person and awakens "Willa Prescott Nedeed," determined to set her house in order. She cleans the filthy basement where she has lived for weeks. Then, carrying the body of her son in her arms, she goes up the steps and pushes open the door leading into her kitchen. Its latch had been accidentally knocked open by Willie when he was helping Nedeed get boxes down from the attic. When Willa steps into the kitchen, she accepts fully the realities of her life with all of her mistakes—she accepts who she is and where she has been, and she takes charge of where she is going. Willa is determined that nothing will hinder her from putting her life in order.

She begins to clean her kitchen, and when Luther tries to stop her, she hits him. When he tries to keep her out of the rest of the house, she grabs him, while still holding on to the child. The three are locked in a fatal embrace—as negative and positive life forces, with the dead child between them. In their struggle they brush against a fireplace, and the train of an old bridal veil that is wrapped around the child's body ignites. Although Willa and Luther are destroyed in a flash fire that sweeps the house, still Willa is triumphant. She has put an end to the Nedeed dynasty and has inspired Willie to continue his spiritual odyssey wherever it leads him.

Linden Hills is an uncomfortable and dangerous book which pricks the conscience. It takes the reader on a perilous pilgrimage and forces him to consider the hidden cost of his choices. It strips him of the ease of innocence. Naylor has risked much by writing such a disturbing tale.

Her readers may view her subject too narrowly. If they do, she could lose a black audience that feels unjustly challenged and a white audience that thinks the novel's hard questions are not meant for them. Naylor also risks offending modern sensibilities that regard an allegory about moral accountability too medieval for their tastes. But because Naylor knows who she is, where she has been, and where she wants to go, she dares to tell her tale and dares the reader to reckon with it.

Notes

1. *Linden Hills* was published by Ticknor & Fields in 1985. Naylor's first novel, *The Women of Brewster Place* (1983) won the American Book Award for the best first novel.
2. For further studies of Dante's influence on American writers, see La Piana, Paolucci, Giametti, and Vickery.
3. Pellegrini's *American Dante Bibliography* is published annually in Dante Studies and lists articles that discuss Dante's influence on the American writers mentioned in this paper.
4. There are no heretics in Linden Hills because Naylor's sinners are at odds with themselves and not necessarily with God. Luwana Nedeed might be considered an exception, but she is actually worse than a heretic.
5. Naylor omits the vestibule of the neutrals, Dante's Circle One, and places her neutrals on First Crescent Drive. There is no plateau for the virtuous unbaptized pagans in Naylor's version. She considers Lester, her one pagan, as a neutral and places him in the first circle. Heresy and failure to be baptized are offenses against belief, and Naylor is not concerned with belief as much as she is with choice.
6. Luther's house number is 999. In a letter to me, Naylor says that she gave the house this number because in Linden Hills, where up is down, 999 "is really 666, the sign of the beast."
7. Naylor derived the name Nedeed from an inversion of "de eden." She felt the name was appropriate because the Nedeeds are the Satanic rulers of this false paradise (Interview with Cromie).
8. Naylor equates Willie Mason's and Willa Nedeed's ideas of success with salvation (Interview with Cromie).
9. These long leases represent eternity (Interview with Cromie).
10. Like Willie and, to a lesser extent, like Lester, Naylor too turned her back on formal education for a while. After finishing high school, she turned down a scholarship to college and spent seven years as a Jehovah's Witness minister. But at twenty-five she gave up her religion and entered Brooklyn College, after which she went to Yale (Interview with Cromie).
11. A heavenly messenger came to help Dante at a similar place in Hell. Dante could not get into the City of Dis without assistance because the descent was too steep. The implication in both versions is that one does not end up in the depths of Hell through inadvertence. It takes a conscious effort to get this far down in Hell.
12. Lester is both a good pagan and a neutral. He has not really accepted the American social system, having refused to attend college. Thus he is unbap-

tized. He is a neutral, too, because he is able to choose but has not done so, and he suffers from the punishments of Dante's neutrals.

13. Roxanne is an inversion of the heroine in *Cyrano de Bergerac*. The original Roxanne was loved by two men, one openly, the other secretly, with the secret lover helping to win Roxanne's hand. Naylor's Roxanne is loved by Xavier, who refuses to admit his love to her. He is discouraged from pursuing his love by Maxwell Smyth, who believes that romantic love is a luxury that the ambitious cannot afford. Cyrano, on the other hand, sacrifices all for love.

14. Naylor, like Dante, considers gluttony a more serious sin than lust because gluttony is a solitary form of self-indulgence, while lust is shared.

15. The hostile, depressed Hollis represents the consequences of total indulgence, while the cold, dispassionate treachery of Nedeed is the product of his universal and absolute malice. The only thing he can love is himself or an image of himself. Both men live at the lowest spot in their section of Linden Hills, and both serve the subdivision in an official capacity. Their home numbers (Hollis, 000, and Nedeed, 999) mock each other.

16. Dante includes a number of subtypes of sinners in the lower circles of Hell. Naylor omits this further classification of sinners.

17. The symbolism of Braithwaite's first name is clear. The name Daniel alludes to the Old Testament prophet who was among the captives taken from Jerusalem to Babylon. Because of his power of divination he became a minister to the Babylonian kings. Braithwaite's last name may refer to William Stanley Braithwaite, a well-known English teacher at Atlanta University. Braithwaite, who lacked a degree in higher education, was also a minor poet, a critic, and an editor. See Butcher's two articles, which trace Braithwaite's achievements.

18. Naylor quotes extensively from T. S. Eliot's "Gerontion" at this point in the novel. Braithwaite is an obvious parallel to the "old man" in a "decayed house," "Being read to by a boy," Willie.

19. Willie's three dreams may be parallels to Dante's dreams in the *Purgatorio*.

◆◆◆◆◆◆◆◆◆◆◆◆◆◆

Gothic and Intertextual Constructions in *Linden Hills*

KEITH SANDIFORD

Grandma Tilson, I'm afraid of hell.
Ain't nothing to fear, there's hell on earth.
I mean the real hell where you can go when you die.
You ain't gotta die to go to the real hell.

This paper attempts to define the generic and structural nature of Gloria Naylor's *Linden Hills* (1985) by explicating specific formal and ideological features of that novel that link it to the tradition of gothic fiction, and by investigating how the novel's multilayered narrative structure works to produce its final textual integrity. In choosing to preface this article with four lines of dialogue from the novel's ten-line epigraph, I mean to appropriate the aptitude and felicity of an image that foregrounds the thematic and structural concerns of the ensuing discussion. Both in form and content those four lines adumbrate larger novelistic issues and strategies. The epigraph's dialogic (dialectic) form prefigures Naylor's fictionalist strategy of opposing divergent textual categories and their implicit assumptions to explore the nature of textual authority and its relation to knowledge, gender and power. Grandma Tilson, the speaker of the second and fourth lines, was the only woman, indeed the only person of any gender, to oppose the patriarchal authority that furnishes the figure and shape of villany in *Linden Hills*. In its totality, the epigraph typifies the contrapuntal quality of discursive engagement among those divergent textual voices that give the novel its distinctive polyphonic character.[1] Abstracted, Grandma Tilson's lines assume a power that is at once strategic, definitive, prophetic; on the whole, the full ten-line exchange foregrounds a structure of text and context that fittingly supplies both prolegomenon and apologia for Naylor's fiction.

Two fundamental assumptions, therefore, will guide this inquiry. The first is that *Linden Hills* defines itself as a gothic fiction by refiguring the traditional idea of evil into the shape of a modern patriarchy, obsessive in its preoccupation with lineal continuity, androcentric in its definition and pursuit of political reality, and thus engendering a pervasive climate of terror, repression and entrapment in order to disvalue and exclude female and androgynous subjectivities from access to power. The second assumption is that Naylor adopts certain polyphonic strategies to accommodate a diversity of textual voices, providing thereby a ground for engagement between her novel's overvoice and the legitimized, canonical voices of the novel's intertexts, opening up new "discursive spaces"[2] for "other" (unlegitimized, uncanonized) voices to represent themselves in texts that are often radical and extraliterary.

The conjuncture of these two assumptions institutes a marriage of gothic form and intertextual strategies; it provides a fecund context for a variety of dialogic engagements: the overtext discourses generally about texts and authorship, the intertexts discourse polemically among themselves, sometimes sympathetically, sometimes oppositionally.[3] The deployment of this gothic-intertextual structure illuminates how texts function to embody, perpetuate, supplant and/or reform notions of knowledge and power. The gothic-intertextual paradigm may also serve to represent Naylor's authorial relationship to *Linden Hills* as well as the relationship of all the novel's other "authors" to the novel's intertexts. In Naylor's case the relationship is signified by a renunciation of her own authorial prerogative to univocity in exchange for the moral authority to unlock (deconstruct) the closed texts of patriarchy, and place them in oppositional interaction with "other" texts, transforming an otherwise monologic structure into a "dialogic confrontation."

Some reflections Naylor shared with Toni Morrison in a *Southern Review* conversation clearly evidence that, in composing *Linden Hills*, Naylor privileged the dialogic over the monologic, polyphony over univocity. She explained that she gave her characters full freedom to make their own choices, to discover and exercise their own voices, to be authors in their own right, thus fictively assuming the subordinate role of merely providing a mirror in which they could see themselves reflected. This legitimization of "other" voices attests to the Barthean construction of writing as an open, democratic process that gives meaning to history.

Once again, the epigraph is apropos. Grandma Tilson's matter-of-fact declarative enacts a distinctly historicist, if subjective, performance. It demystifies and displaces the eschatological category "hell" in the intertext of her exchange. Similarly, the novel's overtext extends the referential value of the same category, distributing it throughout the novel's diverse intertexts.

By the author's own acknowledgment, the physical and spiritual topoi of Linden Hills were suggested by Dante's richly allusive vision in the *Inferno*. However, in accordance with the requirements of the novel's modern mythology, Naylor's project had to transcend mere appropriation. It therefore exploits and transforms the signs and references derived from the *Inferno*. The effect is primordially illustrated in the representation of Nedeed patriarchy.

Founding the ancestral homestead in a mortuary establishment at the universally contemptible dead end of Wayne County, in close proximity to the cemetery, and willfully electing to share the neighborhood with an equally despised assortment of social outcasts (murderers, root doctors, carpetbaggers, bootleg preachers), Luther I sets about defining himself as a demonic quantity by his peculiar physical features and his monomaniacal dream of personal and racial power.[4] The infernal associations are further amplified in the rapid expansion of the Nedeed real estate domain along a clearly suggestive topography of eight residential crescents or circular drives wherein upward mobility is accomplished by a downward movement, and ultimate social "arrivance" marked by the damned soul's proximity to 999 Tupelo Drive, the most socially desirable address in the evil empire. The basis for the Nedeed intertext is thus laid by inverting the conventional rules of order and cynically subverting a (mainly black) middle-class faith in the possibility of racial progress. However compellingly these moral and philosophical inferences may emphasize the intersection of Naylor's novel with the *Inferno*, Dante's work is not its sole signifying system. Certain other specific themes and motifs characterizing the central narrative of the Nedeed saga are clearly drawn from a gothic family romance intertext. The Nedeeds' identical physical features of pale skin, bulging frog eyes, and squat bow legs and their self-isolation in a large white clapboard house with basement morgue, surrounded by a moat and drawbridge, supply the outward visible formations of inward evil deformations. But these by themselves would amount to little more than the familiar, stereotyped apparatus of gothic fiction. The gothic intertext develops with rather more sophisticated complexity in the patriarchy's gradual accretion of power (unassailable even by the town's mayor and council), in its monomaniacal obsession with architectural projects (particularly of the funerary sort), and in its all-male progeny stretching through four generations, each successive heir sharing an identical first name, each fashioning his own legendary status by individual heroics. These signifiers of monomania—concern for name, lineage, and political continuity—point to the qualitative conditions of crisis and anxiety that constitute the psychological substructure of gothic.

Still other factors illuminate the relation of the Nedeed family romance to gothic fiction. Nedeed's apostasy irrevocably commits each heir to the pursuit of ultimate secular power objectified in marble, mortgages, and mammon. The Nedeeds materialize as latter-day Vatheks, damning themselves and holding out an equal opportunity for countless other hopeful residents to cooperate in realizing the Nedeed Faustian psychotic vision and working out their damnation: "Because when men begin to claw men for the rights to a vacuum that stretches into eternity, then it becomes so painfully clear that the Omnipresent, Omnipotent, Almighty Divine is simply the will to possess. It had chained the earth to the names of a few and it would chain the cosmos as well."[5] Systematically engineering the demographic qualifications for residence in Linden Hills to lure applications from both blacks and whites in Wayne County and from persons of various ethnicities from all over the country and the Caribbean, Nedeed assays a new social myth of classlessness and racial harmony, which offers to all an equal opportunity to realize the hellish paradox of an earthly paradise: "Of course Wayne County had lived in peace with Linden Hills for the last two decades, since it now understood that they were both serving the same god. Wayne County had watched the wedge of earth become practically invisible—indistinguishable from their own pathetic souls."

In their headlong career to reach 999, Linden Hills residents invert the normal rules of order governing social mobility, to move up in the world is to move down toward Nedeed, to rise socially is to fall spiritually toward dehumanization, self-extinction and spiritual death.[6] Nedeed's studied Satanic ability to make the hopeful believe down is up marks him as the consummate fictionalist.

The dual signs of gothic and intertextual strategies converge also in the Nedeed fixed rites of copulation. On the one hand, the objective and operation of the protocols are rigidly prescribed to produce a determinate genetic result (all male offspring) and to devalue and exclude female participation. As gothic structures, the protocols reflect the male gothic text's preoccupation with patriarchal values, privileging male over female. This question will be more fully canvassed in the section analyzing texts that exemplify female and androgynous subjectivities. On the other hand, the inscription of these rites in astrological charts and journals, all bound and locked away in a rolltop desk, constitutes the formal textualization of Nedeed patriarchy. Embodying the procreative rituals, those journals are canonical texts, producing the Nedeed intertext as a closed system, determinate of reference and restrictive of access, these documents consist with Barthes' definition of a classical text as "a body of writing that cannot transcend the knowledge of its period, and is therefore, capable of being written only once." In like terms, the relationship of each successive Nedeed male to these artifacts is that of an ecrivant, a practitioner whose writing (or reading, in the case of each Nedeed after the original patriarch) targets purely pragmatic and utilitarian ends intended in this instance to prescribe and regulate the conditions of coitus and geniture. Insofar as they deny Nedeed mothers any active role in the socialization of their sons, and insofar as the rules interdict the begetting of female progeny (thus preempting any possibility of infusing new strains and extending the bloodlines), the texts effectively exclude female voices from semantic authority. Given their unique quality, definition and intent, such texts are neither capable nor desirous of making themselves writable to a diverse reading public, as they preclude possibilities of "continuing fabrication of meaning." Ritually encoding absolutism, tyranny and monomania, they define themselves as monological and univocal: they do not assume a potential interlocutory audience (witness the passive-submissive role assigned to woman).

These characteristics are dramatically personified in the total behavior of Luther V, the Nedeed who presides over the main action of the novel. In language, emotions, work and moral complexion, he exemplifies the hereditary male rationalist principle encoded in his guiding maxim, "It's always been done that way." Inflexible in his commitment to ancestral decree, he approaches sexual matters with a sterile, clinical precision and discharges his other spousal responsibilities with passionless severity. Above all, though, it is in his language that all the most vital moral signs of his lineage coalesce, primarily those that reveal his misogyny. In a moment of solitary reflection, he delivers himself of this maxim from the patriarchal text: "breaking in a wife is like breaking in a good pair of slippers. Once you'd gotten used to them, you'd wear them until they fell apart, rather than go to the trouble of buying another pair." While his attribution identifies the text as patriarchal in origin, the situation and the signification also characterize it as monological, not only because he has no physical audience, but, more importantly, because he desires none, nor would brook interlocution if there had been one. Decoded, Nedeed's speech reveals that he is incapable of switching texts/voices, even for public discourse. His exhortations to Winston Alcott on Alcott's wedding day preserve the ironic ambiguities of the patriarchal rhetorical register: "You're burying one way of life for another. But if you'll suffer me a further metaphor, after every death is a resurrection, hopefully one to paradise." Not only are the metaphors here familial in origin, but they are also charged with the ironic ambivalences (resonances) of the Linden Hills myth. At the wedding reception later that day, his rhetorical register is equally ceremonial, stiff; in language (text) and gesture, his public presentation of a mortgage to Winston for a house on Tupelo Drive binds Winston more securely into the text of Nedeed imperium. Lester Tilson—who is observing all these ceremonial proceedings with voyeuristic curiosity—likens Nedeed's oratory to something "straight out of a gothic novel."

Besides the formulas of his speech, the rituals of his work also enshrined the signifiers directly referable to the hereditary text. In the preparation of female cadavers for burial, "He had to undress those bodies, move his hands slowly over the skin to check the flow of the formaldehyde. Those weren't breasts, thighs, hips; they were points of saturation. He was a technician." Distinctly patrimonial (Nedeed had learnt his art at his father's side), this discourse with the self accompanies his skilled, controlled movements about the mortuary lab. Its vocal quality echoes the preceptor text in the manner of a diligent (but not too imaginative) pupil rehearsing a teacher's instructions: "Standing by his father's side being told to forget all the nonsense he had learned in school about cosmetic techniques and procedures: female bodies were different. With the proper touch you could work miracles. Their skin wouldn't remain rigid and plastic if the fluid was regulated precisely. Just the right pressure and resistant muscles in the face, neck, arms and legs gave themselves up completely to your handling. Moved when you made them move, stayed where you placed them. Attention to the smallest details—edges of mouth, curves of wrists—could bring unbelievable life into the body before you. But it was a power not to be abused; it took gentleness and care to turn what was under your hands into a woman." Decoded, the collective signs of discourse, movement and action in these passages manifest recurrent gothic and intertextual modalities. Down to the insertion of the fish head into the female vagina, the rites are executed without the slightest variance from the letter of the patriarchal canon. His precision and fidelity mark him as the consummate gothic technician. His relation to the corpse, especially the female corpse, was that of an illusionist, a veritable makeup artist, a true fictionalist of the mortuary art.

Though this production of the female body (with its manifest associations of dominance-submission, perversion and necrophilia), as a voiceless, plastic object, is the supreme metaphoric figuration of female value in *Linden Hills*, to an equal extent all other bodies in *Linden Hills* are similarly defined and subsumed beneath the tyranny of the Nedeed text's logocentric, determinate body. However all-consuming this may seem, the Nedeed text is, ultimately, only an intertext of *Linden Hills* and, as such, is inevitably brought into dramatic confrontation with the voice of another text. In the verbal collision at the Dumont home on December 23, Nedeed's fixed determination to evict Laurel is met with her equally stubborn resolve to continue residing in her nuptial home despite an imminent divorce. The formal terms of the interview underline the irreconcilable oppositions of voices, the radical points of view of two conflicting myths. Characteristically, Nedeed's language is formal, legalistic; the voice is monological, basing its authority on text of Mr. Dumont's lawyer's divorce notice and the sympathetic concurrence of the sexist mortgage covenant of the Tupelo Realty Company. Immediately grasping the patriarchal political assumptions of Nedeed's discourse, Laurel opposes them with her own dialogical interlocutory text/voice:

(Luther): "I don't think you understand, Mrs. Dumont. This land was only leased to the Dumonts in 1903, and subsequently the Tupelo Realty Company underwrote the mortgage for the house that was built on it. Now, that gave them the right to live here for a thousand years and a day, which in effect is a small eternity, but it is still a lease. And under our stipulations, if the Dumonts no longer wish to reside here and there are no children to inherit the lease, the property reverts back to the original owners: my family—the Nedeeds. That decision has been made, Mrs. Dumont.

(Laurel): "No, let's back up a minute, Luther. Howard Dumont made that decision, not Laurel Dumont—not me. And this Dumont is telling you that she is going to stay here.".

(Luther): "The Decision isn't yours, Mrs. Dumont."

(Laurel): "You're damned right it's mine." Laurel leaned over. "Don't come in here bringing any of that crap from the Middle Ages. You see, I know how it is in your house, Luther. But Howard speaks for Howard, and I speak for me. We're in the twentieth century up here at Seventy-Two Tupelo Drive. And I have as much say about the future of this property as he does."

(Luther): "You're in Linden Hills, Mrs. Dumont. Read your lease. And this property belongs to the Tupelo Realty Corporation."[7]

The interview reveals several things. Laurel Dumont defines Nedeed's discourse as anachronistic, unreal; she denies it any textual validity, indeed denies the very existence of a discourse, annihilating it with her own intertext: ("This conversation isn't taking place"). She refigures the nature and terms of the discourse: ("There is no way that this conversation is taking place in my living room, with this man . . . telling me that I don't exist. That I don't live in this house"). The subtle shift in rhetorical voice and register denotes the flexibility and adaptability of her text to meet changed discursive demands: she moves from an ironic second-person familiarity ("I know how it is in your house") to third-person (impersonal) distance ("There is no way that this conversation is taking place in my living room, with this man . . . telling me that I don't exist. That I don't live in this house"). Her discourse therefore claims authoritative parity with Nedeed's and with the other cooperating structures that undergird it. The parameters of her speech extend the limited issues of power and property raised in Nedeed's text to include the very issues of reality and ontology themselves.

While Laurel Dumont's remonstration with Nedeed dramatizes most explicitly the vulnerability of Nedeed's hegemonic text, hers is not the only overt challenge to Nedeed's voice. On the previous day, at Lycentia Parker's funeral, the Rev. Michael Hollis had enacted another episode of Naylor's texts-in-conflict paradigm by opposing his improvised sermon to Nedeed's sterile clichéd eulogy. The rhetorical confrontation that results resembles Dumont's in polemical weight and intertextual significance, but the more public nature of the material discursive space (a congregation of mourners at the Sinai Baptist Church) and the participation of a full choir with Sister Wilson as musical accompanist render Hollis' stratagem markedly dialogical, while isolating and exposing Nedeed's flat, uninmaginative presentation as monological ("His voice droned on and on"). Hollis' true motives for switching from a prepared sermon to an extemporaneous text were face-saving (he was too intoxicated to read his prepared text), cynical (he wanted to "signify" upon his shared unworthiness with the deceased and all her Linden Hills mourners), and political (here was a calculated attempt to assert power and precedence over Nedeed). This oratorical moment also provides Naylor with the right context for signifying the extenuation of the Nedeed patriarchal voice and the spiritual effeteness of the whole Linden Hills myth. Where Nedeed would have assuaged the mourners' sorrow with the baroque power of the Bach funeral canon, Hollis' changed format stirred their snobbery with the more culturally relevant gospel strains of "Amazing Grace." Nedeed's eulogy was a banal, conventionalized text prepared to flatter Lycentia Parker's social and civic life. Hollis publicly and contemptuously shreds his prepared text and meditates vehemently on the very notion of preparedness, casting ironic aspersions on the spiritual preparedness of the deceased and of all Linden Hills dwellers. Where Nedeed is staid, formal, and stiff, Hollis is histrionic, unseemly, and excessive (rocking Lycentia's coffin and screaming at her corpse).

The minister's Biblical scholarship might be penetrating enough to decode the mortician's diabolical design from the signs of his house address (999), but Hollis' claim to spiritual superiority over Nedeed (by virtue of residing at 000) is as hollow as the spaces in the middle of those O's. His desire to arrogate to himself the morality (perfection) and divinity (the Holy Trinity) he attributes to the numerological sign 000 only thinly masks his deeply troubling sensations of private guilt over his marital infidelity, advanced alcoholism, and a rapidly plummeting credibility among his congregation. His is, in fact, a voice which has itself lost force, power: "his field of energy had dwindled and receded farther to the back of the church." Dumont, for all the self-possession and legitimacy of her challenge to Nedeed, is riven internally by guilt over her phenomenal career success and her failed marriage. She is, in fact, a woman on the verge of suicide.

Undeniably, both the Hollis and Dumont verbal assaults on Nedeed authority work to deconstruct the Linden Hills myth and weaken the patriarchal voice. Still, at the end of each successive episode, neither the challenger nor Nedeed holds the balance of moral power.

The interpolation of such voices, then, ought not to be conceived as ascribing any privileged value to the texts they represent. In keeping with John T. Matthews' formulation, we may interpret the process of intertextual confrontation exemplified above as a dialectic of one social presence (intersection of certain coded forms of behavior and utterance) striving to burst into the verbal space of another social presence by "rupturing and dissolving" the coalescences in order to assert an "individual sense of uniqueness." Put differently, these voices merely attempt to carve out particular verbal spaces; they are staking proprietary claims to textual parity, rather than attempting to establish some absolute moral order in a textual hierarchy.

As a group, the four Nedeed wives, whose voices speak through the intertexts of *Linden Hills*, produce texts that qualitatively illustrate this notion. They assert social presence by striving to rupture and dissolve the formidable coalescences of (Nedeed) patriarchal texts. Willa discovers her voice as she resurrects the burried voices of three former

Nedeed wives. The four voices are then transmitted on the main frequency of the novel's overtext where they take an irruptive stance against the Nedeed narrative. The resultant structural shape of these female intertexts is a *mise en abyme:* Naylor—producing—Willa—producing—other Nedeed women.[8]

Written as covert responses to tyranny and loneliness, the Nedeed wives' texts define themselves unequivocally as gothic forms by their nature and mode of production. In each case the female author forges a text out of her self-division and entrapment which is finally read by another woman, the last Nedeed wife, in her time of similar extremity. Imprisonment within the "flawed enclosures of family and household" causes self-division and ultimate insanity, but ironically, it also frustrates the intentions of Nedeed misogyny by radicalizing these women, awakening their consciousness to the true nature of their status and function within the Nedeed patriarchy. The Nedeed females' texts challenge social and political reality. Each female author creates a structure that helps her to achieve self-expression, while at the same time employing techniques of subterfuge and subversion, with either a literal or metaphoric relation to subterranean spaces. The mode of these texts' production is calculated to dethrone prescriptive univocity or, as Hillis Miller terms it, "inside becomes outside, outside inside, dissolving polarity." It is principally here that Naylor's narrative-within-narrative achieves its most powerful effects, and the contest sharpens between these female voices and the absolute voice of the patriarchy in which they are trapped. The problematics of authorship for Nedeed women are highlighted not only in the restraints placed on their voices but also in the prohibitions imposed on their capacity to wield power and control the products of their own bodies. Their texts are never permitted to see the light of day; they lack full (equal) control over their sexuality, their offspring, and their households. Thus, they are doomed to remain mothers, never fathers, of their own work.[9]

Including letters, diaries, photo albums and cookbooks, recipes, cosmetic concoctions and love potions, the Nedeed female texts represent widely diverse forms of the gothic genre. As Fleenor observes in *Female Gothic,* "there is not one gothic but gothics." The texts' relation to this genre is also self-evident by the gender of their authors and the gender of their readers. By virtue of their total identity as Nedeed property, all these women are entrapped in the Nedeed patriarchy and cut off by marriage from nurturing female support systems. The narratives of their lives refer slightly or never to their mothers; they are either motherless or appear to be so.[10] Furthermore, their wifely duties severely limited their contact with wider family, placing them in a condition of total dependency on the Nedeed power structure not only for their material subsistence but also for self-definition and validation. Fleenor calls this condition "the reflected self motif."

Luwana Packerville's life is buried in at least three significant inter-textual remains: her Bible (the gift of a slave mistress), her letters and notes (placed between the books of that Bible), and her wedding veil. Luwana's being a bondswoman to the Packervilles in Mississippi and then bondswoman-wife and mother to Luther I and Luther II, respec-tively, initiates the gothic female experience of all the Nedeed wives that were to follow her. Though literate and lucid, her writings are the scribblings of an abused, rejected wife whose role and voice in the family are gradually whittled away until she is denied communication with her son and accorded only the most formal courtesies from her husband. Not only is she alienated from that narrow family circle, but she is also alien-ated from herself. Verging on insanity from the privations and self-divi-sions, she resorts to clandestine journal- and letter-writing (discourses with the self); this awakens her consciousness to the reality of a ne-glected self ("the true horror is that I am becoming a true stranger to myself") and to the existence of an alter-ego, the only audience she can have for such a blatantly unauthorized discourse. The reinvention of voice in epistolary discourse with the alter-ego reveals the conflict be-tween the obedient loyal wife and the radical consciousness about her own oppressed condition and about her precise relation to the Nedeed design ("I fear that I have been the innocent vessel for some sort of unspeakable evil").

Luwana Packerville articulates early in her narrative the problemat-ics of female authorship. In the face of vacuity and inertia, she must turn to reading as her "sole pleasure." Even as she writes her journal entries, she is painfully aware that she lacks an audience ("I write to no one and am missed by no one on this earth. . . . But sometimes I do indeed wonder what it is like to have someone to care about what you will say"), expressing thus a poignant sense of the female's disability in a world where only male authorship is valued or legitimized. The manner of writ-ing and defining a space for her reflections is especially remarkable. In-terleaved as they were between the books of the Bible, these thoughts occupy a series of interstitial spaces, constituting themselves as in-tertexts. As such, they open up spaces for an "other" voice, a female voice to speak to, dispute with, render inclusive, and continue that most patriarchal of Judeo-Christian texts. These features represent the quint-essential liminality of female texts as a genre. Also nontraditional in their message and manner of production are the 665 lines Luwana tattoos into her skin with a pin and her own blood to record the number of times her husband and son speak to her after a year of absolute silence. These lines suggest stripes of self-flagellation inflicted out of Luwana's victimized feelings of self-division and guilt. The number 665 is significant, just one short of the unspeakable numerological sign for Nedeed. This subversive, polemicist attitude ends in Luwana's outright denial of God: "There can be no God," a legend she has inscribed on the inside cover of her Bible.

Luwana's texts are undoubtedly dialogical; searching for their own voice and placing it into creative engagement with other voices, her texts covertly resist the monologic of Nedeed's and kindred patriarchal systems. In their assumptions and rhetorical character, Luwana's writings are open and accessible, desirous of an audience: From this aspect—and especially in their interstitial relationship to the Bible—they are seen to accomplish a critical textual transformation, an act Barthes describes as "an impetus to perpetuate the plural nature of writing. . . . a desire to continue works that appear to have been continued or finished." That Evelyn Creton's texts derive from those precise circumstances that engender the female gothic is manifest from the dichotomy between the social role she so efficiently performed and the private hunger she suffered from unsatisfied sexual and emotional needs. Publicly, she fulfills all her domestic roles with quiet dignity and meticulous efficiency: "This woman never had a curl out of place, a ribbon knotted loosely, a stick of furniture not glowing with lemon oil. She gave the right parties at the right time for the right people." Privately, she struggles with the ache of her husband's personal neglect and desertion of the marital bed. In the Nedeed context of deformation and moral evil, the otherwise distinctive marks of a proud housewife's personal order and method dissolve into behavior that is aberrational and obsessive. Evelyn is driven to physiological self-abuse (binge-purge syndrome) and psychological madness. Her compulsive recording and revision (with only minor variation) of the recipes for each meal, together with the purchase dates of foodstuffs, and her purchasing and cooking massive quantities of food ("The woman cooked as if she were possessed") evidence characteristic female gothic guilt about her (mistaken) responsibility for her husband's failure to yield her intimacy and affection. Similarly, she concocts inordinate quantities of cosmetic preparations for her hair and skin in an attempt to enhance her appeal and lure Nedeed. Again, the nature and processes of production involved here are noteworthy. Evelyn's texts are being elaborated even as she creates her recipes. A recipe is in itself a a very specific kind of composition: first a particular arrangement of components is conceptualized in the mind, then those mental and verbal concepts are given concrete form as a consumable artifact. This is the very analogue of textual composition.

Of all the Nedeed wives, Evelyn most clearly illustrates the relation of gothic to archaic consciousness. As she reverts to the folk epistemes of her female forebears, she brings that legacy of herbological and occult lore to bear on her quest for a way to resolve her desperation. The signs of witchcraft—use of incense, oils, bull testicles, orchid root, ginseng and the menstrual fluid of virgins—are all the raw revelations of "the relentless accuracy with which this woman measured her anguish." Such desperate measures also betray Linden Hills' failure to acknowledge the peculiar subjectivity engendered by the oppressive space of Nedeed life and provide remedial resources for the psychological abnormalities immured within that space. Her recipe books "exposed such raw and personal needs that the woman herself had probably wanted to forget them."

By resorting to occult practices she most probably inherited from her womenfolk, Evelyn aligns herself with a source of power that circumvents and subverts the secular, material and male rationalist principles of Nedeed dominion. Evelyn's development consists closely with that gesture, described by Fleenor, of the female at odds with the male structured universe ("It seems that whenever women reach back to find a form to convey protest, or rage, or terror, or even humor, they find the Gothic. It seems that the Gothic allows us—as readers and writers—to express the conflict for which patriarchy has had no name"): Embracing this archaic belief system, she displays the very ground and origin of her voice. Rooted in the need to find a language and an ethos that would expressly validate her own subjectivity, her obsessive-compulsive compositional processes (written, culinary and occult) are attempts to invent a discursive space of her own.

Though by no means identical in form (indeed, they defy conventional textual form), nor as extensive as Evelyn's recipes, Priscilla McGuire's family photos represent an equally radical textualization of her voice in its confrontation with the Nedeed patriarchal voice. The photos of her in single womanhood are suffused with freshness, spontaneity and zest. Willa's reading extrapolates from the photographic texts of these early years the irrefutable marks of personal autonomy: Priscilla's involvement in liberal-progressive social and political causes manifests her native passion for life. With her marriage into the Nedeed family, though, Priscilla's photo-history begins to chronicle a gradual suppression of those vital spirits and that native will to self-determination. As her yearly lilac-ink inscriptions on the family photos record the birthdays and growing presence of the Nedeed child, they also document her own inversely proportionate absence as a political quantity from the Nedeed equation. The heavy dark Nedeed hand laid repressively on her shoulder, combined with the heavy dark shadows cast by her son, unites gothic and intertextual signs. The hand functions as a proprietary signifier to oppress and exclude. Spanning her reproductive and vocal organs, the shadow achieves the exclusionary design of the Nedeed text to muzzle "other" voices, even as it asserts typical gothic control over Priscilla's sexual, procreative and discursive potentialities, damming them up forever, now that the single male offspring has been delivered. Hand and shadow are thus metaphors for the continuing gothic discourse on control of sexuality and procreation, yea, dread of female sexuality.

To complete the description of the Nedeed women's voices and constitutive intertexts, it only remains to define Willa Prescott's role and relationship to them and to *Linden Hills'* larger gothic and intertextual processes. Last of the Nedeed wives, Willa is uniquely situated to play the role of historian/redactor of the texts of all the women who preceeded her. Her place in the tradition defines her as one of those writers who, as Barthes describes them in *Le Degre Zero de L'Ecriture*, is destined to become "the unhappy consciences of their historical moment." Within her single voice, she unites the functions of reader, narrator and interpreter, transforming herself into the historian of these women's lives and experiences. As she seeks to impose meaning on the texts and make sense of her own cruel fate at the hand of Luther Nedeed, she discovers and adopts for herself the initial impetus that formed these women's voices, that impulse not to be lost to history, to matter in a way that Nedeed's objectives sought to deny her and them. In reading the texts of Luwana, Evelyn and Priscilla from her subterranean locus of exile, she reads (writes) the text of her own life within the flawed structure of Nedeed patriarchy. Her project is at once the reconstruction of Nedeed female voices and the deconstruction of the Nedeed male voice to render Nedeed history truthful and entire. The texts and her continuing structuration of them unfold for her new revelations about the meaning of her name (Willa equals will, resolve) and help her to rediscover the shape of her face. The process allows her to grow in authority over her emotions and to find the will to resist and repudiate the Nedeed imperium over her (even as the tyrannical voice invaded her discursive space via the basement loudspeaker): "She listened numbly . . . There was no meaning to those patterns of empty noises. Their words didn't connect to any history or emotion. She was past being moved to disbelief, frustration, or anger. The power of that voice was gone."

While Nedeed means his imprisonment of Willa to assert punitive-political hegemony over her as his wife, Willa transforms that isolation and exclusion (as the other Nedeed wives before her did theirs) into an opportunity for introspection and discovery; gothic and intertextual strategies conflate in both these processes. As Willa reflects upon the very sound of her name and specific memories of her girlhood, she understands that the accidents of gender and socialization had mapped out this fate for her from the very moment of her conception. Now motherless and fatherless, she intuits that her victim status in relation to Nedeed had been defined from the beginning, that she had started walking down those basement steps from the second she was born. Nedeed's capricious exercise of the power to ration her food and water and, his tormenting accusations of infidelity and treachery serve to instill the same mental and emotional traumas that had produced madness in Evelyn and Luwana. Appearances notwithstanding, Naylor clearly does not intend her form of insanity to be an expression of extreme cognitive incapacitation: Willa exploits her madness as a political response to patriarchal terror, discovering in her subterranean exile the power of absence, a passive yet potent method of resistance. The very thoughts she thinks and the texts she reads become convert subversions of the Nedeed system, ultimately forcing Luther to violate his ancestral Christmas rites for the first time ever in Nedeed history. Thus Willa confers value and legitimacy on a set of female experiences commonly defined as madness and widely supposed by Freudians to arise from fundamental female biological and sexual causes. All these she transforms into productive, heuristic events that feminist scholars like Chesler affirm as an attempt by the biologically, sexually, and culturally castrated female toward a "doomed search for potency."

As a practitioner of intertextual processes, Willa authorizes her own distinctive voice in ways that show her developing consciousness about the imperatives for a female writer in her condition. When she uses Luwana's wedding veil to furnish forth the winding sheet of her dead child, she pronounces a kind of defilement and defiance on Nedeed structures. When she assents to Luwana's apostate creed ("There can be no God") etched in the Bible swathed by that same veil, she not only signals her solidarity with Luwana, but she also defines Linden Hills as a moral universe from which the principle of regular order has removed itself. These actions manifest her conscious dissociation from the Nedeed myth.

Reading these texts Willa opens up hitherto interdicted structures of subjectivity to gain self-knowledge, clarity and, above all, resolution. Reading these women's writings, she releases their voices from a long enforced silence, and rekindles a discursive process that had been extinguished by the heavy hand of Nedeed authoritarianism. In a characteristic writerly gesture, Willa continues the process of structuration by the order and shape her reading/writing confers on these texts. Her project is not merely to reproduce the discovered texts in fidelity to their originals but also to complete them by imaginatively supplying those places where the texts are silent. For example, she derives such an intimate understanding of Evelyn's motives and dilemmas that she is able to complement that author's text by interpolating vividly imaginative sketches of Evelyn's furtive visits to the railroad depots and to the dingy backrooms of grizzled old women who supplied the raw materials (bulls' testicles, menstrual fluid, etc.) for her recipes and potions. Interpreting the emotions and imagining the sense of helplessness Evelyn must have experienced, Willa continues Evelyn's writing as she reads: "She probably lay awake in that empty canopied bed, preparing a thousand explanations in case he discovered their presence; but she would have been hard-pressed for the language to explain their need. She had watched the twentieth century bring a multitude of new words to Linden Hills without one to validate these types of desires in a Mrs. Evelyn Creton Nedeed."

While the Nedeed women's persecution experiences may be attributed to their gender-role relationships to Nedeed male power, Naylor does not posit strict biological identity or female gender-specific behaviors as the sole cause of those gothic and intertextual structures that openly challenge Nedeed authority in *Linden Hills*. Through certain dissonant male voices, Naylor broadens the basis of her novel's argument for the plural nature of history and subjectivity. Willie Mason holds a relationship to the production of these male voices similar to Willa's participatory and mediative role in producing the women's. Reputed in his neighborhood as a "'deep' dude," Willie gestates hundreds of poems in his head, never committing any to writing because of his deep distrust of the written word, especially white-controlled media. Social and economic deprivations combine to nurture in Willie a dissident poetic sensibility that marginalizes him from Linden Hills society and places him in resolute antagonism to Luther Nedeed. His intense and instinctive curiosity about Laurel Dumont and Willa Prescott defines his as a sympathetic or androgynous consciousness (he is the only one to hear Willa's piercing wail from the basement).

In two separate episodes of particular relevance to Nedeed and Linden Hills, Willie assumes the narrative consciousness through which the reader's understanding of rhetorical moment and meaning is illumined.

At the wedding of Winston Alcott and Cassandra, Willie and his friend Lester Tilson watch the wedding guests from the kitchen through double glass doors. That point defines his outsider status in Linden Hills, but it also affords him the advantages of invisibility and penetration—all at once. With his peculiar intuitive cognition, he reads and interprets the signs of gothic and intertextual value, especially as they emerge in the rhetorical and ceremonial parts of the proceedings.

Winston's decision to marry was instigated primordially by patriarchal anxieties. His father feared that a blackmailer's threat to expose Winston's homosexuality would jeopardize Winston's social standing in Linden Hills and in his law firm. Luther Nedeed himself urged the marriage as "a step which would ensure the stability and growth of Linden Hills." Nedeed's compulsive gothicism transformed the wedding into yet another manifestation of Linden Hills' evil and horror. Driving Winston and his best man David to the church, Nedeed couches his paternal reassurance about married life in the terms of a funereal analogy: "You're burying one way of life for another. But if you'll suffer me a further metaphor, after every death is a resurrection, Winston—hopefully, one to paradise." Later, at the reception, the heavy dead hand of Nedeed officialdom continues to prescribe and shape events. His oratorical performance at the reception was true to Nedeed style: formal, brief and businesslike, he laced his speech with elegant archaisms and he crowned it with the richly symbolic presentation to the newlyweds of a mortgage on Tupelo Drive, a necklace and matching cuff links, the three gifts symbolic of their bondage to Nedeed.

Both the symbolic and material signs of Nedeed's performance were calculated to reinforce Nedeed's terms of order and ratify Nedeed's political potency over Linden Hills affairs.

However, the next toastmaker, David (Winston's erstwhile male lover, now his best man), frustrates the Nedeed impulse to univocity by appropriating a text of Walt Whitman ("Whoever you are holding me now in hand") to challenge and deconstruct Nedeed's performance, as well as to pronounce his distaste and hostility upon those traditional codes that made his eight-year-long affair with Winston impossible of consummation.

Whitman's poem's polyvalent signification accords suitably with David's polyphonic design. By introducing certain subtle variations into his rendition of the poem, David deploys Whitman as a writable text, appropriating its indeterminable signs and references to diverse targets in the audience. Ostensibly, David offers the verses as a tribute to the bride, but this gesture is purely for the consumption of a public "that had given him no words—and ultimately no way—with which to cherish . . ." the "joys" and "communion" he had shared with Winston. His prefatory remarks anticipate and comprehend plural significations rather similar to those in Whitman's poem: "Mr. Nedeed addressed Mr. Alcott and so I would like to direct my remarks to the other half—and as some would say, the better half—Mrs. Alcott." In asking Cassandra to imagine that his voice is Winston's addressing the poem to her, he really attempts to produce the emotions and desires that Winston might have liked to convey to his bride and Linden Hills guests:

> The whole past theory of your life, and all conformity
>   to the vibes around you, would have to be abandon'd;
> Therefore release me now, before troubling yourself any further
>   Let go your hand from my shoulders,
> Put me down and depart on your way.

The intention is to convict Winston with his own self-deceit, while dissociating himself from that deceit. Fully cognizant that Winston's decision was forced on him by an unwritten Linden Hills tyrannical decree, David resists that authority and the values it preserves. To Nedeed and Linden Hills, David brandishes these verses as his imperative weapon of self-invention. Where Winston, by succumbing to pressures from his law firm and Nedeed, acquiesces in their image of the organization man, David, by deconstructing Whitman, finds a weapon to resist those forms of coercion and assert the self as antidote to the organization man.

David clearly intends to oppose his oratory as a dialogical response to Nedeed's monological performance. And Willie, with his privileged knowledge and intuitive understanding, appreciates this immediately. Marking Winston as their particular target, he points out to Lester the potent ironic ambiguities David is appropriating in both his remarks and Whitman's verses. In addressing "the other half, the better half," David pays tribute to the homoerotic part of Winston's identity, too fearful to be comprehended in the rigid prescriptions of Nedeed's univocal text or in any of the other comfortable fictions (the made man, the good son, the promising young lawyer) Linden Hills had constructed around Winston.

What David as orator and Willie as voyeur/invisible audience bring to this scene is their common androgynous subjectivities which subvert the superficial trappings of Nedeed-Linden Hills ritual and respectability. Each man is able to combine his individual consciousness and his esoteric understanding of the adaptive possibilities of language to expose Linden Hills' dark underside of contemporary evil and horror. In Whitman, David finds a voice to dramatize the deficiencies of the Nedeed system and to repudiate the self-division, uncertainty and horror that system occasions in Winston by coercing him into a conventional marriage. With voyeuristic acuity, Willie perceives Winston's private discomfort as he smiles and dances with his bride ("why that guy looked like someone had punched him in the stomach and his lips sorta froze up that way") and unmasks all other Linden Hills guests to reveal the horrific substructure of this social event. The meal concluded, he observes to Lester: "They might look like birds of paradise, but they sure ate like vultures."

In the definitive character of antagonists to the novel's fictive reality and intertextual polemicists to the Nedeed text, David and Willie enact in this episode Linden Hills' most emphatic representation of the contemporary gothic vision. Each discovers and engages something deeply terrifying in Nedeed's earthly paradise. David understands it as something soul-killing, antithetical to truth and passion. Willie reads it as glimpsed vision of nightmare and repressed desire in the physiognomic and rhetorical images informing the nuptial ceremonies and writes it as his latest addition to the poems collected in his head. In this respect, both these male figures manifest their spiritual affinity with the Nedeed women, effectively controverting those gender divisions assumed in the Nedeed text, divisions that would traditionally have inhibited these males' "apprehensions of [Linden Hills'] deep disorders and fears." *Linden Hills* thus illustrates the gothic's radical shift away from exclusive ascriptions of rationality and order to males; it bears out Doody's observation that "In the gothic novel, heroes and heroines share the nightmare and the nightmare is real."

The discursive moment captured in this wedding assembly exemplifies the evolutionary process by which gothic transcended its eighteenth-century origins and limits. *Linden Hills* affirms latter-day critical reinterpretations that argue gothic's continuing relevance to contemporary issues. It affirms the gothic's thesis that the world of form and substance is illusory and unreal, masking its horrific properties beneath such benign inducements as a mortgage on Tupelo Drive. Skarda and Jaffe write: "Evil can parade as good even amid fashionable people of wide experience. No one is protected from the problem of evil in himself and in society."

If the novel accomplishes the highest expression of gothic form in the discursive space of a matrimonial rite dramatizing gothic's concern with complex issues and questions that prove difficult or impossible of resolution, Naylor's deployment of plural voices and plural meanings in the discursive space of those macabre rites surrounding Lycentia Parker's wake ratifies Kristeva's definition of text as "a productivity, . . . a permutation of texts; an intertextuality," a space wherein "several utterances intersect and neutralize one another." At the wake, Naylor yields the canonical space traditionally occupied by the voice called "author" to a voice traditionally designated "character."

Willie Mason, that voice, is a poet in his own right, but a poet whose poems exist only in the textual space of his own head, a space radically differentiated from the space of those voices intersecting with his own, the long-standing Nedeed adversarial voice and now the collusive voice of Wallace Stevens.

The same intuitive consciousness that enabled Willie to transform the guests at Winston Alcott's wedding from "birds of paradise" into "vultures" now transforms the diners at Lycentia Parker's wake from a solemn assembly of middle-class mourners into macabre images of self-devouring cannibals. From his vantage point of invisibility on the upstairs banister of the Parker home, Willie observes the wake diners seated at the banquet table. With heads bowed over reflecting glass plates, they are not only consuming portions of rare roast beef, but they are also consuming the reflected images of themselves consuming rare roast beef. This *mise-en-abyme* effect, coupled with the click-scrape of silverware on glassware, is not lost on Willie; it immediately opens up a space in his penetrative head for the subjectivity of Wallace Stevens' poem "Cuisine Bourgeoise." The lines

> These days of disinheritance, we feast
> On human heads. . . . This bitter meat
> Sustains us . . . Who, then are they seated here?
> Is the table a mirror in which they sit and look?
> Are they men eating reflections of themselves?

furnish a definitive image, a kind of objective correlative of the scene he is witnessing. J. Hillis Miller has observed that Wallace Stevens catches in his poetry "a vision of ultimate being," not from some transcendental realm removed from the visible objects of the physical world, but from "within things as they are . . . in the presence of things in the moment." And this is distinctly the nature of Willie's poetic talents. His function at the wake, as elsewhere in *Linden Hills*, is to catch being in a way that no one else can. Willie's deconstruction of this ceremony is the penultimate gesture in the total narrative operation of deconstructing Nedeed.

It is altogether apposite that in the final denouement of this narrative, Willie Mason, the "deep dude," should be the one who hears Willa's mournful wail; it is he who ultimately releases her from her subterranean dungeon within the Nedeed gothic enclosure and it is his instinctual intelligence that finally unmasks Nedeed's true nature. In Willie and Willa (the nominal likeness symbolizing their kindred spiritual affinitiy and their common antagonistic relation to Nedeed authority) the gothic and the intertextual finally converge; they alone in their generation attain the final terror-riven knowledge of Nedeed's real hell signified in Grandma Tilson's apothegm. Naylor's harmonization of form and strategy not only achieves the ultimate deconstruction of the Nedeed text (Nedeed destructs himself and the seat of his empire in the novel's climactic inferno), but also achieves the dissolution of her own narrative and her own discursive authority through those very irruptive processes that subvert Nedeed's.

Notes

1. My use of the term "polyphonic" in this paper derives from Bakhtin's notion of the polyphonic novel as a discourse involving diverse voices interacting and competing with each other. See Mikhail Bakhtin, *Problems of Dostoevsky's Poetics*, trans. R. W. Rotsel (Ann Arbor: Ardis, 1973), 181–204.
2. Jonathan Cullers, *The Pursuit of Signs: Semiotics, Literature, Deconstruction* (Ithaca: Cornell University Press, 1981).
3. Julia Kristeva, "The Bounded Text," *Desire in Language: A Semiotic Approach to Literature and Art*, trans. Thomas Gora, Alice Jardine, and Leon Roudiez, ed. Leon S. Roudiez (New York: Columbia University Press, 1981). This interplay (colloquy) of diverse texts theoretically enacts the post-structuralist idea of continuous structuration. More elementally, it offers a clear example of that relation between texts which Kristeva describes as "a productivity . . . a permutation of texts."
4. Though Naylor's depiction of successive Nedeed males renders them virtually indistinguishable, I have assigned each Nedeed an ordinal number (Luther I, Luther II, etc.) to facilitate references to the text.
5. All textual references to *Linden Hills* are to the Penguin Books (1985) edition.
6. In symbolic numerology, primarily in the Book of Revelation, the number 999 is the sign of the beast.
7. Dialogue format and emphasis throughout this extract are mine.
8. J. Hillis Miller, "Stevens' Rock and Criticism as Cure," *Wallace Stevens*, ed. Harold Bloom (New York: Chelsea House Publishers, 1985), 36.
9. I am applying here the problem of the female author's relationship to her work as defined by Juliann E. Fleenor, ed., *The Female Gothic* (Montreal and London: 1983), 16.
10. The Nedeed wives are effectively rendered motherless by their marital entrapment in the patriarchy. This motherless condition has its definitive arche-

types in Milton's Eve and Mary Shelley's Frankenstein. For a further discussion of this interpretation, see Gilbert and Gubar, *The Madwoman in the Attic: The Woman Writer and the Nineteenth-Century Literary Imagination* (New York and London: Yale University Press), 243.

11. Phyllis Chesler, *Women and Madness* (New York: Avon, 1972), describes the incidences of "madness" in women as forms of cultural castration and women's responses thereto as a search for potency.

◆◆◆◆◆◆◆◆◆◆◆◆◆◆

Reconstructing History in *Linden Hills*
TERESA GODDU

"... the past is all that makes the present coherent ..."
—James Baldwin, *Notes of a Native Son*

African-American women's writing repeatedly foregrounds the theme of self-understanding. Often a personal journey toward self-revelation depends on an exploration of a group history as well.[1] Those who return to their roots, such as Avey Johnson in Paule Marshall's *Praisesong for the Widow* (1983), rediscover their selfhood; those who remain alienated from their past, like Helga Crane in Nella Larsen's *Quicksand* (1928), never find their liberating identity. In her novel *Linden Hills* (1985), Gloria Naylor also takes the relationship between personal identity and cultural history as her theme. By setting her story in Linden Hills, a "buppified" suburb where members derive their self-worth from the location of their house, Naylor focuses on a community of soulless people who, in climbing the corporate ladder toward a brighter monetary future, become disconnected from their cultural past. Through her female protagonist Willa Nedeed, who is buried alive in the cellar of the Nedeed house until the end of the book, Naylor outlines a recuperative vision of history, a vision which opposes the willed cultural amnesia of Linden Hills.

Willa Nedeed's personal journey toward self-discovery begins with an immersion in her maternal past. As Willa reads her foremothers' records, she writes her own story, turning cultural history into personal autobiography. Naylor would seem to use Willa's autobiographical relationship to history as the novel's model of efficacious history-making. However, to understand fully the nature of Willa's revisionary female model, the novel's alternative versions of history must first be examined: Luther Nedeed's mythic, Daniel Braithwaite's objective, and Willie Mason's poetic histories. Beginning with Luther's and Braithwaite's authorized white, male accounts, histories which deny the female subject and cover over a cultural past, I will then turn my attention to Willie's and Willa's opposing black female-centered stories, subjective histories that exhume the past in service of the present.

I. Mythic History

Myth has the task of giving an historical intention a natural justification, and making contingency appear eternal.

We reach here the very principle of myth; it transforms history into nature.
—Roland Barthes, *Mythologies*

Luther Nedeed, the founder and patriarch of Linden Hills, creates a mythic model of history. Not only does Luther live in the "dead" center of Linden Hills and in a realm of static time—"[nothing] [changes] in the white clapboard house at the bottom of Linden Hills"—but his history, told in the novel's undated prologue which lies outside the chronological progression of the other chapters in the book, also claims the timelessness of myth.[2] The Nedeed family history, which chronicles four generations of Luther Nedeeds, is based on repetition and replication instead of progression through difference. Each generation produces a single child: a "short, squat, dark" son who is a carbon copy of his father. Through the repetition of male promogeniture, the Luther Nedeeds create their own male myth: "[i]t surprised no one when the baby was male and had his father's complexion, protruding eyes, and first name—by now it had come to be expected." By making a contingent event appear eternal—that the child will be a boy, not a girl, black and not white—the Luther myth transforms history into nature, turning each individual Luther Nedeed into a single mythic man.

Luther's male myth, which claims the justification of nature, is exposed as an ideologically contingent story through the birth of a white son. The boy's whiteness undermines years of patrilineal transmission since he resembles his pale-skinned mother instead of his dark father: he looks like his "grandmother. And the mother before that." This son represents the rupture that begins the process of revisioning Luther's patriarchal myth. With this rupture in Luther's repetitive history, the novel moves out of its timeless prologue back into chronological history and begins to give an identity to the generations of women which Luther's myth has reduced to a single sign—the pale-skinned bride. Luther, however, refuses to accept the female difference which contradicts his master narrative; instead of admitting the mother's son into his system, he represses the rupture by denying the mother's son his name and by burying both mother and son alive. Luther's only recourse when faced with difference, then, is to reject, not incorporate, it.[3]

By refusing the maternal rupture, Luther not only adheres to a phallocentric model of history but also accepts a white version of the world as well. According to James Snead in "Repetition as a Figure of Black Culture," black culture is built on a "metaphysics of rupture and opening." Unlike white European culture which emphasizes the continuity of repetition, black culture allows for a break—or a "cut"—to occur in its cycles of repetition. For instance, the trickster figure, who is emblematic of black culture, works by "signifyin(g)," to use Henry Louis Gates, Jr.'s term, against the sanctioned system, "*repeat[ing] and simultaneously revers[ing]*" that system "in one deft, discursive act."[4] Unlike the signifying trickster figure who gains liberation through "repetition with a *signal difference*," Luther's repetition without a difference cannot dismantle the white word.[5] Instead of signifying against a white paradigm, Luther mindlessly borrows the terms of the white culture; he deals "with the white god who would one day *own* that sky" on that God's own terms.

Naylor's rewriting of the genesis myth in the opening pages of the book highlights Luther's inability to play the role of trickster. Luther's creation myth is a de-creation, a de-eden:[6]

> He [Luther] sat there every day for exactly seven days—his thick, puffed lids raising, lowering and narrowing over eyes that seemed to be measuring precisely the depth and length of light that the sun allowed *his* wedge of *their* world. . . . As the sun disappeared on the seventh day of his vigil . . . all the bushels [of apples] facing Nedeed's side of the road had fruit worms in them.

Luther's attempt to find a place of agency within the white world, no matter how small the wedge, ends up re-enslaving him in gold chains rather than iron to another white master—consumerism. His version of genesis does not dismantle the hierarchy inherent in a system of binary oppositions (black/white, hell/heaven, for instance): instead, it binds him even more deeply to these oppositions. If Luther cannot be God he will be Lucifer; if he cannot have eden, he will take hell; if he cannot rule "he sure as hell [can] ruin." In "Criticism in the Jungle," Henry Louis Gates, Jr., formulates this negative gesturing as follows: "To think oneself free simply because one can claim—can utter—the negation of an assertion is not to think deeply enough. . . . It is to take the terms of one's assertion from a discourse determined by an Other." Instead of transforming the system, Luther and his community end up being reinscribed within it.

By choosing to build over instead of on their past, Luther and all the lost souls in Linden Hills not only lose their signifying powers to transform the white man's world but also buy into a system which naturalizes black inferiority. When the occupants of Linden Hills in their whitewashed houses spell "real progress in *white capital* letters," they accept the white world and a white-class paradigm and, in so doing, they lose their interior self along with their cultural identity to an exterior sign of white consumerism. By permanently burying "any outside reflections about other beginnings," by rooting out those who believed "that Africa could be more than a word; slavery hadn't run its course; there was salvation in Jesus and salve in the blues," Linden Hills erases its difference and hence loses its power to rupture the dominant script. Ironically, by refusing to step into history ("step outside Linden Hills and you've stepped into history—someon else's history about what you couldn't ever do"), Luther and Linden Hills accept the white man's myth—and a whitewashed version of their own history.

II. Objective History

Our discourse always tends to slip away from our data towards the structures
of consciousness with which we are trying to grasp them.
—Hayden White, *Tropics of Discourse.*

[A] paradigm is prerequisite to perception itself. What a man sees depends
both upon what he looks at and also upon what his previous visual-conceptual
experience has taught him to see.
—Thomas Kuhn, *The Structure of Scientific Revolutions*

In its penultimate section, "December 23rd," *Linden Hills* explicitly
foregrounds the role of history in its presentation of Daniel Braithwaite,
a history professor who lives at the end of Tupelo Drive. At first glance,
Daniel Braithwaite would seem to view history differently than Luther.
Instead of covering over Linden Hills' origins as Luther does, Braithwaite copiously records Linden Hills' beginnings and subsequent evolution. In his den crammed with such books and journals as "[t]he entire
set of the Federal Works Project's slave narratives . . . every *Crisis* in
existence . . . Booker T. Washington's *The Negro in Business*, . . . [and]
Du Bois's *The Philadelphia Negro*," Braithwaite would appear to act
as the articulate kinsman for Linden Hills.[7] However, by choosing an
"objective" model of history, Braithwaite, like Luther, buys into a logocentric model of history that not only makes maleness normative but
whiteness as well.

Like Luther's myth, which claims the justification of nature, Brath-
waite's history invokes the authority of fact. If Luther thinks that he
can step outside of history, Braithwaite believes that he can escape subjectivity. Arguing that "history [is] a written photograph," Braithwaite
claims that he can record an objective reality; he assumes he can get
"the whole story, the real story if you will." However, Braithwaite himself exposes the subjectivity inherent in his objective stance when he
describes his role as a photographer of history: "Put your subject too
much in the shade, too much in the light, dare to have even a fingernail
touch the lens or *any evidence of your personal presence*, and you've
invalidated it." What Braithwaite fails to take into account is the perspective of the viewer; subjectivity enters this experiment as soon as the
scientist picks up the camera and looks through its lens.[8] As a product
of Luther Nedeed (Luther finances his education, gives him his house,
and allows him access to the records he needs), Braithwaite's eye is
conditioned to see from Luther's perspective: his house, which is among
the "final set of houses on Tupelo Drive" and closest to Luther's, allows
him the "privilege of seeing what Luther Nedeed has seen." Moreover,
by living within Linden Hills and participating in its functioning, he
introduces a variable into his closed experiment—himself.

Like Luther's myth, Braithwaite's objective history, which universal-
izes his own subjective perspective, is phallocentric. Instead of repre-

sessing the rupturing female difference as Luther does, Braithwaite simply fails to see female subjects with his male gaze. He might balance out the records he gets from Luther with other sources such as "county court transcripts, the minutes of the state realty board, personal interviews . . . et cetera," but he never takes into account the unofficial records which memorialize women's lives. When Willie notes that "Braithwaite would have gotten a much different picture all these years" if he had kept his desk up against the window which looks down toward the Nedeed house instead of up toward the rest of Linden Hills, he finds Braithwaite's blind spots: first, that he looks at Linden Hills from Luther's upward phallocentric perspective, and second, that he fails to see what goes on in Luther's house, namely Willa's imprisonment. Although he claims he "miss[es] nothing," Braithwaite does miss just that— nothing—when he fails to read the absences and the silences in the female position. Even though his real-life namesake, William Stanley Braithwaite, an early twentieth-century black poet and critic, wrote a biography of the Brontë sisters, Daniel Braithwaite misses the madwoman in the basement. Without the unofficial records of the community, the diaries Willa digs up in the basement of the Nedeed house, Braithwaite's history is revealed as just that—his story.

Moreover, by choosing an objective model, Braithwaite necessarily writes a white version of history. When he takes a neutral stance in relation to history, Braithwaite forfeits his racial perspective.[9] In response to the question "Was slavery wrong?" for instance, he declines to answer in the affirmative, replying instead that "[i]t would depend upon who you were talking to and when—black or white." Refusing to judge history from his black perspective, Braithwaite fails to act like a trickster. Instead of reinterpreting the American past through a racial lens, Braithwaite subsumes black history under a white rubric: under his pen Luther's history becomes just another Horatio Alger story. By focusing on Luther's individual achievement rather than the collective accomplishments of Linden Hills, Braithwaite transforms a communal history into the myth of a single, "special" man.[10] Braithwaite, then, simply replicates Luther's version of Linden Hills instead of signifying against it.

It is the replicating and spectating nature of Braithwaite's model, a history which can only "hope to record . . . not rectify," that the novel calls into question. By watching Laurel Dumont dive to her death, Braithwaite is finally no different than Luther—both feed off the lost souls of Linden Hills. While Luther makes money from their headlong rush into damnation, Braithwaite gains his reputation (and perhaps a Nobel Prize) from his "exclusive access" to "priceless information" about the community. Able to detect that his "studies were . . . the record of a people who are lost," Braithwaite refuses to "bemoan that fact" or to "applaud it" but merely continues to compile the data which "Luther brought [him]." Using his objective stance as an excuse from nonparticipation, Braithwaite becomes complicit in Luther's lie; for, by replicating Linden Hills in his detailed photographs instead of rupturing it, Braithwaite acts not to change the history of Linden Hills, but to perpetuate it.

Willie's question, *"After such knowledge, what forgiveness?"* reveals the inhumanity of Braithwaite's position. In fact, the novel's allusions to T. S. Eliot's *Gerontion* emphasize the inadequacy of Braithwaite's view of history. Braithwaite is the *"old man in a dry month/Being read to by a boy, waiting for rain."* He is another one of Eliot's hollow men, spiritually and sexually empty, waiting for redemption. Braithwaite's gnarled, dead willows, whose skeletal branches will never bud again, symbolize the sterility which results from his objective project. This blind, passionless man isolated from his past and present cannot redeem his community; the *"decayed house,"* an emblem for the crumbling civilization of Linden Hills, cannot be saved by a tenant who only rents.[11]

III. Poetic History

To reassemble fragments, of course, is to engage in an act of speculation, to attempt to weave a fiction of origins and subgeneration. It is to render the implicit as explicit, and at times to imagine the whole from the part.
—Henry Louis Gates, Jr., *The Signifying Monkey*

History . . . is a nightmare from which I am trying to awake.
—James Joyce, *Ulysses*

Willie Mason, the unemployed poet from the neighboring town of Putney Wayne, who works his way through Linden Hills doing odd jobs to earn extra Chistmas money, acts as the true trickster figure of the novel, not Luther or Braithwaite. Willie's alliance with an oral tradition—he memorizes his poems since the "written word dulls the mind, and since most of what's written is by white men, it's positively poisonous"—his lower-class status, and his marginal sexuality (the novel allows for a reading of Willie as gay) all emphasize his relationship to the dominant system: he is an outsider in every sense.[12] Positioned on the margins, Willie signifies against the system as he journeys through Linden Hills.

Willie's journey is twofold: first, he reads against the socialized signs of Linden Hills and recuperates a black vernacular history; second, he sees the absences in Linden Hills and recovers the female subject. These two projects are interdependent. By reading from a black perspective, Willie writes a history which allows for rupture and which encodes absences; by imaginatively reconstructing the female face, he deconstructs white logocentric history. Acting as a trickster, Willie locates the absent center of the novel—Willa; however, it is Willa's rupturing presence which finally tears down the system that Willie has been signifying against. Revising the nonracial nature of Luther's and Braithwaite's histories as well as their phallocentricity, Willie's history, then, accounts for the *other* side of the story.

Although Willie's history-making depends on Willa, he only gradually comes to accept her rupturing presence. When Willie first hears Willa's howl in Lester's room, he shuts the window, refusing to respond to Willa's call: "The wind brought the cry again, but it went unheard by Willie as it rattled against the closed window and then returned back over the tree tops and houses below. . . . Down to die in the aching throat of a woman who was crouching over the shrunken body of her son."[13] By shutting out Willa's howl, Willie represses the female voice, much like Luther and Braithwaite. At this point, Willie is not yet ready to face the rupture which will destroy his reality, so he shuts the window and turns on the light to make sure that "the world he understood was still intact."

Willie, however, remains haunted by Willa's howl in his dreams. For example, on the night of December 21, he dreams about the very words Willa is uncovering. Evelyn Creton's question "Will he eat it?" is transposed by Willie's dream-work into his statement "Willie eat it." Chronicling what he has *not seen* that day in Linden Hills, Willie's dreams arise out of his haunting sense of Willa's absence, an absence he can taste in the cake that Luther brings to Lycentia Parker's wake, an absence which he constantly probes: "Do you ever *see* [Luther's] wife?" asks Willie of Reverend Hollis. By understanding the connection between his nightmares and his own waking reality, Willie's history will record what Braithwaite's does not—the woman in the basement.

In order to make peace with his night images, Willie creates a poem—his story of what he has seen and not seen in Linden Hills. Significantly, Willie's poetic history is centered in the body: "[h]is poem only made sense in his ears and mouth. His fingers, eyes, and nose" and his poetic process is akin to masturbation. Willie's bodily history-making not only accounts for his personal perspective—his poems push themselves up from "his center"—but also insists on a participatory stance: "once [the poem] was out of his mouth to be heard by his ears, *he knew he was committed*."[14] Instead of writing an objective history, then, Willie produces a subjective story. Moreover, by taking responsibility for his story, Willie moves away from Braithwaite's nonparticipatory stance toward a self-involved history.[15] In order to rectify history, he must identify himself with the life he records—Willa.

As Willie draws closer to discovering Willa and to participating fully in her plight, he becomes more feminized. The scene which begins with Willie worrying that his brothers will ridicule him for wrapping his Christmas presents like a woman, ends with him wondering about whether he really is turning into a woman. As Willie thinks about Willa and how "she was waiting for him," he shudders, "now [I] really [am]

turning into a woman—[I sound] like somebody's superstitious old aunt."
Yet, it is when Willie most fully takes part in Willa's history (enabling
her escape from the cellar) that he is turned, if only for a moment, into
a woman. After unwittingly sliding the bolt back from the cellar door
while at Luther's house, Willie looks into a mirror and sees "what Willa
saw," finding her face in the mirror instead of his own. Willie's total
identification with Willa, then, allows for the possibility of his seeing as
a woman.

Although Willie, in identifying with the faceless women that he
dreams about, escapes his male gaze, it finally remains up to Willa to
reconstruct the female face. Willie's vernacular poem, "There is a man
in a house at the bottom of a hill. And his wife has no name," might
attempt to reinsert the woman back into history, but it fails finally to
name the woman. His poetic story might revise Luther's and Braithwaite's logocentric histories by insisting on a subjective rendering of
reality situated in the body and by signaling a move toward a female-
centered story, but finally the novel only allows Willa to reconstruct a
female history—only she can give a face and a name to the women buried
at the bottom of the hill.

At the end of the novel, having witnessed the emergence of Willa
from the cellar and the deconstruction of his reality, Willie is left without
any ready-made formulas: "[w]here were the guidelines with which to
judge what they had left behind that door?" he asks. Freed from the
binary system which imprisons Luther, Willie, as Jeffrey Masten argues,
moves out of Linden Hills in search of a "middle ground"—a world of his
own re-creation somewhere between black ghetto and white middle
class.[16] Leaving "a world where reality [has] caved in," Willie and Lester
walk hopefully out of Tupelo Drive into the waning days of the year.
However, even though Willie might be able to imagine a new class model,
he finally remains unable to reconstruct a female history for he still does
not know Willa's name.

IV. Autobiographical Herstory

*It was a conversation. I can tell because I said something I didn't know I
knew. About the "dead girl." That bit by bit I had been rescuing her from the
grave of time and inattention. Her fingernails maybe in the first book: face
and legs perhaps the second time. Little by little bringing her back into living
life. . . . She is here now alive. I have seen, named and claimed her—and oh
what company she keeps.*
                                        —Toni Morrison, "A Conversation"

To rename is to revise, and to revise is to signify.
                        —Henry Louis Gates, Jr., *The Signifying Monkey*

Through Willa, Naylor completes the revisioning process of history
that Willie begins: a phallocentric, objective model of history is replaced

by a female-centered, subjective one. In discovering the names and histories of the "many mothers that Luther never talked about," Willa not only recovers the identities of the women who are effaced in Luther's mythic history, who are left out of Braithwaite's objective account, and who Willie's poem cannot yet name, but she also reclaims from the mythic sign of Mrs. Nedeed her own "singular identity." In the everyday records of her foremothers' lives—the Bible, the cookbook, and the family photograph album—Willa discovers autobiographical accounts which, in recording the very absence of these women, give testimony to their presence. Only by recovering and identifying with her past can Willa reconstruct the fragments of her own face and claim a future for herself.

Willa's story begins when Luther imprisons her in the basement.[17] The basement, which doubles as a morgue, symbolizes Willa's confinement within patriarchy; for here Luther controls her water, food, and light, and here, in the same place that he molds the bodies of dead women into specimens of perfect womanhood, he plans to transform Willa from a "whore" into the ideal "wife." Willa, however, refuses Luther's objectification. Instead of becoming the perfect wife, she recovers a history which deconstructs the myth of marriage, a myth which creates women as ghostly absences and naturalizes their namelessness.[18] Instead of blocking out her origins, as Luther and Linden Hills do, Willa recovers her foremothers' identities which lie under the name of Mrs. Nedeed and with them her own selfhood.

Willa's journey toward self-recovery begins in her effort to mourn her son. By having the "courage to mourn," Willa faces her memories and does not cover over them. Her howl of despair in fact begins her history-making. The howl, as Mae Henderson describes it, allows Willa to find a vantage point outside of patriarchal language.[19] Like Willie who refuses the white man's written word, Willa situates herself outside of the patriarchal word. Her story, for instance, is written in the interstices of the novel's dominant story line, its absence foregrounded in heavy, bold type. Like the trickster Willie, Willa writes a signifying story, one that ruptures the dominant story line even as it encodes her absence from it.

This signifying history, however, dates back to the first Mrs. Nedeed, Luwana Packerville. Luwana acts like a trickster, working to dismantle the patriarchal word, when she writes in a "fine, webbed scrawl . . . crammed onto the gold-edge tissue paper that separate[s] one book of the Bible from another." By personalizing biblical stories, she makes history autobiographical. For example, she writes "the sorrows of never knowing her own mother next to the Book of Ruth; her fears of being a new bride before the Song of Solomon." Evelyn Creton, the second mother-in-law, also writes an autobiographical history but this time in the modern-day woman's bible, the cookbook. Not only does Evelyn write her own personalized versions next to the codified recipes in *The Joy of*

Cooking, changing onions to mushrooms, for example, but in two, black, nameless volumes where Willa finds recipes "crammed together so tightly they were almost a blur," Evelyn also rewrites these same recipes with a signifying difference—now adding shameweed and pubic hair. Beneath her meticulous writing, then, lies a subversive message. The last foremother which Willa recovers, Priscilla McGuire, uses the family photograph album to personalize her history. Again, her pictures (which are very different from Braithwaite's) contain a signifying difference— they record her face as it disappears in the shadow of the two Luthers who frame her on either side.

Against this positive signifying heritage, which gives voice to silence and a presence to absence, Willa recovers a history of self-mutilation. Like Willie who creates poetry out of his body, Willa's foremothers use their bodies as a place to mark their own history; however, unlike Willie, these women use their bodies not as the source of their spoken stories, but as memorials to their silence. No longer able to voice her subversion in the Bible, Luwana Packerville turns to recording her presence in her body, memorializing each moment she is called on to speak by carving a line in her body with a silver hat pin. The correspondence between Willie's 665 poems and Luwana's 665 marks of silence points to the difference between male and female signifying: whereas Willie can create poetry out of his body, giving voice to subversion, Luwana remains silent, turning her body into a painful poem. Paradoxically, she can only claim her presence through self-mutilation.

Evelyn Creton also records her painful history in her body. Through a regime of overeating and purgation, Evelyn eats herself to death. Turning the conjure which was meant for Luther inward against herself, she literally transforms herself into a ghost, becoming thinner and thinner, "her face . . . becoming sunken, her arm skeletal," until she makes her last recipe—vanilla ice cream and prussic acid. Finally, Priscilla not only records the growth of her absence but participates in her own loss of identity when she decapitates her photographic image (the face she removes is the size of a large *thumbprint*) with hot grease, cleaning fluid, and bleach. In scrawling the word "me" over the empty hole, Priscilla shows that she can only assert her selfhood through a self-mutilating absence. It is this female model of history—an autobiographical history written in the body—that Willa must learn to write; yet at the same time it is this cycle of disfigurement which she must rupture.

Like Willie who tries to shut out Willa's howl, Willa at first refuses to identify with the history she recovers. She sees her own marriage in terms of Luwana's slavery and draws parallels between Evelyn's conjure and her own modern-day magic, makeup, yet she ultimately refuses to identify herself with them: "[s]he wasn't like these other women; she had coped and they were crazy." But also like Willie, Willa cannot proceed forward until she recognizes the continuity between her mothers-in-law's "sad, twisted lives" and her own. She finally recognizes herself as the "other" in the mirror—or in this case the photograph—when, in looking into Priscilla McGuire's "soft, compassionate eyes," she sees the reflection of her own being: a modern, independent woman imprisoned in marriage. Only by allowing the past to dissolve into the present and by accepting her mothers-in-law's nightmare as her own reality, then, can Willa begin to re-create the features of her own face. Seeing her image, Eve-like, reflected in a pot of water, she recovers her identity, her name and her will. By tracing how she consciously came "to be exactly where she was," Willa claims responsibility for her own history. Her autobiographical act, in turn, empowers her, for if she had "walked down twelve concrete steps . . . whenever she was good and ready, she could walk back up."

Just as Willa physically inscribes her pain in her body (the "blood from the open scars [her memories] dripped down behind her eyes"), she records her self-authentication there as well. Willa gives birth to herself, as Willie begets a poem, from the "center of her being." Willa's resurrection is described in evolutionary terms:

> She breathed in and out, her body a mere shelter for the *mating of unfathomable will to unfathomable possibility.* And in that union, the amber germ of truth she went to sleep with conceived and reconceived itself, splitting and multiplying to take over every atom attached to her being. That *nucleus of self-determination* held the tyrannical blueprint for all divisions of labor assigned to its multiplying cells. Like other emerging life, her brain, heart, hands, and feet were being *programmed to a purpose.*

In recording her self-determination in her genes, Willa reclaims her essential nature. Instead of inscribing her absence by deforming her body, Willa chronicles her presence by re-forming it. As the "great Amazon" queen ant, the metaphor used to describe Willa throughout the rest of the book, Willa reclaims the matriarchal role that patriarchy denied her and her mothers-in-law.

Willa's history-making, then, would seem to draw on the enabling parts of her foremothers' histories while refusing the destructive victimization inherent in their model. Willa would seem to offer a version of history as "repetition with a signal difference." The novel's ending, however, severely limits any radical reading of Willa's history. In the end, when in her determined effort not to be forced back down into the basement she unknowingly catches her bridal veil on an ember and starts a fire, Willa neither acts willfully in burning down the house of patriarchy nor lives to tell her story.[20] Willa's self-determination, like all female history in this book, ends in self-destruction and disappearance. She is carried out of the house, faceless, as part of "one massive bulk," which contains the perverted trinity of Luther, Willa and their son. Moreover, not only does the fire erase Willa's identity, but it also burns all the records in the basement. Female history literally goes up in smoke at the end of this book.

The troubling question that the novel leaves unanswered is why it ends without a viable model of female history?[21] To put it another way, why must two Adams go forth from the ruins of this inverted paradise and no Eve? By focusing on Willie's journey toward a "middle ground" at the end of the book, Naylor would seem to write an optimistic and perhaps even radical ending. Yet why does the ending posit the possibility for a reconstructed black male history but not a female one? Why must Willa serve only as a conduit for the real reconstructor, Willie? Since women end up with so little in a book that seems to promise them so much, Naylor's own dreamlike ending remains haunted by what is still denied—the woman's story.

The problem lies, I think, in Naylor's essentialism.[22] Her essentialistic model of womanhood, centered in a biological self-determination ("[e]very cell in [Willa's] body strained against [Luther's] hands"; her path is "coded into her being"), errs in the same way Luther's mythic model does. By describing Willa as a powerful queen ant, Naylor recreates an historically contingent subject as a mythic matriarch. Like Luther's myth, Naylor's essentialism threatens to invert but not to dismantle patriarchy. By merely flipping the binary oppositions of a patriarchal/matriarchal system, Naylor fails to free Willa from a system which defines her as an absence: Willa might escape the basement but she never leaves the house. In the end, Naylor's seemingly radical revisioning of history proves to be limited. Willa's autobiographical history recuperates her past and her self-identity, but it posits no alternative system, no movement beyond. Willa might deconstruct the system, but it is Willie who offers a vision of a new order. As the efficacious historian, Naylor can finally only imagine a black male poet.[23]

Notes

1. The connection between cultural history and self-understanding in black women's writing is a theme which many critics have discussed. Susan Willis, for instance, writes: "History gives topic and substance to black women's writing. No one can read a novel by Toni Morrison or Alice Walker or Paule Marshall without confronting history, feeling its influence and experiencing the changes wrought by history. . . . The answer to why Selina is the way she is, or why Sula is Sula, or why Meridian is Meridian involves reconstructing the development of the character's individual personality in relation to the historical forces that have shaped the migrations of her race, the struggles of her community, and the relationships that have developed within her family." See also Barbara Christian and Catherine Ward.

2. Naylor emphasizes the mythic qualities of Linden Hills in her own literary borrowings. Not only is the exact location of Linden Hills unknown, but with its eight curved roads winding downward to the "dead center" where Luther Nedeed lives, it also resembles Dante's hell. See Catherine Ward for a discussion of Naylor's use of Dante's *Inferno* and Margaret Homans for Naylor's use of Virgil, Dante, and Plato.

3. Unlike Luther, Ruth and Norman understand how "rupture strengthens the rhythm" of history. Their marital history is an example of the way rupture functions to strengthen, not weaken, a bond. Due to Norman's sickness, their lives revolve around seven seasons and then a rupture—the return of the pinks. Because Norman destroys everything during this time, they cannot accumulate material things; hence, they concentrate on the process of living between the moments of rupture, not the achievement of an end-product: "They filled the vacant spaces in the apartment with the memories from long walks in the park, bus outings to the beach, and window-shopping for that new home . . . with a whole, safe year and then that summer, fall, and winter before the next pink spring." By making room for Norman's disease inside the system of their own seasonal repetition, they accept the nightmare which occasionally rips through the fabric of their reality. Whereas Ruth incorporates Norman's nightmare as her own reality—"Norman!" It was the wail of a woman embracing a nightmare. "Scrape. Them. Off"—Luther represses the "ghostly presence" of his son which threatens to destroy his reality. Fittingly, it is at Ruth and Norman's house where Willa's wail is first heard.

4. See Lawrence Levine's *Black Culture and Black Consciousness* and Houston Baker's *Long Black Song* for discussions of the trickster figure in black culture. Also, see Henry Louis Gates, Jr.'s *The Signifying Monkey* for a full explanation of the term "signifyin(g)."

5. Naylor gives two wonderful instances of signifyin(g) in the description of how "White Willie" (Willie K. Mason) and "Shit" (Lester Tilson) get their names.

6. Naylor makes a connection between the Nedeed name and "de-eden" in an interview she gave for National Public Radio (discussed in Ward).

7. Here I use Robert Stepto's term from *Behind the Veil*. According to Stepto, the articulate kinsman seeks tribal literacy in order to ameliorate his own solitude. By immersing him/herself in a tribal past (usually in a trip south), s/he comes to understand his/her tribal past and hence him/herself. As I will argue, Willa, not Braithwaite, is the articulate kinsperson of this text. In recovering her female past, Willa begins articulate in the ways of her "tribe."

8. The subjectivity of the scientific cameraman is also exposed in the episode when Maxwell, Xavier, Lester, and Willie are looking at a *Penthouse* photograph. The eight-page spread pictures a "lush, tropical forest and a very dark-skinned model" dressed in "thin leopard strips" and chained at the wrists. The progression of the photographs shows the model as she wrestles with the "invisible hand off camera" that holds the chain, and as she brings the holder to her feet in victory: "One leg was raised in victory on the shoulder of a scrawny white man in a safari outfit, and his thick bifocals had slipped below the bridge of his nose." Maxwell misses the point when he thinks that this photograph speaks a liberating message of black supremacy. The photographic sequence actually unmasks the supremacy of the male gaze. Instead of figuring her victory, the last picture shows the woman caught in another gaze: Maxwell's, Xavier's, and Lester's (Willie has left by this time). Both the white cameraman and Maxwell construct the black

woman to fit their own subjective fantasy: the exotic object or the revolutionary conquerer. Moreover, when Maxwell presses "his finger on the photo, leaving behind a damp smudge," he reenacts the physical oppression taking place within the photograph: the woman might have subdued the white male, but she is still under Maxwell's thumb. Hence in spectator events, which in Braithwaite's case includes the writing of history, the meaning lies less in the action than in the watching.

9. Braithwaite's historical namesake, William Stanley Braithwaite, also denied his black perspective. By accepting a formalist model of poetry instead of Dunbar's vernacular one, W. S. Braithwaite chose not to write as a black poet or about racial themes. According to J. Saunders Redding and others, W. Braithwaite rejected his blackness when he competed with white writers on their own terms. Redding describes William Braithwaite's poetry as "unintelligibly esoteric and deficient in racial feeling" and claims that he was "the most out-standing example of perverted energy that the period from 1903 to 1917 produced." Like his namesake, Daniel Braithwaite also isolates his work from his world and refuses connection to his race. See Harris and Butcher for further background on W. Braithwaite. I am indebted to Ward for first drawing my attention to this connection.

10. When he tells his history of Linden Hills in terms of Luther Nedeed's individual achievement ("The Nedeeds kept going because they felt our people needed a role model"), Braithwaite places himself in what August Meier and Elliot Rudwick term "the Builders and Heroes" school of history. This school, headed by Carter G. Woodson whose book, *The Negro Professional and the Community*, D. Braithwaite has in his library, believes in highlighting the outstanding contributions of "special" black people. Like Braithwaite's description of Luther's building up of Linden Hills ("I watched them build this place up from practically nothing. A handful of illiterate and unskilled people came here and prospered because of them"), Woodson's work stems from a "petit-bourgeois philosophy of individualism and business striving" rather than an overall racial philosophy. Such an ideology, as Meier and Rudwick point out, focuses on the victimization, rather than the creative survival of the black race. For example, Braithwaite blames the white community, not Luther Nedeed, for the sold souls in Linden Hills: "they've sold nothing; pieces of themselves were *taken* away." According to the new black historians, however, Woodson's objective, scientific approach to history, like Braithwaite's, fails to use history as a "valuable instrument in the struggle for black autonomy, self-definition, and self-determination."

11. Eliot's old man, like Braithwaite, is only a renter as the following lines show: "We have not reached conclusion when I/Stiffen in a rented house." Ward also notes the sterility of Braithwaite's model: "his knowledge," she writes, "is sterile because it is irresponsible."

12. Jeffrey Masten reads Willie's marginality in terms of his sexuality. Because of his "liminal position in the sex-gender system," Masten argues, Willie can read against and subvert the bourgeois ideology of Linden Hills. Using gay and lesbian theory as his model for Willie's signifying, Masten focuses on the intersection of sexuality and class in the novel. See Henry Louis Gates, Jr.'s "Significant Others" for a reading of *Linden Hills*, which addresses the connection between class and race: the novel, Gates writes, "depicts the irruption of class politics into the terrain of race politics."

13. This is actually the second time Willie has heard Willa's howl, but this is the first time that the novel focuses on his reaction.

14. Masten makes clear the difference between Braithwaite's objective and Willie's subjective histories. He writes: "The process of poetic creation is for

Willie solipsistic, and this is what marks its difference from Braithwaite's objectivist history. Braithwaite's methodology is unable to account for the self in the process of writing; Willie's bases itself in the realization that all formulations, all compilations of data, are centered in the self. Masturbation becomes the appropriate metaphor for his poetics . . . [since] the onanistic aspect of Willie's poetry emphasizes its unabashed perspectivism." Although I agree with Masten that Willie's poetic history gives a subjective rendering of reality, I would not term it solipsistic. Unlike Braithwaite who voyeuristically looks out on Linden Hills through his telescope, Willie is connected to and participates in the history he writes.

15. Willie's commitment to Willa becomes evident in the last pages of the book. Unlike the rest of Linden Hills (Braithwaite included), Willie does not merely look on as the Nedeed house burns; instead he tries to run inside to save Willa. He says to Lester, "Don't you understand? *She's* in there."

16. Lester and Willie discuss a "middle ground": "'Maybe,' Lester said softly, maybe there's a middle ground somewhere. For me as well as you . . . I don't know why it must be one or the other—ya know, ditchdigger or duke. But people always think that way: it's Linden Hills or nothing. But it doesn't have to be Linden Hills and it doesn't have to be nothing—ya know, Willie?" Masten argues that Willie and Lester not only deconstruct bourgeois mythology but that they also "propose a movement beyond" the bourgeois paradigm. Moreover, Masten points out that "the characters not strictly within heterosexual 'norms' are the spokespeople for this 'middle ground.'" Having already subverted "middle-class norms of sexuality," Willie and Lester can move "out of the bourgeois paradigm into a realm of unexcluded middles" at the end of the novel.

17. Willa's journey differs from Willie's in the same way that Linda Brent's escape from slavery differs from Frederick Douglass's: women must act within confined spaces, whereas men may roam wide open areas. Naylor explains the difference between male and female acts of self-authentication when she describes how she wrote *Linden Hills*. Writing the book in Spain, Naylor, as a single woman, was taken for a prostitute and constantly harassed on the streets. She describes her subsequent self-confinement to a boarding house in Cadiz as follows: "I was free to write as much as I wanted, but not to roam the streets . . . And I'm going to be honest—I resented that; I was bitter that I couldn't have the world like they had the world." Naylor emphasizes the female position—a lack of geographical freedom—in Willa's imprisonment. In a very real way, then, Willa's ability to escape the basement literalizes her self-discovery.

18. In her white wedding gown, Willa looks like a "ghostly image" as the dense veil causes her face to disappear: "she could barely see out and surely no one could see in." Moreover, Willa's red gold wedding band, which matches the color of her dark skin as Luwana Nedeed's platinum ring does her lighter skin, completes her disappearance. As her ring becomes indistinguishable from her finger, marriage is naturalized and the individual Willa Prescott is replaced by a mythic Mrs. Nedeed.

19. These remarks were made in a lecture at the University of Pennsylvania entitled "Black Women Writers: Speaking in Tongues."

20. Naylor points to her own problems in writing the ending in her conversation with Toni Morrison: "She [Willa] liked being a wife and mother and she was going upstairs to claim that identity." And I said, "Oh, Lord, woman, don't you know what the end of this book has got to be? You've gotta tear that whole house down to the ground, or my book won't make any sense." Through the accidentally lighted veil, Naylor would seem to achieve both

ends: burning down the house of patriarchy without wrenching Willa out of her character. Significantly, Grandma Tilson, another validated female subject in the novel, also does not burn down her house; instead she leaves that task to her grandson Luther.

21. Homans is also bothered by this question. "Whatever the reason," she writes, "it is striking that the novel institutes no countertradition of strong womanhood to oppose the destructive legacy of patriarchy. The dead Mrs. Nedeeds . . . can expose the destructive truth, but they offer no hints for constructing a new one."

22. Masten offers another way to read the ending: that Naylor adheres to a "radical humanist" model which centers consciousness in a stable and self-evident subject. He notes that Grandma Tilson's silver mirror of the soul serves as "the novel's pervasive metaphor for a humanist subjectivity" since it reflects a "true" self. Arguing that *Linden Hills* inscribes an attempt to subvert the bourgeoisie from the "self-authenticating" margin, Masten discusses how this humanist vision is a product of the very bourgeois ideology it seeks to subvert. Homans discusses this same double bind as it applies to feminist critiques: "feminist criticism . . . tend, like Willa Nedeed looking in her mirror, to view the recuperation of subjectivity in the form of female identity as the best defense against androcentrism"; however, as Homans argues, this "is too simple an answer, because, as Peggy Kamuf points out, such a project may 'remain caught as a reflection of the same form of nineteenth-century humanism from which we have inherited our pervasively androcentric modes of thought.'" By reclaiming her identity in a mirror, then, Willa resumes not only her "self" but, as Henry Louis Gates, Jr. argues, "the identity Luther has imposed upon her." As always, moving from the margins to the center is a difficult business. In claiming the centrality of her story, Willa loses her signifying difference; moreover, once her subscript is subsumed within the dominant story line her self-authentication is soon silenced.

23. I wish to thank Professor Houston Baker for his insightful comments on earlier drafts and Jeffrey Masten who generously shared his work with me and offered many suggestions along the way.

◆◆◆◆◆◆◆◆◆◆◆◆◆◆

"Shakespeare's Black?": The Role of Shakespeare in Naylor's Novels

PETER ERICKSON

The attempt to rewrite the Renaissance has been a major strand in criticism in the 1980s. At least four Renaissances are being vigorously reinterpreted. The current reconsideration of the English and European Renaissance of the sixteenth and seventeenth centuries is exemplified by the collection *Rewriting the Renaissance*, whose title articulates a much wider effort.[1] Three American versions of renaissance are also being reconstructed. F. O. Matthiessen's classic *American Renaissance* has been challenged by a series of critics.[2] Gloria T. Hull's study reassesses the Harlem Renaissance.[3] In conversation with Gloria Naylor, Toni Morrison applies the term renaissance to contemporary black women writers: "It's a real renaissance. You know, we have spoken of renaissance before. But this one is ours, not somebody else's."[4] Yet work by critic Hazel V. Carby (discussed later in this essay) suggests that this most recent Renaissance is being rewritten even as Morrison formulates it.

My specific concern here is points of contact between the first and fourth of these Renaissances as represented by Gloria Naylor's use of Shakespeare. My paper is offered as a contribution to what might be called canon studies, and my purpose is to show the need for detailed, in-depth analysis of particular cases. A related goal is to expand the possibilities for talking about race within the field of Shakespeare studies. *Othello* continues to be the primary focus for the discussion of race and racism in Shakespeare; Karen Newman's essay on the play demonstrates the extremely valuable results that can be produced from such a focus.[5] Shakespeareans, however, should not be limited to instances of black characters; responses to Shakespeare by a later black writer such as Gloria Naylor are also relevant. Canon studies that cross-period divisions provide another avenue for considering Shakespeare's work in relation to questions of race.

I.

Gloria Naylor's series of novels, eventually to be a quartet, is linked by a set of internal cross-references to characters and places.[6] Shakespeare, however, provides a second set of connections, for he figures in all three novels to date, and the range and depth of Shakespearean allusions has increased in Naylor's most recent novel, *Mama Day*. My starting point is the question: what is Shakespeare doing here? Why does Naylor so consistently evoke the Shakespearean reference point?

As an epitome of the literary master and as a representative of the main line of the inherited literary tradition, Shakespeare provides Naylor with a counterpoint to the emergent tradition of contemporary black women writers. The presence of Shakespeare allows Naylor to explore the relation between these two traditions, which she experiences not only as distinct but also as split, divided, opposed:

> The writers I had been taught to love were either male or white. And who was I to argue that Ellison, Austen, Dickens, the Brontes, Baldwin and Faulkner weren't masters? They were and are. But inside there was still the faintest whisper: Was there no one telling my story?

Because of the absence of her story, it was "a long road from gathering the authority within myself to believe that I could actually be a writer." In Naylor's development, this authority comes crucially from her immediate predecessor Toni Morrison: "But for me, where was the *authority* for me to enter this forbidden terrain? But then finally you were being taught to me."

The perception of two traditions—one that omits black women, one that focuses on them—creates for Naylor an irreducible gap. The new tradition produces stories that are "'different but equal,'" with the stress falling on both terms. They are equal and not minor or second rate, but they are also still different. Naylor resists the pressure of the logic that if they are truly equal, then they cannot be fundamentally different since all works of the first rank are judged by a single standard and thereby incorporated into a single canon.

Naylor's energies are directed rather toward preserving and dramatizing the signal differences between the dual traditions of which Shakespeare and Morrison are emblematic. Naylor's bond with Morrison as the originator of an alternate, non-Shakespearean tradition makes Morrison a more important resource than Shakespeare; Morrison provides an identity and a voice, which Shakespeare is powerless to do. Yet Naylor's primary allegiance to Morrison does not lead to the exclusion of Shakespeare. If, sustained by Morrison, Naylor need not approach Shakespeare with disabling reverence, neither does she simply reject him, as her evident attraction to Shakespearean language testifies. Naylor's involvement and negotiations with Shakespeare occur in an intermediate zone that conveys a delicate tension in Naylor's double perspective on Shakespeare: she appreciates Shakespeare while at the same time she is determined critically to rewrite him.

Naylor's attention to Shakespeare serves to raise the question of Shakespeare's changed status when seen from the vantage point of the emergent tradition in which Naylor is a participant. By putting into play and testing both positive and critical attitudes toward Shakespeare, Naylor's work dramatizes with particular fullness the conflict between established and emergent traditions.

II.

In Naylor's first novel, *The Women of Brewster Place* (1982), the Shakespearean moment is located in the "Cora Lee" story, the fifth of seven sections. The moment exemplifies the delicacy of tone with which Naylor approaches Shakespeare: her humor is too finely textured—too sympathetic and poignant—to be merely satirical.

Cora Lee, overwhelmed by her sole responsibility for her children, takes refuge from her burden in a heavy dose of TV soaps. This pattern is temporarily disrupted when she and the children are invited to a black production of *A Midsummer Night's Dream*. Shakespeare as cultural event inspires in Cora Lee an unprecedented outburst of energetic determination: "It would be good for them. They need things like Shakespeare and all that," "They would sit still and get this Shakespeare thing if she had to break their backs." The specific incentive is defined by Cora Lee's association of Shakespeare with school, career aspiration, and upward mobility: "Junior high; high school; college—none of them stayed little forever. And then on to good jobs in insurance companies and the post office, even doctors or lawyers."

Naylor matches the comedy of *A Midsummer Night's Dream* with her own mischievous comic mood. She builds up the Shakespearean motif of the dream by linking Bottom's and Puck's references to dreaming with allusions to Mercutio's set piece on Queen Mab and Prospero's "We are such stuff as dreams are made on." Using this Shakespearean background, Naylor plays off two meanings of dream—genuine hope and futile fantasy—against each other in the immediate context of black urban poverty. Though Mercutio's apparently genial speech comes from an early moment in *Romeo and Juliet* before the tragic current has taken hold, Naylor does not ultimately block out the tragic implications of Cora Lee's situation. The "night of wonders" that Shakespearean comedy creates for Cora Lee proves to be only an interlude. The evidence of "hopeful echoes" she finds upon her return home are summarily canceled: "Then she turned and firmly folded her evening like gold and lavender gauze deep within the creases of her dreams. . . ."

The discrepancy between hopeful dreaming and dead-end finality is abruptly brought into focus by her child's questioning: "'Mama,' Sammy pulled on her arm, 'Shakespeare's black?'" Naylor's gentle ironies become painful ones as she directly poses the issue of the relevance of Shakespeare's pastoral to black urban landscape. We are forced to ac-

knowledge not only that Shakespeare is white but also that, even when
"'brought . . . up to date,'" his translation into a black cultural idiom is
neither automatically assured nor unambiguously benign. Moving up
from the low culture of white-produced TV soaps to the high culture of
black-produced Shakespeare no longer seems an answer.

The problematic aspects of Shakespearean inspiration are intertwined
with the paradoxical position of Kiswana Browne, who issues the invitation to Cora Lee to attend the Shakespeare play produced by her boyfriend Abshu. Unlike the others "who came because they had no choice
and would remain for the same reason," Kiswana, having rejected her
middle-class family situation in Linden Hills, is the one woman in Brewster Place who is there by choice. Kiswana's renunciation is subsequently
vindicated by Naylor's own condemnation of Linden Hills in her second
novel. Yet there is pointed irony in Kiswana's being the intermediary
who arouses in Cora Lee a Shakespearean dream of upward educational
mobility when Kiswana herself has already deliberately rejected it, having dropped out of college: "'Those bourgie schools were counterrevolu-
tionary'"; "'What good would I be after four or five years of a lot of
white brainwashing in some phony, prestige institution, huh?'" When
she does take courses again at a community college, Shakespeare is not
in her curriculum.

Kiswana's appeal to come to the performance of *A Midsummer
Night's Dream* is her second invitation to Cora Lee; the first is a request
that she attend the meeting of a tenants' association that Kiswana is
organizing. Naylor does not so much reject Kiswana's political commitment as show its limits. Kiswana, too, is compromised by the double
meaning of dreams as hope and as lack of realism: "She placed her dreams
on the back of the bird and fantasized that it would glide forever . . .
she watched with a sigh as the bird beat its wings in awkward frantic
movements. . . . This brought her back to earth."

When the well-attended meeting in Kiswana's apartment is disrupted
over an objection to the participation of Lorraine, a lesbian, Kiswana is
unable to respond effectively. Her belated apology still expresses this
inadequacy: "'I should have said something—after all, it was my house—
but things got out of hand so quickly, I'm sorry, I . . .'" Kiswana's politics
fail to include the political issue of lesbian relationships. Even in Mattie's
dream sequence at the end of the novel, Kiswana is represented as hesitant to acknowledge the consequences of the hostility to Lorraine's lesbian identity. Confronted with blood-stained bricks that body forth both
Lorraine's violent rape and her retaliatory murder of the defenseless
man who befriends but ultimately cannot protect her against male aggression, Kiswana initially responds with denial:

> She tried to pass a brick to Kiswana, who looked as if she had stepped into
> a nightmare.

"There's no blood on those bricks!" Kiswana grabbed Ciel by the arm. "You know there's no blood—it's raining. It's just raining!"

Ciel pressed the brick into Kiswana's hand and forced her fingers to curl around it. "Does it matter? Does it really matter?"

Kiswana looked down at the wet stone and her rain-soaked braids leaked onto the surface, spreading the dark stain. She wept and ran to throw the brick spotted with her blood out into the avenue.

Kiswana's weeping during this act of symbolic identification marks the final separation from the comic note struck by *A Midsummer Night's Dream*. The "Cora Lee" section containing the Shakespearean episode is strategically placed because of its sharp juxtaposition with the section that follows on "The Two," the lesbian couple. The humor, shifting to a different register, now serves as a medium for releasing and partially transforming suspicion and uncertainty about lesbian sexuality. The attack on Lorraine at the block meeting is defused through humor, but it is a strained, ambivalent humor that conveys tentative acceptance without completely dispelling the underlying discomfort and anxiety:

The laughter that burst out of their lungs was such a relief that eyes were watery. The room laid back its head and howled in gratitude to Ben for allowing it to breath again. Sophie's rantings could not be heard above the wheezing, coughing, and backslapping that now went on.

Lorraine left the apartment . . .

The humor escalates in the wildly comic moment when Lorraine's lover Theresa puts on an angry display with food for the benefit of a disapproving voyeur:

Theresa's sides were starting to ache from laughing, and she sat down in one of the kitchen chairs. Lorraine pushed the bowl a little further down the table from her, and this set them off again. Theresa laughed and rocked in the chair until tears were rolling down her cheeks. Then she crossed that fine line between laughter and tears and started to sob.

The phrase used to express the way humor gives access to hurt aptly charcterizes Naylor's harsher comic action: in moving from "Cora Lee" to "The Two," the novel has "crossed the fine line between laughter and tears."

This crossing can be described as a shift from Shakespeare's rendering of the dream motif to that of Langston Hughes in "What happens to a dream deferred?," the politically charged poem that Naylor uses as the epigraph for the novel as a whole. Naylor's break with the evanescent atmosphere of *A Midsummer Night's Dream* is particularly appropriate because the play's design undermines female bonds: the intimate connection between Hermia and Helena is severed by the marital demands imposed by comic form.[7] Setting aside a comic pattern that cannot be accommodated to her focus on female bonds, Naylor answers Hughes' final line *"Or does it explode?"* with her own word "exploded." Naylor's

explosion dismantles the wall that maintains Brewster Place as an isolated ghetto. By contrast, the removal of the wall in *A Midsummer
Night's Dream* occurs within the concluding play-within-a-play, a carefully circumscribed entertainment that observes firm class distinctions
between the lower-class artisans who perform and the aristocratic audience whom they serve to amuse.

Naylor's fantasy is fiercer, enabling a glimpse of black female action
across differences in class and sexuality. Middle-class Kiswana, moving
beyond her instinctive denial of lesbian identity, participates in a protest
she did not plan that honors Lorraine's sacrifice. Theresa, Lorraine's
partner, joins in: "She grabbed the bricks from Cora and threw one into
the avenue. . . ." Naylor makes clear that this unified action occurs in
imagination only, not in reality, by articulating it as Mattie's dream preceding the actual block party. But the dream vision is so intensely imagined that the daylight reality which succeeds cannot displace it, and this
achievement belongs to Naylor's, not Shakespeare's, imagination.

III.

In *Linden Hills* (1985), Naylor's second novel, the main reference
point from Western literary tradition appears to be Dante's *Inferno*.
However, in a penultimate moment, the two black friends, Lester and
Willie, the latter a struggling poet, discuss Shakespeare. The terms have
modulated from the humorously innocent query "'Shakespeare's black?'"
in *The Women of Brewster Place* to the more pressing issue of "'. . . why
black folks ain't produced a Shakespeare.'"

In these first two novels, the dominant typography is the splitting of
black urban landscape into separate poor and middle-class areas. The
novels' views of Shakespeare are correlated with this internal class division. From the perspective of Brewster Place, Shakespeare belongs to
Linden Hills and the rising middle-class expectations associated with
that privileged space: at the play, Cora "looked around and didn't recognize anyone from Brewster so the blacks here probably came from Linden Hills. . . ." But, on closer inspection in *Linden Hills*, Shakespeare
is not to be found there either, as the exchange between Willie and
Lester testifies:

> "You'd think of all the places in the world, this neighborhood had a chance of
> giving us at least one black Shakespeare."
> "But Linden Hills ain't about that, Willie. You should know that by now."

Shakespeare's location with respect to black society remains elusive and
hence the shift from the relatively playful tone in the first novel's representation of Shakespeare to the more frustrated note in the second.

The phrase "one black Shakespeare" expresses the highest artistic desire as the replication of the Shakespearean model. But to shape one's desire in this way may be to create a self-defeating dependence; Shakespeare comes to symbolize a quest for black recognition that is unattainable within the narrow terms of imitation suggested by the uncomfortable echo effect that ties Willie's name to Will Shakespeare's. Naylor's third novel will move outside this framework through a decisive turn to a wider geographical exploration. The earlier counterpoint between poor and middle class is subsumed by a larger structure of tensions between Northern urban and Southern rural that gradually emerge into prominence over the course of the three novels.[8] The increasing emphasis on the North-South contrast leads, I shall argue, to a different kind of engagement with Shakespeare because the Southern terrain of *Mama Day* makes possible a literary mapping wherein Shakespeare can be not only emulated but also outmaneuvered.

The Women of Brewster Place dramatizes its Southern origins through Mattie Michael, whose story both begins in the South and begins the novel. Though left behind in the move northward, the South has a powerful residual presence because a crucial part of the network of female bonds is formed there: Mattie's friendship with Etta Mae Johnson is established before their arrival in New York as is Mattie's relationship with Ciel. Partly because of this Southern connection, Mattie can be seen as a prototype of Mama Day in Naylor's third novel. While lacking Mama Day's specific knowledge of magic, Mattie nonetheless has a maternal force and communal authority that parallel Mama Day's. Mattie's care of Ciel after the death of Ciel's child is analogous to Mama Day's concern for Cocoa: "The black mammoth gripped so firmly that the slightest increase of pressure would have cracked the girl's spine. But she rocked."

Mattie differs from Mama Day in two crucial respects: she remains permanently in the North with no prospect of returning to the home base in the South she has been forced to leave, and her reunion with Ciel is fulfilled only in a dream. But Mattie's dream organizes the women of Brewster Place in a manner that anticipates Mama Day's more potent art. In so doing, Mattie holds out the possibility of a black alternative to the Shakespearean imagination, an alternative to be realized when Naylor's Mama Day supplants rather than duplicates Shakespeare's Prospero.

The central line of development from Mattie to Mama Day can be traced in *Linden Hills* through the figure of Roberta Johnson, who, as grandmother to Laurel Dumont, is "'the closest thing to a natural mother you got.'" Remaining firmly based in the rural South, the grandmother sponsors the Berkeley education that separates them: "Because all Roberta knew was that she had cashed in her life insurance to send a child she had named Laurel Johnson to the state of California, and it sent her back a stranger." Laurel's engulfment in the "emptiness" of middle-class achievement places her beyond the grandmother's power to rescue her:

"Why did you come, Laurel?"

There was a long pause, and then her voice was barely a whisper. "When people are in trouble, don't they go home?"

Roberta covered her clenched hands gently. "But this ain't your home, child."

Yet in reversing the one-way northward migration, Laurel's attempt to reconnect with a Southern rural landscape in *Linden Hills* prefigures Cocoa's return from New York City to the South in *Mama Day*.

The resource from which Laurel has been cut off involves tradition: "She was taking in the sight of an old woman, the sound of old stories, and the smells of an old tradition with nothing inside her to connect up to them." Roberta evokes the saving power of this native tradition by opposing it to the European art to which Laurel is habituated:

"You can hear the hurt in Bessie or Billie and I just kinda wish that I'd come here and found you playing their stuff, 'cause that man you seem to like so much—that Mahler—his music says that he ain't made peace with his pain, child. And if you gonna go on, that's what you gotta do."

The motif of conflicting Afro-American and Western traditions extends, by implication, to the vexed homage Willie pays to Shakespeare as formulated in the need for "'one black Shakespeare.'" Shakespeare, like Mahler, may be the wrong place to seek artistic salvation.

IV.

Mama Day (1988) picks up where *Linden Hills* leaves off by greatly intensifying both the North-South cultural contrast and the Shakespearean motif. Before turning to *Mama Day*'s treatment of the latter, I want to examine the former through a comparison of *Mama Day* with Paule Marshall's *Praisesong for the Widow* (1983). The correspondences between the two novels suggest a common pattern with four steps.

The first step in this sequence is the protracted struggle to achieve middle-class security. This driving upward mobility is recounted in Part II of *Praisesong for the Widow* in the story of the Johnsons' move from Halsey Street in Brooklyn to North White Plains. The counterpart to Jerome Johnson's rise as an accountant is George's successful New York-based engineering career in *Mama Day*. For Kiswana Browne in *The Women of Brewster Place*, the ultimate proof of "middle-class amnesia" is the existence of black Republicans, a condition she vows to avoid: "'But I'll never be a Republican.'" George in *Mama Day*, viewing his Republican affiliation as a necessary component of his business success, experiences only occasional regret: "Meeting his type always made me ashamed to be a Republican."

A second phase begins with symptoms of malaise after the hard-won attainment of middle-class status, with a growing awareness of the emptiness of arrival. Avey Johnson's perception of being stuck in an impasse propels Marshall's novel forward. George's more muted dissatisfaction with the limitations of his constricted identity is implicitly expressed by his desire to reach out and to incorporate Cocoa's very different background:

> And I wondered if it was too late, if seven years in New York had been just enough for you to lose that, like you were trying to lose your southern accent. . . . That's why I wanted you to call me George. There isn't a southerner alive who could bring that name in under two syllables.

This turning point leads to a third stage, the counter-project of recovering what has been lost in middle-class achievement. The project takes the particular geographic form of leaving behind New York City in order to reclaim a living connection with a self-contained Southern black culture symbolized by an island community. In the case of *Praisesong for the Widow,* the specific locale is Tatum Island, where, as a child, Avey Johnson visited her great-aunt Cuney, who is responsible for Avey's name Avatara.[9] Avey regains her connection with this heritage by literally enacting the meaning in her name—incarnation—in the ritual dance during the festival on the Caribbean island of Carriacou. Not only are Tatum and Carriacou both directly connected with the African origins of their black inhabitants, but also Avey's participation in the Carriacou festival is matched point for point with her recollections of Tatum.

In *Mama Day,* George too "crosses over" onto the Southern island of Willow Springs, a move which for him is equivalent to "entering another world" and which for Naylor marks the boundary of the novel's second half. Both for Avey Johnson and for George, the new realm is governed by a set of beliefs that demand faith and challenge skepticism. Avey manages the process with relative ease: ". . . she had awakened with it [her mind] like a slate that had been wiped clean, a *tabula rasa* upon which a whole new history could be written." George's test of believe is more involuntary and more stressful: "How could I believe?"

Mama Day denies, or fulfills more stringently, the affirmative answer *Praisesong for the Widow* gives to Avey's question:

> Would it have been possible to have done both? That is, to have wrested, as they had done all those years, the means needed to rescue them from Halsey Street and to see the children through, while preserving, safeguarding, treasuring those things that had come down to them over the generations, which had defined them in a particular way. . . . They could have done both, it suddenly seemed to her.

In Marshall's novel, the tragedy—the death of Avey's husband—has already occurred, leaving the novel free to concentrate on transcendence for Avey. *Mama Day,* however, dramatizes the tragic cost through its focus on George's crisis and sacrificial death.

Yet this difference between the two novels becomes less pronounced when the fourth stage of resolution is considered. Whatever George's deficiencies, the novel more than makes up for his inability to believe with its own decisive investment in the character of Mama Day. Despite Naylor's rejection of happy endings ("Grown women aren't supposed to believe in Prince Charmings and happily-ever-afters. Real life isn't about that . . ."), *Mama Day* conveys a strongly positive sense of completion through Mama Day's epilogue. With Mama Day's help, Cocoa finds the peace that eludes Laurel in *Linden Hills:* Cocoa's is "a face that's been given the meaning of peace." Although the transmission of heritage passes through the female line from Mama Day to Cocoa, George is included in this resolution. In spite of his failure, George initiates and shares the peace: "there was total peace." As Mama Day predicts, his bond with Cocoa is maintained after his death through her ongoing communication with him: "whatever roads take her from here, they'll always lead back to you."

A similarity between Marshall's and Naylor's respective endings is reinforced by the way their recovery of the distant past is accompanied by studied neglect of more recent political history. Avey's change in *Praisesong for the Widow* is measured symbolically by the reversal of her initial refusal to sell the White Plains house she achieved with her husband:

> Sell the house in North White Plains as Marion had been urging her to do for years and use the money to build in Tatum.
> It would be a vacation house, and once she retired she would live part of the year there. . . .
> And Marion could bring some of the children from her school. . . . The place could serve as a summer camp.

By this decision, Avey responds to the "mission" bequeathed by her great-aunt Cuney; at the same time, this triumph is partly undercut by the way her language suggests a real estate transaction.

The resolution is romanticized because it is a substitute for a direct confrontation with the images of political conflict in the sixties that Avey has "conveniently forgotten":

> Hadn't she lived through most of the sixties and early seventies as if Watts and Selma and the tanks and Stoner guns in the streets of Detroit somehow did not pertain to her, denying her rage, and carefully effacing any dream that might have come to her during the night by the time she awoke the next morning.

This spirit of denial remains in force; Avey's plan does not undo the repression of her anxiety over political struggle.[10] A similar dynamic is at work in *Mama Day*, where preoccupation with the deep time of the ancestral past squeezes out contemporary political issues from which Willow Springs is portrayed as fundamentally immune. The sixties are bypassed, treated peripherally as high comedy in the tale of outwitting the abrasive white deputy.

Both Marshall's Tatum and Naylor's Willow Springs take on an aspect of pastoral refuge that makes them subject to Hazel V. Carby's analysis of black folk tradition as a romantic avoidance of the present political crisis whose primary focus is urban.[11] In Carby's persuasive view, recent literary criticism has privileged the folk line as the authentic tradition, excluding or minimizing the other, equally authentic black urban mode and thereby participating in the evasion to which folk genres are prone. Like *Praisesong for the Widow*, *Mama Day* abandons New York City without regret: "It was a relief to leave for good." I want to acknowledge the force of Carby's powerful critique but at the same time to argue that *Mama Day* is not simply escapist because it enacts another drama—the cultural political struggle with the Shakespearean past. Though Naylor's presentation will not permit disbelief in Mama Day, her skepticism remains active in relation to Shakespeare.

Much in *King Lear* and *The Tempest*, the two principal plays evoked in *Mama Day*, seems merely to aid and abet the sentimental pastoral tendencies in the novel. Both plays assume the salubrious value of pastoral space—the exposed heath in Lear's case, the magically controlled island in Prospero's. Both plays employ the rhythm of the tempest followed by the restorative calm after the storm; in Naylor's final line, ". . . the waters were still." Moreover, the generic progression from *King Lear* as tragedy to *The Tempest* as late romance serves to reinforce a romanticized version of pastoral.

These congruencies between Shakespeare and *Mama Day* do not tell the whole story, however. Naylor's interest in Shakespeare cannot be satisfactorily treated according to T. S. Eliot's account of Joyce's use of classical tradition as an ordering device.[12] Naylor's sustained engagement with Shakespeare cannot be explained by the image of Shakespeare as an exclusively positive resource, nor is Naylor's action limited to the harmonious adaptation and recapitulation of Shakespearean motifs. Rather, the effect of *Mama Day*'s exploration of Shakespearean heritage is critically to revise and decenter it.

V.

Naylor's reassessment of Shakespeare in *Mama Day* is carried out on two levels. On the first, George's attachment to *King Lear* is probed; on the second, more pervasive level, associations between Willow Springs and *The Tempest* are tested. This twofold approach is correlated with the novel's overall geographic movement from North to South since

George's *Lear* is situated in the former while *The Tempest*'s connections are with the latter.

George's adoption of Shakespeare serves as a badge of his upward mobility. His successive editions of *King Lear* both mark the increasing value of the play as a material object and cultural status symbol and measure the progress of his relationship with Cocoa. He begins with a "worn copy" that he prefers to Cocoa's and ends with "the calfskin and gold-leafed copy" that Cocoa gives him as a birthday present. *King Lear* specifically provides the medium for negotiating George's seduction of Cocoa: "The games people play. I wasn't coming to your apartment the following Tuesday night to talk about *King Lear*."

The chief point of emotional connection to the play is George's identification with Edmund: "It had a special poignancy for me, reading the rage of a bastard. . . ." Edmund's soliloquy—"Now, gods, stand up for bastards"—speaks to George's desire to make it against the odds. George smugly notes Cocoa's naive reading, though he withholds his commentary so as not to impede the seduction:

> And you were so glad I'd turned you on to this. It showed you how hard the playwright tried to convey that men had the same feelings as women. No, that was not true. No way. Along with *The Taming of the Shrew*, this had to be Shakespeare's most sexist treatment of women—but far be it from me to contradict anything you had to say. I didn't want to waste any more time than necessary for you to work yourself up to untying the strings on that red halter.

But George's own misinterpretation is just as bad, for Shakespeare does not stand up for bastards any more than for women.[13] Edmund is defeated by Edgar in the end, and George chooses to neglect his fate.

George's relatively superficial attachment to Shakespeare comes nowhere close to his passionate commitment to football. If Shakespeare's images of women are restrictive, football excludes women entirely. In Cocoa's detached view of football's male bonding: "They line up, bend down, and all of a sudden they're in a pile, smelling each other's behinds." Since Naylor herself shares Cocoa's resistance to George's love of football,[14] one might say that Naylor has paid George back by imposing on him her own fascination with Shakespeare. After the tempest hits Willow Springs, she puts into George's mouth a phrase derived from Prospero's revel speech: "this was the stuff of dreams." But George's understanding of the cue proves inadequate. While his attitude toward football approaches the religious—"And I'm not talking in metaphors—it could create miracles," his response to Mama Day conspicuously denies that this attitude could apply to her female arena: "'Well, you're talking in a lot of metaphors.'" Ultimately his approach to Willow Springs remains on the same order as his treatment of "the symbolism" of *King Lear*.

The novel's second Shakespearean strand, the interplay between *The Tempest* and Naylor's representation of the Southern island of Willow

Springs, involves a much more active encounter with Shakespeare. Naylor rewrites the exchange between Prospero and Caliban concerning ownership, in effect honoring Caliban's accusation—"This island's mine, by Sycorax my mother, / Which thou tak'st from me"— and reinstating his legitimate, female-derived possession. The black islanders of Willow Springs oppose the trend in island development that would reduce them to Caliban-like servility:

> Hadn't we seen it happen back in the '80s on St. Helena, Daufuskie, and St. John's? And before that in the '60s on Hilton Head? . . . And the only dark faces you see now in them "vacation paradises" is the ones cleaning the toilets and cutting the grass. . . . Weren't gonna happen in Willow Springs. 'Cause if Mama Day say no, everybody say no.

Their attitude toward real estate contrasts sharply with that represented by the black developer Luther Nedeed in *Linden Hills;* where Nedeed imitates the white model, Willow Springs rejects it. Nedeed's obsessive concern with the empty ceremony of a traditional family Christmas is replaced in *Mama Day* by the non-Christian observance of the winter solstice that signifies cultural independence: ". . . old Reverend Hooper couldn't stop Candle Walk night. . . . Any fool knows Christmas is December twenty-fifth—that ain't never caught on too much here. And Candle Walk is always the night of the twenty-second."

Naylor's depiction of Willow Springs' resistance to white corporate and cultural control parallels her own resistance to Shakespearean colonization of her art. However, although Naylor teasingly alludes to Caliban—"some slave on a Caribbean island" Cocoa recalls "from her high school Shakespeare," the main line of Naylor's resistance lies elsewhere. As a recent survey shows, twentieth-century attempts to revise *The Tempest* have concentrated on reversing the Prospero-Caliban relationship by imagining a newly empowered Caliban.[15] Naylor's special contribution is her focus on women characters, a focus that adds a reconfiguration of genders to the issues of race and class associated with Caliban. Largely ignoring Caliban, Naylor's subversive strategy is to create a black female equivalent to Prospero.

The force of Naylor's project is implied by the central character's double name: both Miranda and Mama Day. If the former suggests the tie to Shakespeare, the latter breaks it by indicating the possibility of escape from Shakespearean entrapment in the subservient daughter role. The age and experience of Naylor's Miranda not only contrasts with the youth and innocence of Shakespeare's Miranda; Mama Day's scope also encompasses and outdoes Prospero himself. In 1999 at the novel's close, Mama Day, having been born in 1895, is 104 years old and even then her epilogue is not quite ready to seek release: ". . . and when she's tied up the twentieth century, she'll take a little peek into the other side—for pure devilment and curiosity—and then leave for a rest that she deserves." The hyperbole of her age establishes that Mama Day is more than able to compete with Prospero, whose "Every third thought shall be my grave" seems pinched and feeble next to the splendor of her approach to death.

Naylor not only has Mama Day usurp Prospero's role but also redefines that role by altering the prerogatives that go with it. The moral structure of *The Tempest* is carried over into *Mama Day* only in a residual way. Ruby, for example, is a Sycorax figure against whom Mama Day is allowed a spectacular punitive display. However, Naylor's main stress is on the differences between Prospero's and Mama Day's magical powers. The storm at the outset of *The Tempest* is Prospero's concoction, as he reveals with paternal reassurance and pride in act one, scene two. By contrast, Mama Day is powerless to prevent the storm's destruction of Little Caesar, the child whom she had helped Bernice to produce. As Mama Day reflects, "she ain't never tried to get *over* nature." While Prospero may belatedly accept the limits of his magic, Mama Day is mindful of her limitations from the beginning.

The contrast between Prospero and Mama Day is especially sharp with respect to gender politics. Though the relationship between Mama Day and her father Jean-Paul is portrayed as a positive resource, it is nonetheless subordinate to the primary emphasis on strong female bonds—bonds that Miranda's isolation makes impossible in *The Tempest*. Mama Day's central drama concerns the recovery of connections with three women: Sapphira, the slave woman who originated the Day line; Ophelia, Mama Day's mother who, distraught over the death of her daughter Peace, drowned herself; and Cocoa, her grandniece, who has left Willow Springs and now works in New York City.

Like Mama Day, Cocoa has a double name that operates to deny Shakespearean expectations. Cocoa is named Ophelia after her great grandmother, whose death by water recalls the destiny of Shakespeare's Ophelia in the male-dominated world of *Hamlet*. Cocoa's alternate name aids the process of exorcising the burden both of her great grandmother's demise and of the potential Shakespearean connotations. Mama Day's comment about tradition can be applied to the novel's general stance toward patriarchal political structures in *Hamlet*, *King Lear*, or *The Tempest*: "'Tradition is fine, but you gotta know when to stop being a fool.'"

It is true that in its own way *Mama Day* is as determined as any Shakespearean comedy its marital and reproductive drive. Like Prospero, Mama Day orchestrates generational continuity: "I plan to keep on living till I can rock one of yours on my knee." This parallel does not mean, however, that Mama Day derives after all from a Shakespearean analogue. Mama Day is shaped rather by the figure of the black mother as artist described by writers such as Paule Marshall, Alice Walker, and June Jordan,[16] and it is within this distinct tradition that the Mama Day-Cocoa relationship has to be considered.

In Paule Marshall's *Praisesong for the Widow*, the unattributed poetic phrase "my sweetest lepers" comes from Gwendolyn Brooks' "the children of the poor," whose first line chillingly observes: "People who have no children can be heard."[17] This assertion has a resonance with Toni Morrison's *Tar Baby* (1981), where the unattached and childless Jadine is presented not as an opportunity but as a problem.[18] In the 1985 conversation with Naylor, Morrison comments: "That's another one of those unreal, I think also fraudulent, conflicts between women who want to be mothers and women who don't. Why should there be any conflict with that? You could, first of all, do both." But Morrison's idea of choice modulates into the imperative of doing both: "No one should be asked to make a choice between a home and a career. Why not have both? It's all possible."

Morrison's comments suggest some of the emotional charge behind the novel's procreational pressure, a pressure exemplified by the quilt Cocoa receives from Mama Day and her sister: ". . . I also knew they hadn't gone through that kind of labor just for me . . . They had sewed for *my* grandchildren to be conceived under this quilt." Cocoa begins as a potential Jadine, but through Mama Day's intervention ends by carrying on the family line, on which the inheritance of land and the survival of Willow Springs depend. The novel's conclusion leaves no room for doubt about Cocoa's commitment to Mama Day's legacy. Yet their bond is not completely idealized; a slight prickliness and tension flickers around the edges. Cocoa's original departure from the island signals her need for psychological separation; she vigorously rejects George's notion of settling in Willow Springs; even when she relocates, she maintains some distance by living in Charleston instead of returning to the island itself.

We have in the end to see Naylor's work in relation to two different contexts, both of which are important for a full view. Naylor's departures from Shakespeare—especially her rejection of the absences and restrictions imposed by Shakespearean images of women—are substantial. By countering Shakespeare, Naylor demonstrates the degree to which Shakespeare does not author us, the extent to which that role has irreversibly passed to others. New problems indeed arise, but they are not Shakespeare's problems nor does his work contain the materials needed for exploring all the possible options.

VI.

The conclusion of this analysis of Naylor's use of Shakespeare is that Shakespeare's cultural reach is diminished, not extended. Shakespeare's work can no longer be conceived as an infinitely expanding literary umbrella, the ultimate primary source capable of commenting on all subsequent developments no matter how far historically removed. Faced with apparently limitless possibilities for interpretation, Shakespeareans have tended to romanticize their critical quandary by investing it with an existential myth of Shakespeare's inexhaustibility, by means of which Shakespeare already anticipates every possible future situation or response. This notion of Shakespearean anticipation amounts to a denial of history, of change, and of our own agency.

Naylor's work provides a valuable test case for how we are going to formulate a multicultural approach to literary studies. Naylor's interest in Shakespeare neither translates into kinship nor supports a model of continuity; the main note is rather one of conflict and difference. As Gloria T. Hull remarks, "Black women poets are not 'Shakespeare's sisters.' In fact, they seem to be siblings of no one but themselves."[19] *Mama Day* owes less to Shakespeare than to a separate tradition of black women writers. Shakespeare does not assimilate Naylor; Naylor assimilates Shakespeare.

The result is that we must give up the assumption that the literary curriculum revolves around Shakespeare. The habits of a Shakespeare-centered universe may inspire ever more elaborate and farfetched attempts at "saving the appearances" comparable to the calculations devised to defend a geocentric system against the encroachments of a heliocentric view. The cultural act of naming newly discovered moons—most recently those of Uranus—after Shakespearean characters may seem to provide confirmation of old patterns; new moons cannot talk back and disconfirm. But new authors like Gloria Naylor can. Her fictions encourage us to direct our energies toward investigations of Shakespeare's place in a reconstellated cultural situation in which his work, while still significant, is no longer the all-defining center of things.

Notes

1. *Rewriting the Renaissance: The Discourses of Sexual Difference in Early Modern Europe*, ed. Margaret W. Ferguson, Maureen Quilligan, and Nancy J. Vickers (Chicago: University of Chicago Press, 1986).
2. Recent work on Matthiessen includes: Jonathan Arac, "F.O. Matthiessen: Authorizing an American Renaissance," in *The American Renaissance Reconsidered: Selected Papers from the English Institute 1982–83*, ed. Walter Benn Michaels and Donald E. Pease (Baltimore: Johns Hopkins University Press, 1985), pp. 90–112; Sacvan Bercovitch, "The Problem of Ideology in American Literary History," *Critical Inquiry* 12 (Summer 1986): 631–53; Donald E. Pease, "F. O. Matthiessen," in *Modern American Critics, 1920–1955*, ed. Gregory S. Jay (Detroit: Gale, 1988), pp. 138–48; William E. Cain, *F. O. Matthiessen and the Politics of Criticism* (Madison: University of Wisconsin Press, 1988).

3. Gloria T. Hull, *Color, Sex and Poetry: Three Women Writers of the Harlem Renaissance* (Bloomington: Indiana University Press, 1987).

4. Gloria Naylor and Toni Morrison, "A Conversation," *Southern Review* 21 (Summer 1985): 567–93; quotation from p. 589.

5. Karen Newman, "'And Wash the Ethiop White': Femininity and the Monstrous in *Othello*," in *Shakespeare Reproduced: The Text in History and Ideology*, ed. Jean E. Howard and Marion F. O'Connor (New York: Methuen, 1987), pp. 141–62. Naylor glances only briefly at Othello in *Mama Day*, where she finds other points of entry into Shakespeare more useful.

6. The fourth novel, *Bailey's Cafe*, is mentioned in Bronwyn Mills' interview article, "Gloria Naylor: Dreaming the Dream," *Sojourner* (May 1988): 17.

7. A full analysis of this aspect of the play is given in Shirley Nelson Garner's "*A Midsummer Night's Dream*: 'Jack shall have Jill;/Nought shall go ill,'" *Women's Studies* 9 (1981): 47–63.

8. The resonance of the Southern location is increased when its autobiographical dimension is added: though born in New York City, Naylor "returned to the town of Robinsonville, Mississippi, where her family originated, to research folk medicine for *Mama Day*."

9. In her Introduction to her 1967 short story "To Da-duh in Memoriam," in *Reena and Other Stories* (Old Westbury: Feminist Press, 1983), p. 95, Marshall links the character Aunt Cuney with Da-duh, Marshall's grandmother. The balance of forces between New York City and black island culture to the South is quite differently portrayed in the two cases. The granddaughter's triumph in the short story is reversed sixteen years later in the novel, which awards power to the grandmother figure.

10. This criticism of *Praisesong for the Widow* is not intended as a generalization about Marshall's work as a whole. Her previous novel about Barbados, *The Chosen Place, The Timeless People* (1969), exhibits an acute political awareness; there is nothing inherent in a Caribbean island location that automatically excludes sensitivity to political questions.

11. Carby's argument is presented in "The Quicksands of Representation: Rethinking Black Cultural Politics," the final chapter in her *Reconstructing Womanhood: The Emergence of the Afro-American Woman Novelist* (New York: Oxford University Press, 1987), pp. 163–75; and elaborated in "Ideologies of Black Folk: The Historical Novel of Slavery," in *Slavery and the Literary Imagination: Selected Papers from the English Institute, 1987*, ed. Deborah E. McDowell and Arnold Rampersad (Baltimore: Johns Hopkins University Press, 1989), pp. 125–43, and "The Canon: Civil War and Reconstruction," *Michigan Quarterly Review* 28 (Winter 1989): 35–43. The critical reassessment of the central folk line defined by the Alice Walker–Zora Neale Hurston connection is exemplified by Mary Helen Washington's reconsideration of *Their Eyes Were Watching God*: "'I Love the Way Janie Crawford Left Her Husbands': Zora Neal Hurston's Emergent Female Hero," in her *Invented Lives: Narratives of Black Women 1860–1960* (Garden City: Doubleday, 1987), pp. 237–54.

12. The account occurs in Eliot's Review, "Ulysses, Order, and Myth," in *The Dial* 75 (November 1923): 480–83.

13. For a discussion of the sexual politics of women's roles in *King Lear*, see my *Patriarchal Structures in Shakespeare's Drama* (Berkeley: University of California Press, 1985), pp. 103–15.

14. Naylor comments in her own voice on football in the boxed inset, "Keeping Up with the Characters," accompanying the review of *Mama Day* in *The New York Times Book Review* (February 21, 1988): p. 7.

15. The survey is Alden T. Vaughn's, in his two articles "Caliban in the 'Third World': Shakespeare's Savage as Sociopolitical Symbol," *Massachusetts Review* 29 (Summer 1988): 289–313 and "Shakespeare's Indian: The Americanization of Caliban," *Shakespeare Quarterly* 39 (Summer 1988): 137–53. Thomas Cartelli's "Prospero in Africa: *The Tempest* as Colonialist Text and Pretext," in *Shakespeare Reproduced*, pp. 99–115, is wholly occupied with the dynamics of the Prospero-Caliban relationship.

16. The mother is identified as an artist in Paule Marshall, "Shaping the World of My Art," *New Letters* 40 (October 1973): 97–112 (subsequently incorporated in "From the Poets in the Kitchen," *New York Times Book Review* [January 9, 1983]); Alice Walker, "In Search of Our Mothers' Gardens," *Ms.* Magazine (May 1974); and June Jordan, "Notes of a Barnard Dropout (1975)," *Civil Wars* (Boston: Beacon Press, 1981), pp. 96–102.

17. Just as Toni Morrison acknowledges Paule Marshall as a predecessor, so Marshall names Gwendolyn Brooks as a precursor: see Marshall's contribution to "The Negro Woman in American Literature," *Freedomways* 6 (Winter 1966): pp. 23–24.

18. For a detailed analysis, see my "Images of Nurturance in Toni Morrison's *Tar Baby*," *CLA Journal* 28 (September 1984): 11–32.

19. Gloria T. Hull, "Afro-American Women Poets: A Bio-Critical Survey," in *Shakespeare's Sisters: Feminist Essays on Women Poets*, ed. Sandra M. Gilbert and Susan Gubar (Bloomington: Indiana University Press, 1979), pp. 165–82; quotation from p. 165.

◆◆◆◆◆◆◆◆◆◆◆◆◆◆

The Ornamentation of Old Ideas: Naylor's First Three Novels

JAMES ROBERT SAUNDERS

In 1982, when Gloria Naylor exploded onto the scene with her award-winning novel, *The Women of Brewster Place*, it was only the beginning of a career in which the artist would continue to draw substantially from other writers' works to enhance her own presentation of novelistic ideas. Henry Louis Gates has characterized this strategic style as "signification," that is the utilization of others' characters and themes to provide a foundation from which to springboard off into one's own variations. Slave narrators did it with their reinforcement of certain themes such as an oppressive South, the value of education, and flight to northern freedom. The brilliant Ralph Ellison, with his *Invisible Man* (1952), did it as he drew upon Richard Wright's *Native Son* (1940) to create his own version of the black American male. In more recent years we have seen Alice Walker relying on Zora Neale Hurston's *Their Eyes Were Watching God* (1937) to provide, in *The Color Purple* (1982), her own rendition of the quest for self-actualization.

The literary process of borrowing ideas has been going on for quite some time, but Naylor is one who has perfected the technique. One need only have read Ann Petry's *The Street* (1946) to be struck by the similarity between it and *Brewster Place*. First of all, both novels ended with a terrible death that contributed to a most profound meaning. In Petry's novel the death involved protagonist Lutie Johnson killing lecherous Boots Smith, a black nightclub entertainer who promised himself to do all that he could to get Lutie's body. He had promised her a singing job, and at one point pulled his car to the side of a deserted road and held her "so tightly and his mouth was so insistent, so brutal, that she twisted out of his arms, not caring what he thought, intent only on escaping from his ruthless hands and mouth." So desperate was he to achieve his goal that when physical force failed he concluded that "if he couldn't get her any other way, he'd marry her," not due to anything even faintly resembling love, but as yet another means whereby he might attain the object of his lewd desires. He was no different from the white business proprietor, Old Man Junto, who warned, "Leave her alone. I want her myself." No different from the janitor, William Jones, who planned to rape her. No different from Mr. Crosse, of the Crosse School for Singers, who stipulated, "If you and me can get together a coupla nights a week in Harlem, those lessons won't cost you a cent." Lutie picked up an inkwell

and hurled it at that propositioner's face, "the ink paused for a moment
at the obstruction of his eyebrows, then dripped down over the fat jowls,
over the wrinkled collar, the grease-stained vest." She dared to strike
back, but her reaction, at that time, was against only one of the despica-
ble male characters. When a half crazed Boots finally resorted to extreme
violence, declaring, "Maybe after I beat the hell out of you a coupla
times, you'll begin to like the idea of sleeping with me," Lutie picked up
an iron candlestick and:

> kept striking him, not thinking about him, not even seeing him. First she was
> venting her rage against the dirty, crowded street. She saw the rows of
> dilapidated old houses; the small dark rooms; the long steep flights of stairs;
> the narrow dingy hallways . . . the smashed homes where the women did
> drudgery because their men had deserted them. She saw all of these things
> and struck at them.

Bludgeoning Boots in this way, she imagined she was destroying all the
dreadful obstacles that had prevented her and other black women in like
situations from attaining respectability.

In *Brewster Place* the killer resides in a housing project and is a
lesbian who has just been raped by C. C. Baker and his cohorts. C. C.
and the other gang members escape but Lorraine kills Ben, a janitor
who years earlier had been a cause for his own daughter's turn to prostitution. That daughter had come to Ben and told him about the sexual
improprieties she had been forced into under the auspices of doing maid
work for a white landowner. Ben resolved "that if he sat up drinking all
night Friday, he could stand on the porch Saturday morning and smile
at the man who whistled as he dropped his lame daughter home." Notwithstanding the social inequities in force between black and white men,
it is evident that Ben could have done more before his daughter fled,
leaving a note that stated, "If she had to earn her keep that way, she
might as well go to Memphis where the money was better." In a literal
sense Ben's death is accidental, but from another perspective, his death
is symbolic of an end to the same phenomenon Petry's Boots represented,
the lack of proper action when proper action was so desperately needed.

Kathryn Palumbo is pessimistic in her article, "The Uses of Female
Imagery in Naylor's *The Women of Brewster Place*," where she maintains that Naylor "offers her characters no hope and no power beyond
daily survival." But in actuality the final section of the novel serves
notice that a new way of life may be on the horizon. At first conceived
as a means of raising money to pay for a tenants' association lawyer, a
well-planned block party takes on even greater significance as:

> Women flung themselves against the wall, chipping away at it with knives,
> plastic forks, spiked shoe heels, and even bare hands. . . . The bricks piled
> up behind them and were snatched and relayed out of Brewster Place past
> overturned tables, scattered coins, and crushed wads of dollar bills. They
> came back with chairs and barbecue grills and smashed them into the wall.

* * *

That wall was the place where C.C. had led five others in rape. It was where a dazed Lorraine had killed Ben. This was the wall that separated all project residents from the rest of society, and now in the drenching rain while "all of the men and children . . . stood huddled in the doorways," the women dismantled this wall of seclusion and opened the way for possibility.

Petry had a somewhat similar depiction of black sisterhood. In fact, the Georgia-born outcast, Mrs. Hedges, saved Lutie from rape. Interestingly enough, it was the janitor (building superintendent) who forced her down toward the basement until:

> A pair of powerful hands gripped her by the shoulders, wrenched her violently out of the Super's arms, flung her back against the wall. She stood there shuddering, her mouth still open, still screaming, unable to stop the sounds that were coming from her throat. The same powerful hands shot out and thrust the Super hard against the cellar door.

Yet in spite of that aid, Mrs. Hedges is less than satisfactory in terms of supplying a solution for young women out on the street. Her answer was for them to become prostitutes.

Mrs. Hedges does not offer the optimum solution, but upon considering how Lutie had been abandoned by virtually all of the men in her life, we wonder what exactly Petry had in mind for black women's progress. Lutie's husband became mired in an adulterous affair. Her father chose alcohol and loose women over contributing to a suitable environment for his young grandson. And then there was that child himself who, while albeit not at an age to be fully responsible, had already become susceptible to "gangs of young boys who were always on the lookout for small fry Bub's age, because they found young kids useful in getting in through narrow fire-escape windows, in distracting a storekeeper's attention while the gang light-heartedly helped itself to his stock." After Bub was caught and taken into police custody, Lutie could only contemplate how "the little Henry Chandlers," such as those she had cared for in the plush Connecticut suburbs, "go to YalePrincetonHarvard" while "the Bub Johnsons graduate from reform school into DannemoraSingSing." The cycle of disappointments seemed bound to continue.

As Petry had done thirty-six years earlier in her novel, Naylor likewise has three generations of males fail Mattie Michael who, first of all, has gotten pregnant by a man who won't marry her. When she refuses to tell her father who the baby's father is, Mr. Michael "held her by the hair so she took the force of the two blows with her neck muscles, and her eyes went dim as the blood dropped down her chin from her split lip." Mattie continues her refusal and the father keeps on with his punishment, beating her with a broom until it "had broken, and he was now kneeling over Mattie and beating her with a jagged section of it that he had in his fist." Shortly thereafter, she leaves home and gives birth to a son she names Basil. Time passes quickly as he becomes a young man and Mattie realizes she had:

> never met any of Basil's girlfriends, and he rarely mentioned them . . . and it suddenly came to her that she hadn't met many of his male friends, either. Where was he going? She truly didn't know, and it had come to be understood that she was not to ask.

Just as the hardworking Lutie had lost her son, Bub, to the street with all of its illegal distractions, Mattie loses Basil to a barroom brawl. After he is arrested, Mattie seeks legal help. "Thank God for ignorance of the law and frantic mothers," her lawyer says to himself. Lutie's attorney had been just as calculating, thinking, "Now why in hell doesn't she know she doesn't need a lawyer?" as he gave her three days to get two hundred dollars.

One is tempted to reconsider if indeed Mrs. Hedges would not be a better alternative to such devastating results. But Petry made her too much a flawed character. On the other hand, Naylor has Mattie develop into a great source of strength without losing her morality. Forced now to live at Brewster Place, she nevertheless does not exploit in the manner of Mrs. Hedges. Naylor has her strongest woman character giving an abundance of love, the sort of love that makes her wait up late for Etta Mae out on a date with the opportunist, Reverend Woods, who is attracted to Etta, strictly in the physical sense. Mattie had tried to stop Etta from going but she also understood:

> Sometimes being a friend means mastering the art of timing. There is a time for silence. A time to let go and allow people to hurl themselves into their own destiny. And a time to prepare to pick up the pieces when it's all over.

When Lucielia Louise loses both of her children and subsequently wishes to die herself, it is Mattie who gently rocks her back toward a healthy consciousness.

> She took the soap, and, using only her hands, she washed Ciel's hair and the back of her neck. She raised her arms and cleaned the armpits, soaping well the downy brown hair there. She let the soap slip between the girl's breasts, and she washed each one separately, cupping it in her hands. She took each leg and even cleaned under the toenails. Making Ciel rise and kneel in the tub, she cleaned the crack in her behind, soaped her pubic hair, and gently washed the creases in her vagina—slowly, reverently, as if handling a newborn.

It is the notion of the fulfillment of sisterly love that separates Naylor from Petry. In *The Street* Lutie finally fled New York City, and there is utter sadness as we think of her loss. The women of Brewster Place also have suffered immensely, but they "still wake up with their dreams misted on the edge of a yawn. . . . They ebb and flow, ebb and flow, but never disappear." We have seen the tragedy of these women's lives but anticipate prospects for a better future.

Many in our society have come to regard the massive movement to suburban-type environments as the key to progress. So it is apropos that Naylor's next novel should examine an exclusive black neighborhood where residents have gained economic success. Naylor narrates:

> Practically every black in Wayne County wanted to be a part of Linden Hills . . . somehow making it into Linden Hills meant "making it" . . . only "certain" people go to live in Linden Hills, and the blacks in Wayne County . . . kept sending in applications to the Tupelo Realty Corporation—and hoping.

However, on the very first page of *Linden Hills* (1985), we are given reason to suspect that not everything is as it should be. Linden Hills "wasn't a set of hills, or even a whole hill," but the northern face of a plateau that led down into the town cemetery. The main proprietor of the Tupelo Realty Corporation is one Luther Nedeed, an old, rather spooky dark man who has assumed the ownership of his father's undertaking business, an establishment which that father had inherited in turn from two previous generations of Luther Nedeeds.

One might assume in this case that an analogy can be made between moving up in terms of socio-economic prosperity and a geographic moving up within the context of Linden Hills. But on the contrary, movement downward is what these residents seek, although once reaching the bottom they mysteriously disappear. Still, "none of the applicants ever questioned the fact that there was always space in Linden Hills." Residents at the very bottom are disposed of in some way by Nedeed, whose inverted name, "de eden," means false paradise.

Naylor would have done well enough just to have depicted the superficiality of those lost in the quest for material possessions. However, she chose to innovate and use Dante's *Inferno*, written in the fourteenth century, as the framework for her twentieth century tale. Dante's version of Hell is best conceptualized by imagining ten descending layers of circles. At the top are virtuous but unbaptized pagans. The second circle consists of inhabitants who have been lustful. Those who have been gluttonous compose the third circle. Followed, in the fourth, by both those who have been avaricious and those who have been prodigal. Then come the wrathful, the heretical, the violent, the fraudulent, and the traitorous who are trapped in circles five through nine respectively. The Devil himself, frozen from the waist down in a lake of ice, makes up circle number ten, the most frightening of all Dante's levels.

Drawing on that model, Naylor has eight concentric circles composing Linden Hills. Lester Tilson lives with his mother and sister on First Crescent Drive in "the smallest house on a street of brick ranch houses." They live on the fringe but are nevertheless part of the Linden Hills community. As Catherine Ward has asserted, "Here, like the neutrals in the vestibule outside Circle One of the *Inferno*, live those who are neither good nor evil, the uncommitted who chase after banners." The full import of that statement is realized as we view the Tilson home where:

> Its two-story wooden frame had been covered with light green aluminum siding, and three brick steps led up to a dark green door. . . . Willow-green print furniture sat on jade carpeting and there were green-and-white Japanese porcelain vases arranged on the tables in the living room. The curtains in the hallway and living room had avocado stripes and fern prints, and with the light coming through them, they gave a whisper-green tint to the white walls.

The color green dominates, emphasizing the degree to which money itself becomes a god. Even house walls appear green when the sun shines through avocado-striped, fern-printed curtains. Inside, the carpeting is jade; outside, the wooden frame is covered with green aluminum siding, a clue to how artificiality has covered what was once natural.

Further down on Third Crescent Drive lives Maxwell Smyth, assistant to the executive director of General Motors, whose "elaborate series of humidifiers and thermostats enabled him to determine the exact conditions under which he would eat, sleep, or sit." His life is so calculated that "the only thing his bathroom lacked was toilet paper, which he kept in the closet and brought out for rare guests since he never needed it." As Naylor says, "His entire life became a race against the natural—and he was winning." The decision whether even to smile at his secretary was one that he considered with great gravity.

On the sixth level down we come across Mrs. Laurel Dumont, who is likewise losing touch with her most valuable possession, her own inimitable soul. As an eight-year-old child she had loved the water although "she didn't swim a lick." Grandmother Roberta saw to it that young Laurel learned; in time, the youth came to be quite proficient, as comfortable in a country swimming hole as when her head was "resting in Roberta's lap, the crickets and bullfrogs competing as hard to give the light." But as Laurel grows older she finds herself first in college and then married to Howard Dumont. "And when she finally took a good look around, she found herself imprisoned within a chain of photographs and a life that had no point." The last time we see her alive she is consciously diving from a thirty-foot board into the twenty-foot end of an empty swimming pool.

In characterizing Laurel, Naylor builds on the feminist statement that was so much a part of her first novel, *Brewster Place*. Laurel was indeed trapped in a life dictated by her husband's social position and standards perpetuated by Linden Hills. But it is as we continue on with our downward movement that we get to the most disturbing portrayal of sexist oppression as we are told about the four Nedeed wives. Luwana

Parkerville Nedeed bore a dark-skinned son for her husband and then faded into an obscure life of privately composing letters just to herself. A generation later, Evelyn Creton Nedeed bore the traditional dark-skinned son, thereby becoming expendable, and then starved to death. Priscilla McGuire Nedeed had the requisite son and then watched as that son cast a deeper and deeper shadow across her face, first as she observed it in family photographs and then in reality. As Ward puts it, "Without a fight, she watches as the shadows of her husband and son blot out her soul."

The latest in the line of Mrs. Nedeeds is Willa Prescott Nedeed, who wore:

> Saddle oxfords in grade school, maroon loafers in high school, platform heels in college. . . . She imported the white satin pumps that took Willa Prescott down the aisle six years ago and brought her back up as Willa Prescott Nedeed. Her marriage to Luther Nedeed was her choice, and she took his name by choice. She knew . . . that there were no laws anywhere in this country that forced her to assume that name; she took it because she wanted to. That was important. She must be clear about that before she went on to anything else: she wanted to be a Nedeed.

Her desperation to be married had been so great that she did not consider the exact nature of her compromise. Nedeed had gone to his tenth college reunion to choose from among "those who had lost that hopeful, arrogant strut," someone "more than willing to join the life and rhythms of almost any man." Willa Prescott had been just such a woman. She wanted to be a Nedeed and "walk around and feel that she had a perfect right to respond to a phone call, a letter, an invitation—any verbal or written request directed toward that singular identity." Her fate will be linked to the other Mrs. Nedeeds who preceded her, but she is the most tragic of all, for upon giving birth to a son who turned out to be light-skinned, her husband locked both her and that son in the basement where, during a six-year period, the son slowly died and the mother slowly lost her mind.

Naylor has cleverly altered the Dantean concept of Hell to include what can be experienced in this mortal life. Willa Nedeed suffered through it, as did the other three Nedeed wives. Linden Hills is Hell, and in place of morality lies the single-minded thirst for financial success. As was true in the *Inferno*, the price paid is in human souls.

The Roman poet, Virgil, led Dante through an afterlife Hell, and Lester leads Willie Mason through Linden Hills. It is, of course, significant that Lester is a poet who occasionally earns five dollars for getting a poem published in a local newspaper. However, Willie does not write his poems. He serves the same function as an African *griot*, perpetuating a culture through phenomenal memory. Willie had:

> already memorized 665 poems and this last one just wasn't working out. Would he have to start writing them down? He couldn't imagine that. Poetry

wrote itself for him. If he had to pick up a pen and paper, he just knew there would be nothing to say . . . His poems only made sense in his ears and mouth. His fingers, eyes, and nose. Something about Linden Hills was blocking that.

Willie is unable to memorize more than 665 poems, which bodes well for him, considering 666 is a sign of the Devil. The young poet had wanted to continue with his craft but is appropriately wary in approaching Linden Hills. Lester is thus essential as a guide though dangerously relaxed in this evil territory.

In Canto XXI of the *Inferno* we had also seen recklessness on the part of Virgil, so sure that demons who once threatened would now let them pass. A demon chief even offered them escorts. Virgil handled all of this in matter-of-fact fashion while Dante asked the vital questions:

"O Master, what is this?" In fear I spoke,
"Alone, if thou the way know, let us start.
Such escort's aid I care not to invoke.
If thou beest wary, as wontedly thou wert,
Dost thou not see them, how they grind their teeth
And with bent brows threaten us to our hurt?"

Virgil ignored Dante's apprehensiveness on that as well as on several other occasions.

In spite of such difficulties, however, they made it through the Inferno and on to Purgatorio for a rendezvous with the illustrious Beatrice, a woman the author Dante himself first saw when he was nine years old and she was eight. Although they were never involved in any kind of physical romance, Dante did envision her as his ideal. Stewart Farnell offers insight:

Virgil is Dante's immediate guide, but it is Beatrice who has sent Virgil to Dante. Just as Virgil is even himself, the Roman poet, and also, symbolically, much more, so Beatrice is herself, the real Beatrice whom Dante loved and who was for him a revelation of the divine glory, and she is also a symbol. Beatrice symbolizes revelation, spiritual illumination, grace, theology, salvation, and even Christ.

This would explain Virgil's flaws. Though ordained to lead Dante, he was not on a par with Jesus Christ or Beatrice, who might have been designed to symbolize either Christ or goodness in pure form.

Naylor's version of Beatrice is Ruth Anderson, previously a resident of Linden Hills but now living on Wayne Avenue and married to Norman Anderson who comes down with "the pinks" once every year and nine months. When that psychological fit occurs it leaves him desperate to scrape off imaginary slime. "He resorted to his teeth and bare nails only after everything else had failed—jagged sections of plates and glasses, wire hangers, curtain rods, splinters of wood once part of a dresser, coffee table, or her grandmother's antique music box." Nevertheless, Ruth stays with him in their sparse apartment "with its bare floors, dusted and polished, and with the three pieces of furniture that sat in three large rooms: one sofa in the living room, one kitchenette set with plastic-bottomed chairs on uncertain chrome legs, one bed." Like Beatrice, she is reminiscent of Christ who lived only with the barest essentials and with those most despised, like the lepers.

Just as Beatrice had sent Virgil to Dante, so too does Ruth suggest that Lester guide Willie through Linden Hills, in this case to look for odd jobs. When they run into difficulty with a policeman, she somehow knows of their dilemma and sends Norman with a story the police will accept. "Norm, you must have been sent from the gods," Willie says, to which Norman replies, "Ruth had a feeling that you two might get yourselves into a mess, walking around down here." Virgil led Dante through the levels of Hell, but Christ was the source of love and wisdom. So too with Ruth. While Luther Nedeed has held his wife in captivity six years for the most insignificant of reasons, Ruth celebrates six years of being with someone she had every reason to leave. "I rule in—," Norman starts to say before Ruth catches him as they drink from their Styrofoam cups. "Love rules in this house," he corrects himself with Christian words.

The prospect of pure love is also at the heart of Naylor's most recent novel, *Mama Day* (1988). The novel's basic structure consists of briefly rendered sections in which a formerly widowed woman and her dead first husband narrate alternatively. Ophelia recalls, "Six months of looking for a job had made me an expert at picking out the people who, like me, were hurrying up to wait—in somebody's outer anything for a chance to make it through their inner doors to prove that you could type two words a minute, or not drool on your blouse while answering difficult questions about your middle initial and date of birth." She is cynical about her move from Willow Springs (off the coasts of South Carolina and Georgia) to New York City, and it is most evident as she seeks gainful employment after two years of business school in Atlanta and seven years with an insurance company that folded because of its "greedy president who didn't have the sense to avoid insuring half of the buildings in the south Bronx—even at triple premiums for fire and water damage." She now sits alone in a restaurant, pondering her tenuous situation.

Seated at another table is George Andrews who, in his first dialogue from beyond the grave, confides, "Our guardians at the Wallace P. Andrews Shelter for Boys were adamant about the fact that we learned to invest in ourselves alone." In accordance with that institutional standard, George matriculated at Columbia University and, upon graduation, went on to become a partner in his own engineering firm, Andrews & Stein. Still, he suffers from an identity crisis caused by parental circumstance. His mother had been a prostitute; his father had been one of her customers.

There is a vague resemblance, even this early on in the novel, to Shakespeare's Prince Hamlet whose mother Gertrude committed adultery with his Uncle Claudius and then married him less than one month after that uncle killed King Hamlet in pursuit of the throne. Prince Hamlet was devastated and railed in a soliloquy:

> Frailty, thy name is woman!—
> A little month, or ere those shoes were old
> With which she followed my poor father's body,
> O God, a beast that wants discourse of reason
> Would have mourn'd longer.

It is possible that Hamlet's grievance against his mother became transferred to women in general, making it difficult for him to conduct any kind of relationship with members of the opposite sex.

Naylor's George, who is indeed quite fond of Shakespeare, has been seeing one woman for five straight years, but their relationship has become stagnant. And then when Ophelia arrives on the scene, seeking employment at Andrews & Stein, George is attracted but still recommends that she try another company where, unbeknownst to her, a lecherous boss lurks in waiting. She nonetheless avoids sexual harassment by contriving a story and "a couple of coffee breaks with the office gossip and then everyone knew about my breaking up with a man who I found out had been committed twice for homicidal rages and who now took to slinking around my apartment building." This keeps the lecher out of her personal life so she can accomplish that for which she is being paid.

Some readers might wish that Shakespeare's Ophelia could have had only half so much cunning and strength so that when Hamlet demanded, "Get thee to a nunn'ry," she might have withstood it better. For was it proper to blame her, the pawn of Hamlet's testers? On the other hand, can we really blame Hamlet for retaliating against someone he saw as a spy?

Bernard Grebanier, in a rather provocative study entitled *The Heart of Hamlet* (1967), noted the wide variety of ways in which scholars have viewed Hamlet's supposed rejection of Ophelia. Many have thought that Hamlet rejected her because of his mother's inappropriate remarriage that distorted his own perspective on women. Others conclude Hamlet just was not in love. Then there is the view that Hamlet was a man of such limited energies that he could not have engaged in courtship and planned vengeance too. Some say that in earlier versions of the Hamlet story Ophelia was a prostitute. Finally, there is the opinion that Hamlet was a man so consumed with himself that he was incapable of loving anyone else.

Having presented those possible explanations, Grebanier then does something of an about-face in proposing how it was most likely Ophelia who did the rejecting. "Fear it, Ophelia, fear it, my dear sister," Laertes had advised with regard to her relationship. "Do not believe his vows, for they are brokers," added Polonius. And Ophelia apparently gave in to those entreaties, rejecting Hamlet and then reporting how she "did repel his letters, and denied his access to me." By the time she fell into the "weeping brook," we were not even sure whether she had committed suicide or accidentally fallen in. But we did know she was victimized by an ongoing state of affairs that made love a quite tangled prospect.

Writing for the *Richmond Times-Dispatch*, Robert Merritt criticizes *Mama Day* and assesses, "the clarity the story demands has faltered in what seems to be a misguided effort to make the story more structured for accessibility." *Brewster Place* was recently made into a television drama, and the movie rights to *Mama Day* have already been bought. So Merritt might be correct in insinuating that Naylor now writes with an eye toward greater remuneration than mere book sales will allow.

Still, we must consider that clarity in itself was not Naylor's goal as she wrote *Mama Day*. As it is, the woman after whom the book is named is in possession of certain powers that defy explanation. At eighty-five years of age, Mama Day "can still stand so quiet, she becomes part of a tree." The local doctor has to admit that her herbal cures are just as good as what he himself can accomplish with years of medical training. All of Willow Springs knows that she has a gift, but they do not know the gift's source.

Mama Day's great-niece, Ophelia, is another most ambiguous character. As has been mentioned, the novel's basic structure is that of a lengthy conversation between two lovers, one dead, the other alive. The novel's very last lines are, "What really happened to us, George? You see, that's what I mean—there are just too many sides to the whole story." After three hundred and eleven pages we still cannot be sure about the veracity of the events which surround their relationship. Can too many New England Patriot football games, a white ex-girlfriend, and a move to Willow Springs be the source of so much conflict? Or is it the natural order of things that what goes on between a man and woman, presumably in love, is indeed a complex tangled web?

It is this latter point, in particular, that Naylor has drawn from *Hamlet*. Like Hamlet, George is concerned about his place in the world of "movers and shakers." But unlike Hamlet, George marries Ophelia anyway, and we get rapid hints of ensuing difficulty. "It was a pity you didn't like being called Ophelia," says George at one point. Then there is something crucial that Ophelia's grandmother and Mama Day have not told her. Those two elderly women talk, with Mama Day beginning:

> "And we ain't even told Baby Girl about. . . . And we should, you know, Abigail. It ain't nothing to be ashamed of, it's her family and her history. And she'll have children one day."
>
> "There's time before you saddle her with all that mess. Let the child live her life without having to think on them things. Baby Girl—"
>
> "That's just it, Abigail—she ain't a baby. She's a grown woman and her

real name is Ophelia. We don't like to think on it, but that's her name. Not
Baby Girl, not Cocoa—Ophelia."
"I regret the day she got it."
"No, Sister, please. Don't ever say that. She fought to stay here—remember, Abigail?"
"I could forget to breathe, easier than I could forget those months. Sitting
up with her night after night, trembling every time she choked."

In a literal sense Abigail and Mama Day are referring to the day when
Ophelia was born premature, weighing less than five pounds. Born in
1953, when medical technology was not as advanced as it is today, she
indeed had to fight to survive, her success being a minor miracle.

However, there is much more to this matter than the gasps of a
premature child. Naylor wants us to ponder on the challenge undertaken
at the very point when we began living, a challenge that involves reconciling ourselves with the past. Early in the novel we are told about
Sapphira, an African-born slave sold to Bascombe Wade in 1819. Legend
has it that the slave "married Bascombe Wade, bore him seven sons in
just a thousand days, to put a dagger through his kidney and escape the
hangman's noose . . . persuaded Bascombe Wade in a thousand days to
deed all his slaves every inch of land in Willow Springs, poisoned him
for his trouble." Obviously, that narration hinges on something phenomenal, to say the least. We are reminded of the ending in *Hamlet* where
four people meet death as a consequence of the duel between Hamlet
and Laertes, Claudius dying by both sword and poison.

It is, moreover, intriguing that Bascombe's last name is Wade, perhaps alluding to another version of his death, that he walked out into the
Atlantic Ocean after Sapphira "got away from him and headed . . . toward the east bluff on her way back to Africa." We think back to Shakespeare's Ophelia who "fell in the weeping brook" and met her demise.
Perhaps Ophelia *did* commit suicide, and Hamlet might have done the
same had he not had the task of staying for revenge.

Naylor's emphasis is nonetheless on the woman. Being a black woman
herself, she is especially sensitive to this tragic history. Slavery allowed
Bascombe to do a terrible injustice to Sapphira who, in other circumstances, might have been able to give him as strong and pure a love as
was humanly possible. Later, as Mama Day observes, "We ain't had
much luck with the girls in this family," it is as though the females are
all cursed. Mama Day thinks about how:

Most all of the boys had thrived: her own daddy being the youngest of seven
boys, and his daddy the youngest of seven. But coming on down to them, it
was just her, Abigail, and Peace. And out of them just another three girls,
and out of them, two. Three generations of nothing but girls, and only one
left alive in this last generation to keep the Days going—the child of Grace.

Who were the wives of those first two succeeding generations, totaling
fourteen boys? Did they even all get married? We are not fully told, but

we do get the impression that they were not much better off than the four wives of the Luther Nedeed generations. The names are of less significance than the probable fates they suffered as a consequence of the era and circumstances into which they were born.

One whom we get more information about than all the others was the woman who would be the mother of Mama Day. This mother was also named Ophelia and in addition to having Abigail and Mama Day, she gave birth to Peace who, while still a baby, fell into a well. That first Ophelia was so distraught that she actually tried to jump into the well after her dead daughter. She was restrained then but would later go into a trance and wander into The Sound, a relatively narrow but deep body of water between Willow Springs and the eastern United States mainland. She died, in Mama Day's words, "trying to find peace." Naylor's ingenious use of the name "Ophelia" and the action of death by drowning draw on Shakespeare and thereby add a certain power to the message of repeated loss.

Of Ophelia's three children only Abigail and Mama Day are still left. Mama Day has no children; Abigail has had three: Grace, Hope, and yet another Peace. The symbolic import of those names becomes clear as we learn that all three of these daughters are dead. Abigail's Peace died even younger than the first Ophelia's. Abigail's Hope was the mother of Willa Prescott Nedeed; Hope died shortly after Willa married Luther.

So what we are left with is the child of Grace, yet another Ophelia who "came into the world kicking and screaming," an omen of things yet to come. After coming of age, she journeys first to Atlanta and then New York and seems bound to survive rather nicely until upon a return visit to Willow Springs, she is propositioned by Junior Lee and then cursed by his disturbed wife. There is little that Abigail and Mama Day can do as Ophelia gazes into the mirror and sees "flesh from both cheeks was now hanging in strings under my ears, and moving my head caused them to wiggle like hooked worms." Ophelia feels her face and it is normal, but later, as the curse progresses, she conveys:

> it was no illusion that they had begun to crawl within my body. I didn't need a mirror to feel the slight itching as they curled and stretched themselves, multiplying as they burrowed deeper into my flesh . . . they were actually feeding on me, the putrid odor of decaying matter that I could taste on my tongue and smell with every breath I took.

As it turns out, the only thing that can save Ophelia is George's love. It is as though Hamlet has been given just one more chance. Mama Day carts her rooster off to a distant cabin and then summons George to bring her hen from the chicken coop. His instructions are to "search good in the back of her nest, and come straight back" with whatever is found. The hen wages a vicious battle, dealing George several death blows, and he has found nothing but his own "gouged and bleeding hands." What he learns, however, is that with those very hands he can hold on tight to Ophelia, and, metaphorically speaking, never have to let go.

In *Brewster Place* we had been presented with a world in which relationships between males and females were devoid of the required mutuality. *Linden Hills* presented one such reciprocal relationship, rendered through the marriage of Ruth and Norman Anderson. But by casting Ruth in the mold of a Christ-like figure, we wonder what the prospects would have been for average people. Finally, in *Mama Day*, we see how love between a mortal man and a mortal woman can be strong enough to conquer anything.

Lead on with Light

HELEN FIDDYMENT LEVY

[Miranda] finds herself in a vast space of glowing light.
Daughter. The word comes to cradle what has gone past weariness. She can't really hear it because she's got no ears, or call out because she's got no mouth. There's only the sense of being. Daughter.

—Gloria Naylor
Mama Day

The outlines of the wise woman's loving community in America remains an attractive one for the woman writer, although increasingly problematic, given the atomized and regimented social order. As before, this fictional ideal allows the woman writer in America simultaneously to create a model for her own creativity and to point the way to more cooperative, egalitarian community. The evolving body of work of Gloria Naylor suggests that the patterns of plot, characterization, and attitudes toward language persist to the present. Naylor's personal history differs from the other women authors in this discussion in several important respects: she grew up as the child of poor black parents in New York City.[1] The several strands of her cultural background unite to give her writing an emphasis unique among this group, although the underlying imaginative paradigm shares many of the same outlines.[2] Naylor, for example, never accepts the ideal of the heroic individual as a model for her female protagonists. Instead, her first novel, *The Women of Brewster Place* (1980), portrays a woman's community gathered around the maternal figure of Mattie Michael, a community brought together from an urban world of broken neighborhoods and disrupted families. The society Naylor depicts is an infernal mix of uncaring bureaucracies and male violence, a society whose fragmentation is indicated by the work's structure, "a novel in seven stories."

In a famous passage in *The Souls of Black Folk*, W. E. B. Du Bois writes of the conflict of African-American identity: "One ever feels his twoness—an American, a Negro; two souls, two thoughts, two unreconciled strivings." Despite obvious and crucial differences in their respective histories, women in America, like African-Americans, have felt a split in their consciousness between the perceptions of themselves that the dominant cultural discourse attempts to impose and those generated by the testimony of their own experience. Commentators as early as abolitionist Frederick Douglas and DuBois himself have understood the connection in the situations of the two marginalized groups in the larger society. Decades ago, sociologist Gunnar Myrdahl in his classic *An*

American Dilemma detailed the similarity in the stereotypical portrayals of both groups, noting that women and African-Americans both were distinguished from the assumed cultural norm of the white adult male by their appearance, making their isolation from central decision-making groups easily achieved. He points out that they are often characterized negatively in very similar terms, which justify their social subordination. More recently, commentators such as Audre Lorde and Elizabeth Fox-Genovese have noted the difficulties of reconciling the identity of individual promoted by the dominant discourse and the identity of race or gender.

With the African-American woman author, however, the problem multiplies. Lorde, a black lesbian poet and cultural critic, writes of the difficulties particular to the feminism of women of color. As Lorde pungently proclaims, "Black feminism is not white feminism in black-face." The woman of color, whether African-American, Latina, Native-American, or Asian-American, finds it necessary to sort out authentic portions of her self-image and reject the false images projected by sexism and racism, for, as Lorde insists about her ethnic group, black America has no need to repeat the mistakes of white America.

Henry Louis Gates, Jr. writes that the problem of twoness posed by DuBois extends to literature. Black writers learn to write by reading, and the texts that serve as models are those of the Western canonical tradition, therefore works of African-American literature share more resemblances than differences with other Western texts. Naylor herself speaks directly to the problem of literary "influence," which she found a particularly complicated one as a black female child. If women must overcome patriarchal influence to discover an authentic voice, the black woman must overcome patriarchal influence and racial oppression, both of which insist that her contribution conform to the existing models of Western male literary achievement. As Naylor grew up, her literary education offered her no examples of writing black men, let alone black women writers: "I read Emerson, I read Poe, I read Hawthorne, Fitzgerald, Faulkner, Hemingway. My God! Wonderful writers, wonderful writers! And never having read anything that reflected me" (*American Audio Prose Interview*). Like the white women authors in this discussion, Naylor found herself turning to models from classic European and American sources gained in her early literary education and revisioning them into patterns that reflected her ethnic and gender identities. Naylor identifies, for example, the landscape of Dante's *Inferno* as the model for her modern suburban hell in her "apocalyptic" second book *Linden Hills* (1985) and various aspects of Shakespeare's *King Lear* and *Romeo and Juliet* as important influences on her latest book *Mama Day* (1988). As Cather uses classical and biblical sources, as Welty, Glasgow, and Jewett use classical references, and as Porter uses Roman Catholic,

Mexican, and biblical references, so Naylor reaches to her earlier education in the traditional canon.

Only much later did Naylor realize the diversity and richness of the African-American experience in literature and discover the work of women who, like herself, shared the two marginalized identities of female and black. As Calvin Hernton notes, black women writers must cross a sexual mountain, for "the world of black literature in the United States has been a world of black men's literature." Naylor remarks that in the year of her birth, 1950, Gwendolyn Brooks received the Pulitzer Prize, but she never heard of Brooks in school. Not until she was twenty-seven years old did she discover that there were black women literary artists. Toni Morrison's *The Bluest Eye* (1969) was a "watershed" book for the young author, making her aware of a tradition of black writing women (*American Audio Prose Interview*).

Elaine Showalter notes that literary subcultures go through three stages, imitation of the models of the dominant discourse, protest against the morality and standards of those usages, and finally self-discovery, the reclamation of an authentic voice of the community. In the last stage, the existence of an artistically skilled, *and widely read*, body of work gives rise to the beginning of a true, independent literary tradition. Showalter's model serves to illuminate Naylor's career. Her first books show the righteous anger seen in Showalter's protest stage (designated "Feminist" in women's writing) as the author protests both the impersonal indifference of the bureaucratic society to black women's suffering and the harsh models of competitive male achievement, which offer woman as the ultimate trophy and the available conquest; in her latest book she turns instead to the final stage of art (the *female* mode) as *Mama Day* speaks with the voice of the black woman and her community. Black texts, Gates insists, have a crucial difference in their use of the vernacular; the language that Gates presents has significant connections with the oral, pictorial local language of the home place. Through use of the vernacular voice, Naylor achieves the third stage of Showalter's evolution.

The women in the first novel, *The Women of Brewster Place*, are meant, as Naylor asserts, to represent "a tiny microcosm of the black female experience" (*American Audio Prose Interview*). No matter how diverse the women in age, talents, and experience, the wall seals them in behind barriers of racism and sexism, defines the limits of their aspirations, and shields the rest of the city from their influence. Losers all in the social competition, the black women of Brewster Place succeed first in creating a community and finally in tearing down with their bare hands the isolating wall.

Moreover, in *Brewster Place*, Naylor portrays the hate and fear that such men as Eugene hold toward Mattie's influence on "his woman" Ciel, as the author depicts exclusive male possession of the wife as the reward granted to each man, if he chooses to grasp it, in the competitive individualistic culture. And through the brutal gang rape of Lorraine, Naylor connects violence against women directly to the cultural ideal that privileges male aggression, acquisitiveness, and dominance. The fact that Lorraine has chosen to live with her female lover Tee, rather than a man, offers a justification for her rape to the gang; she has committed the ultimate sin in refusing to keep to her "place" as a woman in a masculine-dominated social setting. That the attack represents a homophobic attack is certainly correct, but it also represents an attack on any woman who does not accede to subordinate status in a relationship with a man, who claims primary attachment to a woman, whether that be lover, sister, mother, or friend. Like Jewett's Mrs. Tolland, the refusal of Lorraine and Tee to conform has excited the curiosity and enmity of the conventional women around her, especially the gossiping churchwoman Sophie, who spies on Lorraine and her lover. Barbara Smith has noted the ambivalence at the heart of this story; Lorraine suffers the most violent fate, and the pair are both shown in an exclusively heterosexual context—although Tee often mentions a homosexual social club. Even as she identifies the homophobia motivating the attack, Smith neglects the overreaching sexism that underlies that hate—the Big Man's demand for dominance, which the young men emulate in the dead-end alley.[3]

As Smith notes, Mattie and her lifelong friend Etta are moved by the presence of Tee and Lorraine to examine their own attitudes toward love between women. When Mattie, the elder wise woman, muses that she has loved some women more deeply than any man and that some women have loved and labored for her more earnestly, Etta demurs, insisting that her experience is "different" from that of "the two." But Mattie insists, "Maybe it's not so different. . . . Maybe that's why some women get so riled up about it, 'cause they know deep down it's not so different after all." But both Etta and Mattie, feeling the intensity of their own relationship, retreat, refusing to examine the mingled love, attraction, and responsibility they feel toward each other. As Eve Sedgwick has suggested, in contemporary society close relationships between women are only socially acknowledged after primary allegiance to the male is first sworn; otherwise the relationship is classified as "deviant" and therefore to be shunned. Nonetheless, like Louisa Goddard and Victoria Littlepage of Glasgow's *They Stooped to Folly*, Mattie and Etta share the deepest relationship of their respective lives, yet paternalistic social practice offers no publicly validated form for the celebration of that friendship and love. Love between women having either emotional or sexual intensity, or both, is ignored and reviled, finally attacked as illegitimate. This is the point of Naylor's narrative, and indeed Lorraine is not shunned by Kiswana, the political activist. Even Etta, who rejects

Mattie's discussion of their love, understands that Sophie's attempt to eject Lorraine from a neighborhood meeting attacks female rebellion of all types. (As in Jewett and Cather, the churchwoman acts as the local militia for male leadership, enforcing conformity.)

Naylor connects the street violence on Brewster Place with the violence she perceives at the center of the American ruling bureaucracies. The young men leading urban gangs find no wide fields or deep forest to conquer, no boardroom to dominate as validation of their "success" as men in the social competition; instead they, like such female creations as Wharton's "mannequin" Lily Bart, see themselves as figures of fashion, having their existence primarily through life-style. Naylor shows that violence against Lorraine affirms the leader C.C. as a model of triumphant masculine initiative: "She had stepped into the thin strip of earth that they had claimed as their own. Bound by the last building on Brewster and a brick wall [the true end of the American social order in contrast to the fabled endless nature], they reigned in that unlit alley like dwarfed warrior-kings." Naylor connects the dominance of the CEO with the display of force by C.C. and his followers. In Naylor's view, the neighborhood "dwarfed warrior-king," the socially subordinated male "cheated" of his perceived masculine birthright, asserts his dominance over woman in imitation of the Big Men, who now have expanded technological phalli for scattering "iron seed" into the womb of the supine earth. Naylor offers a suggestion for the cause of urban male violence. Denied the individual notice celebrated in cultural myths perpetuated by daily news and sportscasts, celebrity biographies, and television and movie narratives, without a "stateroom, armored tank, and executioner's chamber" of their own, the disenfranchised male still can find a way to assert his individual dominance within the social dead end of Brewster Place.

In contrast to these men, Naylor creates the fatherly figure of Ben, the gentle janitor who befriends Lorraine and who dies because of the violence against her. In contrast to C.C. and the other male figures who emulate the values of the dominant men, Ben refuses to return the cruelty the white world has visited upon him. In the South from which he fled, Ben has been cheated by the landowner, who promises Ben more land if he will ignore his daughter's sexual abuse by the white man. His wife Elvira accuses him of unmanliness because he will not accede to Mr. Clyde's demands, and ultimately his daughter is lost to the world of Memphis, sending back the money Elvira craves. Ben becomes an alcoholic, a figure of no great influence even on Brewster Place, yet in his compassion he illustrates—as do other masculine "failures" such as Asa Timberlake of *Beyond Defeat*, Mr. Elliott of *Two Lives*, William of *The Country of the Pointed Firs*, and Ray Kennedy of *The Song of the Lark* among others—that men as well as women can shelter and care. Unfortunately, these men spend much of their time shedding the cultural messages of hypermasculinity. But Ben is the one Brewster Place inhabitant who says to Lorraine, "I got nothing, but you welcome to all of that. Now how many folks is that generous?" Together, they form a father-daughter relationship until violence tears them apart.

Mattie herself was started on her long road to Brewster Place by an unmarried pregnancy and a beating by her heartbroken father. She and her son Basil are sheltered by Miss Eva, who takes her in as a daughter. Miss Eva anticipates in her generosity and wisdom the woman Mattie herself becomes in the present time of the story. Despite her age, Miss Eva remains the lusty, humorous woman of her youth. She tells Mattie that she's had five husbands and "outlived 'em all," and her old house still glows with the laughter of her absent son's girl child, the aroma of a pot roast, and the gleam of brightly polished surfaces. She becomes the mother that Mattie, Basil, and her own granddaughter all need so desperately as she bonds together a family from the damaged urban setting. Like Grandmother Fincastle, Nannie and Sophia Jane, Mother Blackett and Almira Todd, Ántonia, and other wise women, Miss Eva holds the warmth of life after the beauty and passion of youth have passed. As Mattie realizes, Miss Eva replaces the mother she lost when she left her home. Thirty years later, as Mattie prepares to take Miss Eva's place, she remembers the lessons the old woman taught her, and she too in her turn takes over the task of sheltering the lost and the weak. Mattie, however, has no home or family of her own now; it must all be redone by will and emotion. Late at night and alone, her prayers are addressed to "the wisdom of a yellow, blue-eyed spirit who had fore-seen this day and had tried to warn her."

Cast aside by a succession of men, Mattie's girlhood friend, Etta Mae Johnson, places her last hope for a "respectable" life on enticing Rever-end Moreland T. Woods into marriage. A rebel like Amy Rhea, Virgie Rainey, and Clara Vavrika, Etta Mae was "a black woman who was not only unwilling to play by the rules, but whose spirit challenged the very right of the rules to exist." Etta is driven out of the small town from which they both come, moving from man to man as she seeks always to better herself economically and socially. She breaks the rules by ac-cepting them with a vengeance; she seeks the big stake by identification with a powerful man. Like her male counterparts, Etta wants to rise in the social scale, and she will do it by treating the opposite sex as a commodity. For a woman, however, the game runs out, and age comes. Abandoned by Reverend Woods after their sexual encounter, Etta real-izes that she is trapped in Brewster Place, that as with Mattie, Tee, and Lorraine, she has no place more to go. As she walks into Mattie's house, she hears Mattie's records, and she realizes someone has waited up for her. Once again, the wise woman gathers in the lost sister, offering love and comfort after the wars of romance and passion. As the three wise women shelter Nelly Deane, as Grandmother Fincastle aids Ada, as Almira Todd comforts Mrs. Tolland, Mattie brings Etta Mae home, into the small woman's space allowed in the modern American city. Unlike the earlier rebels who disappear from the community's history, Etta Mae's life will be difficult, but it will not be solitary because she and Mattie will together keep Brewster Place alive, fighting the conventionality within the community and the indifference and bigotry without.

Like Jewett, Welty, Cather, Porter, Gilman, and Glasgow, Naylor shows a persistent suspicion of the male-led church, although not the faith itself, as an instrument of control for women by the social leadership. In *Brewster Place*, as in Jewett's "The Foreigner," the female churchwoman enforces the morality of the male leadership against Lorraine. And both *Brewster Place* and *Linden Hills* have scorching portraits of male clergy who cynically violate the tenets of their religions through self-indulgence. The "spawning" of the impersonal, legalistic rules of remote complex organizations and the lethal seed of the "dwarfed warrior-kings" contrast with the birth of children and dreams engendered by the women's community. Discord comes from the bureaucratic outside, either directly or through those who accept its judgment of value. Romance, as before, brings the women into unwed maternity, disappointment, or bitter marriage.

Like the domestic novelists so long before her, who created reconstituted female networks, Naylor portrays women of spirit and determination remaking their community and re-forming their families. And in the passion for justice of Kiswana Browne, formerly of Linden Hills, Naylor indicates that Brewster Place will not fall. When she visits, Kiswana's mother is offended by her daughter's repudiation of her suburban Linden Hills existence, and by her daughter's characterization of her own past, but in an emotional exchange, the mother concludes that she raised her children so that no one would ever slight them, and "that's not being white or red or black—that's being a mother." Suddenly, Kiswana has an epiphany similar to that of Vickie Templeton at the end of "Old Mrs. Harris": she "suddenly realized that her mother had trod through the same universe she herself was traveling. . . . She stared at the woman she had been and was to become." (In the taped interview Naylor says that she could not entirely condemn Mrs. Browne, so she put her in the outer ring of Linden Hills.) In *The Women of Brewster Place*, Naylor places a strong emphasis on shared identification between women, while depicting the oppression of the urban bureaucracies. In Brewster Place, threatened by mandates, legalisms, and distant judgmental bureaucracies, the living community embraces black women and men of all ages and circumstances except those tied to the morality of *Linden Hills*. The woman's community, but not the home place, lives despite the urban bureaucracies: "*It watched its last generation of children torn away from it by court orders and eviction notices, and it had become too tired and sick to help them. . . . But the colored daughters of Brewster, spread over the canvas of time, still wake with their dreams misted on the edge of a yawn."*

Naylor's second book, *Linden Hills*, pictures the author's inferno of success, the competitive and isolated lives of the black "winners" of the competitive consumer culture. When asked if Tupelo Drive, the inner circle of her Hell, reflected her southern childhood, Naylor answered that its name represented instead the two pillars found at the entrance of the lower Hell in the City of Dis. Linden Hills represents a male-controlled American dystopia in contrast to the ideal female pastoral of Mama Day's Willow Springs. As with Dante's *Inferno*, the guides to the infernal landscape are a pagan poet, Willie, the unbeliever from the outside, and a young poet seeking salvation from his sinful heritage, Lester. Like Dante, Lester cannot renounce Linden Hills until he has viewed the center of its evil.

Naylor has identified a loss of communal memory and "a geographical center" as a crucial factor in negative self-images of black people (*American Audio Prose Interview*). The author considers that individual identity arises out of a group unity based on a shared oral tradition of family and neighborhood history, out of distinctive local foods, colloquial speech, and codes of behavior. Naylor identifies the loss of the oral tradition, the mother tongue, the family interaction, as dissolving the "communal ties, familial ties, spiritual ties," the connections that shape an enduring sense of individual identity. She recalls that her own family, despite their poverty, gave her a sense of self which came out of their struggles and experiences in the South.

Whereas Naylor identifies the women of Brewster Place as having "very strong communal ties," the black citizens of Linden Hills seek to leave their pasts and their communal identities behind. As they rise in material success and social esteem—both central markers of success in the social competition—they descend ever further down toward the deepest Hell of Luther Nedeed's undertaking parlor. In Naylor's words, these bonds of identity "all melted away the farther they come down." If Mama Day can be said to preside over a harmonious female pastoral, Luther Nedeed rules over a competitive consumerist Hell.

The first Luther Nedeed, he who reportedly sold his wife and children into slavery to get a stake, soon discovered that the future was "white," that the white male leadership would determine the definitions of "success." He decided that success, defined as an acknowledgment of black individual achievement in the market economy, would be the overriding cultural value. A deformed, froglike creature, Luther constantly renews himself through the single son named for himself who is born of a nameless mother. He indicates the nature of marriage at the center, for the son is shaped and schooled by him, and the succession of wives are always and only known as Mrs. Nedeed.

Naylor paints the perfect male material achiever through the limning of Luther Nedeed. With deft satiric touches, Naylor portrays the deity of Linden Hills and, by implication, the modern social leaders, the Big Men, writing that within the social competition it becomes clear that the great power is simply the "*will* to possess. It had chained the earth to the names of a few and it would chain the cosmos as well." The white leaders find no need to destroy the leaders of Linden Hills because they understand that they both serve "the same god."

On the outer rings are such people as Winston and David, lovers torn apart by Winston's marriage, which will "prove" his heterosexuality and thus advance his career; Catherine Ward calls them Naylor's Paolo and Francesca. As a result of his betrayal of David, his bride, and himself, Winston is promised a deed to the deepest rings of Linden Hills. In contrast to Winston's failure of love, Naylor offers us the abiding love between Willie Mason and Lester Tilson, the two comrades who will walk together out of the hell of Naylor's Linden Hills. Like Mattie and Etta in *Brewster Place*, Willie and Lester have the most intense and sensitive relationship in the narrative. They bring to each other their dreams and their fears; together they seek a definition of manhood that will defeat the sterility and calculation of the personal relationships they see on Tupelo Drive. Willie is the oral poet, the living voice of the black community, whereas Lester writes his poems in reflection of his Linden Hills education. Lester's family lives on the outer rings, the space allotted the uncommitted, those who are neither good nor evil.

The Tilsons have had a sure guide in the person of old Grandmother Tilson, who had warned them that the price of living in Luther's infernal suburb will be their souls. The original Luther first tried to buy her land and lease it back to her, but the old wise woman drove him off. As Ward writes, "She warned her children and neighbors that they were in danger of losing the 'mirror' in their souls, of forgetting what they 'really want and believe.'" The Tilson women show the gradual disintegration of the family from the courageous old grandmother to the status-seeking granddaughter. This is the limbo that Lester lacks the will to flee at the narrative's beginning.

The loving relationship of Lester and Willie contrasts as well with that of Maxwell Smyth and Xavier Donnell, the young men on the way up in the corporate structure and on their way down in Linden Hills. In contrast to the young poets' discussions on morality and poetry, the young executives' relationship with each other hinges on such matters as how long each waits to respond to the ring of a doorbell. Maxwell, who is Xavier's "mentor," warns his colleague to avoid marrying black women because they either refuse to assume a subordinate role, or— even worse—they "let themselves go," refusing to be the mannequin they both demand as a complement to the success. In Maxwell's own life, he does not allow himself to have sexual relations often because of the loss of isolation and the potential loss of control. In fact, he has disciplined his body so completely that it resembles the perfectly working machine; as he walks in the cold December air, he "seemed to have made the very elements disappear, while it was no more than the psychological sleight-of-hand that he used to make his blackness disappear." The man who joins the top of the bureaucratic structure becomes the perfection of Weber's rationalized manager, and as Ward points out, ironically enough, this mechanical man becomes a type of the Dantean glutton, his appetite, however, is not for food or drink, but rather for the endless power of the white male leadership.

As the aspirant to this life, Xavier justifies his choice to Lester who tells him that their ideal of progress is spelled "W-H-I-T-E" and that he and Maxwell are merely tokens who allow the system to continue without essential alteration. Xavier responds that a photographic spread in the "men's" magazine *Penthouse* proves him wrong. It features a nude dark woman with a short "Afro" haircut, who is shod with leopard-skin boots and little else. She is pulling on a chain. At the end of the eight-page feature she is shown having reeled in the chain as she stands with her foot on a white hunter. Maxwell says triumphantly that today it's *Penthouse*, but tomorrow the American world. But Lester and Willie realize that the spread implies that black people live in a jungle, that the living woman has been changed into "breathless body," and later Willie remembers that his shame comes from the model's resemblance to his own sister. Where Maxwell sees cultural acceptance in the spread of commodification of black women in the mass media, the young men understand that now both black and white women have a chance to be "sold out." Both Willie and Lester feel their connections to their racial identity and to their female family, despite Lester's rejection of his mother's upwardly striving in the outer rings of Linden Hills.

In the lower rings, Laurel Johnson Dumont dies crumpled in the bottom of her empty winter swimming pool, crushed after taking her arching swan dive into death, her last flight. Lester and Willie find her body by following her grandmother's plaintive call to the child who has been unable to hear her for so many years. As with many previous female characters in this discussion, Laurel has no available parents, her mother dead, her father in love with a selfish young woman. Her grandmother takes her into her small home for wonderful summers. There she discovered her two loves, music and swimming. As with such women writers as Welty, Cather, Chopin, Carson McCullers, and Porter, music and dance, here synchronized swimming, becomes for the protagonist the undiscovered voice: "It was difficult to tell whether her body was making the music or the music her body." Laurel finds the creativity, the harmony missing in her life away from her grandmother's house. In her grandmother's home she reaches the fullest expression of her own personality.

As Laurel moves away, attends university, and attains success, she accumulates the markers of her progress: Phi Beta Kappa key, featured articles in the *New York Times* business pages, a wealthy marriage to a scion of the Linden Hills Dumonts. Laurel slowly realizes how many times she has had no time for her grandmother. Upon her return to Roberta Johnson's home, however, she thinks of it as "little more than a shack" compared to her Linden Hills house, and the grandmother's place smells like old age. Laurel discovers that the woman's space in the competitive social order is small indeed. When her grandmother asks her why she has returned, Laurel responds that when people are in trouble, "[D]on't they go home?" But Roberta Johnson reminds her that the small house is not her home, and Naylor continues, "So Laurel went home. And home was Linden Hills. If she had any doubt, she could look at her driver's license, or call up the post office just to be sure." Home is now defined by bureaucratic designations, not by personal relationships. Her grandmother's world and her life seems dingy and shrunken compared to the jewels, automobiles, and elegant clothes of Tupelo Drive. In many respects, Laurel Dumont's story has parallels with that of Wharton's Lily Bart. Like Lily, Laurel feels a tie to the small personal space allowed to women within the social structures, but nonetheless finds herself inevitably shaped by the consumer culture. Women here, as there, function as ornaments to their husbands, with the addition of the wives' own success now validating and expanding their husband's own power. Like Lily Bart, Laurel, the prize, is rootless, "the number of places she couldn't claim, dizzying." Despite her accomplishments in the reigning social bureaucracies, Laurel, like Lily Bart so many years before, is finally an object of display.

Bib by bit Laurel tries to get back to her family and her history, but given Naylor's firm contention that the individual identity is shaped by and inseparable from the communal ties, she finds there is no foundation on which to rebuild. She gives up, in their turn, her profession, her social circle, her husband, her possessions. She stays on alone in her husband's empty house. Now she frantically shuts out the world with music, choosing Mahler above all, appreciating music as knowledge, as discrimination, as *expertise*, in contrast to the bodily joy of her youth at her mother's house, within nature. On a final visit to save her child, Roberta makes explicit the woman author's attitude toward language and music when she remarks that Billie Holliday and Bessie Smith communicate emotional truths inexpressible by "plain talk." When the lost modern daughter notes that Holliday and Smith were alcoholics and drug addicts and thus poor examples for her own controlled life, the grandmother asserts connections between generations of black women:

> "No, you ain't never had to worry, like a lot of us did, about Jim Crow or
> finding your next meal, but if that's all you hear in them songs, then you don't

know as much about music as you think you do. What they *say* is one thing, but you supposed to hear is, 'I can.'" Roberta came and stood over her. "'I can,' Laurel, that's what you supposed to hear. It ain't a music that speaks to your head like some of this stuff you been playing, or to your body like the rock music of these kids. But it speaks to a place they ain't got no name for yet, where you supposed to be at home."

Roberta explicitly asserts the passing of experience from one generation of women to another. From the example of female creativity, at no matter how much cost, the daughters learn to live and to create. In her life at the center, Laurel learns to shun their black female messages coming directly through music; instead she listens to the music of European males.

Laurel has lost touch with her heritage as a black woman. In her success, Laurel believes, like other autonomous female protagonists, that she is different, insulated from the failures of the other women in her community. Instead of the Linden Hills demand for excision of her maternal past, the records of Smith and Holliday sing of that past, illuminating the strength of the black women who sing despite the best efforts of the white, male-controlled social bureaucracies to ignore or to trivialize their experience. Those voices, if she would listen, would sing her home to Roberta, connecting her with those before who have joyed in the face of defeat, who have refused to retreat.

Laurel makes a last attempt, begging Roberta to tell her the old stories, to spin out the black female past, and to give her back her own childhood. She has internalized the morality of the massed, materialistic social order around her. The weight of her loss and depth of her entrapment only adds to her depression, as she listens to the stories she realizes that she has "nothing inside her to connect up to them." Finally, like Lily Bart, Laurel's rootlessness overcomes her, she realizes that she has no way back, no solid earth to sustain her growth. When Luther comes to evict her from her house because her husband is gone and she has none of "his" children, she realizes that she has never really had an independent existence separate from that of her husband in Linden Hills. Like so many other dependent women, this modern woman finds herself with no identity that expresses her self and her female history. Her argument with Luther was only a reflex, but now Laurel realizes the meaning of time in hell through Luther's words: "She had never lived in a house in which she had never lived." Unlike Lily Bart and Edna Pontellier, Laurel cannot even dream her way back to the home place in death. In her last moment she can only dream a cessation of pain. Her last hope is a flight to oblivion, "Once she got down, she'd be free."

The deepest rings of Nedeed's inferno are composed of those who have completely renounced that communal memory, Laurel Dumont, Professor Daniel Braithwaite, and finally Luther Nedeed. As Naylor notes, those on the upper reaches lose their family ties, next they lose the social, personal ties, next the spiritual, religious ties, and finally all traces of their ethnic heritage as they strip away all traces of the received communal identities to enter the social competition. The old history professor Dr. Braithwaite occupies the ring well within sight of Luther's undertaking parlor, because he has converted the living memory of the black people into the rational associational language of his own self-advancement: "He's this dried-up voyeur—that's the worst kind of academic you can have, someone who goes through life, sapping and sapping and storing knowledge" (*American Audio Prose Interview*). Unlike the living stories of Mama Day, Dr. Braithwaite disconnects memory from emotion, embalming it into the dry, associational language, trapping it in impenetrable jargon that excludes those who are "outside." As Willie, our poet guide to the underworld, tells us, universities have fences to "get you used to the idea that what they have in there is different, special. Something to be separated from the rest of the world." Willie sees that he must never be a hired pen like the historian. Dr. Braithwaite's language, like the barrier around the university, serves as a fence against the anger of the unheard, the blacks and the women of Linden Hills. If memory of the community is the key to an enduring self for members of marginalized groups as these women writers suggest, then the Braithwaites who rewrite those memories into palatable tales of deserved failure, enduring weakness, and lost rebellions deserve opprobrium. Or even worse, those memories disappear into convoluted language, reified into a social problem within a complicated methodology. For these academics give over, in Mary Douglas's words, the "lineages and ancestral shrines" to the control of the dominant discourse safely sanitized of all emotion. They justify the group's losses, stressing how they could have been avoided, planting their roots in helplessness, showing how "progress" can be measured.

The metaphor for Braithwaite's memory are his dead willow trees. Because they blocked his view of Nedeed and his house, because the living memories of blacks and women separated him from success, Braithwaite had them killed. Now he can imagine they will bloom for half a year, during winter, just as he can believe his histories reflect lives. He has killed his living knowledge of the community so that he could more easily keep the deadly Nedeed in sight. He need no longer suffer guilt. Through the dried, blasted nature of Dr. Braithwaite's grounds, Naylor protests the jargon-filled academic language, which pretends detached intellectualism and erases the pain of experience. Braithwaite's preserved, embalmed trees resemble the perfumed, cosmetic-covered corpses that are Nedeed's true female loves—the ultimate compliant mannequins. The two deadly creations of the two successful men prepare us to enter the vital female pastoral of *Mama Day*.

At the time of the action of *Linden Hills*, the latest Luther has imprisoned his wife and son, who he suspects of "belonging" to another man, in his cellar, an abandoned embalming parlor without food and with only limited water offered in small amounts for "good behavior." After the boy's death by starvation and dehydration, his distracted mother takes a journey back through the trunks holding the abandoned diaries, clothes, and photographs, the only records of the earlier anonymous wives. The first Mrs. Nedeed bemoans her enslavement by her husband as more absolute than that of slavery itself, a later wife begins to cook enormous amounts of food, finally seeking to poison her husband, and a third progressively disappears from photographs of herself with her family. Only in her own extremity does the last Mrs. Nedeed discover their names, finding the female connections that allow her to destroy Luther and his kingdom.

Here, as in the domestic and introspective novels by women, female voices reach out to each other over time and distance, their respective miseries in marriage exposed. Luwana Packerville's diaries turning to madness, Evelyn Creton's domestic labor turning to poison, Priscilla McGuire's photographs turning to blankness, and finally Willa Prescott, through their words and images, turning to the avenging angel who destroys Luther's kingdom in a fiery conclusion on Christmas Eve. Starting in 1837, Luwana Packerville's entries hidden in her Bible begin Willa's journey back. Luwana's writing creates a fictional sister "Luwana" in her loneliness because "together we can weather those tiny tempests that blow through a woman's world." She was first a slave bought by Luther; her son is freed by her husband but not she. Naylor reveals through this circumstance her perception of the truth of upper-class marriage. Slowly, Luwana realizes that she has exchanged one slavery for another, "From his birth, he had been his father's son in flesh and now in spirit. But I tremble daily, for I fear it is even more than that. . . . Believe me, I am not losing my mind but it is not just that he is Luther's son, he *is* Luther." "Luwana" answers that there is nothing in her sister's marriage that "is not repeated in countless other homes around you." Through the buried tales of the successive Mrs. Nedeeds, Naylor builds up a critique of marriage at the social center. Like Chopin, Wharton, Gilman, Cather, and Glasgow, Naylor shows marriage within the material competition placing the wife on a shelf as one of many possessions who display the husband's achievement. As Willa—the present Mrs. Nedeed—regains her strength, she remembers her own shopping trips to New York as she struggled to make "it" change. Naylor parodies the slogans that alienate the woman from her own body through the profitable manipulation of fantasy, "steal a little thunder from a rose," "paradise regained," "say it without a word," and "believe in magic." For all the ministrations of the potions, "it" never changes as she becomes increasingly peripheral in Luther's self-expansion.

At the end, Willa changes from the "she" of the early passages, claiming her own identity. She refuses to be Mrs. Nedeed as she recovers the names and stories of her predecessors and sisters, claiming their strength and histories, finding her way out of his jail of imposed definition. Margaret Homans discusses Willa's emergence from the "cave" as a re-vision of male myth, turning it into a birth tale. Willa finds in their shared domestic tragedies the "mirror," a cooking pot, which will allow her to see herself clearly. Then Naylor brings her character to her own birth through her lost female community; as she sleeps, she dreams herself past the human limitations of material reality. The author rewrites a creation myth, whose destructive power recalls the Great Mother in her negative aspect; through this figure she prepares us for the creative power of Sapphira Wade and Miranda Day: "She breathed in to touch the very elements that at the beginning of time sparked to produce the miracle some called divine creation and others the force of life." She passes beyond the "ovaries, wombs, and glands" to reach the cosmic creativity that will destroy Luther's hell: "Out, toward the edge of the universe with its infinite possibility to make space for the volume of her breath." Naylor tells us that it is a "birth" out of the thunder that Sapphira and Miranda can summon, and she awakes Willa Prescott Nedeed.

That Luther Nedeed anticipates the healing of Mama Miranda Day is suggested by the contrasts between them. He is an undertaker, she is a midwife. He dominates the residents of suburban Linden Hills, she nurtures the neighbors of communal Willow Springs. He values material success, she honors communal ties. He refuses the black spiritual, historical, and cultural past, she keeps its traditions and memories. The final conflagration that destroys Luther, his mad wife, and dead son, an unholy family whose death on Christmas Eve clears the way in Naylor's fiction for the serenity and wisdom of Mama Day's ideal island community. This sequence of books brings to mind Glasgow's last two books, *In This Our Life* and *Beyond Defeat*, in which the venality and impersonality of William Fitzroy's Queenborough yields to the generosity and acceptance of Kate Oliver's pastoral Hunter's Fare. In both, the hellish, unholy family of the male leader is changed into the chosen, blessed community of the female figure of warm autumn.

As with preceding women authors, Naylor turns to the home place in *Mama Day* (1988). In Mama Day's Willow Springs, Naylor summons a separate, democratic community wrested from a white slave-master and landowner by the first mother and wise woman, Sapphira Wade.[4] Through sisters Miranda, again an unmarried "seer," and Abigail, the mother of three daughters, Peace, Hope, and Grace and granddaughter Cocoa, Naylor shows the harmony between the single artist-woman and the mother-woman. As Gilman did so long ago, Naylor insists that biological maternity does not define or enclose participation in motherhood. When Cocoa is threatened by death, Miranda tells George that no mother could feel more pain or pride in "Baby Girl" as she grew. Because the sisters complement each other's femininity, the sisters combine without rancor or jealousy to bring to life and happiness their child, Ophelia-Cocoa-Baby Girl—the daughter's multiple names a litany of love. Cocoa reflects that together they were the perfect mother. In the separate island community, Willow Springs, Miranda works through nature, midwife and death dealer, daughter of the Mother Goddess as she redefines the received categories of gender conventions and rejoins the human community.

Mama Day opens with a narrative celebration of the female seer Miranda, and her foremother, the founder of Willow Springs, Sapphira Wade. A voice tells the reader of the island women's world, found on no map, lying just off the coast of South Carolina and Georgia and then the narrating voice—defined as neither male nor female—in the preface enjoins us to hear the maternal language of Mama Day and Sapphira Wade. Naylor seeks to bring the reader immediately and intuitively into Willow Springs as she insists on direct personal communication. Miranda's voice, or more precisely the voice of the community—she is the oracle—merge with the reader's own emotions and memories, a part that the mainland has taught the reader to ignore: "Think about it: ain't nobody really talking to you. We're sitting right here in Willow Springs, and you're God-knows-where. It's August 1999—ain't but a slim change it's the same season where you are. Uh, huh, listen. Really listen this time: the only voice is your own." The community's voice comes close, enters the reader's experience, demanding that he or she, black or white, young or old, reach back, to remember the wise woman. Although the voice clearly arises from the black community, it invites the reader into the homes as the seer's legend is passed, as the community members fix their autos, prepare their dinners. With the insistence on the oral nature of the printed narrative and its direct, immediate, even telepathic transmission, the writing daughter Naylor attempts to transcend the limits of modern language and summon the connecting strength of myth. And in her refusal to classify the opening narrator as belonging to either gender, Naylor insists that the home place welcomes men as well as women. The mystery of religion is once again merged with the acts of the daily life as the domestic acts and manual labor of the working man and woman are elevated to the sacred.

The narrating voice recollects the college-educated Reema's boy, who returns from the mainland to study Willow Springs's customs and language. This figure allows Naylor to juxtapose Mama Day's maternal language with the impersonal associational language represented by the writing of Reema's boy—he is known on Willow Springs by his mother's name—and the language and calculation of the mainland investors who seek to persuade Miranda to sell the island for "development." Reema's boy "rattled on about 'ethnography,' 'unique speech patterns,' 'cultural preservation,' and whatever else he seemed to be getting so much pleasure out of while talking into his little gray machine." When the academic books arrive, the inhabitants discover that Reema's boy writes condescendingly of Willow Springs's legends, calling it "asserting our cultural identity" and "inverting hostile social and political parameters." The narrating consciousness laughs off the corrupt and limited modern language, which separates itself from the morality and emotions of the maternal home and prepares us for Mama Day's own narrative of her salvation of her beloved Cocoa. Tracing the woman's lineage back to the first mother, the narrator looks forward to the next century. The author relinquishes control of the narrative, telling us that the story comes from within, from our own memories, our own voice.

In *The Signifying Monkey*, Henry Louis Gates, Jr. contrasts the "speakerly text" of Zora Neale Hurston with the ideal of the individual text found in Richard Wright. Gates posits that difference in voice comes from the attitudes of both toward the black culture around them, Wright, in Gates's opinion, believing that the only representative of "the ideal individual black [self]" was the author himself. Further, Gates observes that Wright's humanity is "achieved only at the expense of his fellow blacks." Accordingly, Wright uses the strategies so prominent in the white male canon, the recourse to "realism" or the depiction of social arrangements as they exist and the recreation of the self-made man. Hurston, in contrast, allows the community to speak for itself through the agency of the author herself, creating a "transcendent, ultimately racial self, extending far beyond the merely individual." Gates depicts Hurston and Wright at opposite poles of African-American literature, fellow artists who carried on a critical debate through reviews as well as through the fiction itself.[5] A trained anthropologist and folklorist, Hurston understood the power of the language of the black community from her own intellectual work; in addition, her protagonist Janie Crawford of *Their Eyes Were Watching God* as a woman of color—the member of two marginal groups, understood the consolations offered by her woman friend, and she suspected the romantic attentions of material achievers like Jody Starks, who would view her as a possession. Unlike Wright's acceptance of competitive individualism, Hurston understood the terrible isolation of the single human being and reached toward connection. If, as Calvin Hernton contends, the black literary tradition has until this point been as dominated by male voices as the white canon, this poses even more difficulties for the black woman facing white male structures.

Hurston's language itself reflects the attempt to bring the mother tongue into literature, to bridge the gap between reader and author and fictional community. Indeed, the local language arises from groups who retain some of the communal identity within the bureaucratic society.[6] In line with Gates's theory of transmission of fictional patterns, Naylor acknowledges Hurston's influence when she came to write the crucial storm scene in *Mama Day*. She gained confidence in the ability of the communal voice to carry the narrative through her reading of the flood scene in *Their Eyes Were Watching God*. As Andree McLaughlin writes, African-American women must refuse the Western images and ideas that deny full humanity to those who in their persons or their lives challenge white, male, Christian dominance, and the materialistic pyramid. McLaughlin calls for black women to redefine themselves in their entirety, which includes, as do the other visions here, the men, children, and natural world: "By symbolmaking, ideamaking, and worldmaking, they are creators in a preeminent sense." The critic concludes that these women along with other women of color can defeat that dominant world view by recourse to "the traditional world views and fearlessness of their maligned foremothers." Along with other feminist critics and women artists, McLaughlin identifies these new constructions as leading to "real change in the real world through real means."

Naylor's *Mama Day* moves toward this ideal as the author seizes the voice of the community. The communal voice of Hurston, her courageous defiance of both black male and white definitions, has empowered Naylor, as well as other African-American women authors, to write out of their experience of doubled marginality as woman and black, and like Hurston, Naylor reaches back to the local language, which exists at the margins of the competitive bureaucratic social order. By refusing the authority of the scientifically detached introspective author, Naylor, like other women here, negates the idea of the self-created genius and instead insists on the vitality of woman's communal voice.

Hidden away from the American mainland, connected only by a fragile bridge, Willow Springs enriches the New York of Cocoa and her husband George. As with Porter's "Pale Horse, Pale Rider," the bridge demarcates the separation of the two worlds, a function served by the mountain in Glasgow's *Vein of Iron*, Gilman's *Herland*, and Welty's *The Optimist's Daughter*, the vast plains in *My Ántonia*, and the ocean in Jewett's *The Country of the Pointed Firs*. In all, the natural world shelters the other place at the same time as the author indicates the imaginary nature of the hidden home as well as its different relationships and beliefs.

As with Van of *Herland*, George serves as the reader's guide to Willow Springs. A city man, George grew up without a mother or father; instead he received the just and impersonal guidance of Mrs. Jackson of the Wallace P. Andrews Shelter for Boys. She teaches her charges the affective rules for survival in the city: "Our rage didn't matter to her, our hurts or disappointments over what life had done to us. None of that was going to matter a damn in the outside world, so we might as well start learning it at Wallace P. Andrews. There were only rules and facts." Mrs. Jackson is the perfect mother of the abandoned children of the bureaucratic society; she offers fairness and promises control as long as her children follow the rules. Although harsh, her punishments for misdeeds are dispassionate; emotional reaction and personal relationship will only hinder her charges in the city outside. George represents the man of the regimented social order; like Mr. Elliott of McIntosh's domestic novel, he must learn the morality of the home place. When he meets the mothers of his bride, George realizes that he has come back to a home he never knew, but at some level mourned. As he crosses the bridge from the mainland, that good man knows that he enters "another world," the other world in which nature enters the breath and blood of each person, spanning the divide between environment and human being. George knows that "it all smelled like forever," and when Abigail blesses him, he realizes that no woman had ever called him her child before. As Cocoa tells him, he has come home.

Naylor suggests that George's lonely life represents the emotional costs to men as well as women of the mother's loss. Although Hazel Carby calls for a return to the urban setting for verisimilitude in the portrayal of the lives of urban blacks, Naylor's career suggests that portrayals of black rural communities, even the ideal home place, represents more than a facile "romantic" vision of the folk, just as in the earlier white women's writing it represents more than simple "nostalgia." As Barbara Smith notes, Alice Walker, Toni Morrison, Margaret Walker, and Zora Neale Hurston incorporate such folk arts as root working, folk medicine, midwifery, and conjure into their narratives to capture the distinctive experience of black history and community. Smith offers this concise observation: "The use of Black women's language and cultural experience in books *by* Black women *about* Black women results in a miraculously rich coalescing of form and content and also takes their writing far beyond the confines of white/male literary structures." Smith concludes that critics would find many connections within bodies of work by African-American women. White women too can find segments of their experience and history in books by black women; there are many roads to and from the home place.

Although Mama Day still believes in the male deity as the first creator, she imagines a powerful female partner. In Miranda's extremity, when Cocoa is threatened with death, she knows she must summon the Mother, but she cannot name her. Her name has been lost. To free her mind, Mama Day sets her house in order, prayer mingling with and arising out of her domestic rituals. Frantically, she searches through a catalog of names, "Samantha," "Sarena," "Salinda," "Savannah," as she moves around her home touching the sacred cooking vessels, asking her familiar, Cicero the rooster, cleaning away the outward dust of male experience to get back to the creator. She prays to the "Father and the Son as she'd been taught. But she falls asleep, murmuring the names of women. And in her dreams she finally meets Sapphira." Through her prayer, her devotion to the homely tools of her power, Miranda finally reaches back to the mystic ancestress who first won the island from the white slaveowner. The goddess whose name is never "literally said" is the "guiding spirit for that island" *(American Audio Prose Interview)*. Arising out of a historical memory, a racial memory as well as a female memory, Sapphira's name comes only when Miranda passes through rationality, through male myth, coming at last through dreams to the first seer. As she sleeps, in dreams, Sapphira comes, nourishing Miranda, calling her "daughter," giving her the female power of working with nature. Naylor makes it clear that Sapphira Wade, like any deity, cannot be described except through her identity as a conjure woman of African ancestry. Like the Virgin Mary in her many manifestations, Sapphira takes on the complexion of the worshipper: "satin black, biscuit cream, red as Georgia clay: depending on which of us takes a mind to her." Unlike Mary, the ever-virgin handmaiden, however, the fully sexual Sapphira, like all the female demigoddesses in this study, is independently creative and restorative within her own realm: "She turned the moon into salve, the stars into a swaddling cloth, and healed the wounds of every creature walking on two or down on four."

Now Miranda can command the thunder in the thrilling storm scene as the mother deity and the seer battle the false arts of obsessive passion. As Naylor has remarked, she originally feared that this central scene could not encompass the symbolism and power of the storm if it was written in the community's voice. Depicting the turmoil in the mother god's community as the daughter passes toward death, the hurricanes arise from the coast of Africa, Sapphira's birthplace. Naylor intends this hurricane to serve as the central metaphor of the Middle Passage, and she wondered as she contemplated this sophisticated metaphor if the local, communal "world view" could carry it to completion. Then remembering Hurston's flood in *Their Eyes Were Watching God*, she gained the confidence to allow the community to speak for itself.

Like the female elders in Jewett, Porter, Welty, and Glasgow, Sapphira and her female descendant Miranda guard the gates of birth and death, bringing her healing powers of growth to the natural world. Like the male deity, Sapphira has her own day of commemoration, Candle Walk, whose nature implicitly comments on the mainland's commercialized Christmas, a holiday most notably portrayed in Naylor through Luther's fiery demise. The story of Candle Walk's founding comes from a local legend, which says that when God threw down the island from heaven, he brought along some stars. The mighty conjure woman, Sapphira Wade, tells the deity to let them stay, so that she can lead on with light. Thus the ritual of celebration asks each member to carry a candle and a gift as they walk from house to house in a ceremony something like the Mexican *posada*. Instead of exchanging purchased gifts among friends, the members of the community carry a gift, however modest, as long as it is homemade or the product of the earth. These gifts are given to the needy and the lonely as the givers walk about on Candle Walk.

In Willow Springs the women carry the memory, the magic, and the creative power of the ideal community. Together Sapphira, Cocoa, and Mama Day form a sort of woman's trinity with mother, daughter, and spirit. The antagonist of the narrative is Ruby, a woman jealously in love with a younger man, transformed into an evil sorceress; Naylor portrays Ruby's obsession as the source of disorder and evil within the community. The supposed conjure man, Doctor Buzzard, is in fact an ineffectual figure of fun.

Naylor implies that the home place, existing in "no state," enriches the America outside despite its distance and isolation. Cocoa, for example, sees New York not as a city, but as a collection of small towns; her childhood experience of the mothers enables her to humanize the impersonal urban setting. Her experience with Willow Springs accompanies her to the city, but George's childhood leaves him unable to understand the mores of Mama Day's island as his experience with the gambling circle illustrates—he exposes and defeats an ancient male charlatan, robbing the old man of one of his few illusions. When the mainland developers seek to buy the island, promising jobs and prosperity for Willow Springs, Miranda sends them packing from her women's world because "even well-meaning progress and paradise don't go hand in hand." The regimented, impersonal society and its language gain no foothold on Sapphira's island.

At the narrative's climax, Naylor depicts the wise woman struggling to convey her meaning in modern language. When Miranda tells George that he must undertake a quest to save his wife, Cocoa, who is bewitched and dying from Ruby's sexual jealousy, the city man replies that she is talking in metaphors. Through Miranda's anguish, Naylor portrays the modern emptying of effective ritual communication from literature, as she dismisses the elegant, aesthetic concept of metaphor as belonging to the present leisure entertainment of intellectual literature. She concludes that she is speaking of efficacious ritual speech and acts: "The stuff folks dreamed up when they was making a fantasy, while what she was talking about was *real*." Naylor portrays the shared symbolism that holds the bonding power of the community, that ritual language charged with emotion when understood and underlined with belief. The language Miranda summons is literature in its truest sense, possessing force and consequence in the real, natural world; it breaks out of the library's walls; it defies explanation and explication. Naylor evokes the language of the face-to-face woman's community, calling up the immediate emotion, the efficacy of shared ritual. In Mama Day's "paradise," communication and law come from old tales and memories, lived ties between neighbors, and continuity between the female generations; by recourse to both Miranda's creativity through the garden—work with the natural world and through the quilt—art through the spirit, Naylor returns to the metaphors found in many writers from the beginnings of women's introspective fiction in America. The characterization, the ongoing generations of women, their bodies and spirits, and the setting, kitchen and garden, recall previous women's work. In *Mama Day* we envision, along with George, "paradise," but the author locates her haven in an island found on no American map.[7] Through the other-worldly content, magic and metaphor, and the rejoined generations, contemporary women authors like Naylor restore the home place to the American literary landscape.

We pass through death and violence to come back where we started with Miranda in the future August, waiting the daughter's return, waiting for the millennium's end, easily in the past and memory as she communicates with her dead sister through the rustling of the trees and the unspoken language. Like Cather's hidden Ántonia or Glasgow's isolated Kate Oliver, Miranda is aged, tired with her prodigies of work, but she still lives and still summons in living memory her dead, like Miranda of "Pale Horse, Pale Rider" and Laura of *The Optimist's Daughter*. And she still waits for the daughter's return.

Notes

1. I use the term "black" in reference to Naylor's heritage and writing since that is her preference.
2. The books on African-American feminism consulted are Joanne Braxton and Andree Nicola McLaughlin, eds., *Wild Women in the Whirlwind*, Hazel Carby, *Reconstructing Womanhood*, Audre Lorde, *Sister Outsider*, Barbara Smith, "Toward a Black Feminist Criticism" in Elaine Showalter, *The New Feminist Criticism:* 168–85, and Alice Walker, *In Search of Our Mothers' Gardens*.
3. Naylor insists that there is enough agony in Brewster Place to make comparison obscene. Is Lorraine's rape more tragic than Ciel's loss of her child? Is Ciel's loss of her child to be judged worse that Mattie's betrayal by her son?
4. In her recorded interview Naylor promises that her fifth book will center on the narrative of Sapphira Wade.
5. *Mama Day* illustrates the problem of multiple group identities. As Elizabeth Fox-Genovese writes in *Within the Plantation Household*, the African-American woman in the slavery era remained caught between the gender rules of the dominant white Southern community and the gender conventions of the slave community.
6. Marget Sands, a scholar on Native American women's sacred writings, has suggested similarities between the morality of the home place and attitudes toward community in those writings.
7. In my teaching, two works elicit the same love, there is no other word for it, *Mama Day* and Cather's "Neighbor Rosicky." These works seem to send the readers back to their own histories.

◆◆◆◆◆◆◆◆◆◆◆◆◆◆

Black Sisterhood in Naylor's Novels

LARRY R. ANDREWS

In the conclusion of her study of twelve novels by black women over the last four decades *(No Crystal Stair: Visions of Race and Sex in Black Women's Fiction)*, Gloria Wade-Gayles, speaking about the female characters, says:

> [E]ven when the women understand that they share a sisterhood of oppression, they often do not act on the belief that "sisterhood is powerful." They do not come together to talk about their common history and their common reality. When they do attempt to communicate as women, they fail to sustain the sisterhood.[1]

A number of writers have portrayed strong friendships between black women (e.g., Morrison in *Sula*, Walker in *The Color Purple*), but these bonds are often broken or slackened by competitiveness, betrayal, and physical or socioeconomic separation, Gloria Naylor, in her first three novels—*The Women of Brewster Place* (1982), *Linden Hills* (1985), and *Mama Day* (1988)—devotes considerable attention to the special bond that can exist between women characters, including women of different generations. In the first two novels, this bond derives its power from the women's previous sense of isolation, from their mistreatment by men, and from their regenerative discovery, through suffering, of the saving grace of shared experience. In *Mama Day* the power comes from folk tradition, from "foremothering," and from nature, as Naylor moves into the realm of matriarchal mythmaking. At its best this bond among women confers identity, purpose, and strength for survival. And the possibility of its achievement grows in the course of the three novels. But although it is dramatized in the novels as clearly desirable, the success of female friendship, of the black womanbond, remains limited and potential.

Naylor's exploration of black sisterhood is clearest in *The Women of Brewster Place*, where she focuses almost entirely on women. In the prologue ("Dawn"), she presents the female residents of the tenement as a vibrant community:

> Nutmeg arms leaned over windowsills, gnarled ebony legs carried groceries up double flights of steps, and saffron hands strung out wet laundry on backyard lines. Their perspiration mingled with the steam from boiling pots of smoked pork and greens, and it curled on the edges of the aroma of vinegar douches and Evening in Paris cologne that drifted through the street where they stood together—hands on hips, straight-backed, round-bellied, high-behinded women who threw their heads back when they laughed and exposed strong teeth and dark gums. They cursed, badgered, worshiped, and shared

their men. . . . They were hard-edged, soft-centered, brutally demanding, and easily pleased, these women of Brewster Place.[2]

At the end of this "novel in seven stories," despite numerous conflicts, she unites the women in Mattie's dream of the block party (which may come true). They join in an act of protest against the power of men over women (the gang-rape of the lesbian Lorraine) and, more broadly, against the barriers of racist and class oppression (the bloodstained wall) that distort relations between the sexes. Even after Brewster Place has been condemned and abandoned in the epilogue ("Dusk"), the women carry on:

> But the colored daughters of Brewster, spread over the canvas of time, still wake up with their dreams misted on the edge of a yawn. They get up and pin those dreams to wet laundry hung out to dry, they're diapered around babies. They ebb and flow, ebb and flow, but never disappear.

The women are a collective repository of dreams, a resilient source of strength for continuing survival if not yet conquest.

In *Linden Hills*, which continues the fictional world of *Brewster Place* but moves up in social class to the black bourgeois housing development dominated by the mortician Luther Nedeed, Naylor places a more balanced emphasis on both men and women. At the same time, there seem to be far fewer possibilities of female community. Despite their college educations and, in some cases, professional careers, most of the women are isolated and vulnerable. Yet here, too, a sense of community comes to play an important role in the plot. When she is locked in the basement morgue with her dead child, Willa Nedeed's emerging discovery of the suffering of her female predecessors in the house gives her strength to survive, accept herself, and take revenge on her husband. Furthermore, the hope is more clearly developed in this novel that the sensitive black male, in the person of the poet Willie Mason, can begin to bridge the gap of understanding between men and women and to support women in their quest for identity.

In *Mama Day*, both the contemporary and the historical bonds between women are important, for connection to the past helps make possible a connection in the present. Naylor develops the three main characters (Mama Day, Ophelia, and George) much more fully that any of her previous characters as she explores a family related to Willa Nedeed from *Linden Hills*. Here female community becomes empowered by natural forces and religious tradition in the coastal island community of Willow Springs. The bond between women does not arise as a refuge from isolation, mistreatment by men, or loss of identity in the white and black bourgeois worlds. It predates and transcends these modern conditions. Most important is the historical connection that runs from the legendary free spirit who founded the community, Sapphira Wade, through Miranda (Mama Day) to Miranda's great-niece Ophelia. This connection among women is related to nature through Miranda's extraordinary powers of intuition, "magic," and fertility as well as through the cyclical sense of time that pervades the island community. At the climax of the novel, this form of sisterhood is affirmed and strengthened. At the same time, sisterhood can still be jeopardized by the seductions of modern America and the evil and divisive jealousy of someone like Ruby, who nearly succeeds in killing Ophelia with night shade poison.

In all three novels Naylor uses a unified physical setting, a spirit of place—just as Gwendolyn Brook does in *In the Mecca* and Morrison in *Sula*—to provide a communal framework for the varied descriptions of the women who come to live in it. Like the Mecca tenement, Brewster Place offers close physical contact that makes the women's confrontation with each other inescapable and their mutual support compelling. In *Linden Hills*, however, the women are physically isolated in houses and separated by status distinctions. The possibilities for sisterhood here are less spatial and contemporary than temporal and historical. In *Mama Day* the rural South, alternating with New York scenes between George and Ophelia, offers a setting for a healing community with roots in female folk tradition and nature.

In *Brewster Place* a friendship based on the shared experience of black womanhood exists sometimes in the form of the mother-daughter relationship. One of the problems several women face is that in their isolation they come to focus all their needs on their children and define themselves exclusively as mothers, thus enacting a male-defined, exploitive role. This tendency has both negative and positive consequences. The book is dominated by Mattie Michael, whose presence is felt in all of the individual character studies. Given the weak model of her parents' marriage and her desire for Butch, she rejects the timid suitor her stern father favors and at the same time harbors no expectations that Butch will show responsibility for her or their baby. After the violent scene with her father and her ejection from home, she quickly converts from lover to mother. Miss Eva, with whom she later shares a household and whom she regards as a surrogate mother, finds Mattie's excessive mothering and sexual continence unnatural. Mattie sleeps with her son Basil and channels all her needs into mothering him. In fact, she renders him incapable of responsibility. When he skips bail and she loses her house, she faces a tragic awakening.

The positive effect of her mothering emerges later, however, in her influence over other women in Brewster Place, above all in the powerful healing scene in which she rocks and washes Ciel Turner from despair back to life:

> Like a black Brahman cow, desperate to protect her young, she surged into the room, pushing the neighbor woman and the others out of her way. . . .
> She sat on the edge of the bed and enfolded the tissue-thin body in her huge ebony arms. And she rocked. . . .

> . . . Mattie rocked her out of that bed, out of that room, into a blue vast-
> ness just underneath the sun and above time. She rocked her Aegean seas so
> clean they shone like crystal, so clear the fresh blood of sacrificed babies torn
> from their mother's arms and given to Neptune could be seen like pink froth
> on the water. She rocked her on and on, past Dachau, where soul-gutted
> Jewish mothers swept their children's entrails off laboratory floors. They flew
> past the spilled brains of Senegalese infants whose mothers had dashed them
> on the wooden sides of slave ships. And she rocked on.
>   She rocked her into her childhood and let her see murdered dreams. And
> she rocked her back, back into the womb, . . .

The female connection here participates in a whole history of mother-
sorrow, black and white. But the bond is not just that of mother and
daughter, even though Mattie had helped raise Ciel years earlier. It is
woman-to-woman. Their similar suffering makes them equal. Lucielia
had come to look on her own daughter Serena as "the only thing I have
ever loved without pain." Just before Serena electrocutes herself, Ciel
has detached herself emotionally from her unreliable man Eugene, who
has too many problems of his own with "the Man." What Mattie and Ciel
come to share in Mattie's act of primal mothering is their isolation, their
burden of responsibility as mothers, and the loss of their children.

Another mother-daughter relationship that becomes sisterhood
emerges not from suffering but from the daughter's discovery of her
mother's sexuality. Kiswana Browne is "healed" in her conflict with her
mother by coming to identify herself with her mother as a woman. Kiswana has allied herself with the only thoroughly positive male character
in the novel, Abshu, and with the now moribund black militance of the
sixties. Her mother, from middle-class Linden Hills, pulls her up short
when Kiswana accuses her mother of being "a white man's nigger who's
ashamed of being black!" Her mother reacquaints her with a tradition of
pride and strong mothering in the example of her great-grandmother—
a full-blooded Iroquois "who bore nine children and educated them all,
who held off six white men with a shotgun when they tried to drag one
of her sons to jail for 'not knowing his place'"—and in her own example
as a mother toughening her children to meet the world. But despite this
reestablished bond of women over generations, the clinching moment for
Kiswana comes only when she notices for the first time her mother's
bright red toenail polish, like her own:

> I'll be damned the young woman thought, feeling her whole face tingle.
> Daddy's into feet! And she looked at the blushing woman on her couch and
> suddenly realized that her mother had trod through the same universe that
> she herself was now traveling. Kiswana was breaking no new trails and would
> eventually end up just two feet away on the couch. She stared at the woman
> she had been and was to become.

From the moment of their parting laughter she begins a productive new
life in organizing rent protest among the women of Brewster Place and
returning to school.

Kiswana can also now bring sisterly nurture to Cora Lee, another woman unbalanced in her mothering. Strangely obsessed with doll babies as a child, Cora Lee bears numerous children by the many "shadow" men in her life who slip in and out of her bedroom at night. Much as she desires *babies*, she is bewildered when they start growing up and she simply cannot manage them. But the friendship of Kiswana Browne, through an invitation to Shakespeare in the park, rekindles her old dreams of education. The act of friendship and offer to help, once Kiswana gets beyond her own initial condescension, contributes to restoring Cora Lee's self-esteem both as a person and as a mother. Her new mothering energy will be directed toward her children's education, and she has found a sisterhood in Kiswana that lifts her out of her isolation.

The best example of sisterly friendship without the maternal connection is Etta Mae Johnson's relationship with Mattie. A woman weary but "still dripping with the juices of a full-fleshed life" in Preacher Woods' eyes, Etta returns to Mattie and Brewster Place as a homecoming herself:

> She breathed deeply on the freedom she found in Mattie's presence. Here she had no choice but to be herself. The carefully erected decoys she was constantly shuffling and changing to fit the situation were of no use here. Etta and Mattie went back, a singular term that claimed co-knowledge of all the important events in their lives and almost all of the unimportant ones. And by rights of this possession, it tolerated no secrets.

After Preacher Woods' one-night stand shatters her brief illusion that she might achieve her dream of quick respectability as a preacher's wife in the front pew, she returns again to Mattie as to a center: "She laughed softly to herself as she climbed the steps toward the light and the love and the comfort that awaited her." With no worthy object for her flamboyant spirit, Etta yet has the deep friendship, support, and even moral judgment of Mattie in warding off loneliness and despair.

The love between Etta and Mattie is described more pointedly in a key passage in the later chapter about the two lesbians, Lorraine and Theresa. But first a word must be said about this pair of lovers. This marriage of the timid and the tough is fraught with as much hostility as love. Alternating between fostering and fighting, these two young women are still struggling to find their identities. Lorraine hates the cynical gay bars that are Theresa's element and wants to feel at one with her neighbors in Brewster Place. Theresa resents Lorraine's vulnerability yet is uncomfortable when Lorraine acquires firm convictions. Each seeks a different community. When Lorraine discovers an accepting listener in the alcoholic janitor Ben, Theresa insists on their own mutual dependence as outcasts, and Lorraine rebels. After their final quarrel, when Theresa lets Lorraine go to the party by herself, there is no more opportunity for them to resolve their conflicts and reaffirm their love. Lorraine is physically and psychologically destroyed by C. C. Baker and his gang, and in her derangement she murders her only friend, Ben. Because of its unresolved tensions and concern over power, this relationship between two women, despite its seeming intimacy, remains less successful than that between Mattie and Etta, who generously accept and nurture each other.

That there is a connection between the two relationships is brought out significantly in the key passage referred to earlier. After a block association meeting where Mattie and Etta have defended the lesbians against the gossip Sophie and the others, Mattie feels uncomfortable about the lesbian relationship and ponders with Etta the nature of female friendship:

> Mattie was thinking deeply. "Well, I've loved women, too. There was Miss Eva and Ciel, and even as ornery as you can get, I've loved you practically all my life."
> "Yeah, but it's different with them."
> "Different how?"
> "Well . . ." Etta was beginning to feel uncomfortable. "They love each other like you'd love a man or a man would love you—I guess."
> "But I've loved some women deeper than I ever loved any man," Mattie was pondering. "And there been some women who loved me more and did more for me than any man ever did."
> "Yeah." Etta thought for a moment. "I can second that, but it's still different, Mattie. I can't exactly put my finger on it, but . . ."
> "Maybe it's not so different," Mattie said, almost to herself. "Maybe that's why some women get so riled up about it, 'cause they know deep down it's not so different after all." She looked at Etta. "It kinda gives you a funny feeling when you think about it that way, though."
> "Yeah, it does," Etta said, unable to meet Mattie's eyes.

What Mattie comes to realize, through the insight of her own experience, is that the deep bond she has felt with some women may have a wholeness and power (including the sensual) comparable to that of the lesbians and perhaps superior to any relationship that seems possible with a man in the distorted world of black gender relations. This is surely the central expression of black sisterhood in the novel.

The strength of this sisterhood can be explained partly, but not entirely, by the men's failures in love. In a conversation with Toni Morrison (published in *The Southern Review*), Naylor speaks of her concern lest readers exaggerate her treatment of the male characters:

> I bent over backwards not to have a negative message come through about the men. My emotional energy was spent creating a woman's world, telling her side of it because I knew it hadn't been done enough in literature. But I worried about whether or not the problems that were being caused by the men in the women's lives would be interpreted as some bitter statement I had to make about black men.[3]

Most of the men in the novel may indeed be so ego-crippled by racism as to be unable to love their women, but Naylor still holds them accountable: the irresponsible Butch, the enraged father who is ready to kick his pregnant daughter Mattie to death, the father who rejects his lesbian daughter Lorraine, the transient "shadows" in Cora Lee's bedroom, the hypocritical Preacher Woods, the insecure Eugene, who abandons Ciel, and, above all, C. C. Baker and his gang, whom Naylor describes with her most sardonic language. Only Abshu and Ben are capable of fruitful relationships with women, and Ben only out of guilt for his impotence in letting his wife sell their daughter into concubinage with a white man. Generally, therefore, the men abandon the women to double burdens of work and domestic life without support. Women become the victims of class, race, and sex, as Wade-Gayles points out. In this condition the friendship of other women is not only a saving grace but a political necessity.

Can the women move beyond haphazard friendships to any larger sense of community? The only collective sisterhood larger than that of the pairs discussed so far is the block association. Yet it is riven by conflict over allowing the lesbian Lorraine to be the secretary, and its political power is shown only in embryo. But the powerful denouement of the novel, even if expressed as dream, draws all of the women intuitively together in a common gesture of outrage as they try to eradicate Lorraine's and Ben's bloodstains from the brick wall.

No such community of action closes the plot of *Linden Hills*, but a similar act of exorcism based on a *sense* of female community does take place. In this novel a variety of women characters again appears, but they rarely communicate with each other for mutual support. Among the minor characters are two older women (one with a matriarchal aura), several respectable wives and mothers of middle age, and several well-educated young women of the third, rising generation. Grandma Tilson is the stern guardian of traditional values comparable to Mattie Michael, but she is no longer alive. She had fought Luther Nedeed as the maverick of his upward-striving black community, and she had provided the catfish heads the Luther Nedeeds used to make their female corpses seem alive, as if passing on some principle of female vitality. Yet she is significant not just as a woman or for women, as Mattie is. Her warning against self-betrayal and loss of identity (selling "that silver mirror God propped up in your soul"), so often ignored by the middle-class residents, is meant for women *and* men, and Lester and Willie are its most receptive audience. The other older woman, Roberta Johnson, Laurel Dumont's grandmother, gives good advice about finding one's center, too, but she is ultimately ineffectual in preventing Laurel's suicide.

The second-generation mothers of Linden Hills share an ambition for a better life, but they are not shown as coming together out of a fellow-feeling and creating a genuine community. Like many of the men, they are out for themselves and their own families. Their acquisitiveness, like that of Silla Boyce in Paule Marshall's *Brown Girl, Brownstones*, isolates them and stifles a vital part of their identity. Lester's mother, Mrs.

Tilson, is the most fully characterized. From Lester's point of view her ambition killed his father under the weight of two jobs; she has betrayed the values of black integrity by wanting an easier life for Lester in his struggle for dignity and power in a white world. Lycentia Parker, now dead, apparently took a more destructive stance in heading a petition drive to keep poor blacks out of Linden Hills, and her feelings are shared by the women at her wake, including Xavier Donnell's aunt. All of them are concerned with material status, with appearance, but derive little human sustenance from each other despite these shared values. Willie's mother, from the lower-class Putney Wayne, has been beaten by his alcoholic father, and, given a chance at Linden Hills, might have ended up like the others.

The young women tend to fare badly and remain isolated from each other also. Roxanne Tilson, at twenty-seven, wants to marry rich and black, and she clings to Xavier Donnell at the price of some humiliation. Though Xavier loves her, he is fearful of the commitment and anxious because the upward career he aims for as a GM manager makes marriage to Roxanne imprudent. Marie Hollis, originally sharing her preacher husband's distaste for up-tight, middle-class congregations (despite her Cambridge-Radcliffe background), grows away from him when he receives the plum post in Linden Hills and begins philandering, and she eventually leaves him. Barely mentioned Cassandra is made the victim of another status marriage with the gay Winston Alcott, who betrays himself and his lover David for respectability as an attorney.

Laurel Dumont's tragic story is the most developed among those of the minor characters. She has chosen, instead of the swimming and music she loves, a career as a top IBM executive and a status marriage with the district attorney Howard Dumont. Her increasing emptiness leads her to divorce and withdrawal from life. Unable to find her "home," her place in life, she makes a last attempt to reach out for support from other women. Since she has difficulty responding directly and openly to her grandmother, she tries to call Mrs. Nedeed, who, however, has been locked in the cellar morgue by her husband. She does reach Ruth Anderson and talks with her for hours about old times (a dialogue not reported, hence de-emphasized). But Ruth, not feeling well, sends her husband with the Christmas gift, and the direct supportive contact between the two women is never achieved. The combination of the snow and Luther Nedeed's reclaiming of her house, the only "home" she has, pushes her into taking a high dive into the empty Olympic-sized swimming pool.

Ruth Anderson is the only one among the young women who has anything close to a successful relationship with a man. And since she and Norman are everything for each other, the issue of black sisterhood seems to have less relevance. Her dreams of stability have been shattered by Norman's insane attacks by an imaginary pink slime every two years. But the two have affirmed their love for each other even in the depths of their worst suffering, and they are committed to caring for each other.

The main woman character is, of course, Willa Prescott Nedeed, the young wife of the current Luther Nedeed. She is presented initially as a total victim of her husband and as totally isolated. In his rage at his son's light skin and his wife's supposed infidelity, Luther has locked her and her son in his basement morgue and has indirectly caused his son's death. Much of the book is the story of Willa's gradual awakening to her position and to her power in a pattern reminiscent of slave narratives, as Calvin Hernton illustrates in discussing *The Color Purple*.[4] This discovery comes about as Mrs. Nedeed, near death from grief and starvation, finds stored documents from three previous generations of Nedeed wives. Her contact with these women through their documents is a genuine if indirect experience of black sisterhood. The 1837 Bible scribblings of the first, Luwana Packerville Nedeed, reveal a young wife's discovery that her husband regards her as little more than chattel. Willa sees in this woman's usurpation by a housekeeper and total isolation from husband and son as a parallel to her own enslavement to a later, equally sexist, Luther Nedeed. In her growing insanity Luwana had created a correspondence with a fictitious sister of the same name, so desperate was her need to communicate with an understanding woman. Willa is stirred to remember particularly the way Luther has come to dominate her and separate her from her former girlfriends. At this point she can finally begin to express her mourning for her child.

The second encounter, with the recipes of Evelyn Creton Nedeed, leads to Willa's discovery that Luther, not she, had the sexual inadequacy that explains his physical coldness toward her. Evelyn's sexual frustration and self-hatred were expressed in an obsession with cooking, first crazily huge amounts, then small furtive doses of aphrodisiacs designed to make her husband attracted to her, then bulimic purgatives, and finally rat poison to kill herself with on Christmas Eve. The connections are again numerous. Willa, too, has been brainwashed into feeling sexually inadequate: "His coldness and distance, the feeling that things weren't the way they should be must lie in something that she just wasn't doing right. If she hung in there long enough, he would change."[5] She, too, put on weight after their marriage, sought help from expensive perfumes, and is now starving. She, too, will die on Christmas Eve, but she will take her husband with her. In the midst of this stage of discovery, she barely manages to stifle the memory of seeing Luther embalming one of his female corpses. Intuitively she begins to recognize Luther's perverted potency: like his forebears, he exercises all his tenderness on making his dead women look alive, like satisfied lovers, yet he deadens his living wife. The ironic parallel between the two processes is all the more grim because they both concern his vaginal insertions. Willa's response is rage as she rips up the cookbooks and recipe files and scatters them over the room; she is emerging from apathy and returning to life.

Willa's third encounter, with Priscilla McGuire Nedeed's photo album, leads to her reaffirmation of her own identity, her freedom, and her sense of responsibility for her own life. The series of annual photographs demonstrates graphically how a previous Luther and his son gradually overshadowed his spirited woman's selfhood until she began removing her face from all of the pictures. Willa's recognition of shared experience is again immediate:

> Staring at the gaping hole that was once Priscilla McGuire, she reached her hand up and began to touch her own face, her fingers running tentatively across the cheeks and mouth, up the bridge of the nose, and spanning out over the eyes and forehead.

She finds a Grandma Tilson mirror of her identity, first in her hands, then in a pail of water:

> She now closed her eyes and used both hands, trying to form a mirror between her fingers, the darkness, and memory. What formed in her mind might be it, but she needed to be sure.

> Rimmed by light, there was the outline of her hair, the shape of the chin, and if she turned her head slowly—very slowly—there was the profile of her nose and lips. . . . No doubt remained—she was there.

Naylor explains this moment to Morrison in "A Conversation":

> After she had dug up the remnants of the other Nedeed women, I created a way for her to see her own reflection in a pan of water because she had no self up until that moment. And when she realized that she had a face, then maybe she had other things going for her as well, and she could take her destiny in her own hands.

The final stage of regeneration is the rediscovery of her first name (which we now learn for the first time in the novel) and the acceptance of what she had become, a good wife and mother in a limited circumstance:

> But Willa Prescott Nedeed was alive, and she had made herself that. . . . Her marriage to Luther Nedeed was her choice, and she took his name by choice.

> Upstairs she had left an identity that was rightfully hers, that she had worked hard to achieve. Many women wouldn't have chosen it, but she did. . . . whenever she was good and ready, she could walk back up.

Her journey back upstairs, however, runs afoul of Luther, who intercepts her as she tries to clean house with her dead child in her arms. Her act of self-affirmation instantly becomes an act of revenge: she clasps Luther to her in a feral death grip and the three burn in the Christmas tree fire.

The conclusion of Willa's journey to self-discovery is a dead end, but she has brought to an end the Nedeed dynasty. She has achieved selfhood and poetic justice with a strength derived from recognizing the accumulated suffering of the Nedeed women. Thus a kind of sisterhood has been established over time, between Willa and her dead predecessors who haunt this house. She is restored briefly to life and strength only through her recognition of a common bond with these other women. The power she achieves is hair-raising.

From the recital of the women's stories it should be clear again that the men often mistreat the women and that sisterhood is often a reaction against men. Yet the men here are dramatized more fully and sympathetically than the men in *Brewster Place*. Even the monster Luther Nedeed and his forebears reveal inner conflicts, disillusionment, and loneliness. In their desire for power, many of the men betray their race and their ability to love. But not all of them. In Willie Mason, the young poet-protagonist, we see a sensitivity to women's suffering that suggests potential communication between the sexes. It is he who first hears and reacts to Willa's mourning wail wafted up to the top of Linden Hills. He has an idealistic crush on Ruth, he sympathizes with Mrs. Tilson where Lester cannot, he worries about what Winston is doing to Cassandra, he is ashamed of the black Penthouse centerfold that Maxwell Smyth claims as a sign of racial progress, he is a witness to Laurel's suicide and is deeply disturbed by it, and he first wonders about Mrs. Nedeed and suspects foul play. Near the end he has nightmares about women that he can exorcise and reduce to order only by creating the first line of a poem: "There is a man in a house at the bottom of a hill. And his wife has no name." In juxtaposing his and Willa's scenes Naylor suggests an intuitive bond between them. He is the link between the crushed "no-face" of Laurel and the "no-face" of Priscilla in Willa's thoughts. His nightmare phrase "Willie eat it" echoes Willa's thoughts about Evelyn's cooking, "Will he eat it?" Even their names—Willie and Willa—seem mysteriously connected. And it is Willie who accidentally unbolts the basement door just when Willa arrives at the top step. And yet for all this, at the moment of crisis Willie cannot act on behalf of Willa. He and Lester let themselves be put out on the porch because they are too stunned by Willa's appearance, too daunted by the powerful Luther, and too young to take full, responsible action. After failing to rouse the sadistic neighbors to call the fire department, they can at best end their odyssey of initiation by escaping the dead-end street at the bottom of Linden Hills, by climbing Nedeed's chain-link fence, much as Mattie imagines the women of Brewster Place attacking the wall at the end of their cul-de-sac.

For, otherwise, death is the end of all these people's striving in this topsy-turvy world. Upward mobility for these black bourgeois men and women is ironically a Dantesque descent—an allusion Naylor explains in "A Conversation"—down Linden Hills to the cemetery, to a frozen lake, to the mortician, to a dead end. Brewster Place is also a last resort for most of its lower-class residents, but, less complicated by self-betrayals and more easily supported by each other, they continue to nourish their dreams in a community that rests on the solid possibility of love.

In the far more positive *Mama Day* Naylor emphasizes generational or historical sisterhood even more, reflecting what Susan Willis calls the predominant theme of contemporary black women writers: "The journey (both real and figural) back to the historical source of the black American community."[6] Yet at the same time she ties its success increasingly to the resolution of tragic tensions between men and women and between the community as an organic whole and outside influences that threaten its values.

Female power and wisdom are vividly incarnated in Miranda, the title character, a further development of Mattie Michael and Grandma Tilson and comparable to many grandmother figures in black women's fiction (e.g., Eva Peace in Morrison's *Sula* or even Lutie Johnson's grandmother in Petry's *The Street*). Forced prematurely into a nurturing role in her family after her mother's suicide, Miranda eventually becomes not only a mother to her grandniece Ophelia but a "Mama" to the whole island community of Willow Springs. For decades she is not only the community's midwife but also its guardian of tradition and its central authority figure: "Mama Day say no, everybody say no."[7] She is a powerful conjure woman with special gifts derived, in the community's view, from "being a direct descendant of Sapphira Wade, piled on the fact of springing from the seventh son of a seventh son." She feels the burdensome responsibility of her intuitive powers and her knowledge of nature and uses them only to advance the cause of life (making Bernice fertile or calling down lightning to punish the murderous Ruby).

Miranda's womanpower is thus presented as an expression of natural forces (note her gardening ability) and as an inheritance from the legendary ur-mother of the community. When Sapphira Wade liberated herself from her white husband and master, Bascombe Wade, in 1823, she initiated a tradition of female power as well as a religious tradition (Candle Walk) and strengthened the myth of the great conjure woman on hand at God's creation of the island. She was also legendary for bringing into the open the unresolved tensions between men and women. Miranda feels largely an unconscious sisterhood with Sapphira through various intuitive experiences of knowledge and power. For example, when she handles Sapphira's fabric while making a quilt for Ophelia, she has a sudden premonition that George will not be coming, and when she finds Bascombe's undecipherable ledger and Sapphira's bill of sale, she has vague dreams that lead to a way to save Ophelia's life. On the other hand, Miranda feels a more *conscious* bond of sisterhood with her mother. And her mother's madness and suicide, described partly as an escape from her husband, connect her mother and hence Miranda to Sapphira again.

Thus female power is *there* in the legendary past for the females of

Willow Springs to learn, to accept, and to draw strength from in their own lives. As Willis says, "For black women history is a bridge defined along motherlines."[8] Sisterhood here is not a relationship that arises for the nonce as a *response to* a particular condition, such as oppression. It is a force that transcends particulars and is allied to nature itself. Miranda is the role model for the full acceptance and living of this power.

Miranda's blood sister Abigail shares some of Miranda's knowledge, and the bond between them is, on the surface, the best example of sisterhood in the novel. The two became inseparable after the death of their sister Peace. For eighty years they have greeted each other the same way ("You there, Sister?" "Uh, huh"). Ophelia says that "those two didn't breathe without telling the other what it felt like," and they always write joint letters to Ophelia even though they fight over the wording. George finds their head angle and laughter identical. And they are still connected in spirit after Abigail's death. But Abigail is the more timorous and conventional of the two and does not possess the conjure power Miranda has. As surrogate parents for Ophelia, Abigail and Miranda present balance—Abigail dotes and spoils, Miranda enjoins values.

The sisterly bond, then, is shown as stretching back into a shadowy past and also existing in the present relationship of the two sisters. But the plot of the novel is focused on the way this bond is to be passed on to the future, to Ophelia. Like her cousin Willa Nedeed, Ophelia ("Cocoa" or "Baby Girl") is the inheritor of a female tradition. Whereas Willa's predecessors had all been isolated victims of men, Ophelia's predecessors had transcended men. Though they had also suffered, they had achieved a power that could be passed on directly. Although Ophelia has been raised in Willow Springs by Miranda and Abigail, she is not fully aware of her foremother tradition or open to her instincts or alert to the evil represented by New York or by Ruby's jealousy. She resists hearing the voices at the graveyard, she fails to understand the message of her dreams, and she scoffs at Miranda's power to get her the New York job (though it is the peculiar dust from Abigail's stationery that makes the job possible). The knowledge and power of sisterhood are yet to be fully transmitted to her and accepted by her. She has spent her twenties uncertainly pursuing a career in New York, but she still draws on the connection with Miranda and Abigail and her community by returning to Willow Springs each August for two weeks of its summer lushness. Ophelia finds at home the "living mirrors" of her identity and her continuity with her past. In contrast to her foil Selma, she is only partly uprooted, partly corrupted in her power of belief.

On one of Ophelia's visits she and Miranda go both literally and figuratively "in search of their mothers' gardens," as Alice Walker describes in her famous essay the process of discovering black women's artistic traditions.[9] When Miranda takes her gardening to the old Wade homestead (the "other place," where Sapphira's original garden is located),

Miranda begins to pass on more of the sisterly bond from the past by telling Ophelia about her own family tragedy. As Marjorie Pryse points out, such passing on of the oral tradition with its elements of genealogy, magic, and naming, is a particularly female tradition that empowers the women who inherit it.[10] Significantly, Miranda calls her by her proper name, Ophelia, for the first time, and Ophelia then realizes her connection to her great-mother Ophelia (who had drowned herself) and to her mother, Grace, who had named her Ophelia in revenge for the desertion of her husband. Soon after, when Ophelia visits Willow Springs with her new husband, George, she can consciously recognize that she is a child again in this place and that her bond with Miranda and Abigail is eternal: "My bond with them was such that even if hate and rage were to tear us totally apart, they knew I was always theirs." Miranda sees Ophelia as probably the last woman of the family line but a worthy descendant of the "great mother" Sapphira:

> And now she strides so proud, . . . The lean thighs, tight hips, the long strides flashing light between the blur of strong legs—pure black. Me and Abigail, we take after the sons, Miranda thinks. The earth men who formed the line of Days, hard and dark brown. But *the* Baby Girl brings back the great, grand Mother.

When Ophelia in turn tells George about the legend of Sapphira, he too affirms the living connection:

> But it was odd again the way you said it—she was the great, great, grand, Mother—as if you were listing the attributes of a goddess. . . . Places like this island were ripe for myths, . . . You were, in spirit at least, as black as they come. No, you could have easily descended from the slave woman who talked a man out of a whole island.

Ophelia has inherited the power and now, through Miranda, the knowledge of her foremothers.

When Ophelia's life is threatened by Ruby's nightshade, Miranda herself gains knowledge of this tradition; she discovers even more of the continuity in the line of women than she had known before. She sees Ophelia's illness in terms of the whole tradition of suffering women, from Sapphira's slavery to Miranda's mother's grief. After finding Bascombe Wade's ledger, Miranda is impelled to uncover the well where her sister Peace had died, in order to confront and understand her mother's tragic sorrow and suicide. Once Ophelia is restored to life, Miranda feels that there are no more secrets for Miranda herself to learn, that the rest of the past will be discovered by Ophelia: "The rest will lay in the hands of the Baby Girl—once she learns how to listen." The sisterly bond is suggested when the grieving Ophelia goes on Candle Walk between Miranda and Abigail, but the promise of Ophelia's future wisdom and power is only fully imaged in the final paragraph, when Miranda sees Ophelia on the hillside:

It's a face that's been given the meaning of peace. A face ready to go in search of answers, so at last there ain't no need for words as they lock eyes over the distance. Under a sky so blue it's stopped being sky, one is closer to the circle of oaks than the other. But both can hear clearly that on the east side of the island and on the west side, the waters were still.

Both are united with nature in a listening posture, open to its power and to the future. This union beyond words is a further development of the storytelling sisterhood that connects Gayl Jones' *Corregidora* women and frames Hurston's *Their Eyes Were Watching God.*[11]

If Ophelia will achieve full identity through an inherited sisterhood, Naylor shows less confidence in sisterly friendship among other women of similar age. The picture of lonely black women in New York looking for men understandably lacks any sense of community. But the young women in Willow Springs also find little support in each other. Frances suffers a breakdown over the loss of Junior Lee to Ruby, and no one can help her. Bernice, Ophelia's former best friend, is temporarily restored to belief and to a bond with traditional sisterhood through Miranda, but loses her faith and her child. Ruby, in defining herself solely as a possessor of men, has rejected all ties with women and seeks to do them harm.

These failures of female community on the island reflect tensions within Willow Springs and between it and the outside world. Hostile values, for example, infect Bernice's marriage through her mean-spirited mother-in-law with her hypocritical Protestantism. Harmony is restored at Candle Walk, but its traditions are changing too. The children increasingly clamor for Christmas instead, and some adults simple forget old customs over time. The organic wholeness of Willow Springs as a community, however, is less important than its acceptance of a larger organic wholeness in nature, which is not only cyclical and stable but also pardoxically full of change and development. Already the traditions of Candle Walk are different from what they were generations earlier, but Miranda voices a healthy acceptance of this change and other changes in the future as natural occurrences:

> It'll take generations, she says, for Willow Springs to stop doing it [Candle Walk] at all. And more generations again to stop talking about the time "when there used to be some kinda 18 & 23 going-on near December twenty-second." By then, she figures, it won't be the world as we know it no way—and so no need for the memory.

True sisterhood for Miranda and Ophelia implies being one with their community but also one with the larger reality of nature.

Full sisterhood in *Mama Day* also implies working out relationships between women and men. Ophelia will die and the historical line of conjure women will die out unless she is saved by George. Only through his sacrificial death can Ophelia recover from Ruby's conjuring and inherit the sisterly legacy from the past. George's death also makes it possible for Miranda to die in peace exactly when she plans to at the beginning of the new century. Naylor does show that the women can transcend men and have power of their own, but often at the price of tragic loss for men. The men in the novel tend generously to support the women up to a point and are respected by Miranda for uprightness and strength. Bascombe Wade had freed his slaves out of love for Sapphira, yet he could not let her go, not get beyond the possessiveness of male love. John-Paul, Miranda's father, was a sensitive woodcarver who despaired over his wife's madness but could not let her go. Bernice's Ambush and Ophelia's George offer their wives a rich love, but George is limited to childhood insecurities and certain masculine attitudes toward women that cause miscommunication.

In her climactic effort to save Ophelia, Miranda tries to bridge the gap between the genders in the name of life and wholeness by tying George to Bascombe Wade (the ledger) and John-Paul (the cane) in his quest for whatever is in the nest of the vicious hen. *Her* way would redeem the male element but also allow George to survive and love Ophelia. Unfortunately George goes *his* way, in rationalistic unbelief and relying on his own strength alone, and he succumbs to a heart attack from the hen's violence. Ophelia has reiterated the female pattern of "breaking a man's heart" as her intuitions foretold. Thus the gender conflict seems unresolved at the end, with only a hint from Miranda of how it might be resolved. Only in Ophelia's "conversations" with the deceased George's spirit fourteen years later do we see an ideally open communication between them, as she discovers and accepts his point of view. Although she clearly transcends her second husband in Charleston, she achieves in these colloquies with George the added power and wisdom that Naylor portrays in the optimistic final paragraph cited earlier.

In the three-novel progression, then, *Mama Day* arrives at a more complex vision of sisterhood. Naylor has moved steadily from the merely naturalistic to the symbolic and mythical modes as well, as she adds historical depth to the presentation of the female bond. She has moved away from an exclusive focus on females to an exploration of the relationship between sisterhood and the resolution of male-female conflicts. She has moved from a view of the power of sisterhood as a refuge from oppression to a celebration of sisterhood as empowered by folk tradition, by nature, and by abiding spiritual forces. She has moved from the severely limited and tentative possibility of sisterhood to a richer and more positive glimpse of its reality, even if it is not yet fully dramatized in action, for example, as it is in a community of women like those in Walker's *The Color Purple* or Marita Golden's *A Woman's Place*. If such a community of women is real to her imagination, perhaps she will grace us with it in her next splendid effort.

Notes

1. Gloria Wade-Gayles, *No Crystal Stair: Visions of Race and Sex in Black Women's Fiction* (New York: The Pilgrim Press, 1984), p. 237.
2. Gloria Naylor, *The Women of Brewster Place* (New York: Penguin, 1983), pp. 4–5.
3. Gloria Naylor and Toni Morrison, "A Conversation," *Southern Review* 21 (July 1985), 579.
4. Calvin C. Hernton, *The Sexual Mountain and Black Women Writers: Adventures in Sex, Literature, and Real Life* (New York: Doubleday, 1987), pp. 5–7.
5. Gloria Naylor, *Linden Hills* (New York: Ticknor & Fields, 1985), p. 148.
6. Susan Willis, *Specifying: Black Women Writing, the American Experience* (Madison: Univ. of Wisconsin Press, 1987), p. 57. Also, see Christian Barbara, *Black Women Novelists: The Development of a Tradition, 1892–1976* (Westport, Conn.: Greenwood, 1980), p. 239.
7. Gloria Naylor, *Mama Day* (New York: Ticknor & Fields, 1988), p. 6.
8. Willis, p. 6.
9. Alice Walker, *In Search of Our Mothers' Gardens: Womanist Prose by Alice Walker* (San Diego, New York, and London: Harcourt, 1984), pp. 231–43.
10. Marjorie Pryse and Hortense J. Spillers, *Conjuring: Black Women, Fiction, and Literary Tradition* (Bloomington: Indiana Univ. Press, 1985), pp. 4–5, 12–15, 20.
11. Willis, pp. 51–52. See also Pryse, p. 14.

Essayists

LARRY R. ANDREWS is an associate professor of English at Kent State. He has written extensively on Russian literature, as well as on Gwendolyn Brooks and Ann Petry.

MICHAEL AWKWARD is an associate professor of English and Afro-American and African Studies at the University of Michigan, Ann Arbor. He is the author of *Inspiring Influences: Tradition, Revision, and Afro-American Women's Novels* and the editor of *New Essays on Their Eyes Were Watching God*.

LUKE BOUVIER is an assistant professor at Ithaca College.

BARBARA CHRISTIAN is a professor of African American Studies at the University of California, Berkeley. Her books include *Black Feminist Criticism: Perspectives on Black Women Writers* and *Black Women Novelists: The Development of a Tradition 1892–1976*.

PETER ERICKSON is the author of *Patriarchal Structures in Shakespeare's Drama* and *Rewriting Shakespeare, Rewriting Ourselves*, and co-editor of *Shakespeare's "Rough Magic": Renaissance Essays in Honor of C. L. Barber*.

CELESTE FRASER is a member of the English department at Duke University.

TERESA GODDU is an assistant professor of English at Vanderbilt University, Nashville. She is completing a book on American Gothic and Afro-American literature.

MARGARET HOMANS is a professor of English at Yale University. Her works include *Bearing the Word: Language and Female Experience in 19th-century Women's Writings* and *Women Writers and Poetic Identity: Dorothy Wordsworth, Emile Bronte, and Emily Dickinson*.

HELEN FIDDYMENT LEVY is a professor of English literature at George Mason University in Fairfax, VA. She is the author of *Fiction of the Home Place*.

JILL L. MATUS is assistant professor of English at the University of Toronto. She is writing a book on versions of the sexualized woman in nineteenth- and twentieth-century fiction.

KEITH SANDIFORD is an associate professor of English at Louisiana State University, Baton Rouge. He is the author of *Measuring the Moment: Strategies of Protest in 18th Century Afro-English Writing*.

JAMES ROBERT SAUNDERS is an assistant professor of English at the University of Toledo.

LAURA E. TANNER teaches American Literature at Boston College. She is the author of *Intimate Violence: Reading Representations of Violation in 20th Century Fiction*.

CATHERINE WARD is a professor of English and Director of Women's Studies and Support Programs at Western Kentucky University in Bowling Green.

Chronology

1950	January 25: Born Gloria Naylor in New York, NY, daughter of Roosevelt Naylor, a transit worker, and Alberta (McAlpin) Naylor, a telephone operator.
1968–75	Works as a missionary for Jehovah's Witnesses in New York, North Carolina, and Florida.
1975–81	Works as a telephone operator in various hotels in New York City.
1981	Receives a BA in English from Brooklyn College of the City University of New York.
1982	Publishes *The Women of Brewster Place*.
1983	Receives an MA in Afro-American Studies from Yale University. Writer in Residence at Cummington Community of the Arts. Receives American Book Award for Best First Novel (*The Women of Brewster Place*). Receives Distinguished Writer Award from the Mid-Atlantic Writers Association. Visiting lecturer at George Washington University 1983–84.
1984	Contributing editor, *Callaloo*.
1985	Publishes *Linden Hills*. Receives National Endowment for the Arts Fellowship. Works as a cultural exchange lecturer for the United States Information Agency in India.
1986	Receives Candace Award from the National Coalition of 100 Black Women. Scholar in Residence at University of Pennsylvania. Visiting professor at New York University. Visiting lecturer at Princeton University 1986–87.
1987	Visiting professor at Boston University.
1988	Publishes *Mama Day*. Receives Guggenheim Fellowship. Fannie Hurst Visiting Professor at Brandeis University. Senior Fellow in Society for Humanities at Cornell University. Member, Book-of-the-Month Club Select Committee.
1989	Receives Lillian Smith Award.
1992	Publishes *Bailey's Cafe*.

Bibliography

"Black Women Novelists: New Generation Raises Provocative Issues." *Ebony* (Nov. 1984): 59–61.

"The Women of Brewster Place." Ebony (March 1989): 122–26.

"Until Death Do Us Part." *Essence* (May 1985): 133.

Awkward, Michael. *Inspiring Influences: Tradition, Revision, and Afro-American Women's Novels.* Columbia University Press, New York, 1991.

Bob, Jacqueline, and Ellen Seiter. "Black Feminism and Media Criticism: *The Women of Brewster Place." Screen* (Fall 1991): 286–302.

Collins, Grace E. "Narrative Structure in *Linden Hills." CLA Journal* (March 1991): 290–301.

Eko, Ebele. "Beyond the Myth of Confrontation: A Comparative Study of African and African-American Female Protagonists." *Ariel* (Oct. 1986): 139–52.

Gates, Henry Louis, Jr. "Significant Others." *Contemporary Literature* (Winter 1988): 606–23.

Gilchrist, Ellen, Josephine Humphreys, Gloria Naylor, Louise Shivers, and Willard Pate. "Do You Think of Yourself as a Woman Writer?" *Furman Studies* (Dec. 1988): 2–13.

Inoue, Kazuko. "Gloria Naylor's Narrative: Looking Past the Losing." *Language and Culture* (1990): 157–76.

Kelly, Lori Duin. "The Dream Sequence in *The Women of Brewster Place." Notes on Contemporary Literature* (Sept. 1991): 8–10.

Naylor, Gloria. "Love and Sex in the Afro-American Novel." *The Yale Review* (Fall 1989): 19–31.

Palumbo, Kathryn. "The Uses of Imagery in Naylor's *The Women of Brewster Place." Notes on Contemporary Literature* (May 1985): 6–8.

Pearlman, Mickey. "An Interview with Gloria Naylor." *High Plains Literary Review* (Spring 1990): 98–107.

Reckley, Ralph. *Twentieth Century Black American Women in Print: Essays,* ed. by Lola E. Jones. Copley Publishing Group: Acton, MA, 1991.

Sisney, Mary F. "The View from the Outside: Black Novels of Manner." In Bowers, Begel, and Barbara Brothers, eds., *Reading and Writing Women's Lives: A Study of the Novel of Manners.* University Microfilms International (Research Press: Ann Arbor, 1990): 171–86.

Wagner-Martin, Linda. "Quilting in Gloria Naylor's *Mama Day." Notes on Contemporary Literature* (Nov. 1988): 6–8.

Wells, Linda, Sandra E. Bowen, and Suzanne Stutman. "'What Shall I Give My Children?': The Role of Mentor in Gloria Naylor's *The Women of Brewster Place* and Paule Marshall's *Praisesong for the Widow." Explorations in Ethnic Studies* (July 1990): 41–60.

Acknowledgments

"Women Together." Review of *The Women of Brewster Place* by Annie Gottlieb from *The New York Times Book Review* (22 August 1982), © 1982 by the New York Times Co. Reprinted with permission.

Untitled review of *The Women of Brewster Place* by Dorothy Wickenden from *The New Republic* 187 (Sept. 6, 1982), © 1982 by The New Republic, Inc. Reprinted with permission.

"The Circular Driveways of Hell." Review of *Linden Hills* by Mel Watkins from *The New York Times Book Review* (3 March 1985), © 1985 by the New York Times Co. Reprinted with permission.

"Roots of Privilege: New Black Fiction." Review of *Linden Hills* by Sherley Anne Williams from *Ms.* 13 (June 1985), © 1985 by Fairfax Publications (U.S.) Limited. Reprinted with permission.

"Black Laughter in an Offshore Showoff Novel." Review of *Mama Day* by Rita Mae Brown from the *Los Angeles Times* (6 March 1988), © 1988 by Rita Mae Brown. Reprinted with permission.

"Black Roots, White Culture." Review of *Mama Day* by Linda Simon from the *Women's Review of Books* (September 1988), © 1988 by Linda Simon. Reprinted with permission.

"There Are Four Sides to Everything." Review of *Mama Day*, by Bharati Mukherjee from *The New York Times Book Review* (21 February 1988), © 1988 by the New York Times Co. Reprinted with permission.

Untitled review of *Mama Day* by Rachel Hass from *The Boston Review* (June 1988), © 1988 by the Boston Critic, Inc. Reprinted with permission.

Untitled review of *Mama Day* by Rosellen Brown from *Ms.* 16 (February 1988), © 1988 by Fairfax Publications (U.S.) Limited. Reprinted with permission.

"Saving Lost Souls: Gloria Naylor's *Bailey's Cafe* Stands between Despair and Hope on Infinity St." by Karen Joy Fowler from the *Chicago Tribune* (4 October 1992), © 1992 by Karen Jay Fowler. Reprinted with permission.

"The Woman in the Cave" (originally entitled "The Woman in the Cave: Recent Feminist Fictions and the Classical Underworld") by Margaret Homans from *Contemporary Literature* 24 (Fall 1988), © 1988 by the Board of Regents of the University of Wisconsin System. Reprinted with permission.

"*Linden Hills:* A Modern *Inferno*" (originally entitled "Gloria Naylor's *Linden Hills:* A Modern *Inferno*") by Catherine C. Ward from *Contemporary Literature* 28 (Spring 1987), © 1987 by the Board of Regents of the University of Wisconsin System. Reprinted with permission.

"Gothic and Intertextual Constructions in *Linden Hills*" by Keith Sandiford, © 1990 by Keith Sandiford. Printed with permission.

"Reconstructing History in *Linden Hills*" (originally entitled "Models of History in Gloria Naylor's *Linden Hills*") by Teresa Goddu, © 1990 by Teresa Goddu. Printed with permission.

"'Shakespeare's Black?': The Role of Shakespeare in Naylor's Novels" (originally entitled "'Shakespeare's Black?': The Role of Shakespeare in the Novels of Gloria Naylor") by Peter Erickson from *Rewriting Shakespeare, Rewriting Ourselves* (University of California Press), © 1991 by Peter Erickson. Printed with permission.

"The Ornamentation of Old Ideas: Naylor's First Three Novels" (originally entitled "The Ornamentation of Old Ideas: Gloria Naylor's First Three Novels") by James Robert Saunders from *The Hollins Critic* 27 (April 1990), © 1990 by Hollins College. Reprinted with permission.

"Lead on with Light" (originally entitled "Lead on with Light: Gloria Naylor") by Helen Fiddyment Levy from *Fiction of the Home Place* by Helen Fiddyment Levy, © 1992 by the University Press of Mississippi. Reprinted with permission.

"Black Sisterhood in Naylor's Novels" (originally entitled "Black Sisterhood in Gloria Naylor's Novels") by Larry R. Andrews from *CLA Journal* 33 (September 1989), © 1989 by the College Language Association. Reprinted with permission.

Index

This is one of six volumes of literary
criticism launching the
AMISTAD LITERARY SERIES
which is devoted to literary fiction
and criticism by and about African Americans.

◆

The typeface "AMISTAD" is based
on wood and stone symbols
and geometric patterns seen throughout
sixteenth-century Africa. These hand-carved
motifs were used to convey the diverse
cultural aspects evident among
the many African peoples.

◆

Amistad typeface was designed
by Maryam "Marne" Zafar.

◆

This book was published with the
assistance of March Tenth, Inc.
Printed and bound by Haddon Craftsmen, Inc.

◆

The paper is acid-free
55-pound Cross Pointe Odyssey Book.